Psychology FOR MODERN EDUCATION

By the Same Author

EDUCATIONAL PSYCHOLOGY

THE PSYCHOLOGY OF SECONDARY-SCHOOL TEACHING

THE PSYCHOLOGY OF MUSIC

PRINCIPLES OF EDUCATION

Psychology
FOR MODERN EDUCATION

James L. Mursell
TEACHERS COLLEGE, COLUMBIA UNIVERSITY

NEW YORK
W · W · NORTON & COMPANY · INC ·

PRINTED IN THE UNITED STATES OF AMERICA
FOR THE PUBLISHERS BY THE VAIL-BALLOU PRESS, INC.

Contents

Preface

In the present book I have endeavored to bring the content of educational psychology to a focus on the proposition that the essential reality of education is the shaping of personality. This idea has of course long been recognized as true, is implied in much modern educational thought and practice, and is thoroughly compatible with our present-day psychological outlook. Yet it too often is buried in a mass of information that may lack vital internal coherence, with the result that teachers in service and those preparing to teach fail to derive from their study of psychology a central interpretive idea at once sound and illuminating.

The purpose and general plan of the book have called for a treatment of motivation and of dynamic aspects of learning somewhat more extensive than usual. Beyond this, however, I have found it not only possible, but necessary to retain most of the well-established topics of educational psychology. The mechanisms by which human personality is shaped and molded are clearly those of learning, transfer, and growth. The problem of individual traits and abilities remains germane. Above all, the question of how teaching and the curriculum can and should affect personality becomes crucial. So established topics are fully treated, although with the special emphasis necessarily involved in relating them to the focal conception.

Since my prevailing purpose has been to present convincingly a way of thinking about education, I have avoided loading the book with technicalities. I have concentrated references to the quite extensive research material on which the book is based in a final bibliography, in order to achieve a clear-running text. I have tried to write simply and directly; and I have prevailingly omitted proper names, extensive statistical tabulations, accounts of experimental procedures, and so forth. For the advanced student and the specialist such matters are, of course, important. But the great majority of students and teachers need above everything else an intelligent point of view brought into practical application upon their work; and for them technical details can often be a cause of confusion and obscurity.

My attempt has been, not to defend any special and, as it were, partisan psychological viewpoint, but rather to present the common ground of present-day psychological thought. It is my conviction that essential agreements among various schools of psychology bulk much larger than differences between them. For this reason my treatment of various theories of learning has been brief, although obviously the student should be made aware that such various theories exist. My prevailing purpose, however, has been practical, in the sense of helping the student to achieve a clear and valid understanding of the true nature of human education, and to see how such an understanding bears upon what ought to be done in the classroom and the school.

James L. Mursell

Psychology FOR MODERN EDUCATION

1

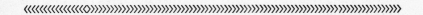

The Meaning of Psychology for Education

EDUCATION AND PERSONALITY

WHEN A psychologist asks himself what he means by education, the most comprehensive and satisfying answer he is likely to find to the question is this: *Education is the shaping of personality*. This answer summarizes the controlling viewpoint of the present book.

It is obvious that the answer is true in a broad and general sense. If at first sight it seems at all surprising, the reason is its very simplicity and obviousness. Whenever we say that a person is being "educated," whether the "educating" goes on in a school classroom, or on a football squad, or in a fraternity house, or in a social group, or anywhere else, we surely mean that he is being "made over" to a certain extent. The change in his personality is the real educative effect. He becomes, in some degree and in some way, a different person. So it is hardly more than common sense to say that education is essentially the shaping of personality.

This idea has a central place in a great deal of modern educational thought and practice, even though it is not always put in precisely the words used here. Moreover, the idea is anything but novel. It is, in fact, very old. Centuries ago it was expressed in the words: *Non scholae sed vitae.* Not schools, but lives! In all the years that have passed since that utterance, no one has arisen to deny it. So all that modern psychology does is to take a very old and very obvious doctrine, and try to explore its meaning and implications.

The very first step in this exploration must be the defining of our central term. What do we mean by a man's personality? Often we talk about personality very vaguely. But if we are to use the concept as the focus of our thinking, we must get rid of this vagueness as far as we can.

The author of one of the best books on the subject has pointed out that the word *personality* can be used in three somewhat different, though related, senses (466).*

1. When we speak of a man's personality, we may mean the impression he makes on us, or his "impact" upon us, to use a familiar expression. His personality, in this sense, is his unique individuality, the pattern of qualities which make him different from other people. We look at the man, so to speak, from the outside; and we sense, and perhaps try to describe in words or even in statistics, his peculiar and special flavor as a human being.

2. When we speak of a man's personality, we may mean the inner organization of his traits and tendencies. We may, for instance, wonder what makes a teacher so harsh and severe, and decide that he is very harsh because he is not at all sure of himself, so that he tends to overcompensate. If we think in this way, we try to look inside the man, as it were; and we regard his personality as a complex organization of psychological factors.

3. When we speak of a man's personality we may mean the

* Numbers in parentheses refer to the bibliography at the end of this book.

ways in which he deals with circumstances, his ways of reacting to persons and things, his ways of behaving. We watch him as he copes with the problems and challenges of life, and with the innumerable stimuli of his environment. We note whether he copes with them intelligently or stupidly, confidently or hesitantly, emotionally or calmly, consistently or inconsistently; and we call these ways of acting and reacting his personality.

You can use the word personality quite correctly in any of these three senses. None of them is wrong. They are not sharply distinguished, and they are not inconsistent. Our main emphasis in this book, however, will be upon the third, because it seems the most suitable and fruitful. The same idea has been expressed by saying that a child's personality is "the sum total of the satisfying ways he finds to adjust his biological inheritance to his circumstances" (757, p. 314). This is simply a more complicated way of saying that a child's personality is the sum total of his modes and methods of dealing with circumstances. There might be some objection to the use of the term "sum total," because a human being's personality is not a mere collection, but an organized and interrelated pattern. So our prevailing conception will be that a man's personality is *the total pattern of his ways of dealing with the challenges and problems of life*, although the other two senses of the word will not be, and in fact cannot be wholly excluded. The central problem of psychology brought to bear on education is to explain how this pattern of ways of dealing with life's problems is acquired. This is what we face when we try to interpret education as the shaping of personality. How do people come to act as they do act? Such is our focal question!

SOME IMMEDIATE IMPLICATIONS

There are some immediate implications a brief discussion of which will help us to a better understanding of our controlling point of view.

1. You will notice that the concept of personality in any or

all the three senses which I have explained above is a very broad and inclusive concept. When one thinks, in one way or another, of a man's personality, one is thinking of the man as a whole, as a total unit. So what we have to do is to bring to bear all available information in order to try to understand human beings as total units. For this reason it has been remarked that an adequate general psychology really amounts to a psychology of personality (466).

In the same way, an adequate educational psychology really amounts to a psychology of the shaping of personality. So when we try to interpret education as the shaping of personality, we do not disregard everything that has already been said and written. We do not clean the slate and get off to a brand-new start. We take the data which have been accumulated, the insights which have been achieved, and point them up to a new focus. What we get is not an entirely novel kind of educational psychology, but rather a new perspective on a familiar scene. This, however, has great value, as I shall now proceed to show.

2. If we think of education as the shaping of personality, we center our thinking on essentials rather than on externals. Subjects, courses, marks, promotional plans, extracurricular activities are among the externals, the machinery of education as it goes on in school. But its reality consists in what actually happens to people. Certainly the educational machinery cannot be ignored. But neither can it be treated as though it were an end in itself, with its own intrinsic values. For instance, the question of what is a good classroom method is meaningless if it is considered in isolation. The real question is what is likely to happen to human beings under such and such a classroom regime. What impulses and desires are touched off? What trends of development are helped or hindered? What differences are likely to be produced in the personalities concerned? The same approach holds good in dealing with any of the educational machinery—with the marking system, or the program

of intelligence testing, or the arrangements for promotion, for example. The psychologist cannot disregard the institutional apparatus of education, for personalities are not shaped in a vacuum. But he cannot for a moment accept the idea that the essential and central problem of education is the efficient running of the apparatus.

3. Once again, it is very clear that if education is to be considered as the shaping of personality, then education means vastly more than schooling. The home, the clique, the neighborhood, the community, the nation, friends, enemies, associates, and, indeed, an innumerable multitude of influences and contacts go to make people what they are and what they become. This means that all of these are educative influences. Indeed, once we think of education as the shaping of personality, it becomes clear that all life is educative. This, in fact, is precisely the point of view that the psychologist is bound to take. So a really complete psychology of human education would be a vast and far-ranging subject indeed. It could not stop short of dealing with the sweeping question of how life forms and molds our natures.

4. However, there are good reasons for the psychologist to limit his field, and to pay special attention to schools and schooling, which is perhaps a lucky thing! Certainly all life is educative, but the school is an educational institution of a very important and very special kind.

In the first place, the school is an institution deliberately set up to have a dominating influence on the lives of young people for many of their most formative years. Between the ages of six and eighteen (at least), going to school is a youngster's chief job. We recognize this by calling him a pupil or a student, just as later on he will be called a mechanic, or a clerk, or a physician. Moreover, the school is the agency in which conscious and deliberate educational planning is most feasible, and upon which psychological ideas can best be brought to bear. These reasons alone would make it quite proper for the psychologist to give particular attention to the influence and effect of the school.

But there is something more. The school is an educational institution which undertakes to teach a planned curriculum, and to conduct classroom learning. No one can doubt for an instant that, as a matter of plain fact, these have been its chief social responsibilities from time immemorial, and that they are likely to remain its chief functions for as far ahead as we can see. So the school presents a very intriguing psychological problem, and a problem that is very important, not for any theoretical reasons, but because of the realities of the situation. What is the relationship between curricular achievement and classroom learning on the one hand, and the shaping of personality on the other? Any psychologist who undertook to discuss education while ignoring this problem would clearly be dodging what everybody knows is the crucial issue. In principle the solution of the problem turns upon the broad conception of personality which I have already set up; and in the pages that follow much attention will be devoted to developing this solution.

Primarily, then, the meaning of psychology for education is the establishment of a point of view, a mode of approach, a focus for thinking and planning. To consider education from the psychological viewpoint means cutting through the details, getting below the external machinery, and centering always on this question: *What actual effect are we having on the personalities of young people?*

DESIRABLE PERSONALITY TRAITS

The moment we say that education is the shaping of personality, we run head on into the question: What sort of personality do we want to shape? Unless we know what kind of personality we want, the whole idea of shaping, molding, and developing personality remains very vague and even rather meaningless. Yet the question is remarkably tricky and difficult.

At least it is a tricky and difficult question for members of a society like our own. Educational authorities in totalitarian regimes have very little trouble in laying down specifications for what they would consider the right sort of human beings. Hitler, in one of his speeches, described quite definitely the characteristics of the "national socialist man." Among other things, he said that national socialist men should be "lean as greyhounds" and "hard as Krupp steel." The top Communist leaders, too, have no hesitation in saying what sort of a person the "new Communist man" ought to be. Totalitarian educators take these statements, amplify them into a bill of particulars, and set up a program to produce the desired type of human creatures. So, in a sense, totalitarian educators have a rather easy time of it.

But with us it is not so easy. We have no ready-made stereotype. We are committed to a respect for human personality as such. We believe in the importance and value of variety. We cannot say that we want nothing but extroverts, or rotarians, or joiners, or hard-headed realists, or conformists, or conservatives, or radicals, or reformers, or liberals. A couple of quotations define our position very well. "It inheres in the philosophy of a democracy that those social institutions and processes are esteemed most which contribute most to the full maturing of a maximum of the population. In such a society, the primary aim of educational institutions must be to provide the best possible conditions for the development of all children, rather than to standardize the personalities entrusted to them to meet some social aim, such as procuring good soldiers or effective robots" (172, p. 193). And again: "The ideal of mental hygiene for the schools of a democratic society may be described as equality of opportunity for personality development in relation to individual potentiality" (530, p. 4). One might boil down these two statements and others like them by saying that, in the shaping of personality, our business is to try to make all human beings as truly human as possible.

Now this way of putting the case really does seem like an educational version of the basic tenet of our society, namely, respect for personality as such. The trouble is that it is extremely vague. To talk about "equality of opportunity for personality development" sounds very fine. But just what does it mean when we come down to cases? arithmetic for everybody? compulsory athletics for everybody? or just a grand policy of educational laissez faire and free electives? Again, just what is the particular meaning of being "as truly human as possible"? What are the characteristics of the "truly human" human being? Is it possible to say? If we cannot say, then will not our educational system and practice be dominated only by good intentions instead of being directed towards definite goals?

Fortunately, there is a constructive answer to these questions. To be sure, we have no inspired autocratic leader to tell us in a few short sentences just what sort of folks we ought to be. But our psychologists have come very successfully to the rescue. They have described very helpfully and understandably the characteristics of a good and satisfactory personality—the characteristics, that is to say, that are proper to a human being in a society whose fundamental tenet is the worth of human personality as such. Here in summary is what the psychologists have to say.

1. We want people who deal with the challenges and problems of life by dint of what are often called the "higher mental processes," i.e. reasoning, drawing inferences, analyzing and understanding experience, inventiveness, creativeness (357).* The vital importance of developing people who will act on the basis of thought, reasoning, and evidence has always been one

* Later on I shall argue that the expression "higher mental processes" is unfortunate, because even a "lower mental process" such as memory really depends upon insight—a fact that must always be remembered in dealing with memory properly. For the moment, however, we may accept the expression, because the idea in it is all right.

of the main themes of American education. The founding fathers supported and advocated schools because they saw the necessity for a literate electorate. The same thought has recently been put in these words: "To bring home to each and every individual the importance of critical thinking as a prelude to social action is to help to preserve and enlarge the democratic way of life" (20, p. 47).

But much more than social or political action in the ordinary sense is involved. We want people who will act intelligently (i.e. in terms of insight, evidence, and information) in dealing with *all* the problems and challenges of life, not just the political and social ones (138). Ultimately we want this because of our basic social tenet—respect for personality itself; for only the person who is capable of making rational decisions and inclined to make them is capable of independent self-direction. "The purpose of guidance," it has been said, "is to assist the individual, through counsel, to make *wise* choices, adjustments, and interpretations in connection with critical situations in his life in such a way as to ensure continual growth in *ability for self-direction*" (352; the italics are mine). Pray do not think that these pleas for the development of *thinking people* are only empty words. They point straight to a program of action in the schools. "If the higher mental processes of application of principles and inference are really to be cultivated, learning conditions appropriate for their cultivation are necessary" (357, p. 17). What these conditions are we shall consider later.

2. We want people with a varied range of living interests and vital concerns. Just what these interests should be in the case of any individual, it is not possible to say. The important thing is that a person should have *some* genuine interests. A very extensive survey of a large number of economically underprivileged young men showed that many of them seemed to have no constructive interests at all. They spent their spare time lounging, loafing, visiting in barber shops or pool halls,

and usually they did not like their jobs (42). It is just such narrow, uninterested personalities that the psychologist considers undesirable, and they are certainly a reproach to education.

Of course no one can be interested in everything, but it is very important for everyone to be interested in something. "In brief, it is neither possible nor desirable that all our activities and contacts in our complex social order should penetrate beneath the surface of our personalities. But unless we try deliberately and persistently to affect our destinies at certain points, especially where broad political policies are concerned, we are not democratic personalities, we have no balance, or wholeness, and society undergoes proportionate stultification" (9, p. 127). The author of these words goes on to express the belief that everyone should have a strong participating interest in some aspect of what he calls six "value spheres"—the political, the economic, the recreational, the religious, the cultural-scientific, the domestic. If we accept this proposition, then, clear as day, it is full of implications for practical educational planning.

3. We want people who have a common body of experience, understanding, knowledge, belief, and aspiration; who have, that is, a common and shared outlook, however much they may differ and vary individually. Benjamin Disraeli long ago said that England was made up of "two nations" who could hardly understand or communicate with each other—the nation of the leisured and cultivated rich, and the nation of the poor and the oppressed. Not only England was weakened because of this division; the individual personalities on both sides of the fence were weakened and impoverished too. Now we know that social and economic status tends to perpetuate itself over the generations, because underprivileged homes produce underprivileged children (42, 138). So one of the great obligations of the school is to create the common bonds of understanding, outlook, and aspiration which knit a society together and enrich

individual lives. In our free society we want many, many diverse kinds of personalities; but also we want all the creatures of this diversity to be akin in vital matters.

4. The mental hygienists have given particular attention to the question of what kind of people we want and what kind of personalities we should try to develop. Their general answer to the question is that we should try to develop what they call "wholesome personality" in young people. Obviously the idea needs to be defined, and one of the best summaries of its meaning is as follows.

(*a*) Wholesome personality is a consistent or integrated personality, free from serious contradictions and conflicts. (*b*) The wholesome personality is marked by an objective outlook towards oneself. This means a willingness to recognize one's own abilities, limitations, failures, and attainments for what they really are. (*c*) Wholesome personality involves a good and satisfactory social adjustment. On the objective side this means the achievement of a stabilizing social status, a place in the world of human affairs, a vocation in the broad sense. On the subjective side good social adjustment means the satisfaction of the inner need for social recognition and respect. (*d*) Wholesome personality involves a working adherence to social ideals (172).

You will, no doubt, notice some overlappings in the above statement with the three points previously made. But also you will notice several new considerations of great importance. What has been said under all the four headings of this section is a summary, very brief to be sure, of the opinions of psychologists about the sort of people we want, the sort of personalities we ought to try to develop.

ADJUSTMENT

I have said that the very essence of education, psychologically considered, is the shaping of personality; and also I have tried to give at least a rough idea of the kind of personality we want to shape. Now another question arises. How is the shaping done?

Obviously this is a very practical question, because unless we have a good answer to it we do not know how to set to work. Also, it is the question with which the psychologist, by profession, is most concerned, and to which he has most to contribute. There are educational issues which go beyond psychology. For instance, a psychologist may insist that we ought to try to develop thinking people, and he may believe that he can say something worth-while about how to develop them. But when it comes to the question of what people should think about, he may have his opinions as a private citizen, or as a general student of education, but in a strict professional sense the question is beyond his range. Again, the psychologist may insist that we should develop personalities with common loyalties and understandings, and it is definitely his job to try to show how to develop such personalities. But to decide in particular just what these loyalties and understandings should be goes beyond his professional province, though he may have a share in the decision. Or once more, the psychologist may maintain that the "wholesome personality" is integrated or consistent, and it is his responsibility to show how integration is developed and what it means. But the specific focus of desirable integration is once more beyond his professional range. The business of the psychologist in serving education is to block out a general picture of the desirable personality, and above all to explain the process by which personality is shaped.

All the chapters in this book deal with various aspects of this process. But I want at the very outset to present a brief outline description of the process, and to give enough illustrations to make the description reasonably clear. This process is, in many respects, exceedingly complex and baffling. Our understanding of it is far from complete, and many of its details are obscure. But its determining and essential features can be very simply stated.

The shaping of personality always depends upon two related but distinguishable conditions. First, the person concerned must strive to deal with a challenge that is relevant to his interests, a challenge that has for him what is sometimes called "ego-relevance" (9). Second, in striving to meet this challenge, he must achieve a new organized mode of dealing with his environment. To put the idea in simpler but somewhat less precise language, the shaping of personality depends first on the arousal of the *will,* and second on the finding of a *way.*

In the chapters that follow we shall have to study each of these two conditions at considerable length. But before going into any detailed analysis I will give a number of varied illustrations to show what the conditions mean, how they operate, and how the shaping of personality depends upon them.

Let us begin with the case of a child who has been made very dependent by oversolicitous parents, and who is baffled, or frightened, or resentful when he is faced with school requirements. We say that such a child manifests unfortunate personality characteristics. How were they acquired? The answer in general is quite clear. In his preschool life he has faced many "developmental tasks," many challenges which are relevant to his interests, which have "ego-relevance"—dressing himself, washing himself, feeding himself, playing games in which small difficulties and frustrations may arise, coping with other children who may at times annoy him, and who show him no particular consideration. Here is the arousal of the will, the first of our two conditions. Now for the second condition. His parents have made easy for him an organized, and in a sense a reasonable way of dealing with these challenges—by running to mother, or by telling father. These ways of acting have become part of his repertoire for dealing with his environment. When he comes to school he simply applies the lessons he has learned at home, or at least applies them as well as he can. We call the result a set of unfortunate character traits.

Perhaps if this child does not achieve a sufficient emotional re-education, and if parental overconcern is continued, he may manifest a deep psychological insecurity later on in life. His reactions to the opposite sex may be compromised and warped. Or he may develop a set of neurotic symptoms, such as irrational fears, peculiar compulsions, obsessions of one kind or another, and so on.

One way of explaining these unfortunate reactions would be to say that he was dominated by a repressed maternal attachment. But another, though by no means conflicting analysis of the situation is perhaps more illuminating. For it has been shown that phobias, obsessions, rationalizations, and neurotic symptoms generally are precisely learned ways of dealing with environmental problems. They are poor and ineffective techniques, of course, and this is what one means in calling them neurotic or pathological; but they were learned as solutions for problems, as methods of dealing with imperative challenges in just the way we have described (147). If our "maladjusted" child, now grown up, comes under the care of a psychiatrist, the expert will have to work back to the original conditions and situations in which the abnormal and unfortunate ways of acting and feeling were acquired, and to help his patient to acquire new and better ways.

To take a contrary case, a child who manifests independence, self-control, and courage in the face of difficulty has acquired these character traits by precisely the same process and mechanism. He, too, has faced many ego-involved challenges. But he has been enabled to meet them by the exercise of his own initiative. He has not merely been allowed to make his own choice, though of course permission and opportunity would be essential. He has also probably been helped, encouraged, and guided in his choosing. So he has also found a way of dealing with environmental problems which manifests itself as a set of character traits.

An instance of far-reaching re-education in which the school played a vital part is a very good illustration of the process by which personality is molded and shaped. A boy transferred into the third grade of a certain school. Within a week the teacher realized that she had a difficult problem. He turned out to be antagonistic and hostile. He refused, as far as he dared, to obey her instructions. He would not co-operate with the other children. He would not do his lessons. He frequently expressed the opinion that school was "the bunk." The teacher seemed to be able to do nothing with him.

About a month after the start of the term the third-grade group undertook a unit on Indians and Indian life, including a number of Indian songs, the words and music for which were to be composed by the children. At first this boy remained contemptuously aloof; but from some chance remark he let fall the teacher gathered that he thought very poorly of the songs that were being produced, and believed that he himself could do much better. Tactfully she planted in his mind the idea of composing a song of his own and bringing it to school with him. This he did. The song turned out to be surprisingly good. Everyone liked it, and the group learned to sing it with much pleasure. Within another week this refractory and difficult boy was the heart and soul of the project. His attitude towards the teacher, towards the other children, and before long to school itself was transformed. He became, almost literally, "another person." He had been gripped by a will-arousing challenge. He had found a satisfactory and constructive way of dealing with it. He had learned a new and successful technique for dealing with his environment (471).

A closely comparable case, in which, however, the person concerned was an adult, has been reported in connection with a workshop for the training of group leaders. One of the men who enrolled was known to have constant difficulties in dealing with others in group relationships. It became apparent that the source of these difficulties was his autocratic and domineering attitudes. The essential training program involved two related lines of attack. First, the concepts and techniques of democratic group leadership were explained and discussed. Second, the method known as "role-playing" was utilized. Briefly this means that the trainees acted out the role of group leader, making it possible for them to see how the general ideas that had been explained might apply in practice, and also making it possible for the workshop staff to criticize and help. In the particularly difficult case here described, what might almost be called a conversion took place. The man's attitudes both towards others and towards himself were deeply changed, his methods of working were transformed, and his effectiveness as a group leader was greatly increased.

The analysis of this instance is clear enough. Here was a man who was struggling with the challenges involved in group leadership. He was meeting those challenges as well as he could —by issuing orders, by trying to control everything himself, by domineering, by autocratic behavior. Left to follow his own devices and such glimmering lights as he had, he could see no other method of dealing with the situation. General verbalized explanations of other possibilities probably would not have got very far, for he would have tended to brush them off, and to call them impractical and silly. It was only when he was actually shown how to operate on quite a different basis that he was able to reach a better solution. He had the will. He needed to be helped to find the way (194).

Now let us consider an example of quite a different kind. A certain artist has for many years been conducting a studio in which he teaches artistically untrained adults how to draw. He has a definite system which proves very successful. First, he instructs his pupils to observe very carefully the over-all contour outlines of the objects or models they want to represent. Second, he insists that when they put pencil to paper they must avoid small broken movements and must make a continuous sweep, taking the consequences of any mistakes which may at first appear. The application of these working principles leads to some very impressive and interesting results. Here once more our two familiar conditions appear. The artist-teacher undertakes to enable his pupils to find an organized, effective *way* of acting. And since the adult pupils come to the studio and pay their money of their own free choice, the *will* has already been aroused. The mere will to draw would not in itself be enough, and however good the method might be, it could not be effective with a person who simply did not care.

Given these two conditions, it is surprising what rapid changes can be brought about. For instance, one hundred and fifty graduate students in educational psychology were given ten minutes practice a day for six weeks on rapid reading. Before the practice sessions they were assured that improvement was possible, and told to eliminate useless movements such as whispering and pointing, to relax and avoid a sense of strain, to concentrate and avoid thinking of anything else, to try to see the printed material in large units, and to try to anticipate what the author was going to say instead of assimilating it passively. In six weeks there was an average increase in speed of 15–20%, which is remarkable for such a short time, particularly with graduate students who might be expected to be well up to their maximum. But the wish to read faster was very strong and genuine with these people, and when they were shown the way, success came quickly (706).

You may think that learning to draw and learning to read faster are instances of the acquisition of skill rather than changes in the personality. Of course, new skills were acquired. But when a person who can't draw learns to draw, he becomes to some real extent a new person "all over," because he has found a new way of expressing himself. The same thing is true of a person who becomes able to read 20% faster than he could six weeks ago. The effect of these changes on the total pattern of ways of dealing with life's challenges may not be enormous, but it is certainly not negligible, and it should not be despised or discounted. There can be gains in self-confidence and self-satisfaction, and a realization of new possibilities and new horizons.

A more profound and far-reaching effect produced by our two basic conditions is shown in an experiment in which three-, four-, and five-year-old children were given special help in singing. The children, of whom thirty-three in all were involved in the experiment, were taken in small groups, usually of three members. In working with these small groups there was an intensive effort to help the children to learn to sing songs. When a new song was presented it was sung to them. Then the children sang it. Special difficulties received attention as they appeared. Various devices were used to enable the children to catch the right pitch. Often the experimenter would hum songs that the children had already learned, and the children would be asked to identify them, the purpose being to develop tonal memory and a grasp of melodic pattern. Songs that would be suitable and attractive were carefully chosen. The words of the songs were explained and discussed. In addition to actual singing, the children listened to numerous songs. The training periods were brief, and the work went on for a total of forty days.

The results reported are extensive and striking. The children became more and more interested in trying to learn. They gained noticeably in self-confidence. There was a marked expansion of general musical interests. It was noted that the children found an increasing enjoyment in the musical activities of the nursery school and kindergarten, and showed a growing comprehension of music as a field of knowledge. The school which these children were attending already had what would be regarded as a good program of musical activities, but there were no such results with the pupils who did not receive the special opportunity. The authors of the experiment believe that the general musical influences were "too thinly spread, too unchallenging, too unaware of the child's capacity to respond"

(692, p. 130). In other words, where there is no real challenge, no effective arousal of the will, no constructive revelation of an effective way, the desired results do not appear. But when the necessary conditions are fulfilled, the effect is likely to be far-reaching, deep-going, and often quite rapid.

These are probably enough illustrations to make clear, at least in a preliminary way, the meaning of our outline description of the process in and through which personality is shaped and molded. Quite possibly you may already suspect that what I have been describing and illustrating here is nothing more nor less than the process of learning. Up to a point that suspicion is perfectly correct. But there is one important qualification. The process here described and illustrated includes a good deal more than what is ordinarily meant by learning. It is perfectly true that learning depends on will, and that without the aroused will nobody learns. But usually one thinks of the arousal of the will, or of what is frequently called motivation, as a condition precedent to learning rather than as part and parcel of the process of learning itself. This may be an unfortunate and unduly limited way of thinking, but it is common and familiar.

Of course, the issue here has to do simply with terms and definitions, and it would not be unjustifiable to define the learning process as including both the will and the way. But if such a definition were set up, we would have to remind ourselves constantly that we were speaking of the learning process in an unusually comprehensive sense. For learning as ordinarily understood has to do rather with the finding of the way, the achieving of an organized mode of response, than with the arousal of the will. So instead of calling the process by which personality is shaped and molded the process of learning (although this way of speaking could be justified), it may save confusion if we call it the process of *adjustment*. And that process, to repeat, involves two conditions—first a striving to meet and deal with an ego-involved challenge, second the discovery of an organized mode of behavior in dealing with that challenge.

A CO-ORDINATING VIEWPOINT

There are four major viewpoints in present-day educational psychology. Superficially these viewpoints seem decidedly different, and even in some respects conflicting. As might be expected, these differences cause a good deal of confusion and partisanship. Some people do not quite know what to think. Other people attach themselves passionately to one viewpoint, and denounce some if not all of the others. So a reconciliation, if one is possible, would be a very good thing all round. As a matter of fact, a reconciliation is not only possible, but quite easy, for all the four viewpoints deal with our process of adjustment, and the differences between them are due to approaching that process in different ways and to concentrating on different aspects of it.*

1. One viewpoint in educational psychology which is widely represented is that of mental hygiene. Mental hygiene, as it is understood nowadays, aims not so much at curing mental and emotional ills, as at promoting "wholesome personality." I have already explained what mental hygienists mean by wholesome personality, and now I will point out what they think the promotion of wholesome personality comes to in the actual work of the school.

To be specific, you have to teach reading in the elementary grades. At the same time you want above all to develop this "wholesome personality" in your pupils. What, then, should you have in mind? What should you do? A recent study on the teaching of reading will give you an excellent answer. First of all, you should bear in mind that many of your pupils will find reading hard to learn, not because they are stupid or naughty, but because they are shy, reserved, flighty, unable to concen-

* Discussions of the content and role of educational psychology will be found in bibliography items 60, 61, 71, 82, 83, 129, 682, 683.

trate for long at a time. If you want them to learn to read, you must try by patience, tact, and kindness, to help them overcome these personality difficulties and limitations. Moreover, you must also remember that although many of the children find learning to read difficult, it is also very important for them. To be able to read is important for a child, not merely because reading is a very useful skill, but also because his self-esteem is involved. If he is a very poor reader or even a non-reader by the third or fourth grade, his failure is likely to be very humiliating and disturbing to him.

So instead of simply teaching reading as a skill, you should try to get the children to want to read and to believe that they can manage to read. You can do this by choosing suitable materials, by creating the right atmosphere in the classroom, by making everybody feel comfortable and at home. That is to say, you should treat the children, not merely as learners of a technique, but as personalities up against a challenge that is both difficult and intriguing. Such, in substance, is the advice of the author of the study, and he brings his recommendations to a close by saying: "Mental hygiene is the very heart of modern education" (55).

This specific example fairly represents the sort of thing that the mental hygienists think should be done everywhere. At first sight it seems rather radical, for it breaks completely away from the old-fashioned formal drill on narrow and stilted content. But you can easily see that it emphasizes one aspect of our process of adjustment. It places great, and quite legitimate emphasis on the *arousal of the will*.

2. Another viewpoint in educational psychology places its chief emphasis upon mental growth and development. For this reason it is often called the "developmental approach." In another book of mine I have summarized the central belief of this way of thinking in the words: "All power comes from growth" (470, p. 3). Psychologists who hold this viewpoint insist that it is the process of mental or personal growth which

makes all of us what we are and what we become. From this it follows that the essential business of education is to foster, promote, and guide the process of mental growth.

What brings about this process? Those who believe in the mental growth theory answer that children grow up towards maturity by dealing with "developmental tasks." Children "have to learn to walk, to talk, to dress themselves, to get along with groups, to behave like boys and girls, to act conventionally in a thousand situations, to read, write, figure, and spell, to use money, to respect property, to accept the values that are characteristic of American life, to find a way to earn a living, to select and win a marriage partner, to fulfill civic responsibilities, to arrive at a satisfying explanation of the meaning of life and of the universe—and much else" (613, p. 10).

Children, it is pointed out, tend to work at such tasks when they reach appropriate maturity, and are disturbed and more or less warped and impeded when they fail. So the great educational aim must be to help children and young people deal constructively with these developmental tasks or challenges. "Understanding teachers know what these tasks are; their sequence and timing in relation to physical, social, and mental maturity; what complications often arise as personalities with different characteristics and different backgrounds work at them; and what conditions, relationships, and experiences are most helpful to children in mastering them" (613, pp. 10–11).

As you read the long list of developmental tasks in the first of the two quotations—a list that is admittedly quite incomplete, you may perhaps wonder whether any tasks are nondevelopmental, and if so, what tasks and why. Later on we may be able to throw some light on this puzzle. For the moment let us say that a developmental task is a genuine, or ego-relevant challenge, and a child learns and grows, his personality is shaped, by attacking these significant, ego-relevant challenges. The significance, the reality, the force of any challenge for any child is determined quite largely by that child's level of maturity. Here is our idea of the arousal of the will as the first condition of adjustment all over again, with one new but perfectly consistent idea added—that a child's will to attack any problem cannot be aroused until he is mature enough.

3. Education has also been approached and surveyed from the standpoint of social psychology. Social psychology deals with the behavior and mentality of human beings as members of social groups and classes. Attempts to bring it to bear on educational problems are comparatively recent, and have not yet grown into a systematic body of doctrine. But there is every reason to think that such attempts will go forward, and that they are highly significant.

One of the most challenging of recent educational applications of social psychology insists that our schools are very ill-suited to socially underprivileged children. Although supposed to be schools for everybody, they are, according to this study, geared very definitely to what its author calls a "middle class" mentality. He holds that the chief reason why many children from the lower social strata do very badly in school, leave early, and are hard to handle while they are there, is that the school as now organized and run has little to offer them that is related to their way of life. So far as such children are concerned, the present curriculum is pretty much meaningless stuff. Also, the standards of behavior, the scheme of values, the mores, and the social and psychological atmosphere of the school are foreign to the outlook of children of these social classes (138).

Here it is clear that the social psychologists also are emphasizing the first of our two conditions of adjustment. What they say in effect is that the school can do very little to shape or influence the personalities of boys and girls from certain social strata because what it has to offer does not grip them, does not impress them as important, does not seem to bear on the real issues of their lives. The author of the study to which I have referred calls for a complete revamping and reconstruction of the school as it now exists, and he even suggests much less emphasis on reading than is customary. Just what the school ought to offer to the underprivileged and ill-oriented boys and girls he writes about is a question that goes beyond the province of psychology. But if we look at education as the shaping of personality, at least some comments on the author's suggestions are possible. First, we should remember that we want to develop in *all* boys and girls certain common understandings, ambitions, enthusiasms, and loyalties. It is probably quite true that the school at present is more class-oriented than we realize. But the answer is not simply another kind of class orientation. Second, there is no doubt that the great weakness of the school is its failure to grip, to interest, to motivate large numbers of young people. If this weakness is to be corrected, we must take into account the human background and real life needs and problems of these young people far more thoroughly than we do. This, however, may not call for such a radical change in the *content* of the curriculum as has been suggested; but it certainly means connecting the curriculum more closely with life as it is actually lived.

4. Another line of approach in educational psychology, which is by far the longest established, centers on classroom learning and subject-matter achievement. Its working assumption is that the essential service of the psychologist to education is to make classroom learning and subject-matter achievement more efficient. How do pupils learn the curricular subjects? How can we account for differences in subject-matter achievement? What differences in subject-matter achievement actually appear? These have seemed to be the vital questions on which psychology should bear. Up to perhaps ten or fifteen years ago they were certainly the problems to which psychologists devoted by far the greatest part of their attention.

This point of view has come in for many attacks. It is said to be narrow, or "formalistic," and to ignore the most important things about education. Mental hygienists, developmental psychologists, and social psychologists do not say that the content of the curriculum does not matter, but they do not give it the first place in their thoughts, and they certainly do not believe that good classroom learning is the central problem. They tend, indeed, to ask some very searching questions. Let us suppose that we manage to organize the learning of long division, or algebra, or French, or history, very efficiently according to psychological principles. Perhaps this may be worth doing. But what relationship, if any, will the better learning of long division, or French, or algebra, or history, have on the establishment of wholesome personality, or to mental development through significant tasks, or to the adaptation of the school to underprivileged children? The answer that is often at least suggested is: No relationship at all! At any rate, the question is a very cogent and searching one.

So at first sight, at least, there seems a striking cleavage between emphasis on classroom learning and subject-matter achievement, and emphasis on personality values—between the fourth of our psychological approaches and the other three. Moreover, the same cleavage runs all through educational thought and practice. We make what seems a sensible distinction between the curriculum as a body of knowledge, and extracurricular activities which affect character, and another and similar distinction between teaching which is supposed to have to do with subject-matter learning, and guidance which is supposed to be concerned with the broader issues of personality development.

The same cleavage is reflected in the attitudes of teachers in their dealings with pupils. It has been shown again and again that when teachers and mental hygienists estimate the seriousness of various undesirable character traits, there is not much agreement between the two lists of ratings (458). In one investigation, for instance, teachers indicated stealing, heterosexual conduct, and the passing of obscene notes as among the worst traits that any child could have. But mental hygienists took these traits far less seriously, and put unsociableness, suspiciousness, and unhappiness at the top of their list.

Again, teachers rated talkativeness as a very objectionable and serious characteristic; but mental hygienists considered it rather trivial. In general, teachers tend to object most strongly to assertive, aggressive, obviously difficult and challenging behavior, and are likely to think that there can be nothing gravely wrong with the quiet, shy, shut-in, introverted child. But the judgment of mental hygienists is often just the reverse (723).

The point, of course, is that teachers think in terms of character traits likely to disturb orderly classroom routines and to make conventional classroom learning difficult, whereas mental hygienists are thinking in terms of traits that indicate deep emotional disturbance and inadequacy and that may warp the child's future development. So the cleavage appears once more. It sometimes almost seems as though the school were dominated by two conflicting conceptions of education—subject matter in the classroom, personality development everywhere else.

Various attempts have been made to heal this breach, but they are not always as wise and helpful as one could wish. For instance, a recent writer has eloquently urged elementary school teachers to do everything they can to "de-emphasize the three R's," and never to allow a child to gain or lose status because of his success or failure in the basic skills (390). But this seems to rest on the assumption that the three R's are a sort of necessary evil which ought to be minimized. The author does not say this flatly, but it is hard to see what else he could have in mind; and it is, to put it mildly, a dubious proposition.

It has also been said that: "In our eagerness to place a book in the child's hands as soon as possible, we tend to overlook the larger aspects of training in personality growth" (305, p. 91). No doubt this is very true, but still the question remains —what do we do about that book? It has been pointed out that, "Academic standards and subject-matter objectives are insisted upon quite frequently, even though they do real damage to some children. We know, too, that often school routines are adhered to in such ritualistic fashion as to deny children the opportunities for experience or self-expression that would establish their faith in themselves or afford them insights into life and social processes which they sorely need" (530, p. 137). Again one willingly agrees; but still one would like to know what kind of subject-matter objectives and school routines might be desirable. The trouble with these pronouncements (and many more in the same vein could easily be cited) is that they do not really meet the issue. They merely accentuate the cleavage.

The real solution is to go back to our process of adjustment and its two conditions. Adjustment, as we have seen, depends upon the arousal of the will and the finding of the way. The learning process, to which many psychologists have devoted so much attention, is the finding of the way. When we say that a child has really learned long division, we do not (or should not) merely mean that he can pass a long division test with a mark of 85. We mean that he can use long division to meet a whole array of life's challenges which otherwise he could not meet. When a child really learns American history we do not (or should not) mean that he can now recite a great many facts. We mean that his ways of thinking, acting and feeling about his country have been more or less deeply affected.

When anything is really learned, it affects the way people live. And the only means we have of affecting the way people live and to shape their personalities is to get them to learn things. Indeed, unless people do learn—unless they find the way—the arousal of the will is unavailing, because it is stultified by failure. The author of a remarkable book on prison life says that many prisoners are extremely patriotic in a vociferous and flag-waving sense. But these men certainly do not act as though they loved the commonweal; and the reason is that they have never really learned how to act in such a way in dealing with the problems of their lives.

The only justifiable criticism of psychologists who have concentrated on classroom learning and subject-matter achievement is that they have concentrated on techniques and methods of learning without considering the arousal of the will. Of course this is a serious criticism. Yet the problem of classroom learning and subject-matter achievement cannot be shirked. After all, a school is not a general welfare agency or a psychiatric clinic. Its main business, in the immediately practical sense, is to teach a curriculum. So a book which undertakes to interpret education as it actually goes on in the school as the shaping of personality, will not read like a general treatise on mental hygiene or a textbook on psychiatry. Such a book must show how the things that the school actually does can and should affect personality. And among the things that the school actually does, the teaching of a curriculum unquestionably has a central place. But it is necessary to understand the teaching of the curriculum in terms of the whole process of adjustment; we must not think in terms of learning alone, ignoring the arousal of the will.

So we go on to deal with the two necessary conditions of the process of adjustment—the arousal of the will, and the finding of the way.

QUESTIONS FOR DISCUSSION

1. Can you think of any other universally desirable personality characteristic besides those listed in this chapter? Consider whether such other characteristics as you may have in mind are not mentioned in some other form or else clearly implied by those listed in the chapter.

2. Select from your own experience some striking experience or learning which had a definite effect on your personality. Are the two basic conditions of adjustment involved in it?

3. Teachers often try to make pupils learn by pressures of various kinds. Do these pressures effectively and genuinely "arouse the will"?

4. Collect and discuss some instances about which you have personal knowledge of how the learning of a new skill has shaped and affected personality.

5. What would be the probable effects on the personalities of children of forcing them to take a required course which was extremely unpopular?

6. Carefully consider all the personality characteristics listed and discussed in this chapter. Do you find any overlappings? Any inconsistencies?

7. Can you suggest some definite interests which the school should promote as widely as possible? Why do you consider these interests important?

8. Find some concrete instances of the meeting of life challenges by thought and intelligence, and also some contrasting instances of life challenges met in other ways. Discuss these instances, showing the importance of thinking in the course of daily life.

SUGGESTED READINGS

Allport, Gordon W., "The Psychology of Participation." *Psychological Review,* LII (1945), 117–132.

Betts, Emmett A., "Social and Emotional Readiness for Reading." *Educational Administration and Supervision,* XXX (1944), 65–86.

Buswell, Guy Thomas, "The Function of Subject Matter in Relation to Personality." *16th Yearbook,* National Council of Teachers of Mathematics (1941), Chap. 2, 8–19.

Prescott, Daniel, *Emotion and the Educative Process.* American Council on Education, Washington, D.C., 1938, Chap. 6.

Zachry, Caroline B., "Personality Growth." *Journal of Educational Sociology,* XVII (1943), 85–89.

2

The Sources of Motives

THE PROBLEM OF MOTIVATION

We have seen that the first of the two conditions which are necessary for the shaping of personality is the evocation of purpose or will. People learn and develop, and personality is molded, through the facing of challenges; and challenges which do not engage the will are not challenges at all. One reason why social contacts at school have such a profound effect on a child is that the challenge of dealing with the other children grips him. Contrariwise, one reason why a school subject like history, in spite of its great possibilities, may have a very small and temporary effect on the same child is that it does not grip him at all. Indeed, for him the actual challenge of history may be to get a passing mark with minimum trouble; and then the real effect of history upon his personality may be the very opposite of what it could and should be. The shaping of personality—the process of adjustment—involves more than the evocation of purpose. But motivation, or the evocation of purpose, is an essential part of the story.

The problem of motivation, put in the simplest language, is

the problem of what makes people do the things they do. Why is one child fascinated by arithmetic while another child sitting right beside him hates it? Why is one boy a constant trouble-maker, while another is rather too good to be true? Why is one high-school student determined to become a doctor, and perfectly willing to face all kinds of difficulties, deprivations, and hard work to achieve his goal, while another seems to have no idea what kind of job he wants, if any? Why do many students find football so much more engrossing than geometry? Or, to put the matter more generally, why are human motives what they are? These are the sort of questions with which we now have to deal.

Clearly such questions are of the very first importance. Anyone who wants to deal successfully with human beings must do his best to understand their motives, and must operate in terms of those motives and try to control them. This is true of parents, salesmen, journalists, advertisers, administrators, executives, politicians, and so forth. And for the teacher it is particularly important to understand human motives and to know how to shape and direct them, because the teacher's job is precisely the shaping and molding of personality, a job which cannot be done without the control and direction of purpose. So the importance of the topic of motivation is abundantly clear.

Almost equally obvious is the difficulty of the topic. Human purposes are endlessly varied and complicated. The springs of human action are often obscure and peculiar. To understand why one boy likes algebra and is bored by football, while another boy loves football and detests algebra, may seem a formidable challenge to human insight and wisdom. So indeed it is! Yet a vast amount of thought and work have been brought to bear on problems just like these—upon the problems of motivation—and it has not gone for nothing. Assuredly we cannot give pat answers to all questions. But a reasonable working comprehension of the nature of human motivation can be had, and such a comprehension is both illuminating and practical.

ITS TWO ASPECTS

If a person stands and watches a brook, there are two general questions which might very well occur to him. First, what makes the brook flow at all? Second, what makes it take the particular course which it actually does take? These are two of the most general questions one can ask, not only about brooks, but also about human motivation. In the case of the brook, the reason why it flows at all is the action of the force of gravity. There is a constant tendency for the water to flow toward the center of the earth. But the actual course it takes will depend upon all sorts of varying and shifting circumstances. These circumstances determine and shape the course of the brook.

So, too, with human motives. They are undoubtedly shaped and determined by circumstances, and later on we shall have to ask how the shaping is done. But the question immediately before us is whether there is in human nature anything corresponding to the force of gravity, any constant tendency which, so to speak, makes us have motives or purposes at all. So the problem of motivation falls into two divisions, and has to do first with the sources of motives, and second with the shaping of motives. It is with the first of these questions that we are now concerned.

The question of the sources of motivation is a very interesting one theoretically. But also it is of immense practical importance. If you want to change the course of a brook, so that it will flow where you want it to flow, you must take the force of gravity into account. It would be useless to dig a trench above the water level, or perhaps running uphill. No matter how beautiful the trench might be, the water would not go into it.

If there is in human nature a force comparable to gravity, which, so to speak, makes us have purposes or motives or goals, and which perhaps determines their general direction, then you must take account of this force if you want to deal successfully with human beings. The most beautifully and carefully planned course in social studies, or science, or mathematics will not have the desired effect if it is wrongly related to the springs of human action. It will be just as futile as a well-dug trench running uphill from a brook. This very mistake is all too often made in the planning of schoolwork. On the other hand, a situation can come about without any planning, which nevertheless has a tremendous effect because it is vitally related to the springs of action. For instance, a vicious clique spirit can develop in a school or in a classroom; and that spirit can engross the pupils, and have more real although unfortunate educative effect—more effect on their personalities—than all the planned teaching that goes on. That would be like carefully digging a beautiful trench uphill from the brook, but accidentally leaving a gap at the low end through which all the water would rush.

So if there is in human nature any constant, any gravity-like tendency which is the ultimate source of motivation, it is very important for us to understand that tendency or force.

CONCEPT OF BASIC NEEDS

On the basis of our present knowledge it seems reasonable to believe that there is such a force. It is the force which originates in what many psychologists today call *basic human needs.* If this is so, then the power of human motives and purposes comes from these basic needs, just as the power of the flowing brook comes from the influence of gravity. Moreover the comparison can be carried further. For just as gravity always gives a general downward direction to the flow of the brook, in spite of all its twists and turns and wanderings, so the constant pressure of basic needs gives a general direction to all human purposes, in spite of their variety.

This brief preliminary statement about the sources of human motives may perhaps seem unduly dogmatic. It is not so intended. I should warn you frankly that the doctrine of basic needs as the origins of motivation is a theory, or hypothesis, and that no one should accept it uncritically. It has not been proved beyond the possibility of questioning, and probably cannot be so proved. Nor is it universally accepted. The most that can honestly be claimed for it is that it is reasonable, tenable, and enlightening, that it helps us to understand human nature and to deal intelligently with human beings. Perhaps this is all one has a right to ask. In any case, a number of critical questions will have to be raised about the doctrine, or the hypothesis, whichever one prefers to call it. But before raising any such questions, it will be helpful to look at one of the best and most convincing of all listings of basic needs. Whether or not this particular listing seems perfectly satisfactory (and there is no necessity to commit ourselves to it in all its details), it will at any rate give us something specific to think about and discuss.

The listing of basic needs which we shall consider is that presented by Daniel Prescott in his celebrated and influential book, *Emotion and the Educative Process* (530). According to Prescott, there are three main types of human needs.

First, there are *physiological needs.* These are needs created by the demands of the organism. Prescott here mentions needs for essential materials and conditions upon which life depends, or more specifically, needs for air, food, and shelter. Also he mentions here needs for recurrent periods of rest and activity. Reproductive or sexual needs should certainly be included, although Prescott himself does not refer to them.

Second, there are what Prescott calls *needs for status.* By this he means what might be rather more loosely called *social needs.* More specifically he mentions here a need for affection, a need to feel oneself as belonging to a social group or social groups, and a need to resemble other people in one's general behavior.

Third, there are what Prescott calls *ego needs,* or *integrative needs.* Here again he subdivides this general classification into a number of more specific items. Thus under ego needs, or integrative needs, he mentions the need for contact with reality, pointing out that people find it unsatisfactory to live constantly in an imaginary or dream world, and seem to crave experiences which bring them into touch with an objective environment. Again, he mentions a need for what he calls "harmony with reality." By this he means a need to reckon with and to understand the world about us as it truly is, in contrast to being dominated by superstition, rationalization, and fantasy. Third, he mentions a need for what he calls "progressive symbolization." Here he means a need to develop explanations of the world about us and of experience. What he has in mind are explanations of the kind that are to be found in natural or social science, explanations in linguistic terms or linguistic symbols. Hence his word "symbolization." But he might also relate the idea of progressive symbolization to the arts, if the arts can be regarded as means of symbolizing emotional values. You may ask why Prescott includes the above-mentioned specific needs under the general class or category of "ego needs," or "integrative needs." His answer would be that unless a person faces the real world about him, reckons with it, understands it to some extent, and has some kind of rational explanation of his own experience, he cannot develop a stable, consistent, effective selfhood.

This list of needs is quite provocative, and immediately stimulates all kinds of questioning and comment. But we had still better postpone our discussion of the general topic of needs for a little while, until we have seen just how this account of human motivation bears on educational problems.

Whatever we think of this account offered by Prescott, it is certainly highly suggestive. Granting, for instance, that everyone has a general need for status which can be further subdivided into more specific needs, then we have an idea full of implications. This might be taken as one of the chief reasons why youngsters in school persistently tend to organize themselves into cliques and closed groups of various kinds, why one of the great pleasures of such groups is the exclusion of allegedly unworthy persons, and why the allegedly unworthy seem to find exclusion so distressing. On a more constructive plane, the effect of status needs would help to explain the delight and enthusiasm which many young people take in co-operative leadership. Also, it would help to explain the wish for athletic prominence. It might have much to do with the prestige of the college-preparatory curriculum, and with the willingness and indeed the strong desire of many young people to undertake such a curriculum, even though they have no passionate interest in the subjects they have to study, or any particular belief that those subjects are of any great use in the world.

Furthermore, if we grant the reality and potency of status needs, we can see at once how harmful it can be for a child to be put up against inevitable failure in his school work. Such potential implications are, indeed, almost endless. All in all, the concept of status needs is so fruitful that one is sorely tempted to accept it out of hand, and to abandon the critical caution which suggests that the explanations offered may just possibly be too easy to be true.

Once again, the notion of integrative, or ego, needs suggests much about subject matter. May not the study of natural science do something to meet the personal need for contact with and harmony with reality? If such is the case, then how should natural science be organized and taught in order to bring it into relationship with this pattern of basic needs? May not literature and the social studies offer interpretations of life and of experience which can be very helpful and very significant, if, indeed, there is a real need for progressive symbolization? Once again, how should literature and the social studies be taught if they are to be means for the satisfaction of such a basic need? If the shaping of personality depends on purpose, and if purposes are determined by some such basic needs as Prescott lists, then we begin to see, at least dimly and partially, how education can be an agency for the shaping of personality.

FURTHER DEFINITION

But is Prescott's list of needs, or any other such list, really tenable? Is it a well-founded and sound account of the sources of motivation? That, by all means, is the crucial question. Before attacking this question directly, however, the concept of need must be more precisely defined, and certain wrong interpretations must be guarded against. So we now raise a number of critical questions.

1. How did Prescott decide on this particular list of needs? He tells us very clearly. He examined and studied a large number of case histories—accounts, that is to say, of children who seemed to be maladjusted and showed certain difficulties or abnormalities in their behavior. Always he asked himself this question: "Just what is the child or young person trying to bring about by each item of observed behavior?" Thus he built up his list of needs. Prescott here makes a modest and honest statement. There was little of the paraphernalia of science about his procedure—no tests, no statistics, no formal experiments. He was operating as a student of what one might call the natural history of human behavior, using a descriptive method, and trying to understand the facts as well as he could.

Quite possibly this is about the level on which a great deal of psychologizing is bound to operate at the present time, for pretentious intricacies are far from guaranteeing results which are significant, or approximately true, or even invested with the saving grace of common sense. In any case, Prescott's account of his own method eliminates from one's mind the uneasy suspicion that he might have been cheating—that he might have started off with a conception of education as he thought it ought to be, and then proceeded to discover a set of basic human needs to fill his bill of particulars and justify his prejudices. What he did was to make a broad survey of human nature in action, and to attempt to understand and explain the spectacle. It is by no means an unreasonable method.

2. Is Prescott's list of basic needs plausible? The answer seems to be, Yes. This is particularly true if one thinks of his broad, threefold classification. There might be considerable disagreement about some of the more specific needs which appear within the three main classes. It might be argued that Prescott has omitted some important ones which ought to be added. Some of those which he mentions might be eliminated. There might be different combinations and also changes in the wording here and there. But on the whole the three main classes seem to bear scrutiny quite well.

Most people would agree about the reality of physiological needs. That human beings really do need air, food, shelter, and alternations of activity and repose; and that these needs operate as basic and more or less continuous motives would be hard to dispute. A few additions to Prescott's list might seem justified, particularly the addition of sexual needs. But apart from such qualifications, which are of minor importance, the physiological needs appear to be fundamental and universal human concerns.

Some psychologists would have a different interpretation of the physiological drives, and instead of calling them basic needs, would regard them as responses to internal stimuli, such as stimuli produced by contractions in the walls of the empty stomach, the sensations of which we feel as hunger. But this alternative interpretation really stems from a general psychological position. It is at least debatable. Its advantages, if any, have not been proved beyond a doubt; and there is no necessity for agreeing that it invalidates the hypothesis of basic physiological needs.

As for the need for a sense of status in human affairs, most social psychologists, abnormal psychologists, and mental hygienists would probably agree that this is a basic and universal drive, although there might well be different ways of phrasing the idea. Under the general heading of status needs, Prescott, as you will remember, specifically mentions a need for affection, for a sense of belonging, and for behavior similar to that of other people. Some might wish to add a need for recognition or admiration or respect. But such a need might perhaps be included under the need for social belonging, and the whole issue may be no more than a matter of words. Apart from such detail, however, there is certainly a wide belief among informed and expert persons that human beings are motivated by a craving for status among their fellows, a craving which exists among children, among adults in our own culture, and in primitive human groups as well. You, as a teacher, will see much in the behavior of your pupils which makes the assumption of such a need seem very reasonable; and if you assume that such a need does exist, it will help you to understand your pupils and also to handle them.

At first sight Prescott's ego needs, or integrative needs, might seem more doubtful. Do human beings really crave contact with reality, harmony with reality, and progressive symbolization? Perhaps one might hesitate. But let us remember what made Prescott believe that there really are such basic needs. He studied the behavior of many young people. He found among these young people a seeking for explanations, a seeking to come to terms with things as they really are. He was forced to believe that the explanations, the viewpoints, the patterns of interpretation which these young people achieved were of great importance in determining their conduct and shaping their personalities. You too can see the same thing. If a youngster becomes a Communist it affects his actions, his feelings, his whole life, his whole personality. It is a focus of integration about which everything in his personality tends to center. The same is fortunately true of other patterns of interpretation or of symbolization than that of Communism.

A wide survey of human nature makes Prescott's ego, or integrative, needs seem very plausible. The nature theories of primitive peoples strike us as crude and absurd. We call them myths and superstitions. But they are attempts to come to terms with reality. Primitive tribesmen take such nature theories very seriously, use them for guidance and help and warning, and turn to them as integrating influences in their living.

The following little story shows how much progressive symbolization can mean on the purely individual plane. A child alone in his bedroom began to shriek with fear when a thunderstorm came up, and finally an adult arrived to comfort him. The visitor invented a myth on the spur of the moment. Thunder, he said, was caused by little pigs' tails rubbing together, and the lightning was the spark. Black pigs produced forked lightning, and white pigs produced sheet lightning. The child, neither quite believing nor disbelieving, drank the story in, became quite calm and happy, and never feared a thunderstorm again. Perhaps a more scientific explanation might have worked better, particularly if adorned with careful statistics about the improbability of being struck by lightning. But in any case, the story very clearly shows the great power of progressive symbolization over the whole gamut of human responses, including emotional responses.

There is a lesson in this which is of the utmost importance for you as a teacher. When you teach science, or social studies, or history, or literature, much of the content of your teaching will consist of interpretations or symbolizations. If you can believe that young people seek interpretations, need interpretations, then you will see that the symbolizations you teach should never be considered mere bloodless theories, constructs of pure reason to be coolly understood. These interpretations, these symbolizations that you teach can and should profoundly affect the actions, the attitudes, the feelings, the working viewpoints, the lives, the personalities of your pupils. If they do not have this effect, they are not being properly taught and learned, for they are out of contact with a basic need.

William James, at the opening of a famous course of lectures, once said that every person in the audience had a philosophy of his own, and that this philosophy was the most important thing about that person. To translate the idea into Prescott's language, a person's philosophy is the means he has achieved for satisfying his integrative needs. One of your own most vital tasks in the classroom is to help your pupils to achieve a philosophy, an outlook upon life which will be constructive and full of promise for the future. This is one of the ways in which the subjects you teach can be agencies for the shaping of personality.

3. Many writers have presented lists of basic human needs. To what extent are these other lists in agreement with that of Prescott? This is a penetrating and revealing question. If there were extensive and radical disagreement it would tend to undermine the whole concept, for it would at least suggest that the determination of what basic needs really are is a matter of guesswork or personal prejudice. Agreement, on the other hand, would tend to substantiate the concept of needs. The summary answer to the question is that there is substantial agreement among many listings of needs, that there are also considerable differences, but that most of the differences have a reasonable and logical explanation. In making this answer good I shall not attempt to survey all or even a very large number of the listings of needs by various authorities. Instead I shall present and discuss four typical examples. This will be sufficient for our present purpose.

The first of these four lists of basic needs is that presented by Breckenridge and Vincent in their book, *Child Development* (69, pp. 112–113). They mention five needs—needs for affectional security, for friendship and understanding, for respect for authority earned by authority, for privacy of possession and ideas, and for fun. The book by Breckenridge and Vincent assembles and co-ordinates a great deal of material from various other authors. It is, in a sense, a source book. Breckenridge and Vincent present this list of needs, not as their own contribution, but as having been presented by another person in lecture form. Presumably, however, it has their approval. As compared with Prescott's list, their list shows certain obvious similarities, but it is much less objective and complete. One feels that the lecturer was explaining what he himself thought would be good for children rather than studying their behavior and asking himself what motivated it. Fun, for instance, may be very desirable, but whether there is in human nature a general need for fun is quite dubious. Again there is no doubt that people in a culture like our own do desire privacy of possession, but there have been and are many social orders in which property is communal, and nobody seems to mind. All in all, the list presented by Breckenridge and Vincent seems to be a somewhat superficial statement, representing a biased point of view, and an understanding of the meaning of needs distinctly different from that of Prescott.

A second list which is worth scrutinizing is that presented by Lawrence K. Frank (189). Frank thinks that there are two main types of basic human needs. First, there are physical needs—needs for food, shelter, rest, and exercise. Second, there are psychological needs—needs for love, affection, and assurance. Here is a close correspondence with Prescott's physiological needs and status needs, although the latter are less precisely defined. But there is no mention at all of Prescott's ego, or integrative, needs which, as I have tried to show, are both plausible and very important.

A third list which deserves notice is that presented by Arthur I. Gates and his associates in their *Educational Psychology* (208, p. 629). They recognize needs for affection, for a sense of social belonging, for a sense of personal independence, for social approval, and for the maintenance of one's self-esteem. This seems to amount to an expansion of Prescott's status needs, with various further details and distinctions introduced. But once more there is no mention of ego, or integrative, needs. This list of needs must be taken with considerably more seriousness than the two previously discussed. It embodies the judgment of a group of distinguished psychologists, each of whom approaches the problem with a somewhat different background, and it is based on a thorough familiarity with the relevant literature.

Among the four listings here being considered, the one that approximates Prescott's most closely is that presented by Fenton in his book *Mental Hygiene in School Practice* (172). According to Fenton the basic human needs are for a healthy body and sound physique, for feelings of security, for social adjustment and recognition, for feelings of personal competence, for an acceptance of the conditions and realities of life, for experiencing curiosity and pleasure and the acquisition of active and varied interests, and for recognition as a developing personality.

There is more than a hint here of ego, or integrative, needs, and a certain general similarity between Fenton and Prescott. However, if one looks closely, it becomes evident that the working conception of need held by these two men is not quite the same. It seems quite reasonable to believe that there are such physiological needs as the need for food, or for shelter, and that these needs operate as motives. But although a healthy body and a sound physique are very good things, a great many people are certainly not actively motivated to seek them. Or again, look at Fenton's alleged need for acquiring active and varied interests. Active and varied interests are certainly desirable. But there does not seem to be a universal urge to acquire them in the same way that there seems to be an urge to seek social recognition and to achieve social conformity.

To repeat, what I have offered here is not at all a comprehensive survey of listings of basic human needs, but only a selection of representative samples. However it is possible to formulate certain conclusions without being too rash. (*a*) There is considerable agreement among the listings. (*b*) Some of the differences are due to the omission of various categories of needs. (*c*) Some of the differences are due to wording. (*d*) Some of the differences arise because one author may carry his analysis into more detail than another. (*e*) Probably the most important of all the differences among these lists come from differing concepts of the nature of needs itself. It is notable that among the authors cited, only Prescott tells us clearly just how he arrived at his schedule of needs. This is valuable because it shows us how he understands the nature of needs, a consideration which leads to our next major question.

4. Exactly what do we mean when we talk about human needs? This is the culminating question in our analysis of the concept of need, and the most important one too. For if we are going to use the concept of need in an attempt to understand human motives, it is very necessary to define that concept as precisely as we can, and to take care always to use it in the defined sense.

a) The needs listed by Prescott are not needs for specific things. You may say that you need eight hours sleep each night, or a ham sandwich, or a job, or a husband, or a dose of aspirin. This is a perfectly proper way of talking, but you probably do not think of needs of this kind as universal basic human urges, and neither would anyone else. Needs for specific things are not the sort of needs considered by Prescott, nor the sort with which we are dealing. It is perfectly true that the specific things that a person wants can help to satisfy more general and basic needs such as we have in mind. A ham sandwich can satisfy hunger. A job can satisfy status needs. A husband can satisfy both status needs and physiological needs. But the distinction between wants for specific things and basic needs is clear enough, and very important if we are to avoid confusion.

b) The kind of needs we are considering are not needs for specific abilities. In a certain course which was given the title "Functional Science," a unit on how to cure a cold was included. In intention at any rate the unit was very practical. It was pointed straight to one of the emergencies of life; and if the unit really did teach people how to cure colds, it did them a valuable service. But human beings certainly do not go through the world motivated by a general desire to be able to cure colds. The same could be said of innumerable other special abilities—reading, spelling, multiplying, speaking Spanish, typewriting, piano playing. Such abilities may be of great practical value, so that an intelligent person will really want to acquire some of them. They may certainly enable a person to satisfy basic needs. But in themselves they are not basic needs.

c) Basic human needs as we understand them are not things that some person or committee or group of experts or enthusiasts think that other people need. This is a point which you should particularly notice and think about. Human needs are often understood in this sense, and, in fact, we found several instances in the lists which were considered above. But it is not the sense in which we must interpret the concept of need. For instance, an important educational committee undertook to show how science could be taught so as to meet what it called "personal-social needs" (477). As a first step the committee had to decide what it thought those needs were. Among them it included a need for "intelligent consumership," and a need to understand the conservation of natural resources. Most people would be likely to agree that in a certain sense these are important needs, and that they should be part of the mental equipment of a good citizen. Furthermore, it is a very sound idea to redirect science teaching for the sake of supplying this equipment. But it is impossible to believe that human behavior is basically motivated by an urge to become an intelligent consumer or to protect natural resources.

In general it is very important to distinguish between the aims of education and the urges which determine individual conduct. The great psychological problem is how to use the urges to achieve the aims. In the shaping of personality we must start with human nature as it is, and bring our teaching into relationship to its fundamental dynamics.

Out of the four distinctions which have been made there emerges a positive answer to our question, Exactly what do we mean by human needs? Needs, in the sense in which the word is here used, and in the sense understood by Prescott and by others who think as he does, are *permanent trends of human nature which underlie human behavior from birth to death under all circumstances and in all kinds of society.*

THE CONCEPT OF NEED: ITS VALIDITY

Now that the concept of need has been defined and clarified, a much more serious issue must be faced. Is the concept sound? Is it valid? That human behavior is ultimately dependent on underlying needs is, of course, a hypothesis. What reasons are there for accepting this hypothesis?

1. There are numerous facts of behavior which strongly suggest the presence and influence of underlying needs. No one of these facts taken separately is conclusive, but cumulatively they give strong support to the hypothesis.*

a) Often a set of stimulating conditions does not give rise to the response which might normally be expected. The suggested explanation is that the appropriate need is not active. The indifference of a recently fed animal to food is one of the most obvious instances. But there are many other examples. Many writers and creative artists, when so satiated with success that their status needs are in abeyance, simply stop work, in spite of stimuli such as commissions and deadlines which would ordinarily make them go on working. A teacher may present a mathematical problem which she finds very intriguing, only to have her pupils show complete indifference, the suggested reason being that it is unrelated to any of their active needs. A general idea of major significance emerges here, for no problem, whether in mathematics or personal living or elsewhere, is really a problem if it is unrelated to active need.

* The discussion here is based largely on an article by H. A. Murray, entitled "Facts which support the concept of need or drive," bibliography item 468.

b) Common objects can often give rise to unexpected reactions, the suggested explanation being that an active need is present without our knowing about it. For instance, one gives an apple to a boy with the idea that he will enjoy eating it. But if he has been recently bullied or frustrated, so that he has an active urge to assert himself, he may surprise one by throwing the apple away. A similar quirk of behavior occurred in a classroom in a boys' school. The teacher had been wrestling with a serious disciplinary problem, and handling it very badly. Three-quarters of the class had been made to leave their seats and line up along the walls of the room. The seats were long movable benches, each accommodating eight boys; and on one of these benches only two boys remained seated. Their classmates along the walls began to dare these two to tip the bench over. It was pushed further and further back out of the perpendicular while all present held their breath (except the teacher, who did not know what was going on). Finally the bench fell over with a satisfying crash, and the two culprits received an accolade of social approval.

c) Trends of behavior can occur without any external stimulus. For instance, a hungry animal does not stay quiescent until food comes its way, but may start to hunt and explore. Many writers, too, will begin to hunt and explore in a not wholly dissimilar manner when the grocery bill begins to look threatening. A great deal of learning and achievement begins with a sense of something lacking, of dissatisfaction, or unrest, which in turn gives rise to a process of questing and seeking whose end result may be very vaguely envisioned at first. Indeed, such indeterminate, yet urgent seeking and questing is usually found in all problem-solving behavior; and it is not implausible to think that this seeking and questing is due to the energy of an active need.

d) We know by introspection that experiences of desiring and intending usually precede active striving. When a person sets to work to learn the rules for Latin conditional sentences, or to write an English theme, or to fulfill requirements for entering a fraternity, he is apt to be conscious of making up his mind in advance, or of nerving himself for the effort. He certainly feels as though his behavior depended on an urge or drive, and that he is not merely responding to stimulation. Introspection, no doubt, is uncertain, but we have no right to ignore or contradict it without good reason.

e) Introspection indicates that a need may determine the direction of attention. It is difficult to concentrate on work when one is very hungry, because of the effect of a physiological need. Thoughts of an engrossing hobby or a prospective party can persistently intrude in the midst of a lesson. On the hypothesis we are considering, the reason would be that the hobby or the party promise excellent satisfactions for potent needs while the lesson is very feebly related to any needs at all.

f) Introspection shows that sentiments and opinions can be affected by needs. Political and social opinions, for instance, are rarely based on full information and pure reason. A person is likely to be a Democrat, or a Liberal, or a Conservative partly because those with whom he associates are Democrats, or Liberals, or Conservatives, and because he wants to stand well with them. Dale Carnegie's formula for making a person friendly is, essentially, to encourage him to talk about himself, which, in our terms, means influencing his sentiments by satisfying his status needs.

g) Many of the phenomena of abnormal psychology become unintelligible or at least very hard to explain without the concept of underlying need or drive. We know, for instance, that a child can be profoundly and permanently disoriented by lack of parental affection. Why should this be so? What makes the withholding of parental affection matter so much? Again, it is believed that conflicts between motives, and particularly between sexual and social motives, can create life problems of the most serious kind. In attempting to deal with such a problem a person may produce a rationalization, that is to say, an explanation and a way of acting that at least enables him to get along fairly well. Or he may sublimate the conflict by devoting himself to some cause with fanatical zeal. Or he may develop neurotic symptoms. It is hard to see how such patterns of behavior could arise unless there were a conflict between deep and powerful urges.

h) Finally we must take into consideration the remarkable effects of partial frustration and of difficulty. Children, and older people too, will often return to an unpleasant task after an interruption. Opposition at home has led many a boy and girl to work all the harder at some project instead of giving it up, and to accept risks and inconveniences in concealing his persistence. High standards in a school can act as a challenge as well as a discouragement. Inventors, scientists, artists, and writers—Franz Schubert and Anthony Trollope, for instance—have stuck grimly at their chosen undertakings in the face of ridicule and apparent failure. Robert the Bruce's celebrated spider, which kept on spinning its web although the web broke down again and again, is a prototype of a great deal in human experience.

How are such things possible? A not unreasonable explanation is that the person who persists in an undertaking in spite of discouragement, deprivation, disapproval, and even pain, does so because he sees in that undertaking the prospective and to some extent the immediate satisfaction of an urgent basic need.

Such, then, are the chief facts of behavior which support the concept of basic needs. It is true that they might all be explained in some other way. They do not add up to positive proof. But positive proof is certainly very rare in psychology. What these facts seem clearly to indicate is that there are powerful underlying trends in human nature. To this extent they substantiate the hypothesis that behavior depends ultimately on basic needs.

2. We find further support for this hypothesis if we ask

what the position would be if we rejected the concept of basic needs. Let us see what the alternative would be.

A human being, we will say, comes into the world and lives his whole life without any permanent general underlying needs at all. What kind of creature then is he? What capacities will he have? He will be a creature capable of *responding* to a range of stimuli, some, like sensations of vision and hearing, coming from outside his body; others, like the sensations we call hunger and thirst, coming from inside his body. Also, he will be a creature capable of *learning* in and through his responses to stimulation. In particular, all this being's motives will be learned or acquired. This is the position expressly taken by certain psychologists, and it is summed up in the statement: "Desires are created only by the process of conditioning" (687), conditioning being the name attached to the learning of motives or desires.

This account, be it noted, would apply to all kinds of motives or desires, including those desires which Prescott would classify as physiological needs. Thus a human being would not be born with any desire or need for food, but only with a digestive mechanism capable of producing certain sensations when the stomach is empty. These gastric sensations would become attached or conditioned first to the response of eating something, and later on to the more sophisticated response of choosing or preferring or liking this or that nutritive substance. So what may seem to a person a basic need for food would be, in fact, an acquired disposition, very powerful and permanent no doubt, but still the result of learning and experience.

Clearly the case for the hypothesis of basic needs is strongest with the physiological needs, and if it is possible to dispose of these, then it will not be possible to maintain the reality of status needs and ego needs. This is exactly what is involved. "Motives," it has been said, "are almost infinitely varied among men, not only in form but in substance. Not four wishes, nor eighteen propensities, nor any and all combinations of these, even with their extensions and variations, seem adequate to account for the endless variety of goals sought by an endless variety of mortals" (8, p. 193). Motives, in short, are all of them acquired, and there are no basic determining tendencies in human nature except the ability to respond to stimulation and to learn.

No doubt when we contemplate the "endless variety of goals sought by an endless variety of mortals" to which the author of the above quotation so eloquently refers, it does seem difficult to bring them all into relationship with a limited catalog of basic needs. May it not be more promising to try to account for this endless variety of goals as due simply to the endless vicissitudes of life, as established by learning and nothing else? But the question is not whether the hypothesis of needs offers here and now a complete, ready-made explanation of everything in human behavior. Most certainly this is by no means the case. The question is whether the hypothesis that behavior is ultimately determined by basic needs is or is not a better principle for explanation and understanding than the hypothesis that all motives are learned from the ground up. I have already argued that there are many phenomena of behavior which strongly support the hypothesis of basic needs, and this seems to be part of the answer. In addition to this, the hypothesis that all motives and goals are completely determined by learning involves a conception of behavior which is certainly dubious.

No doubt actual motives in human life are enormously varied. Perhaps our author may be justified in calling them "almost infinitely varied." But the emphasis must be upon the word *almost*. For that variety is not infinite. It has its limits. And the hypothesis of learning cannot explain these limits. Once we grant that all goals, all motives, all urges are due to learning, there seems to be no reason why a person could not learn to like, to desire, to dislike, to avoid anything or everything. We find ourselves committed to a sort of Alice-in-Wonderland psychology:

Speak roughly to your little boy,
And beat him if he sneezes;
For he can thoroughly enjoy
The pepper if he pleases.

People persistently seem to like eating, drinking, being admired and respected, finding themselves in tune with their fellows, arriving at explanations which they find revealing and helpful; and it is hard to believe that any kind of training would make them dislike such things. On the other hand they persistently dislike hunger, humiliation, neglect, and mental bafflement; and they almost certainly could never learn to like these things. According to the learning hypothesis, a human being could be as lonesome as a woodchuck, as mean as a rogue elephant, and as unthinking as a hen, and still be perfectly happy and self-fulfilled. This, however, is simply not true. No doubt human nature is flexible, but it is not as flexible as all that. The hypothesis that we are ultimately actuated by basic needs provides, at least in principle, an explanation of the rigid limits of human flexibility, and of the strong and universal trends which seem to show themselves in human behavior. But the hypothesis that all motives and proclivities are completely products of learning provides no such principle of explanation.

To return to our previous parable, no doubt we still have to explain the actual course taken by the brook, and this is due to circumstances, and to the learning that arises from circumstances. But to recognize this is not to deny the existence of the force of gravity, which makes the brook flow in the first place, and which determines its general direction.

3. There is a final question of a more systematic kind which has an important bearing on the validity of the concept of basic needs. Are not basic needs, in the sense in which they have been here defined, essentially the same as instincts? If so, the concept of needs would be seriously undermined, for the idea

that human conduct is to an important extent determined by instincts is no longer generally accepted by psychologists, and for very good reasons.

An instinct is a definite, organized pattern of behavior, which is innate in its origin, and very little or not at all affected by learning. The nest-building or migratory or mating behavior of birds are excellent examples of what the word means. A quarter of a century ago the concept of instinct was widely used in psychology, and applied not only to the behavior of animals but also to that of human beings. Numerous lists of alleged human instincts were drawn up, which on the surface, at least, had a considerable likeness to the lists of needs which we have been discussing. Pugnacity, curiosity, and gregariousness, for instance, were often included among these supposed instincts.

The trouble was, however, that pugnacity, curiosity, gregariousness, and suchlike words, did not stand for clear-cut, identifiable patterns of response, like the nest-building activities of birds, or the food-storing activities of bees. They were mere labels without any definite objective reference at all. Nest-building is a quite unmistakable activity, and no one watching a bird so engaged can doubt what it is doing. But this is not true of pugnacity, which is at best only a vague descriptive word for an ill-defined aspect of behavior. To invent labels of this kind for any and every aspect of behavior is very easy; and an enormous number of so-called "human instincts" was, in fact, invented—instincts for loving children, for warfare, for administration, for writing, for fixing machinery, and so on almost without end. One careful study made a survey of 495 books which dealt with the problem, and its author counted no fewer than 14,046 separate human instincts divided into 5,759 different classes that had been proposed (50). The term instinct, in short, could be brought forward to explain anything, although of course it really explained nothing. The term was a loose term very loosely used, so that finally the whole conception of a set of human instincts became discredited. Clearly then, if basic needs are nothing more than instincts under another name, the concept of needs must be discredited too.

But needs are not identical with instincts. Let us revert for a moment to our general definition of instinct as a definite, organized pattern of response, innate in its origin, and very little or not at all affected by learning. No one has seriously denied that such patterns of response occur in animal behavior. Moreover, the further down the scale of life we go, the more prominent such behavior patterns become, the more rigidly they operate, and the less they seem to be affected by experience or learning. The instinctive activities of insects are wonderfully complex, but they are so rigid that they cannot be accommodated to new circumstances, and as far as we know they require no learning whatsoever. The pecking of chickens is undoubtedly instinctive, but for just a few days after it first appears it does seem to improve and become more accurate because of practice. The hunting of carnivorous higher mammals would also ordinarily be considered instinctive, but it would seem that the parents do quite a good deal to educate their cubs as skillful hunters. Furthermore a bear, or a wolf, or a fox can alter his hunting practices to quite a considerable extent if conditions demand a change. As we ascend the scale of life, instincts become less instinct-like, more dependent on learning, less definite, more flexible.

When we come to human behavior it is quite believable that there would be nothing, or almost nothing, that could properly be called instinct. Human beings are enormously more adaptable psychologically than any of the animals, far more flexible in their reactions, far more capable of learning. Above all, human beings can react in terms of general concepts and symbols to an extent quite impossible to any animal. But still the difference is in degree and not in kind. The capacity to generalize or to "reason" does not suddenly vanish when we pass from man to the higher animals. It merely diminishes and contracts; and it becomes fainter and feebler as we move downwards towards the lowest forms of life, and perhaps becomes too dim for us to notice at some undetermined point in the scale.

Arguing inversely, we would not expect man to have innate behavior patterns as definite as those of insects, or even of bears, or racoons, or monkeys. But we would expect him to have inborn determining tendencies—modifiable, flexible, deeply affected by learning and experience—but still genuine and potent. To call these inborn determining tendencies instincts would be to misname them, for the change in degree has become so great that it almost amounts to a change in kind. That is why the attempt to apply the concept of instinct to human behavior has broken down. But unless man is different in kind from all other living creatures (and everything we know indicates that he is certainly not), innate determining tendencies will still underlie his behavior; and these tendencies can very appropriately be called basic needs.

To clarify this general point let us consider one specific case. It used to be said that human beings have an instinct of curiosity, that is to say, an inborn tendency to find out about things, or to inquire. But this is an idea which will not stand scrutiny. The "finding out" or inquiring type of behavior does sometimes occur. But the truth is that most people most of the time do not seem to manifest any curiosity at all. So the assumption of a general instinct of curiosity explains nothing and even sends us off on the wrong track, because it merely attaches a label to a type of behavior which sometimes occurs, without giving us the least indication of why it sometimes occurs and sometimes does not. If, however, we assume a basic personal need for what Prescott calls "harmony with reality," then the case is entirely different. Every human being does in fact have some sort or kind of point of view, some working interpretation of the world about him. If that interpretation is satisfactory, if it serves as a good enough integrating focus for his feelings and thoughts and acts, then he rests content and goes no further. If the interpretation is to some extent unsatisfactory, then he feels disoriented, and regroups or alters his ideas.

The concept of need, then, is not unrelated to the concept of instinct. But the two concepts are not identical. An instinct is a definite, more or less unmodifiable pattern of behavior. A basic need, on the other hand, is an urge to behave, not in this or that specific way, but in a certain kind of way. The manifestation of an instinct can be affected very little if at all by experience and learning. The manifestations of a need can be very greatly affected by experience and learning. But still it is reasonable to believe that human conduct is shaped by basic needs. This is reasonable partly on the general, or a priori ground that it seems consistent with man's place in the scale of life, and partly because the hypothesis of basic needs seems to be our best explanation of the actual facts of human behavior.

BASIC NEEDS AND SCHOOL PROBLEMS

This discussion of motivation has now reached a point at which it begins to suggest very interesting answers to some of the most important questions connected with school work. Let us consider some of these questions, and see how the concept of basic needs bears on them.

1. Why are there such great differences in the appeal and urgency of different school activities? To make this question more specific, why does membership on the football team or in the high school band often seem much more significant to pupils and lead to much harder work than does the study of most subjects? The answer is that membership in these organizations provides deep and rich satisfactions for many basic needs, whereas the study of most subjects, *as actually organized and conducted* provides comparatively meager and

superficial satisfactions. Why does a boy want very much to "make" the team or the band? Why is he willing to work very hard to keep his place once he has gained it? For one thing, because he finds satisfactions for all his status needs. He is in a preferred position, he is admired, he has intimate subjective support from a team group, he has objective reasons to think well of himself. Then too, membership has a bearing upon ego or integrative needs. There is a team spirit, a group morale, a more or less explicit code of ethics which to some extent operates as an interpretation of life and a practical doctrine for feeling and action. Moreover, there is also at least some relationship to physiological needs, for team membership can actually be, or can promise to be, an economically paying proposition, leading to scholarships, jobs, and special privileges and opportunities. An experienced athletic coach or band director is perfectly well aware of all this, and usually does a great deal to make organization membership an effective means for the satisfaction of basic needs.

On the other hand, the study of most curricular subjects is a comparatively pallid and feebly motivated affair. What actually motivates pupils in the study of history, of French, of geometry, or chemistry? Of course there can be no certain or universal answer, but very often it seems that the drives, such as they are, behind curricular study are for marks which are symbols of social approval, for credits which open up certain social and economic advantages, and for the avoidance of immediate trouble. If this diagnosis is at all correct, it is no wonder that team and organization membership leads to far better learning and has far more effect on personality development than the study of curricular subjects. To say that the football team and the band "appeal to youth" more than history and mathematics is no explanation at all. The football team and the band are organized to have a powerful human appeal, whereas history and mathematics are not so organized, although they could and should be.

2. Why are pupils often so much more ingenious and creative in dealing with out-of-class problems than they are in dealing with problems in the subjects they study? A group of young people may behave with what almost amounts to moronic stupidity when faced with an "original" problem in a geometry classroom. But observe this same group huddled in a drugstore booth, busily engaged in planning a social event. Suggestions pour forth, alternatives are explored, criticisms are bandied to and fro. Why the difference? It turns very largely upon motivation. In the drugstore booth the problem is a real problem—a problem of how best to find satisfactions for urgent basic needs. But in the geometry classroom the problem is hardly more than a pseudo-problem; for a problem that does not matter to the persons concerned is, by definition, not a genuine problem at all.

In the drugstore booth the motivation is urgent and vital. In the classroom the motivation is probably to meet requirements which do not strike much below the surface. Could the problem-solving behavior of the group in the geometry classroom be improved? Undoubtedly! Could the improvement be brought about by teaching the young people some of the techniques of problem-solving—looking for the main point, considering alternative methods, and so on? This procedure, which is often recommended, no doubt has its importance, but in and of itself it is not enough. If some techniques of party-planning were tactfully conveyed to the young people sitting in the drugstore booth, they would probably have a very great effect. But in the drugstore booth the other essential condition for effective problem-solving is present, namely a potent motivation derived from basic needs. This condition must also be created in the geometry classroom if we are seriously to expect any radical improvement in problem-solving there.

3. What is the significance of the distinction which is often drawn between extrinsic and intrinsic motivation—between

studying a subject for the sake of a reward, and studying that subject for its own sake? The distinction, in so far as it is valid at all, is really one between superficial and profound motivation. No subject in the curriculum is interesting per se. But every subject in the curriculum can be interesting, and, in fact, must be interesting if it is to be an agency for the shaping of personality. And a subject becomes interesting by becoming a means for the satisfaction of basic needs.

One can introduce games into the teaching of arithmetic, and songs and dramatizations into the teaching of history. This means that one organizes the learning of arithmetic or history in a manner calculated to provide some satisfaction for some social or status needs. Here are instances of what is ordinarily called extrinsic motivation, or sometimes—and more abusively—designated as "sugar-coating." The danger obviously is that the motivation will be very superficial. But even so, it is far better than none at all, or than motivation merely by marks, which is also extrinsic.

There can be no legitimate psychological objection to procedures of this kind, so long as we are not so pleased with them that nothing more is attempted. What should be done is to reveal arithmetic or history to pupils as interpretations of reality, symbolizations of experience which have profound implications for thought, feeling, and action, and which can serve as foci for the integration of personality. This does not exclude games, dramatizations, songs, pictures, competitions, or indeed any of the apparatus of so-called "sugar-coating." What it does is to carry motivation to deeper levels, and to make the subjects in question more adequate and convincing agencies for the satisfaction of basic needs.

All in all, it should now be very clear that the practical problem of motivation in school is not a problem of small tricks, pleasing devices, and amusing antics. On the contrary, it is the problem of organizing all school activities, both in and out of the classroom, as agencies for the satisfaction of basic needs. This is the primary condition necessary for establishing ego-involvement; and without such ego-involvement the shaping of personality cannot go on.

QUESTIONS FOR DISCUSSION

1. A high-school boy got hold of a textbook on economics. He read it with astonishment, zeal, and fascinated interest. It seemed to open up a new world of thought to him. Evidently he was strongly motivated. What basic needs would you say were being satisfied?

2. Children like to be noticed by teachers and other children, to "shine," to do better than others, to consider themselves superior in some respect. Are these tendencies undesirable? Should the school encourage or discourage them, both in and out of class? Are there any dangers in such tendencies? How can such dangers, if any, best be avoided?

3. The marking system involves very powerful motivations. Try to analyze out and discuss the various needs which are likely to be satisfied by getting good marks in school.

4. Some students of the behavior of children have maintained that human beings are motivated by an "instinct of pugnacity." Certainly there is much in present-day adult behavior that seems to bear out this idea. Analyze the notion carefully. Does an alleged "instinct of pugnacity" really explain the phenomena of behavior that we see around us? What alternative explanation might be possible?

5. Granted that our behavior is motivated by the endeavor to satisfy basic needs, to what extent do you think we are usually conscious of the basic needs which we are trying to satisfy?

6. Enormous numbers of elementary-school children are very much bored and even antagonized by the study of arithmetic. Is this a symptom that the learning of arithmetic is largely unrelated to their basic needs? If so, would this be due to the nature of arithmetic itself, or to the way in which it is organized and taught? Can you think of any reorganized procedures in the teaching of arithmetic which would bring it into touch with basic needs? If this were done, would arithmetic tend to become more interesting?

7. Would you be inclined to add any basic needs to Prescott's list? To eliminate any from it? To rephrase or redefine any of them?

8. The existence of basic needs has been put forward in this chapter as a *hypothesis*. Make your own brief summary of the evidence presented in favor of this hypothesis, and then formulate all the evidence you can assemble on the other side, i.e. against the "needs" hypothesis.

9. Probably the best of all ways of coming to an understanding of the needs hypothesis and to an opinion of your own about it is to observe and try to explain your own behavior. It is difficult to suggest the best possible ways of conducting such self-observation, but you might consider some of your hobbies and special interests and ask yourself just what makes you like them and what basic satisfactions they seem to offer. Why are you willing to work very hard for certain goals? What do you "get out of it"? Can you explain your behavior without any reference to basic needs? Does your self-analysis seem to lead towards any better understanding of other people's motives, and particularly of the motives of children?

SUGGESTED READINGS

Frank, Lawrence, "The Fundamental Needs of the Child." *Mental Hygiene*, XXII (1938), 353–379.

Gates, Arthur I., Jersild, Arthur T., McConnell, T. R., and Challman, Robert C., *Educational Psychology*. The Macmillan Company, New York, 1942.

Murray, H. A., "Facts Which Support the Concept of Need or Drive." *Journal of Psychology*, III (1937), 27–42.

Prescott, Daniel, *Emotion and the Educative Process*. American Council on Education, Washington, D.C., 1938.

3

The Shaping of Motives

NEEDS AND GOALS

HAVING tried to show that the sources of motivation are to be found in basic needs, I now turn to consider the shaping and determining of motives as they operate in our daily lives. To clarify this topic, it is necessary to make a distinction between basic *needs* and *goals.**

Human beings actually want to have, to use, to accomplish innumerable things—a vacation, more pay, a visit to a movie, the purchase of a garment, a friendship, more skill at golf, and so on endlessly. These are the actual *goals* of everyday living, the actual detailed and specific motives that control our conduct. But they are not basic needs in the sense in which we have come to use the term. In contrast to these innumerable and endlessly shifting goals, we regard basic human needs as permanent and universal.

The distinction between needs and goals is essential for clear thinking. Yet needs and goals are related to one another.

* For this distinction see bibliography item 208, pp. 630–631, where it is very clearly made.

The things that we seek always involve or promise to involve the satisfaction of some basic need or needs. Otherwise we would not seek them. A young man plans to take a girl to dinner. This, for the time-being, is one of his goals. Why does he want to do so? Because doing so will provide satisfaction for a number of basic needs—for food, for affection and approval, for self-regard, let us say. The importance of the occasion for him is due to its relationship to such a pattern of needs. A man wants a new car although his present car works quite well. It is not an entirely rational goal, yet it can be a very compelling one for all that. What makes it compelling? Because the possession of a new car satisfies various status needs, and because the new car is a symbol of prosperity which might perhaps bring it indirectly into relationship with physiological needs. Automobile advertisers are very well aware of this bit of psychologizing, as anyone who looks at their output can see. A boy deliberately chooses a high-school course made up largely of Latin, mathematics, English, and history. He may not consider these subjects particularly useful, nor may he find them interesting to any striking degree. Why, then, does he choose them? Because they belong in the college-preparatory curriculum, and the taking of such a curriculum promises many satisfactions for numerous status needs and physiological needs.

There are four clarifying propositions which help to define still further the relationship between goals and needs.

1. Any one single goal that a person pursues, any single undertaking, can satisfy a number of basic needs. The examples just given should make this clear enough, but, as a further instance, consider stamp-collecting. Why do many people find this such an engrossing hobby? If one thinks of the varied basic needs which this hobby can satisfy, one has the answer at once. Stamp-collecting can be economically profitable, and can give one a fine backlog investment; so the owner of a good stamp collection can feel that he will never go hungry, which

relates it to physiological needs. Stamp collectors form a world-wide society, or clique, of their own, devoted to a good deal of mutual admiration, and thus they satisfy one another's status needs. Moreover, stamps themselves are highly educative objects, surrounded with a surprisingly large body of doctrine and erudition, so that they are quite likely to affect the general viewpoint and outlook of the ardent collector. All these considerations go to make stamp-collecting a very good hobby, a very enthralling goal. And the point here is that this specific undertaking is related, not to one, but to many basic needs.

2. The selfsame goal can satisfy very different needs when it is adopted by different people. To one child an ice-cream cone is simply a means of satisfying appetite. But to another it can be a thrilling and unusual symbol of affection, and accepted and valued as such. Going to school can mean quite different things to different children. There is a reported case of a little girl named Ann, who never did well in her studies, but always arrived at school clean, bright, eager, and obviously delighted to be there. Ann's teacher got to know her well, and discovered that she came from an exceedingly poor, barren, and underprivileged home, so that school offered many exciting satisfactions denied to her elsewhere (613). Another pupil, a boy, goes to school dutifully and is punctual, though not outstandingly effective, in all his tasks, but shows no pleasure or active wish to attend. His determining motive for going to school is a wish to stand well with his parents. So I might continue. But the general point is that if we wish to understand human behavior, we must try to look below the surface of the immediate operating goals, and ask ourselves how these goals, or undertakings, or immediate purposes, operate as satisfactions of basic needs.

3. It is entirely possible to commit oneself to goals which really do, to some extent, satisfy needs, but which ultimately lead to conflict and frustration. Gangsters and pathological

criminals are outstanding examples of this generalization. Thus, in trying to select fruitful and desirable goals for ourselves and for others we must take into consideration not only immediate need-satisfaction, but also long-time effects on personality—long-time effects on the process of development.

4. There is a concept which makes very clear the relationship of needs to goals. This is the concept of *channeling*, or *canalization*, which has an important place in the psychology of personality (466). It is an idea that takes us back to our parable of the brook, perhaps with one slight modification. Our basic needs are like the water in a reservoir, which exerts a constant pressure, and always tends to run downhill. But the actual course the water will take depends on what channels are made available. The transmutation of needs into operating goals, i.e. the actual shaping of motives, is brought about by the opening of certain channels of action through which the constant pressure of needs can discharge itself.

This analysis of the relationship between needs and goals leads to a very clear conclusion. Psychologically considered, one of the chief purposes of education must be to secure the adoption of worthy goals, capable of affording constructive satisfaction for basic needs, both now and later on. How can this purpose be achieved? How are goals established? How are motives shaped? This is the question now before us.

ESTABLISHMENT OF GOALS: THE PLEASURE THEORY

Our goals, our working motives, our determining ways of behaving are acquired *in and through the experience of success and failure*. This is the position here taken. Before going on to ask what success and failure mean and how they shape motives, there is a point of the greatest importance to be considered.

For the claim that motives are shaped by success and failure contradicts another account of the matter, according to which the shaping is done by *pleasure and pain*, or by *rewards and punishments*. This second account may be called the "pleasure theory" of motivation, or more technically, the theory of psychological hedonism. The best known and most influential formulation and defense of this theory is that presented by E. L. Thorndike. Many years ago he stated the essence of the pleasure theory in his "law of effect," which he regarded as one among several laws of learning. There are various ways in which the law of effect can be worded, but the essential idea is that satisfaction, or pleasure, or reward, associated with any given act strengthens the tendency to repeat that act when the same circumstances arise. On the contrary, dissatisfaction, or unpleasantness, or punishment, associated with a given act weakens the tendency to repeat that act. Moreover—and this is important to understand—pleasure and pain do not operate by increasing or decreasing the amount of practice or use that one devotes to a given act. They operate directly, as causes in their own right. Pleasant practice will do more to establish a way of acting than unpleasant practice or than practice which is neutral in feeling, even though the amount of practice is the same in all three cases. Pleasure and pain, then, reward and punishment, are regarded as in and of themselves the determining causes of human action and the influences which mold and shape our choices and our motives. This is the essence of the pleasure theory, as embodied in Thorndike's earlier work.

There have been many discussions of this theory, some of the most important of them having been supplied by Thorndike himself. In fact his later experiments led him to quite a crucial alteration of his earlier position. These experiments led him to conclude that punishment (or unpleasantness) has little effect in eradicating a habitual act. But they confirmed his earlier view that pleasure has a strong tendency to establish and reinforce a habitual act. (657, 665)

The pleasure theory is extremely, even dramatically, important. If it is true, then all we need to establish goals and to motivate ways of acting is to reward certain responses, to see that they have pleasant consequences. By this simple means we can channel motives just as we wish. Sugar-coating at once becomes one of the most important and legitimate of educational procedures, and we have a formula for getting pupils to want to do and to like doing anything we please. These are startling claims, but they have been asserted by Thorndike himself, and a recent writer has elaborated them at length (687).

Clearly, then, we must examine the pleasure theory with some care; and the truth is that it does not stand scrutiny very well.

Let us consider first Thorndike's experiments on learning, which are the chief research basis of the pleasure theory. These experiments were very intricate, careful, and extensive, and a brief appraisal cannot do them full justice. However, anyone who examines them is likely to come to certain broad conclusions.

Thorndike required his subjects to learn to associate numbers with words by studying several series of pairs of numbers and words; to learn to associate words with other words; to make dots on a table-top hidden by a screen while touching other dots on the under side of the table which was visible in a mirror; and to perform many other learning tasks of the same kind. Rewards, often consisting of very small sums of money, were given. It was consistently found that the reward expedited the learning. Such, in substance, is the supporting basis for the law of effect and the pleasure theory.

But to draw sweeping conclusions from such experiments seems highly questionable. The tasks were very artificial and very trivial. In and of themselves these tasks could not have much interest or importance for the subjects who were required to perform them. Incidentally, the subjects were often paid for their services. The rewards, too, were quite insignificant, and one cannot tell how pleased subjects were to get them, although this is obviously a crucial point for the pleasure theory. In fact, one is inclined to suspect that these alleged rewards were rewards in name only, and that instead of really giving pleasure, they merely defined success in a dull and unappealing task. Claims that the pleasure theory in general and the law of effect in particular are "proved" as general principles of behavior by experiments of this kind are certainly far-fetched.

Moreover, there is experimental evidence pointing in the opposite direction. In one investigation laboratory-type tasks like Thorndike's (i.e. very simple routine tasks and learnings) were used, but punishment instead of reward was given. Electric shocks were administered to different groups of subjects. It was found that this punishment always tended to expedite learning. When it was associated with a "right" response it helped the subjects to learn this response. When it was associated with a "wrong" response it helped the subjects not to learn this response. The suggestion is that the electric shock, like a small money reward, is a break in the monotony, an underlining of certain responses made in a series of dull and uniform tasks, a way of defining success and failure (465).

The real nemesis of the pleasure theory, however, is the obvious fact that human behavior is not determined merely by pleasantness. Persistence in the face of discouragement, for instance, is not usually enjoyable, and yet it certainly takes place (7). We make a common-sense distinction between business and pleasure, yet most people will put business first. But whether people would persist in spite of long discouragement, whether they would put business first if there were absolutely no prospect of any significant success of any kind, seems very doubtful. A slum boy who has been kicked by a policeman very quickly learns the complicated behavior pattern known as "cop-hating." Granted the circumstances, social and otherwise, of the child's existence, this is in a sense a successful way of meeting the situation. But it is extremely questionable whether he learns it because he finds it pleasant.

Moreover, it is also well known that difficulty, danger, and challenge can be highly energizing—and, in fact, fascinating—examples being big game hunting, death-defying mountain climbs, and gambling for large sums of money. To call these activities pleasant—a word which one would use for a country stroll—is positively silly; and yet they have an irresistible attraction for many people. Two hours before a performance a concert pianist may be in a state of utter misery. Yet he goes through with it, partly because experience has taught him that his present agonies of nervousness will culminate in a tremendous release of energy on the platform. In all these instances the attracting force is not pleasure, but prospective success.

One defender of the pleasure theory and the law of effect has argued that there really is a subtle, hidden pleasure in doing difficult, dull, risky, and unpleasant things—the pleasure, namely, of self-commendation (544). But this is a very strained interpretation, and it ignores the patent fact that the experience of performing a repugnant task is certainly not an experience of pleasure. It does, however, suggest an entirely different account of the matter. For it is quite believable that people climb frightful cliffs, risk more money than they can afford, and follow wounded lions into thickets because in such performances they find satisfaction for basic status needs—because, in other words, such doings give them the experience of success.

All in all then, the pleasure theory does not seem tenable. Teachers cannot expect to shape and mold human motives simply by creating pleasant conditions and offering a variety of rewards or treats. Motives are shaped, not by pleasantness and unpleasantness, but by success and failure.

The experiment described in the previous chapter, in which young children were helped to sing, is a very good instance of the effect of success and failure. You will remember that some of the children in the nursery school and kindergarten were separated into small groups and given intensive help and encouragement in the singing of songs. Not only did these children "find their singing voices," but their whole interest in music was strengthened and broadened. Conditions were made pleasant for them, and, in fact, there is no doubt that they found the whole experience pleasurable. But general conditions in the school were pleasant too, and the music there was handled in a manner that made it enjoyable. Yet no such striking effects were noticed. The determining factor was success rather than pleasure.

Perhaps it should be pointed out that success and failure are by no means the same as pleasantness and unpleasantness. Success, no doubt, is usually pleasant, although perhaps not always so. But the pleasantness of success is a very special kind of pleasantness, quite different from the pleasantness of sniffing Chanel No. 5 or receiving a tip. Moreover, success can be long deferred and still have a profound affect on our actions. Conversely, failure, though usually unpleasant, is not equivalent to unpleasantness. The unpleasantness of failure is not like that of a toothache. The experience of success is not identical with the experience of being rewarded, with which Thorndike's experiments dealt; and the experience of failure is not identical with the experience of being punished. Success is the achievement of a purpose, the conquering of obstacles to reach a goal. Failure is the frustration of purpose. And it is through the experience of success and failure that motives are shaped.

So if we are to be effective in shaping children's motives and goals in school, it is necessary *to organize success experiences in connection with goals which are capable of constructively satisfying basic needs.*

SUCCESS AND FAILURE

Success and failure, however, are ambiguous words. They mean different things for different people. An expert craftsman, for instance, may feel that success means nothing short of the very highest possible perfection, and may consider a piece of work a failure even though most people admire it greatly. For different pupils success in school may mean a passing grade, commendation by the teacher, compliments at home, or the inner sense of mastering a subject. Failure, too, may mean complete frustration, partial but unsatisfactory achievement, or lack of expected recognition and appreciation, and so on. Moreover, successes and failures differ in degree or potency. Some successes are very impressive and encouraging. Others do not seem to matter very much. Also there are similar differences in degree, or potency, in failure. Success and failure, then, do not mean getting an A or a B or a D or an F. They cannot be rated on any external criteria. Success and failure are personal experiences of the person who succeeds or fails.

The feeling of success, in fact, is the feeling that we have when some course of action satisfies some need, or needs; and the feeling of failure is the feeling that we have when this does not happen. We may not be able to say just what the need, or needs, may be. Usually, indeed, we cannot. But we know that there has been an inner satisfaction. The depth and potency of the experience of success depends on the depth and extent of this basic satisfaction. So the practical problem of shaping working motives or goals through the experience of success and failure begins to define itself. There is quite a large, though somewhat scattered, research literature on this subject, all of which is brought into line and related to our practical problem by the general interpretation I have presented.

1. It has long been known that praise and blame have very different effects on human behavior and performance. In fact, the influence of praise and blame has been quite a favorite topic for investigation. A considerable number of experiments have established the valuable effects of approval, helpfulness, and sympathy.

In one such experiment a number of boys were given the

task of sorting a set of cards fifteen times. The boys worked individually under supervision, and an achievement score was kept. On one day the supervisor would take a contemptuous attitude, blame the boys for doing poorly, and announced achievement scores that were lower than the true scores. On another day he would take the opposite line, dealing out lavish praise and encouragement, and announcing faked high scores. After the supervised period, each boy went on with the job by himself in a comfortably furnished reception room; but unknown to him he was under observation. The two types of supervisory treatment produced great differences in behavior. Praise gave rise to much less daydreaming and much more general activity. After discouragement there were many unfinished sortings left over, but after praise there were none. And the experimenter points out that these effects were produced by a single session each of encouragement and discouragement (578).

A similar experiment, using 106 children ranging from the fourth to the sixth grade, was done under a closer approximation to normal school conditions. The children worked at arithmetic, sometimes being praised for success, sometimes being blamed for failure. Here again it was shown that praise produces better results than reproof (327).

It would, however, be very naïve to think that praise and reproof have a sort of intrinsic magic of their own, that they can be administered by formula, and that the indicated results will arrive automatically. The effects of praise and reproof depend on a number of conditions, some of which have been investigated.

a) The effects of praise and reproof depend a good deal upon the sort of person who is praised or reproved. It has been shown that weak students are the ones who gain most from praise and encouragement. But these are just the students who receive the least praise and encouragement (330). Obviously, it would not be right to do in school what was done in one of the experiments described above, namely, to give these students a radically false idea of their own achievement. The solution is to recognize that there can be many kinds of success, and to provide a variety of opportunities. The kindly recognition of sincere effort and of progress, and the organization of chances for weaker students to make their own special contributions to units and projects, would be ways of fulfilling this condition.

Again, there is reason to believe that praise and reproof have different effects on different types of personality. One study undertook to discover these effects on introverts and extroverts. The task was to cancel out all the 7's in lines of numbers. The papers of one group were marked poor, those turned in by another group were marked good, and there was a control group which received neither praise nor blame. A personality test to indicate extroversion and introversion was run on the children in the experiment. It was found that either praise or blame was better for all than being ignored, but that praise affected introverts and blame affected extroverts more constructively (651). One cannot place very much weight on this experiment, because of the doubtfulness of personality tests in general, and of the extroversion-introversion classification in particular. But the result seems reasonable, and the investigation should warn us that the effects of praise and blame depend on the total personality of the individual concerned.

Another study undertook to discover the effects of praise and of competition on persistence, using young children as subjects. Various easy and rather interesting tasks were set up. Sometimes the children were praised, sometimes they competed with one another. It was found that with easy tasks children would persist longer under competition than they would under praise. That is to say, success in terms of competition is more potent than success in terms of praise from a teacher, at least under the conditions of this experiment. But the immediate point is that there were great individual differences in the responses of these children. In the case of one girl, who was spoiled and petted at home, neither praise nor competition had any effect. We might interpret this by saying that there was no active status need, and therefore no goal could be established (741).

b) It is known that the effects of praise and reproof depend to a considerable extent on the continuation of the incentives. Praise tends to have cumulative good effects, and to influence children more and more strongly as it continues. Reproof may have a considerable immediate effect, but its influence tends to wear off. This is about what might be expected. Goals are established in and through success, and continued praise is a form of success. Reproof at first may act as a challenge, but as time goes on it becomes a frustration and does harm (328, 330).

c) The effects of praise and reproof seem to depend a good deal on the person who does the praising or reproving. This has been interestingly brought out in an experimental study. The task here was the use of a code substitution test, i.e. changing English words or letters into code symbols, and vice versa. A large number of subjects were used, ranging all the way from the eighth grade to college. The procedure was for the person who ran the test to give the signal to stop work, to pick up the papers, to pretend to examine them, and then to say either that they were very poor, or very good, or to make no comment. After this had been done, the subjects would try again. Several different people administered the test at different times and with different groups of subjects. Taking the results reported from all subjects by all testers, there was no difference between praise and reproof under these conditions. But there was a considerable difference in the results produced by different testers. Some of these persons seemed to have a more constructive effect on the subjects than others. Moreover, one test administrator found praise giving better results, while another got better results from blame (570).

All this goes to show that praise and blame are neither open-sesames nor abracadabras. They are not magic formulae, but transactions between human beings in which the success of undertakings is defined in terms of the satisfaction of status needs. A person who is praised for what he has done by someone he respects and likes has to that extent succeeded. It may not be the most comprehensive and profound kind of success. But it is success nonetheless, and it tends to establish a goal and to shape motivation. On the other hand, a person whose efforts meet with hostility, reproof, and contempt has to that extent failed; and unless he is experiencing some other type of success—through an inner sense of mastery, for instance, or a persistent drive to assert himself—he is likely to be frustrated. This is why sarcasm and ridicule, particularly in public, are apt to be very frustrating and disintegrating, another point that has been experimentally established.

The outcome of all these various experiments is confirmed quite well by the memories which older people have of their own school days. Three hundred and seventy graduate students in a school of education reported on their memories about the effects of various incentives used by their high school teachers, with results that are tabulated below.

	Effect on Work		
	Better	Same	Worse
Reprimand before others	40.4%	13.3%	46.2%
Reprimand in private	83.1	9.9	6.9
Sarcasm before others	10.0	12.9	77.1
Sarcasm in private	18.2	16.9	64.9
Ridicule before others	7.2	23.8	69.0
Ridicule in private	21.2	15.2	63.6
Friendly conference	95.6	3.9	.4
Public commendation	90.6	8.3	1.1
Work for teacher liked best	95.1	3.8	1.0
Work for teacher liked least	5.9	26.9	67.2

From T. H. Briggs (73).

To be sure, the recollection of adults about their school days can only be suggestive rather than conclusive. But the material squares very well indeed with the proposition that motives are shaped by success and failure, and that the potency and profundity of success and failure depend on the degree to which basic needs are satisfied or frustrated. For the tabulation shows the effect of success and failure defined in terms of status needs upon schoolwork.

2. Another very familiar way of emphasizing and, indeed, defining success and failure is to give rewards for achievement. Giving prizes is a less customary practice in our schools than in some other countries; but marks are, in effect, rewards in so far as their psychological significance is concerned.

There have been a fair number of investigations on the influence of rewards upon achievement. The best known of these investigations are those by Thorndike, some of which I have already mentioned, which had to do with the law of effect. He found that rewards unrelated to the tasks being performed, to wit, money payments of from three to five cents for successful performances, improved achievement just about as much as giving his subjects information about their own success (660). Thorndike also raised the question whether increasing the size of the reward would make his experimental subjects do better. Small increases in the amount of money they were given produced no particular effect (667).

These experiments are interesting as far as they go, but they are no more than suggestive at the best. The tasks which the experimental subjects performed were, as I have previously remarked, very trivial, consisting of learning the English meanings of lists of Spanish words, marking segments of diagrams, connecting words with numbers, and so forth. The rewards themselves were small, and so were the increases, which amounted only to a few cents. Surely there could be no very profound motivation or the satisfaction of many basic needs at a rate of even eight cents per right answer. Even though the subjects did very little better when payments were stepped up from one to eight cents, this does not mean that they would not have done better if there had been the prospect of winning a new Plymouth car or even a scholarship. The interpretation of this work may very well be that, under the experimental conditions and considering the monotonous and trivial tasks required, the winning of a reward constituted in itself a kind of success. But it was a trivial success, without any deep or compelling personal meaning.

In another experiment a very substantial reward was offered, and its influence on achievement was quite dramatic. A group of college freshmen who were fraternity pledges were given a test at the end of a very strenuous five-day initiation period. During these five days the boys were under orders. They had to perform many heavy physical chores in addition to their regular work, and were allowed only two to three hours sleep each night. At the climax of these trials they were given an exacting two-hour written test, and it was intimated to them that those who failed in the test would be rejected by the fraternities. The boys attacked the test with might and main, showed very little drop in efficiency in the closing minutes of the two-hour period, and put up a performance that was twice as good as that of unfatigued seniors taking the same test under ordinary classroom conditions (376). When the reward is important, when the winning of it is tantamount to a really significant success, when there is promised satisfaction of vital basic needs, then the effect upon achievement can be very great indeed.

School marks, as I have suggested above, are tantamount to rewards, and, in fact, to "irrelevant" rewards in Thorndike's sense. Theoretically, marks are objective measures of achievement. Actually, their relationship to achievement is quite uncertain and ambiguous. The basis on which they are computed, and the techniques used in computing them are often none too clear either to pupils or teachers. Marks, in fact, are decidedly impressionistic. Pupils tend to think of them as "given" by the teacher rather than objectively earned, and the notion has considerable justification. So the mark is, in effect, a reward; and the gaining of a good mark is in itself a kind of success.

The importance of that success depends very much upon the status-value of the mark—on what it means to one's family and one's friends and schoolmates, on what it does to one's self-esteem. The policy of most schools is to make success "markwise" as important as possible by relating it to privileges, exemptions, promotions, club memberships, athletic eligibility, and so forth. So for most pupils the prospect of this kind of success is a powerful influence, which certainly does much to shape and determine their choices, decisions, and goals. But it has also been pointed out that where slum children are concerned, success markwise means very little because their parents do not care, and because good marks can actually be a stigma in their neighborhood cliques (138).

One of the very few studies ever made on the withholding of rewards had to do with marks. The experiment was run in grades two and five. Nine teachers in these grades warned the pupils of the possibility of failure, and sometimes made threats that many would fail. Nine other teachers made it clear that everyone in their classes would pass which meant that there was very little incentive of any kind. When the groups of children under these two sets of teachers were compared at the end of the semester, there was very little difference in achievement. Even on the basis of this short description you will realize that this experiment cannot be considered conclusive, because many factors besides the threat of failure were probably operating. But it does suggest that purely negative conditions are likely to have very little effect. The shaping of motives depends on the prospect of *success*, of whatever kind that success may be, rather than on the threat of failure (506).

3. Much attention has been given to the effect of social situations upon achievement. It is possible to define success in terms of some kind of social recognition or approval. There is no doubt that success in such terms as these can be very compelling and influential.

One often mentioned study investigated the effects of competition and co-operation, although the co-operation involved was of a rather limited and special kind. The investigation was extensive, for 814 children in grades five to eight were used as experimental subjects and given special incentives, and 734 children were used as controls without special incentives. The tasks consisted of fairly simple arithmetical computations. Sometimes the children worked "for themselves," that is to say, for individual competitive success. Sometimes they worked in groups, for the sake of the success of their own group in competition with other groups. Also, situations were devised in which they could show whether they preferred to work individually or groupwise.

In every case individual competition turned out to be far more effective. An average of 32.4% more examples were worked out in a twelve minute period under individual competition than under the kind of group "co-operation" that was set up. Under individual competition the curves of work rose during the course of the experiment, while under group co-operation the curves fell. Children under the conditions of group work did better than the controls who were given no special incentives. But those who worked in terms of individual competition did very decidedly better still. When it was made possible for the children to choose how they preferred to work, 74% chose individual competition and 26% chose group co-operation (437).

Another study centered on the effect of rivalry between groups, which, of course, was really involved in the work just described. Children from the fourth, fifth, and sixth grades were used as subjects, and the task consisted of arithmetic problems. One group of these children simply practiced working on the problems. Other groups were organized to compete against each other. During the five days devoted to the experiment, the scores of the children in the competitive groups improved over 40% more than the scores of those who only practiced (329).

Even from these two studies it is clear that success defined in terms of social achievement and recognition is very compelling, and has a powerful effect in determining purposes and shaping goals. But the possibilities and potentials of social experience go far beyond individual competition or the kind of group rivalry which the author of the first of these studies calls "co-operation." I shall deal more fully with the use and management of social situations in a later chapter, but one further piece of investigation should be mentioned here because of its tremendous suggestiveness.

This investigation had to do, not with schoolwork, but with efficiency and productiveness under factory conditions. Efficiency experts have often tried (not without some success, of course) to step up production by incentive pay, properly spaced rest periods, adjusting assembly-line speed, providing good lighting, good ventilation, proper temperatures, and so on. Such plans have been tried out many times. Members of the faculty of the Harvard Graduate School of Business Administration undertook to find out the effect of quite a different influence, namely, the social reorganization of a factory. Workers were divided into small groups or teams. Individual workers had some choice about the team to which they were assigned. Each team was given quite considerable leeway as to how they would operate together, and their decisions were respected and supported by the management. There was every attempt to foster group responsibility and a real team spirit, with leadership in the teams emerging as it would.

To some extent the factory lost the orderly look dear to

conventional-minded foremen. But there was a dramatic and startling increase in production per man-hour. This is a most striking result. The moment it became possible to experience and feel success in terms of working together with a like-minded, interested group of associates, motives were deeply affected and working goals came to a sharp and effective focus. To you as a teacher this investigation can suggest quite a few thoughts about the social organization and layout of a classroom. Perhaps a neat, orderly arrangement of the conventional kind is not best for effectiveness. Order and discipline you certainly must have, but one kind of order can foster the growth of a working team spirit and another kind of order can pretty well inhibit it (705).

4. Psychologically speaking, success can mean commendation from an admired and respected person, the winning of a satisfying reward, or the sense of working with a group and achieving status among one's associates. These are perfectly genuine types of success, and they have very definite effects in the determining of purposes and the shaping of goals. All of them can very properly be used in school. But also, success can mean a sense of achievement in a task that one undertakes. This kind of success and its effects have also been investigated, and many of the studies have dealt specifically with the effects of a knowledge of results.

One of the earliest important experiments on the effect of a knowledge of results was done in the early 1920's. The subjects practiced on four kinds of learning—speed and accuracy in making small letter *a*'s, crossing out letters in a list of Spanish words, substituting code symbols, and two-place mental multiplication. The subjects were divided into two groups of equal ability as far as possible. Each one of these groups would work for a time under an arrangement by which it was kept informed of how well it was doing. Then for a time this special stimulating arrangement was discontinued. It was always found that a group of people who worked with a close knowledge of their results did better than another group working without this knowledge, and that the same people would do markedly better when they knew how well they were doing than when they did not. This was a notable experiment, partly because it was one of the first of its kind, and partly because the experimenters coined a striking and memorable phrase to explain their results. They believed that a knowledge of results improves achievement because it arouses the *will to learn* (67).

Many other experiments of a similar kind have been carried out since then. In one of these experiments, in which high-school students were the subjects, practice was given in good English usage. With some of the students a specially adapted standard test of good English usage was given both before and after the practice periods. The test was emphasized, and the students to whom it was given were urged and encouraged to do better. With others there was no test, but just rather general propaganda on the importance of using the English language properly. It was found that the "test motive" had a very marked effect. In fact the investigators concluded that the "will to improve" generated by the test was equal in effect to five repetitions during unstimulated practice (638).

In another experiment it was found that a knowledge of results is very important if a person is to improve in shooting arrows at a target. The subjects who practiced shooting without knowing how well they were doing made no improvement at all, but those who were informed of their results progressed rapidly (162).

It has also been shown that the fullness and completeness of a person's knowledge of his own achievement has an important bearing on the improvement he is likely to make. College students were given the task of learning to make tallies quickly and accurately. Some of these students practiced without any knowledge of their results. Others were given a partial knowledge, i.e. were told whether they were above or below average.

Still others were given quite full and detailed knowledge by being shown each day their previous paper with corrections and score and an evaluation of their standing in the group on the basis of this score. The investigator concludes that: "A knowledge of the learner's own individual progress, both relative and absolute, and that of the group of which he is a member, is sufficient to give him a distinct advantage over competitors, and the degree of superiority is roughly proportional to the amount of knowledge possessed" (553, p. 611).

Similar effects produced by knowing the results of one's efforts have been found in connection with schoolwork. A total of 358 fourth-grade children were divided into 2 groups of equal ability. Both groups carried out 20 drills in arithmetic, one drill each week for 20 weeks. The total time involved was about 3 hours. One of these groups kept charts of individual and class progress, and used rating sheets to make records of this progress. The other group drilled without making any such records or having any special knowledge of results. In the rather limited time they had, the former group improved 12% more than the latter (510).

In another experiment 138 fifth- and eighth-graders were similarly divided into comparable groups. Both groups drilled on arithmetic 10 minutes per day for 20 days. The only difference was that the experimental group corrected their own papers and made graphs of their own scores. But they showed marked and continuing superiority to the others (78).

In yet another experiment 126 college sophomores worked on code substitutions and on improving their reading speed. Two different kinds of arrangement were set up. Some of the students competed against their own records (which of course they knew) and against the recorded improvement of others of similar ability. Others competed as members of groups against other groups. Also, some of the students were used as controls without any special incentives. The work was carried on 3 times a week for 12 periods in all. On code substitution, practice without incentive led to an improvement running from 36.1 substitutions per minute at the start to 74.8 at the end. Improvement with intergroup competition ran from 36.2 substitutions at the beginning to 74.7 at the end. But when students competed directly and individually with their own records and with the records of those of like ability, the improvement was from 36.2 substitutions at the beginning to 95.4 at the end (596).

Knowledge of results, however, is no magic specific. It certainly will not work automatically. This was shown in an experiment using three sections of a course in elementary philosophy. One section was given a test on each class meeting. Another section was given a test once each week. Another section had no tests at all during the term, but only periodical reviews. On the final examination, which was used to discover what had happened, there seemed to be no particular difference (142).

Teachers can learn a great deal from this body of research, if it is rightly understood. Here I must repeat once more that knowledge of results does not automatically produce improvement. By all means students should know how well they do when tests are given. But this alone is not enough. A test should be a real tryout, a challenge to personal pride and perhaps also to competitive spirit. It must bring the performance of the stated tasks involved into vital relationships with basic human needs. It must, that is to say, have a human imperative instead of being a mere mark-gaining requirement. Furthermore, a good test should show a learner *how* to work better and that he *can* work better. This is just what happened in the arrow-shooting experiment. Working in the dark was hopeless and discouraging. But when the participants began to see where they went wrong and where they succeeded, they felt both able to do better and wanted to do better. A test, in short, should really define successful achievement, and should be devised and administered as a personal challenge to succeed more completely. It should not be, as too many teachers seem to think, an instrument for weeding out the weaklings, but a means for both inciting and helping everyone to do better work.

5. Every investigation of any significance that has been made on the subject has shown that a knowledge of results tends to bring about better results. This is an important finding, and a practically helpful one too, if we interpret it properly. But by itself it can hardly be considered satisfactory. For one thing, you may have noticed that all the tasks set up in the experiments mentioned above were very uniform, routine tasks; improvement could be measured in terms of greater speed, fewer errors, and so forth, so that definite scores could be computed and graphs made. What of more complicated undertakings, such as writing better English prose, solving problems, understanding concepts, planning projects, and so forth? Certainly improvement in such undertakings can take place, and it may help and motivate learners to know that they are improving. But objective reports would not be easy to make. Then again, and this is a more important point, there surely must be some way of encouraging learners to do better besides merely letting them know how well they are doing. For quite possibly, in individual cases, a knowledge of achievement might be discouraging, even though on an average, and taking large numbers into consideration, it is helpful. So we come upon a fifth psychological meaning of the word success, namely, an inner and personal sense of achievement. This personal sense of achievement in an undertaking and its effects have also been investigated.

A group of eighty-two young children were set to work on two series of rather difficult tasks. In the first of these series they had to fit interesting objects of various kinds into a box so that the lid would shut. In the second series they had to try to get attractive toys from under a weighted box. The separate tasks or problems in each series were graded from very easy to quite exacting. At first, each group was not presented with the easy problems first and the harder ones later, and there was a good deal of failure and frustration. Eighteen per cent of these children gave what are described as undesirable reactions under failure, and failure was not uncommon under the first condition of presentation. They would give up, or continually beg for help, or go into tantrums, or smash one of the toys, or concoct some imaginary reason for not succeeding. Then the tasks were graded so that the easy ones came first and so that everyone could succeed at the beginning. Furthermore, when the harder problems arrived, the children were encouraged, reminded of their previous successes, assured that they could go on succeeding. This produced a great change of attitude, and a marked reduction of undesirable behavior. Morale was maintained. There was persistence in the face of discouragement. Children would say, "I'll try and try," or "I'll try all ways," and were willing and, indeed, eager to go on without asking for help (363).

In another experiment a group of kindergarten children were set to work learning to recognize words, the work being organized as a game. Some who failed for several periods began to dislike the job. They would complain, grow angry, run and hide, ask that the game be stopped. At a certain point in the experiment the children were given careful individual instruction, so that difficulties were reduced and successes began to appear more and more frequently. Once more there was a radical change in attitude and behavior. Instead of disgruntlement, retreat, and resistance, liking and enthusiasm for the task emerged and increased (445).

Once again, it has been shown that the experience of success is of great importance and value in problem-solving. This was brought out in an extensive study in which adult subjects had to solve problems by making combinations of figures according to known rules. Problem-solving, as the author of this investigation points out, is a very complex process. One must commit oneself to the job energetically. One must search for new modes of approach. One must draw conclusions from data, and put two and two together in following clues. One must discover where one is going wrong and find out how to get back on the right path. It has been shown that all these complex and varied processes are facilitated and made more efficient by the experience of success. So it is a very great mistake always to emphasize difficulty and error in problem-solving. Everything possible ought to be done to show learners how to succeed, the reason being that success creates an attitude, or a slant of personality, which is of prime value in dealing with such challenges (290).

Notice what is involved in these experiments—help with difficulties and an organization of materials and situations so that individuals can experience the realities of success in their undertakings. Later on in this book I shall have something to say about individualized or diagnostic instruction as a means of making learning more efficient. But individualized or personalized instruction, which grapples closely with the learner's actual problems and difficulties, is valuable not only from the standpoint of efficiency, but also because it brings to the learner the powerful and convincing motivation of success.

What is the relationship of success in the sense of direct achievement to the satisfaction of basic needs? Surely the answer is clear. I attack some new undertaking—learning history, learning contract bridge, learning golf, what you will. At first it seems very baffling, and perhaps I feel inclined to give up. But the person who is teaching me knows his business. He shows me what to do and how to do it. Before very long I feel a sort of stir within me, and say to myself, "Now I'm really getting it." That changes all the prospects. Why? Because I know perfectly well that I am beginning to be able to do something that previously I could not do, to understand something about which I may never have even dreamed before. A new tool for living is beginning to come within my grasp—a new mode for satisfying basic needs. Of course I do not put the situation to myself in any such elaborate words, unless I happen to be a psychologist inclined to think professionally in my leisure time. Still less do I try to enumerate the various needs which my new tool for living may satisfy. But this sense of added and expanded mastery is very real and potent even though I do not analyze it. The strong sense of growing mastery transforms what at first may have seemed a baffling bore into an increasingly impelling goal.

SUMMARY

At this point it seems well to bring our findings together into a complete summary statement. If a person sets out to achieve something, he can feel that he has succeeded if one or more of five things happen: (*a*) if he wins the commendation of persons who have prestige for him; (*b*) if he gains a reward that seems important to him; (*c*) if he has the experience of working effectively with other people in competitive or co-operative relationships or both; (*d*) if he is aware of his own improvement; (*e*) if he has the experience of some measure of competence or mastery in what he is trying to do. These five meanings of the word success emerge from the research literature. Of course there are a great many more published investigations than I have mentioned above; but the five points just enumerated seem to be the main outcomes of all the research.

Success in the sense in which the word is here used—that is to say, in the psychological sense—is primarily a matter of personal experience rather than of comparative achievement. A man may genuinely and convincingly succeed in a hobby like woodworking without ever becoming a first-rate craftsman. A child may succeed genuinely and convincingly in arithmetic without ever becoming a fine mathematician or a lightning calculator, or even without doing better than anyone else in the class. It is only when failure to become a first-rate performer inflicts personal humiliation that it becomes failure in the psychological sense. But in the enormous majority of cases no such humiliation need happen. It is very fortunate that this is so, for otherwise most of us would be living warped and frustrated lives, haunted by a depressing sense of our own insufficiency. Moreover, if succeeding could only mean reaching the highest levels of achievement, schools and teachers could not organize effective success experiences, and there would be no way in which we could shape the motives and evoke the purposes of ninety-five per cent of our pupils.

Schools and teachers can shape the motives of young people, not by making everything as pleasant as possible, but by organizing experiences of convincing success. Since success does not primarily mean high relative achievement, and since there are many ways of succeeding, the organization of such experiences is not so difficult as it might seem. Friendly and considerate personal relationships, the recognition of effort and even of modest achievement, the creation of teaching-learning situations such as diversified projects and units in which different individuals can make different contributions, the creation of situations in which small groups can work together with real responsibility, the management of tests in such a way as to emphasize self-appraisal, expert individual help with difficulties, the choice and grading of teaching-learning materials to convince young people by direct experience that they really can, to some extent, master what they are expected to do—these are some of the practical suggestions involved. They are ways and means of enabling young people to experience success in some and in perhaps all of the five senses that we have considered.

Each and all of these five kinds of success tend to raise a person's morale, to improve his achievement, to make him go on trying, to make him want "more of the same." This is because, when he succeeds in one or all of these senses, he gains at least some positive satisfaction for some basic need or needs in and through what he is trying to do. So the tendency of any or all of these types of success is to determine goals and to shape motives. To return once again to our brook, those types of success remove obstacles from it and open up the way for it, so that the water tends to flow in a certain direction.

QUESTIONS FOR DISCUSSION

1. Some school activities seem to call forth a very strong motivation. Athletics, the school band, or social club doings often do so. Why are such activities so much more strongly motivated than the studying of curricular subjects? Is it because subjects like history, science, or mathematics cannot satisfy basic needs, whereas the strongly motivated activities can satisfy such needs? Or is the difference due to the ways in which goals are established and impulses channeled?

2. Teachers often say that pupils should become interested in a subject "for its own sake." Consider how some specific subject, say English literature, could be made interesting for its own sake. Would this mean that the study of English literature should have no relationship to the satisfaction of basic needs? If not, just what would an interest in this subject for its own sake actually mean, and what would be some of the practical implications?

3. Attempts are often made to interest children in certain subjects by means of little games, pictures, and so forth. For instance, the lines and spaces of the musical staff are often coupled with animal pictures, one being a rabbit, another a duck, and so forth. Attempts of this kind are thought of and indeed called "motivation" as such. Consider and analyze them in the light of this chapter.

4. Some teachers will consistently praise a pupil's work even though it is not very good. Is this a mistaken kindness, or a sound application of psychological principles for the sake of giving the pupil a sense of success? May a pupil who gets such praise still have a genuine sense of failure?

5. In a certain school a group of children constructed an elaborate scale-model of the Mediterranean Sea on a large sand table. Much was learned and a very strong interest was developed. Consider the various types of "success experience" involved in such a project.

6. Review in your mind a conventional course or lesson in some

specific subject-matter field. Consider carefully just what real opportunities for various "success experiences" are actually organized in the situation.

7. Consider and analyze some specific instances of success experiences of your own, and try to decide to what extent they have tended to shape and determine your goals.

8. To what extent do your own memories of the effects of various incentives you have experienced in school, and of the influence of those incentives upon you, correspond to the memories tabulated on page 77?

9. Would you expect that a nicely furnished and well decorated classroom, attractive looking textbooks, and a well-dressed and amiable teacher would be important factors in getting children to work harder and learn better?

SUGGESTED READINGS

Allport, Gordon W., *Personality: A Psychological Interpretation.* Henry Holt & Company, New York, 1937, Chapters 2, 20.

Gates, Arthur I., Jersild, Arthur T., McConnell, T. R., and Challman, Robert C., *Educational Psychology.* The Macmillan Company, New York, 1942, Chap. 18.

Hurlock, Elizabeth B., "The Psychology of Incentives." *Journal of Social Psychology,* II (1931), 261–289.

Keister, Mary E., "The Behavior of Young Children in Failure." University of Iowa Studies in Child Welfare, XIV (1937), 29–82.

Sears, Robert R., "Success and Failure," in *Studies in Personality,* McNemar, Q. and Merrill, M. A., eds. McGraw-Hilll Book Company, New York, 1942.

Tuttle, Harold S., *Dynamic Psychology and Conduct.* Harper & Brothers, New York, 1949, Chapters 5, 7.

4

«««««««««««««»»

Wider Practical Issues of Motivation

In the two previous chapters it was argued that the sources of motivations are basic human needs, and that the innumerable goals or purposes of human life are shaped and determined by experiences of success and failure. In this chapter I shall consider some of the wider practical implications of this account for the school, as it performs its central task, which is the molding and shaping of personality.

POSITIVE AND NEGATIVE MOTIVATION

There are two opposite kinds of motivation, positive and negative. A person may do something because he is threatened, because he fears that he may be deprived or punished in some way if he refuses. Then he is negatively motivated. Or he may do something because he wants to. Then he is positively motivated. A distinguished psychologist has analyzed the effects of positive and negative motivation, and has pointed out that these effects are in sharp contrast in the two cases (395).

When a person does an intrinsically disliked task because he fears not to do it, it is always necessary to *confine* him. This is what happens to animals in many psychological experiments. The experimenter wants the animal to find its way through a maze, or to work the lock on a problem box. But to the animal such doings have no appeal whatsoever, and though one cannot be sure how it feels, the probability is that it finds them objectionable. If it can escape, it will certainly do so, and therefore it must be kept inside the maze or the problem box; it would not stay there of its own accord if there were a way of getting out. This is why the results of many experiments on the mentality of animals are questionable. Under such circumstances the creature is likely to seem more stupid than it really is, and to learn much less efficiently than it would in its natural habitat, where it is positively motivated.

Exactly the same is often true of children in school. We do not actually keep the doors and windows shut for fear the children will run away. But we do keep them under close restraint; and the restraint is necessary because the tasks we require them to perform are just as unappealing to them as problem boxes and mazes are to cats and white rats. Parents, teachers, and everyone else concerned are so used to the idea that children will not go to school unless they are made to go, will not stay there unless they must, will not behave "properly" unless compelled to, and will not attend to lessons if there is a chance to do anything else, that they take it all for granted. If people think about these very evident truths at all, they are apt to say that human nature is that way. But human nature is only that way under certain conditions, and particularly under conditions of negative motivation.

So all the confinements and constraints, psychological, to be sure, but very real, which have to be imposed on children in school are danger signs. They mean that there is something fundamentally wrong with the dynamics of the situation. The offerings of the school, which *ought* to be attractive and challenging, which *can* be attractive and challenging, which *must* be attractive and challenging if they are to do much good, are often just the opposite. So children have to be forced to do what they will never do well unless they want to do it; and they have to be confined by various means and measures if they are not to escape. There is not the least doubt in the world that we have here the crucial reason why classroom learning is very often poor learning, and why subject-matter achievement tends to be poor achievement. And here, too, is the root cause of the problem of discipline.

The dynamics of positive motivation are exactly the opposite. Confinement and "walling in" become needless, or, at least, the need for them becomes less and less as the motivation increases in depth and power. In the last chapter we saw both that the positive shaping of goals is brought about by success, and that there are many kinds of success. A teacher may organize a classroom situation in which there is eager competition, commendation for taking part and making contributions to projects and discussions, and various kinds of recognition for good work and sincere effort. This teacher will have placed before the children real prospects of genuine and satisfying success of various kinds. She will have established a positive motivation, and she can have every reason to believe that she will get much better responses and much better work than if she merely nags, scolds, threatens, and drives. Much of the problem of discipline, which is the problem of restraint or confinement, will evaporate. But under such circumstances it will not entirely disappear. For the teacher will have to take care that some of the children do not find short cuts to success, for instance by cheating, bluffing, or some of the varieties of "apple-polishing." What the children want is success; what the teacher wants is for them to learn. Although the success and the learning are by no means unrelated in this kind of situation, they are not yet interwoven so closely that they cannot be separated.

This, however, does not in the least mean that the types of positive motivation just mentioned are undesirable or unwise. They do, beyond a doubt, have good effects—much better effects than the negative motivation of threats and fear. This in itself is an important point. But there is also another contrast between positive and negative motivation which bears on the question. *Positive motivation strongly tends to develop a momentum of its own, while the influence of negative motivation tends to vanish the moment the pressure stops.*

Any kind of success experience, even a limited one, tends to be germinal and expansive. A child may begin to like a subject because he studies it under conditions of exhilarating competition, or because he is commended for his effort or initiative, or because he sees good chances of at least occasional rewards. All this is to the good so far. But the real promise of the situation is that something has been started which is quite likely to continue rolling along. Soon the child may come to like the subject because he senses that he can do something with it, because he begins to have a feeling of mastery and understanding, because he finds it worth-while in itself.

Negative motivation, on the other hand, develops no such momentum. When a child is forced to carry on with a distasteful task simply by threat, and fenced in so that he cannot escape, the tendency is for the task to become more and more distasteful. For the time-being the child is walled in. But later on in life he is very likely to look back on school studies as boring and hateful experiences, or as necessary evils at the best, and to revenge himself by never having anything more to do with them.

STANDARDS

In educational discussions, both formal and informal, one is likely to come upon much talk about standards. Ordinarily standards are thought of as levels of achievement required or expected by schools and teachers. A teacher marks severely, gives long assignments, and is very critical of the work done by students; such a teacher is said to "have" high standards. Another teacher marks easily, accepts almost anything, and seems rather indifferent about what the learners do; all of this and perhaps more is indicated by saying that his standards are low. Also, there are the same kind of differences among schools, and we call them differences in the standards of the institution.

It is perfectly proper to use the word "standards" in this sense; but it is not the sense, or, at any rate, not the only or most characteristic sense in which the psychologist uses the word. The psychologist thinks in terms of the individual human being, his mentality, and his personality. From this point of view standards are levels of achievement which are not set by the school or by the teacher, but set for himself by the learner.

For psychology the vital question is that of the level of achievement the learner himself wants. Is the learner easily satisfied with what he does? Is he content to jog along without much improvement? Is he ambitious to do better and to achieve more? Are his aims steady or fluctuating? Are his aspirations realistic, or are they far beyond his possibilities? These are the sort of questions that present themselves when we think of standards not as levels of achievement demanded by teachers and schools, but as the aspirations and desires of individual learners. All such questions, it is perfectly clear, have to do with motivation.

The standards a human being sets for himself are among the most important aspects of his personality. If those standards are very low, so that he is satisfied with slipshod accomplishment, they have innumerable unfortunate effects on his behavior, and he will almost certainly fail to develop anything like his full potentialities as a human being. If they are extravagantly high, he is heading towards considerable futile misery and frustrating disappointment.

A good many investigations of the ambitions and hopes of high-school students and college students have reported that these students often set their aspirations far above the level of the possible, wanting to shine as opera singers, band leaders, great athletes, artists, writers, or to enter the most exacting professions. There is no doubt that students often report impracticable ambitions of this kind when they have to answer questionnaires distributed by investigators. But there is a great deal of doubt whether such stated ambitions are not very often mere daydreams, rather than working standards of action which really affect their choices and decisions from day to day.

E. L. Thorndike once remarked that most of us are anywhere from twenty-five to seventy-five per cent below our top potential efficiency in most of our doings, and perfectly satisfied to stay there. With all due respect to the investigators and their questionnaires, this seems like a much better guess about the real situation. The trouble with most children and young people in school is not that they are driven by an insatiable longing for impossible achievements, but that their real working standards are altogether too low. Almost certainly this would be the opinion of most of their teachers, and most of the businessmen who employ them when they get out of school. So when it is said, as it frequently is, that young people in school should be taught the meaning of hard work and thoroughness, and should learn to desire and strive for self-improvement within the limits of their capacity, this looks like a very realistic and sensible statement of the problem of psychological standards.

How, then, can such desires be created? How do children and young people, or indeed people of any age, learn to be reasonably self-demanding? This is not the sort of question that will be answered once and for all by one or a dozen or twenty experiments. Yet some experimental evidence bearing on it has accumulated, and even though that evidence is far from complete or conclusive, it does at least suggest an answer. Most of this experimental work has centered on a concept which has come into prominence in recent years—the concept of *level of aspiration.* A person's level of aspiration is his level of desired achievement, or in other and more ordinary words, the standards he sets for himself. The experimental workers who have tried to investigate the level of aspiration under various conditions have developed a special technique for doing so, the technique of the so-called "discrepancy score." If, for instance, a student has made a grade of C in one test and hopes to make a grade of B in the next, his discrepancy score would be the difference between C and B, and this score would measure his level of aspiration (531, pp. 416–417). Beyond this brief mention and explanation I shall not discuss the concept of the discrepancy score any further here, nor shall I report any of the numerous discrepancy scores which appear in published research. The discrepancy score is a tool of investigation about which some rather serious questions can be raised, but they are of a technical and special kind. The interesting and important question for us is how a reasonable, constructive, desirable level of aspiration can be established.

All the evidence very strongly indicates that a practicable, constructive level of aspiration is established by *successful experience.* One cannot say that this has been proved, but what we know points definitely in that direction, and the idea itself is reasonable. Children who succeed in school tend to want and hope to do better, but do not tend to have a level of aspiration that is abnormally high. Children who fail in school tend either to have extravagant ambitions for themselves or to have a very low level of aspiration. It is thought that one reason why many children who fail seem to have impossible ambitions for themselves is that they compensate in this way for failure. They deal with challenges which defeat them in real life by inventing comforting but impossible dream-solutions (15, 187, 188, 577). In much the same way, it has been found that emotionally maladjusted children often have quite unrealistic levels of aspiration. Their stated hopes and intentions for themselves are either grossly compensatory, or below the level of their actual performance (251).

These brief summary statements based on the research may seem to you meager gleanings, scattered and doubtful gleams of light upon a subject of vast importance. So, no doubt, they are. But as far as they go they really are gleams of light, by which we can see something well worth seeing.

High levels of aspiration are not established by negative motivation. Teachers whose policy it is to impose long assignments, to give frequent and exacting tests, to mark charily, and who think that this policy is equivalent to maintaining high standards are certainly deceiving themselves. A policy of this kind may help and benefit a few pupils, but for the majority it will surely spell discouragement, frustration, and a decline of ambition and morale.

There is no objection to difficulty. There is no objection to challenge. Quite the contrary, indeed, for without difficulty and challenge there can be no learning or development. But there is every objection to a motivation of threat and fear, and to the constant experience of failure. The business of a teacher is not to put learners in constant jeopardy of failure and to let the situation go at that. A teacher's business is to help learners to succeed, to show them how to succeed, to organize situations dominated by the prospect of success. For success has cumulative effects. It is the great shaper of motives, the great morale-builder. It is through success that high levels of aspiration, high but reasonable standards of personal achievement and improvement are progressively established.

INTEREST

The problem of interest, which is a special aspect of the more general problem of motivation, is a very vital one for education. That problem involves far more than "making" a subject or a lesson "interesting," which usually means rather superficial classroom motivation. This is evident at once when we define interest as *a more or less stable and permanent goal which tends to direct if not to dominate behavior* (68). Stamp-collecting, music, or baseball are interests in this sense; and a teacher might certainly consider herself a success if she established the subject she taught as a major interest in the lives of her pupils. Interests are more than preferences or likings, though they are preferences and likings. They are goals in which a person finds avenues of more or less permanent and lasting satisfaction and self-fulfillment. So any idea that interest is only the icing on the educational cake is quite wrong. I have already pointed out that psychologists maintain that a person should have a considerable range of genuine interests in his life. The reason why this is so is very evident the moment we see what interest really is. And when we see what interest really is, and how it affects life and personality, we also see that nothing of more importance can be done for a youngster in school than to help him to find and develop desirable and fruitful interests.

Interests are acquired like any other goals, namely, by the experience of success. Take for instance an interest in woodworking, which many boys acquire in school. A boy elects the course in woodworking, perhaps because he has been urged to do so, or has a free period at the right time. On the opening day he goes into the woodworking shop. The course already has a reputation which affects his attitude. He has heard some of his friends talk about what they have done in it, and has seen and admired some of their products. So there is already a tangible promise of success.

When he gets into the shop, he is shown some definite things that he can do, and helped in the doing of them; and he is given some choice as to what he will make, if the instructor is wise. There are challenges, but they are not impossible challenges; difficulties, but not frustrating difficulties. He can watch with his own eyes the results of his own efforts, even though there are no statistics or test scores. So he has a strong sense of identification with the work—of ego-involvement. As his first project moves towards completion he receives, no doubt, some criticism, but also a meed of appreciation. And when it is done, he has something to take home for the admiration of his friends and family and for his own solitary contemplation.

Woodworking, in fact, if it is properly organized, provides a surprising variety of satisfying success experiences. It offers satisfactions for not a few basic personal needs. No wonder, then, that it often becomes a strong and permanent interest! No wonder, too, that it is a very helpful type of "occupational therapy," and can help to stabilize and strengthen disturbed personalities. If you want to explain the appeal of woodworking, there is no need to refer to a mysterious "something" in human nature or in boy nature. The whole activity can be and usually is organized to promise success and to yield success, and in so doing to bring the satisfaction of basic needs.

Here also is the explanation of why curricular subjects do not usually establish themselves as interests. Algebra and history are no more naturally dull than woodworking is naturally interesting. But all too often algebra and history, among other subjects, are organized in such a way as to defeat interest rather than to promote it. In these subjects as often taught (though not as they might and should be taught) young people find themselves required to master routine techniques and to assimilate masses of facts. There is nothing to give them pride or pleasure in their work, nothing to make them want to do it well, very little of either the promise or the actuality of success. In fact the motivation is likely to be negative; and we cannot very well expect a positive effect from a negative cause. So the study of the subject is made a dull chore instead of an interesting challenge.

It might be replied that the curricular subjects are important and worth studying anyhow, whether pupils find them interesting or not. But this would be to miss the real point of our account of interest. Surely a subject is only worth learning if its effects last. No matter how valuable a subject may be in itself, or in its social implications, that subject will not do a student much good if he dismisses it from his mind the moment the course is over. Clearly, then, we must always try for permanent effects in our teaching. But how can these permanent effects be produced? Details of fact and technique will certainly be forgotten. Such details are always forgotten, both out of school and in school. But if we can kindle an interest, there is a very good chance that the fire will go on burning, and perhaps become hotter and hotter. For a genuine interest has a very strong tendency to be self-perpetuating.

This self-perpetuating character of interest has been brought out in an investigation of problem-solving. The investigator found that after her subjects had worked at a problem for a while, until they began to get the "feel" of it, so to speak, it would stay persistently in their minds, and that they would think about it and work at it until they got a solution (290, 291). The solving of a specific problem is, of course, a short-lived interest, because it has a definite terminal point. But within its limits problem-solving does show very clearly and interestingly the tendency of an interest to perpetuate itself, and to proceed under its own steam.

Taking a very much longer view, this same tendency has also been shown when comparisons are made between the interests of younger and older people. For it has been shown that interests have a high degree of stability in people's lives. It is true that there are characteristic changes of interest with age. Older people are likely to be more sedentary in their pursuits than younger people—to prefer sitting at home, reading a book, going on a quiet automobile jaunt, instead of mountain climbing, tennis, and extensive socializing. But in spite of such differences, the striking feature of interest is permanence and stability rather than transience and capriciousness. Thus a comprehensive study was made of the interests of 2,340 men, ranging in age from twenty to sixty. One of the most important findings of this study is that the older men had, at the time the study was made, a stronger liking for the kind of things they liked twenty-five years ago, and a stronger disliking for the kind of things they disliked twenty-five years ago (619).

So if a teacher wants the material she teaches to have a permanent influence, her very best policy is to do all she can to establish that material as a self-propelling interest. In order to do this she may have to sacrifice some sacred and cherished conventions, such as, ground-covering or excessive drill on fundamentals. But it is often necessary to cut out dead wood for the sake of giving the living growth a chance.

This very marked and very important tendency of interests to perpetuate themselves, and even to become stronger as time goes on, has led to the theory that they may have a wholly independent life of their own. This is called the theory of the "functional autonomy of motives" (8). But although the word "motives" is used by the originator of the theory, it would do just as well to speak of the "functional autonomy of interests." According to this theory, the drive of an interest, or a motive, comes entirely from the interest, or motive, itself. It does not come from basic needs. The interest, or motive, accounts for its own perpetuation.

The most important evidence for the theory of the functional autonomy of interest is the undoubted fact that once an interest is well started, it has the same self-feeding tendency as a forest fire. But this fact could be explained in quite a different way. To make the argument concrete, consider stamp-collecting, an instance I have used elsewhere. As a person goes on with stamp-collecting he finds more and more "in it," he gets to know more and more stamp collectors, he has more and more reason to be proud of his collection. So stamp-collecting becomes a better and better satisfier of needs. Moreover, our stamp collector only has so many hours in the day and so many years to live. Stamp-collecting has become a very satisfying part of his life. It has entered into many of the basic adjustments of his personality. Surely we do not have to believe in a rather magical something called "functional autonomy" to make it seem quite reasonable that he will want to go on and on with his stamps, instead of looking for some quite new avenue of self-fulfillment.

The more one looks at actual interests, the harder it seems to explain them without reference to some pattern of basic needs. The comics, for instance, have an amazing and almost universal appeal. It has been found that children of high and low intelligence seem about equally interested in them, and that really good and attractive reading programs do not supplant this interest. How then can we account for the tremendous fascination of the comics? A very reasonable explanation is that children find vicarious satisfaction for many basic needs in the activities of the dramatis personae. The comics, of course, are certainly not always humorous. There are the incredible feats of Superman and the Batman. In such comic strips as Dick Tracy and Smiling Jack there are dangerous adventures, noble deeds, lofty (if sometimes corny) motives, the triumph of the right, the diffusion of copybook morality. Such tales have had a tremendous human attraction ever since stories first were told; and surely one may very well think that this is because in these stories a person can see himself vicariously as a hero and a conqueror. All that the theory of functional autonomy would have to offer would be that children like the comics because they like the comics. The needs hypothesis may not explain everything, but it explains more than that (186, 618, 735, 737).

Moreover, the self-perpetuating tendency of interest is only a tendency, and that tendency may not manifest itself. Interests can wither away as well as flourish, which seems hard to explain on the basis of functional autonomy. A group of 651 college students were asked to report on the reasons why they lost interest in various subjects that they had studied in high school. By far the most usual reason they gave was that these subjects came to seem to them trivial and insignificant and unimportant (756). These students may, and in fact, probably did have some measure of initial success in their high-school subjects, at least to the extent of getting fairly good marks. But there was probably very little sense of personal achievement, of self-identification, of learning things which could orient one in dealing with life's problems—no continuing consciousness of deeper and deeper satisfaction of status needs or ego needs. Hence the initial interest, whatever it may have been, withered away. It is worth-while noticing that the people who made this report on their high-school interests were all of them college students. If prospective college students tend to lose interest in high-school studies because they find those studies trivial and insignificant, this same tendency is likely to be far more striking and disastrous among high-school students who have no college intentions or possibilities.

Interests, as has been very well said, are "the driving force of achievement" (139). They shape and mold the pattern of life. The effectiveness, the happiness, and the development of any human being is largely determined by his interests. This is why teachers and schools must do everything possible to promote significant interests if personality is to be shaped aright and if the influence of education is to be permanent in human lives.

On purely external evidence there is reason to believe that schools do have an appreciable influence in promoting and developing interests. Some years ago an extensive survey was made in Maryland dealing with the lives and problems of more than thirteen thousand young people between the ages of sixteen and twenty-four, all of them out of school. A much greater range and variety of interests were found among those who had gone on into or completed high school than among those who had dropped out at the end of the sixth grade or sooner. Those with no more than a sixth-grade education on the whole spent much of their time "piddling around, loafing, doing nothing in particular, sitting in the barber shop," and so forth. This suggests that the school has an appreciable influence, although it cannot take all the credit for the difference. Moreover, the survey brought out the fact that a great many of the underprivileged young people who have had limited education heartily dislike their jobs, so that they had no compensating strong vocational interest (42).

But what the schools usually do in the promoting of interest is done incidentally and not as a matter of deliberate policy and intelligent planning. This statement is born out unmistakably by the numerous studies and surveys of adult interests. In all these surveys and studies, a person who is found to have a strong and living interest in any curricular field, except perhaps general reading, is a rarity. Is there any good reason why this should be so? Is not modern science as thrilling and amazing as the doings of Superman? Cannot history furnish as much inspiration and enthrallment as Dick Tracy?

These questions bring us to the very heart of the practical problem of interest in education. The function of the school, properly understood, is not to take a predetermined body of content and trick it up to make it interesting. Its true function is to organize both content and teaching-learning situations with a view to establishing vital interests which tend to go forward and develop. Two applications of this idea will help to show what is involved in it.

The first of these two applications has to do with the case of an overage boy in junior high school which I have reported elsewhere (471). This boy was considerably below average intelligence. His academic work was poor, and he was evidently destined for a rather meager life of routine employment. So far one might say that he was an educational misfit. However, the music teacher in his junior high school very skillfully organized success experiences of great variety and significance in the field of music. She encouraged creative dancing, singing, and even composing. Her work made a really profound appeal to this boy, who developed a genuine passion for music. Here he found, in the midst of his otherwise rather frustrating school environment, a means for the satisfaction of many of his deepest needs. While of course no one can foresee the future, it seems very likely that this boy's music teacher established in his life a vital interest of great potential permanent value to him.

The second application and illustration of the general principle stated above is from a study of the "constructional activities" of a group of men. (Constructional activities, I should perhaps explain, are activities such as woodworking, metalworking, fixing the house, painting, and so forth.) Half the men whose constructional activities were investigated in this study had taken part in such activities when they were children, and half of them had not. Of those who had taken part in constructional activities when they were children, 53% were carrying them on as adults. Of those who had had no such childhood experiences, only 3% were carrying on such activities as adults (482). This is very much a case in point. The sort of handwork and craftwork carried on by children is usually not very highly skilled. There is apt to be little emphasis on technique, and no serious attempt to teach the "fundamentals" of high-level artisanship. But children are given a taste of something which spells, within limits, indubitable and repaying success—something which in some real measure is palpably a satisfier of needs. And the effects last through the years, and have an influence in the shaping of character and personality, and the determination of life-destinies.

Here, then, are two instances of school-originated interests, and indeed of interests originating in the curriculum, for in spite of sundry prejudices, music and shopwork are curricular fields. One finds it amazing, deplorable and indefensible that such instances should be startling exceptions instead of commonplace occurrences.

MOTIVATION AND SOCIAL SETTING

Some of the most decisive influences in establishing the goals which the individual will pursue—goals which are determined by self-fulfilling and successful experience—depend on the general social setting. It is not generally understood how much the general outlook and the effective values of various social and economic groups differ. Yet many of the most baffling of educational problems come from these differences.

Part of the story has been summed up in the following words: "Whereas the middle-class child learns a socially adaptive fear of receiving poor grades in school, of being aggressive toward the teacher, of fighting, of cursing, and of having early sex relations, the slum child learns to fear quite different social acts. His gang teaches him to fear being taken in by the teacher, of being a softie with her. To study homework seriously is literally a disgrace. Instead of boasting of good marks in school, one conceals them, if he ever receives any. The lower class individual fears *not* to be thought a street-fighter; it is a suspicious and dangerous trait. He fears *not to curse*. If he cannot claim early sex relations, his virility is seriously questioned. Thus society raises many anxieties in slum people also, but with regard to the attainment of what to middle-class people seem strange goals. For those who live in a slum community, however, these goals are realistic and adequate" (138, p. 30).

In the terms of our discussion it would be better to change these negative statements into positive ones—to say that the slum child *wants* to get poor grades, *wants* to be at loggerheads with the teacher, *wants* to be a street fighter, *wants* to curse, *wants* to have early sex relationships. The reason for this change from negative to positive is that motives are shaped by success rather than directly by failure or fear of failure. And for the slum child, such doings as have been mentioned constitute successes, i.e. ways of satisfying status needs and also ego needs. But this change makes no essential difference in the purport of the passage or in the diagnosis it presents.

The point of the statement I have just quoted is that the school is *dynamically* out of touch with great masses of young people. It holds out to them success-values which for them are not success-values at all. So it cannot shape their motives, or determine their goals, or constructively determine their interests. In short, it cannot influence these young people positively because it does not have the essential means of doing so. It can only deal with them by using a negative motivation of threat and fear, by confining and walling them in for a time, coping with inevitable rebellion as well as it can; and finally it has to let them go more or less untouched and probably hostile.

It is this failure of psychological dynamics—of motivation—that seems to the psychologist the crucial weakness. One often hears it said that the great trouble with present-day schooling is the content of the curriculum. What, it is asked, can science, or mathematics, or history, or literature mean to underprivileged children brought up in urban or rural slums? How much impression can social studies, as ordinarily taught, make on a boy whose family has realistic dealings with the neighborhood ward politician or the local cop? The author of the above quotation even raises the question whether the great emphasis on reading in elementary education is not a mistake due to class prejudices and class values, and whether reading is really as important for great numbers of children as we think it is. Criticisms of this kind are very familiar, indeed almost commonplace. Yet it could very well be argued that the central trouble with the school is not the content of the curriculum at all, but the feebleness of motivation.

If one seriously set out to make a strictly "non-academic" or "practical" curriculum one would run head on into impossibility. What should be put into such a curriculum? house maintenance, machine repair, shop practice? How far could one get with that without science and mathematics? dietetics and personal hygiene? Surely reading, writing, arithmetic, and physiology would enter in. Dramatics, dancing, singing, ensemble music? The floodgates would be wide open to the anathematized general culture. Wise buying, discrimination in the choice of goods, management of a personal budget? The social and natural sciences would at once invade our classrooms. Should we teach patriotism in our practical school? How could we, with good conscience, teach patriotism except on a basis of understanding rather than of slogans. No! The academic curriculum may be poorly organized and arranged. Its subdivision into innumerable small compartments may be artificial and awkward almost to the point of frustration. The textbooks in which it is presented may be dreary. But its actual content, beyond all possibility of denial or avoidance, is the best rationale of enlightened living which the mind of man has yet devised.

So it may very well be argued that the function of the school is not to find some better substitute for the content of culture, but to bring the content of culture into vital relationship with human living. This can only be done by the shaping of motives, the determination of goals, the creation of vital interests.

A certain young teacher, out on his first job, found himself assigned to a problem class of overage boys in an elementary school situated in the slums of a great city. These boys had been the nemesis of several of his predecessors, and the young man faced the problem with fear and trembling. He realized instantly that there would be no handling the group unless he could really teach them something; and he also saw that this could not be done by force. Baseball, he discovered, was a vital immediate interest of every boy in the class. The young man seized upon this, and by projects, map-making, model-making, class discussions, small group studies, and the like, all related to baseball and the fortunes of various clubs, he taught them far more about the geography of their own country than most children ever learn in conventional classes, even though such children have the indubitable advantages of pleasant homes and normal to high I.Q.'s. The teacher did not abandon cultural content. What he did was to motivate it by creating interest through the organization of success experiences in the only way such experiences can be organized, namely, in terms of the boys' own values.

QUESTIONS FOR DISCUSSION

1. When a teacher steps out of a classroom it often happens that the class explodes into disorder. Analyze this reaction on the part of the class in terms of the motivations involved. Is it a symptom of being "walled in"? If so, what does this suggest about the nature of the motivations?

2. Do your best to analyze the actual motivations that lead pupils to do their homework.

3. It sometimes happens that when classes are subdivided into "fast" and "slow" groups some bright pupils will deliberately plan to get into the slow groups. This clearly is an instance of a low level of aspiration. What might be done to raise the level of aspiration of such pupils?

4. Consider some long-continuing interest of your own in some sport, or hobby, or subject. What got this interest started? Does it seem to you to have gained increasing momentum with the passage of time? If so, why do you think that this increase in momentum manifested itself? Consider whether your analysis of your own experience might be applied to teaching situations.

5. A boy in the third grade became intensely interested in art. He devoted a great deal of time to drawing and painting. Was this to any extent an indication that he had unusual artistic talent and would be likely to do unusually well in the field of art?

6. It is sometimes said that the way to deal with the "problem of discipline" is to avoid having any such problem. That is, the thing to try for is to avoid the motivational conditions that produce rebellion and disorder and call for repression. How, in principle, would a teacher set about doing this, even though she might not always completely succeed?

7. Assemble and discuss from your own experiences and contacts a number of illustrations of an unduly high and an unduly low level of aspiration. Consider the unfortunate consequences produced. How might a realistic level of aspiration be established?

8. One often hears it said that a teacher should try to "make a subject interesting." Does this seem to you a sound idea? How would you set out to make some given subject, such as history, mathematics, or science, interesting? Do you think, in the light of this chapter, that you ought to do so?

SUGGESTED READINGS

Lewin, Kurt, "Field Theory of Learning." *41st Yearbook*, National Society for the Study of Education (1942), Part II, 297–302.

Sears, Paul S., "Levels of Aspiration in Academically Successful and Unsuccessful Children." *Journal of Abnormal Psychology and Social Psychology*, XXXV (1940), 498–536.

Strang, Ruth, "Why Children Read the Comics." *Elementary School Journal*, XLIII (1943), 336–342.

Strong, E. K., Jr., *Changes of Interests with Age*. Stanford University Press, Stanford University, Calif., 1931.

5

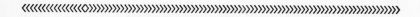

What Happens When We Learn?

DISCOVERY OF TECHNIQUE

THE SHAPING of personality is a process which, for the sake of having a definite single-word name, we have found convenient to call adjustment. Adjustment has two aspects, the evocation of the will, and the finding of a way.

These two aspects of adjustment are very closely related. Indeed, they merge into one another and affect one another in many ways. From what has already been said, it must be obvious that learning depends on motivation; but it may be well to clarify the general connection between the two by bringing out a number of points.

1. No one ever learns anything unless he is faced with a challenge or a problem. Now a challenge is only a challenge if it evokes the will. There must be something that a person wants to do, but as yet cannot do. Otherwise he will simply not be challenged. So far as he is concerned the problem will not be a problem; and then there will be no learning.

2. The true nature of the challenge, the actual goals or motives that are operating, have a great deal to do with what a person actually learns in a given situation. A teacher may set up a situation in which she intends children to learn certain skills or certain facts. But the children may be hostile or bored. Then the real challenge for them may be to "get by" with minimum trouble. So instead of learning the facts or the skills, they learn to shirk or to cheat or perhaps to hate the subject, the teacher, and the school. This is always worth remembering, for the most superlatively perfect teaching methods are quite futile if the motivation is wrong.

3. Motivation determines how well people learn and how long they keep on learning. The moment a person is satisfied with what he is able to do, there is no longer any challenge. The will to learn is shut off, and learning stops. So high standards of achievement cannot be imposed, because they are only possible through constructive and continuing motivation.

These three points, which could be supported by a wealth of experimental evidence, and which can hardly be questioned, go to show the *general* connection between motivation and learning. But the connection between the two aspects of adjustment is even closer and more organic than the three points taken by themselves might suggest. Adjustment starts with the arousal of the will, with an urgent unsolved problem, an insistent dynamic challenge. Adjustment is, for the time being, consummated by finding out how to solve this problem, how to deal with this challenge. And the very essence of learning is the finding of the way. Let us put this proposition in the somewhat more formal language which it deserves because of its importance. The heading of this chapter is the question, *What happens when we learn?* The answer here given is: When we learn, what happens is *the discovery of a method, a technique for dealing with the problem before us.*

Naturally, this is a proposition that takes some defending and explaining. As a matter of fact, everything that I shall say about learning is a defense and exposition of it, for it is my central doctrine. But before taking up various special aspects of the learning process, I shall give some broad reasons why the proposition I have just put forward seems to be true. The present chapter will be devoted to these broad reasons. Much of the evidence comes from technical research, and it must, of course, be considered. But first, let us take some everyday-life illustrations of learning to show more clearly what it means to say that the very essence of learning is the finding of a method or a technique for dealing with a challenge.

A boy starts off for the first time in the school woodworking shop. After a conference with the instructor, he thinks he would like to make a bookcase. This is his general goal, which very soon breaks down into a lot of more special goals. The pieces of wood must be cut square, or the bookcase will not fit together. How does one use a handsaw or a power saw to make square cuts? There are quite a few tricks to doing this, such as double-checking on all the lines that one draws, holding the saw properly if it is a handsaw, being certain that the gauges are properly set if it is a power saw, being sure that the piece of wood is tight against the gauges when one makes a cut, and so on. Skill consists in doing all such things properly. Learning consists in knowing what things must be done, finding out how to do them, and finding out how to make a constant self-check to see that they are done.

Making a bookcase, of course, calls for more than cutting wood on the square. There is planing, for instance, which cannot go well unless the plane blade is properly sharpened, properly set, and moved with, instead of against, the grain of the wood. Other processes, too, will be involved, but I need not go on. Ask yourself just what it is that this boy is learning. Is he learning skill? Yes, no doubt he is, but surely this is rather a vague, over-all description of what really goes on. A more convincing, more tangible answer to the question seems to be that he is learning "know-how," technique, methods of operation. This certainly seems to be what happens when he learns.

A man who has very little public speaking experience takes a position in which it is very important to become a good public speaker, and he learns to become one. You can see that he improves. What makes him improve? I shall not attempt anything like a complete answer, but here are at least some of the factors. He learns always to have a clear central idea, always to decide very carefully on how to open and close a speech, always to avoid confusing his audience by trying to pack in too much, to talk usually to the people in the back of the room, to speak sometimes directly to certain individuals in his audience, to stand still in one place while he talks. You may, if you like, call these the tricks of the speaker's trade. They correspond exactly to the know-how of the expert cabinetmaker. They are ways of acting, techniques, methods of handling a problem and meeting a challenge. Whatever you call them, they are the key points of our speaker's improvement, the true content of his learning as he learns to speak more effectively.

A small child annoys the family friends by always putting on a show in the home when anything annoys him, and by always getting his way by dint of tantrums and whining. Observers say that this child has a nasty disposition and deplorable character traits, which may be a very true description. But what we call deplorable character traits have all been learned. And what the child has actually learned are a variety of techniques for getting his way, for dealing with the various and sundry challenges which life presents to him. Our annoying small child is an even more obvious example than the bookcase maker or the public speaker of the proposition that when one learns anything, one always learns *how to do something.*

You may be interested to apply this proposition to instances of your own finding, and such instances are literally legion. Dry-fly fishing, for example, is really an assemblage of know-how techniques. Riding a bicycle is very largely a matter of discriminating the right cues for balance. Good chess playing means knowing just what to look for on the board. So I could go on indefinitely. How these techniques and methods and items of know-how are acquired is, of course, another question. But that learning itself is, in its essence, the discovery of methods of operating seems so far reasonable and understandable.

The relationship of this analysis to the process of adjustment and the shaping of personality should also now be clear. We face challenges and problems that evoke the will. By dint of learning we discover methods of dealing with these challenges. The totality of all these methods, interwoven with one another, is what we call the personality.

The idea that learning is always *learning how* is a very challenging conception of the learning process, and its practical implications are far-reaching and drastic. It means that what may be called "standard procedure" in teaching subjects in school is quite unrealistic, because it is based on a wrong answer to the question of what happens when we learn. Standard teaching procedure in school is to set up a body of material to be assimilated or "mastered," to divide this body of material into smaller units called courses, to subdivide the courses again into still smaller blocks called lessons or units or some such name, to organize each lesson into a more or less self-contained learning task, and to run tests for the sake of finding out how much is retained. This is the plan followed in most teaching, and the great majority of textbooks are arranged to conform to it.

The basic standard procedure is a very persistent convention. It existed in all essentials long before the textbook-recitation procedure of modern times came into vogue. A hundred years ago schools were not divided into grades on the basis of age. There would be a heterogeneous mob of pupils in each classroom. The practice was for each pupil to study his own lesson independently, and for the teacher to call pupils to his desk one by one to hear them recite. This might seem very different from the sort of recitation we are used to, and there were important differences, especially in the handling of discipline. But the essence of the learning pattern in the old individual recitation method was to study a book and then tell what you knew under test conditions; and all that has happened under our own class recitation practice is to socialize the procedure so that a teacher can handle more children at a time, without altering the basic learning pattern itself.

This basic convention persists in spite of changes in terminology. Nowadays we talk about "units" instead of "lessons," and perhaps about "socialized recitations" instead of the oral quizzes that are supposed to be old-fashioned. But in spite of the new words that come along quite often it is rare to find any radical change in underlying procedure. In one way or another pupils are required to assimilate a certain amount of material for the sake of giving it back in tests. One would certainly seem justified in saying that behind this standard procedure is the idea that what happens when we learn is the acquisition of knowledge, the storing of the mind, or the building of habits. It is very likely that if the average intelligent teacher were caught unprepared and suddenly asked to give a definition of learning, she would say that it is the acquisition of knowledge and/or the building of skills, or perhaps that it is the storing of the mind. If she had recently taken a certain type of course in psychology, she might say that learning is the establishment of connections in the nervous system, but so far as practical implications are concerned, this would be the same idea in more complicated language.

But if what really happens when we learn is the discovery of ways of dealing with challenges, then the conception of learning underlying standard school procedure is highly misleading, and the practices based upon it are highly unrealistic. There is abundant, even overwhelming evidence that this is so. A long series of investigations have shown again and again that the learning of school subjects is slow and inefficient, and that the outcomes of such learning are remarkably transient. To give one typical instance, it is known that when children take up the so-called "subtraction facts" in elementary arithmetic, they have a strong tendency to forget the "addition facts" which were previously learned (84). The situation is just about the same in every subject in the curriculum.

Obviously this means bad and ineffective learning. But the important point is that learning in most curricular subjects is organized unrealistically in view of the desired outcomes. We want children to learn the subject. But what are the actual challenges that are set up, the actual motives behind the learning? Everyone knows the answer to this question—the tests! Children are not motivated to learn in order to master the subject, to understand it, to be able to use it or think in terms of it. They are motivated to learn to pass tests.

No doubt there is a relationship between good tests and knowing the subject, but it is far from a hundred per cent relationship. So passing such tests even with high scores is not equivalent to mastering the subject. Moreover, pupils can always pass tests with quite mediocre scores. What these mediocre scores mean in terms of actual grasp of the material is doubtful, but certainly not impressive. If any proof were needed that tests are the actuating goals of school study under conventional procedures, we have it in the fact that pupils study quite differently for essay tests and objective tests, whereas if they were all working for a direct mastery of the subject, such differences in study methods would certainly be reduced (452, 665).

But test motivation hardly needs research proof. It is accepted as a fact in every cramming school and every fraternity house, and also it is well known to every teacher. Teachers may say that lessons "store the learner's mind" with knowledge, or equip him with valuable habitual skills. But they arrange the dynamics of learning in such a way that what the learner actually works for is to acquire a technique of test-passing. Doubtless there can be a transfer from test-passing to understanding the subject. But one cannot take it for granted.

So learning is still the discovery of technique or method, even when we try quite strenuously to organize it as the storing of the mind. A challenge or a problem which evokes the will inaugurates the learning and gives it direction; and what happens in the process of learning is the emergence of a way of dealing with that problem.

PRACTICE

So far I have tried to explain the proposition that learning is essentially the discovery of technique, and to show its prima facie reasonableness by presenting a somewhat haphazard collection of illustrations. But this proposition is far too important and far-reaching to be accepted without much more careful scrutiny. Do research results, systematically considered and interpreted, support it? This is the question we must now take up.

First, what are the effects and meaning of practice? The word practice as here used means any activity intended to produce learning, so that it includes studying a book as well as practicing a physical skill. What happens when a person "practices" in this inclusive sense? What has experimental research to tell us about the effects of practice? Let us see.

One of the most important investigations of the effects of practice dealt with learning (*a*) to tap fast with a blunt pencil, and (*b*) to remember dictated sets of digits and to repeat them immediately. These are very trivial and routine tasks, but the investigator chose them precisely for that reason. He wanted to use learning tasks in which anything like technique or know-how would be reduced as close to the vanishing point as possible. So this investigation amounts almost to a crucial experiment or test for our doctrine that learning is always the discovery of technique; and, in fact, it was so intended.

The sequence of the experiment was as follows. All the subjects practiced tapping for 3 periods daily for 18 days, at which point the upper limit of improvement seemed to have been reached. Then the subjects were divided into two groups. One of these groups went on with the practice for 76 more days, during which the other group did nothing. At the end of the additional 76 days (94 days in all from the start of the experiment), the group which had not been practicing since the end of the eighteenth day came into action again. At this stage the subjects who had been practicing continuously were much superior to the non-practice group. But within a limit of 17 additional days both groups were on an equality. The point is that a very routine type of learning will turn out just as well if one practices for 18 days, quits for 76 days, and then practices for 17 days as it will if one practices solidly and continuously for 111 days (18 + 76 + 17 days).

This is what happened when the subjects practiced tapping with a blunt pencil, and the results were essentially similar when they practiced the remembering and immediate recall of dictated digits. As the author of the study remarks, the very strong suggestion is that what these subjects acquired during practice was a technique for doing the job (203).

A further finding from this investigation was that after an interval of between four and five months, both the two groups retained about an equal residue of skill from their learning. There was no difference in retention between those who had practiced continuously for 111 days and those who had practiced for only 35 days in all, broken into two periods of 18 and 17 days respectively. As a matter of fact, the loss in skill and efficiency after the four- to five-month interval was very great; and the author expresses the opinion that the loss was great precisely because there was so little in the way of technique to retain.

This last point deserves to be considered carefully, for the facts of long-term retention throw considerable light on what really happens during practice. In one very interesting experiment on long-term retention, the investigator himself acted as subject. In 1907 this gentleman had taught himself to typewrite. He had done so by copying the same paragraph each day, and also copying a new page each day. By this method he worked up to a tested speed of 22.5 words per minute taking 125 days to do so. Then for twenty-five years he did virtually no typewriting at all. During December and January 1932–1933—twenty-five years later—he undertook to regain his skill. On the first day of the new practice he did as well as he had done on the twenty-fifth day of the previous practice, and he reached his original level of achievement in a fifth of the original time (310). Clearly something very permanent had been acquired in those first 125 days of practice. What was it? The reasonable answer seems to be that this permanent acquisition was a technique, a method of using the typewriter—how to use the fingers, how to use the eyes, how to direct the attention.

These experimental findings, and the general interpretation they suggest, are very strongly supported by ordinary undocumented experience. A person learns to speak a foreign language. Then he drops it for many years. He seems to have completely forgotten it. But if he sets to work to regain it, he finds that it comes back to him very fast. Or there is the case of the famous pianist Paderewski, who abandoned the piano for a long and hard career of statesmanship. When he returned to the concert platform, age and care had taken their toll. But in essence the technique and the interpretative power were still there. In each of these cases a way of dealing with a challenging situation had been established. Then for a long time the challenge lapsed. But when it arrived once more, the way of dealing with it could be found again without too long a search.

You may be inclined to say that this quick reconstitution of an ability after a long lapse of time is possible with a physical or motor skill, but that mental acquisitions are usually lost completely and forever. The answer is that the learning of a great many mental abilities is very ineffective if not actually spurious. When a person learns to dance, or to swim, or to ride a bicycle, or to drive a car, or to paddle a canoe, or to make a campfire in the woods, he may never get to be very good, but he does really learn to do something. He acquires a practical technique. He becomes able to meet the challenge of a situation at least well enough to operate.

But when a boy in the tenth grade takes a course in plane geometry, what does he learn? Very often what he learns is how to memorize theorems well enough to get a passing grade. Probably if he took the course all over again twenty years later he would be able to do this particular trick somewhat better. But one cannot quite say that twenty years later he has *forgotten* his geometry, for if we want to talk with strict realism it is quite likely that he never learned any geometry at all worth mentioning. He never, for instance, got to a point where he could use his geometry as even a mediocre canoe paddler can use a paddle—namely, as a means of coping with situations and dealing with problems and challenges. But when geometry, or any other body of intellectual content, is learned so that it is really understood—so that one can bring it to bear on the problems that constantly present themselves in life—there is every reason to believe that it stays learned at least as well as canoe paddling or campfire making.

So we conclude that the improvement brought about by practicing is precisely the discovery and refinement of a technique or a method. This conclusion is sound both in theory and in practice. As a point of possible interest, it is exactly the assumption of every commercial memory system on the market. There are many such systems, and within limits they help. All of them undertake to reveal a technique or method for remembering and recalling.

The general practical conclusion is that all practice, i.e. all activity intended to bring about learning, should be in the nature of an attempt to discover a way of dealing with a challenging situation, or to improve or confirm an already discovered way of dealing with that situation. Good and effective practice should have the quality, not of routine repetition, but of a quest and a discovering.

For instance, we want children to learn to add and subtract. The conventional procedure has been to set up a hundred "addition facts," such as $7 + 5 = 12$, and a hundred similar "subtraction facts," and have the children repeat and recite these facts until they can produce them on demand. It is known, however, that this is a slow, uncertain procedure, with much time wasted on mistakes and forgettings, and much bafflement when it comes to dealing with carrying from units to tens, from tens to hundreds, and so forth. A far better procedure is to create situations in which children will discover how to add and subtract in order to deal with genuine challenges.

Thus, "a kindergarten teacher was observed who endeavored to direct the development of the number ideas of her children in a systematic way. In her room the leader of each table of six children had been in the habit of going to the cupboard within the room for boxes of crayon. In doing so he would look in turn at each child at the table as he selected the box of crayons for that person. The teacher, wanting to lead her children to higher levels of response, placed the crayons out of sight of the children in a small room adjacent to the kindergarten. Although the leaders experienced difficulty at first, they soon learned to count the children at their tables, including themselves, keep the numbers in mind, go to the next room, count out the required number of boxes, and return with them. The teacher varied the experiences of the children by asking them to obtain a given number of sheets of paper, count boys and girls present, set out a certain number of chairs, etc. Thus the development of number ideas were consciously directed by the teacher. Children were carried from the simple level of matching objects with children to that of dealing with total groups" (646, p. 47).

This, of course, would be preliminary to learning addition and subtraction directly; but in the usual drill procedure there are no preliminaries at all. Moreover, the same emphasis on discovering solutions or methods of dealing with situations can be and is continued when addition and subtraction as well as the other arithmetical processes are taken up. Many devices have been invented for helping to continue this emphasis. One of them is the "Unit Board" used by Catherine Stern in her system for teaching elementary arithmetic. The Unit Board is a shallow box ten inches square, into which blocks of various sizes can be fitted. These blocks range from the "one block" to the "ten block," which last is the largest. By manipulating these blocks in the Unit Board, children discover the addition facts for themselves; and Miss Stern has equally ingenious devices for enabling children to learn other arithmetical processes by discovering them (614).

Again, much in the modern teaching of reading turns on enabling and helping children to use their eyes properly when they look at a page. Three discoveries about the movement of the eyes in reading have been crucial in their effects on instruction. These three discoveries are (*a*) that the eyes do not move continuously when a person reads, but that they keep starting and stopping, and that reading takes place only during the pauses; (*b*) that when the eyes are at rest at a normal distance from the page, it is possible to see about an inch and a half of any given line; (*c*) that it is not necessary to see letters or even words clearly in order to read them.

With these facts in mind the suggestion has been made that children ought to be drilled in efficient eye-movement, the word "drill" being used in the sense of directed repetition. There have been some attempts to carry out drills of this sort. But the modern procedure in teaching reading (and it is very successful), is to choose reading material which will tend to require and encourage the right kind of eye movements, and to use this material with the right kind of movements in mind. In this way children find out *how to look* at a page as they read it, although, to be sure, they cannot explain clearly just what they are doing (208).

Reading and arithmetic are usually considered "skill subjects"; and in such subjects it might seem reasonable enough to emphasize ways of acting or doing, techniques for dealing with situations. But is the idea feasible in "content subjects," such as history or social studies, where information is to be acquired? Decidedly the answer is, Yes.

Some years ago an experimental course in architecture was organized in a sixth grade. After the course had been running for several weeks, the class on their own initiative expressed a wish to make a rose window as a group project. No one knew how rose windows were made. Various techniques and skills were obviously required. But a great deal of information was needed too. Acting on suggestions from the teacher, the children proceeded to hunt up and collate this information from reference books, from various libraries which were available, and in conferences with experts. The project turned out to be a great success, and it had many features that are very interesting to teachers. But the point here is that information was a tool or a technique for dealing with a situation, and was used as such. There was a great deal of active and effective learning; and this learning had the character of quest and discovery (32).

Another sixth grade devoted a year to a study of the local textile industry, with a display for a culminating activity. Here again a wealth of information was needed—information about materials, processes, color combinations, business and marketing problems, and so on. This information was not "assimilated" from the pages of a textbook. It was dug up, discovered, formulated, collated, and used for a purpose.

As a matter of ordinary common sense, very few people acquire information merely for the purpose of having it or for the joy of gaining it. Even quiz experts build up a knowledge of facts for a very definite purpose and hunt for those facts far and wide. Everyone who has written a term paper or made a speech in which he had to refer to certain facts ought to be able to see very easily that by far the best way of acquiring information is to hunt it up when and as it is needed and because it is needed. Not only is this the most interesting way of acquiring information, but also the facts so acquired seem to stay with one much better than those which one tries to learn by storing.

So in the light of research it seems justifiable to believe that what practice really does is to lead to the discovery and establishment of a method or technique.

LEARNING APART FROM PRACTICE

But learning does not depend wholly on practice. To say that we learn only by "doing" is simply not true. Some of our very best learning goes on when we are not practicing or doing at all. This fact is interesting and important in itself. It is full of practical suggestiveness for the wise management of the learning process, both in ourselves and in others. But the main point here is that the only way of explaining why learning can and does go on apart from overt practice is to regard learning itself as a process of discovering and establishing methods or techniques for dealing with challenges.

The idea that learning can and does go on apart from practicing, and, indeed, that we must make provision for something more than active "doing" if we are to learn well, may seem strange at first sight. But really it is a common-sense idea, as you can readily see by considering a few illustrations taken neither from experimental research nor from school work.

Think first of a person who intends to make a complicated automobile tour. He gets hold of maps, guidebooks, and brochures, studies them, and probably discusses them. All this one might call practice—a pattern of activities through which the man hopes and intends to learn just where to go and how to get there. But besides such active studying our intending traveler broods over the information he is collecting, considers alternative routes, balances all sorts of possibilities. Certainly he is doing something very important and necessary; and it might be just possible to call such brooding and pondering a kind of internal practicing, although to do so would be to stretch interpretation rather far. But very likely he feels that he must let things hold over for a time, sleep on the matter perhaps for several nights, because he cannot make up his mind at once.

This making up of the mind is the very essence of learning. Yet it is certainly far removed from practicing or active studying, and perhaps has very little conscious thinking about it. Still, important things happen in the seemingly empty interval. Ideas crystallize out. The whole plan of the trip clarifies and reorganizes itself. All this, to repeat, is essentially a process of learning; and while it would never take place if there were no study and active thinking, the sheer passage of time is also essential.

A deep, instinctive feeling that the shaping up of any achievement requires not only hard work and concentrated effort, but also the lapse of time is very common among creative workers. For instance, Arnold Bennett has told in considerable detail about the development and final writing of what is usually said to be his best novel, *The Old Wives' Tale.* The idea first came to him in a Paris chain restaurant where he saw two old women of very contrasting types having dinner together. He began to weave a fantasy about them, and thought of writing it as a long short story of about sixteen thousand words with the title "The Two Old Women." The story, however, would not go as he had planned, but the idea stuck stubbornly with him and kept changing and expanding. New related ideas and new material kept coming into his mind. Scenes from his own past life, accounts of current events from the newspapers (one of them being a description of a public execution) crowded into the pattern. A process of discovery, a quest was going on; and although we might very properly call it a creative process, Bennett's description of what happened is a very good description of learning.

Over ten years passed by from Bennett's first thinking of the idea to the publication of the book. Although *The Old Wives' Tale* is a long novel, he spent only a very small portion of that ten years in actually working on it. During most of the ten years the book was germinating in his mind, clarifying itself, just as the automobile tour clarified itself in the mind of the traveler. Bennett was *discovering* how to write his book. He was *learning* how to write it. And although he had to work on it directly, i.e. to practice, a great deal more than direct and conscious work was necessary.

So, too, a boy in a woodworking shop cannot learn to be an expert in three months, no matter how hard he works or how long he toils. Let us suppose that for those three months he puts in all the time he has, perhaps fourteen hours a day. No doubt he will improve a great deal. But he would be much further along if he distributed the same total amount of time over a year. The same with learning to play golf. A man may play all day and every day and take innumerable lessons, but he will not become an expert in three months. Once more, the same amount of practice time spread over a year would bring him greater returns. The only possible conclusion seems to be that learning is a process of clarification or discovery, and that this process takes not only practice but also time.

So much for the common sense of the matter, which seems fairly convincing. Now for the experimental research. From the very start of experiments on learning, it was noticed that distributed practice yields much better results than massed or concentrated practice, although the significance of this finding was not well understood. The value of distributed practice was demonstrated in one of the famous pioneer studies on memory, which was made by Ebbinghaus and published in 1885. Ebbinghaus worked on the memorization of nonsense syllables, and one of his typical discoveries was that 38 repetitions of a long list of nonsense syllables distributed over 3 days would give as good results as 68 repetitions at a single sitting.

Since that time the general conclusion that distributed practice is much more effective than concentrated, or massed, practice has been confirmed again and again. There is much disagreement among experimental findings on points of detail, such as the degree of superiority yielded by distributed practice or the best plan for distributing practice—whether, for instance, 3 practice periods of 20 minutes each day are better than 4 practice periods of 15 minutes each day. But the general conclusion is thoroughly well established (555). Indeed, in the light of all the extensive work that has been done on the problem, it would seem that in many cases the results of learning depend more on the total elapsed time than on the sheer amount of practice (309). Once practice is started, it seems to set going a process of clarification which proceeds under its own momentum.

Again, in certain experiments on motor learning subjects have been required to work at the task of learning to trace on paper a six-pointed star which they could only see in a mirror. This is a difficult and quite frustrating performance. It is found that lapse of time, particularly in the early stages of such learning, is not only important but even essential. As one traces the star, looking only in the mirror, there is a strong tendency for one's pencil or stylus to go off in the wrong direction at each of the angles, and also a strong tendency to misjudge the angles themselves. To push oneself, to practice continuously and intensively, can lead to complete defeat in the face of these tendencies. It becomes necessary to relax, to "take it easy," to space practice periods quite widely. One has to find out how to look in the mirror and co-ordinate one's actions with what is seen there. A method, a technique of control must emerge. A clarification must be achieved; and this is the reason why time is required (236, 606).

In another case, a celebrated series of experiments done nearly forty years ago revealed the striking phenomenon called "reminiscence" (28). Over 5,000 school children performed various memory tasks in these experiments. One of their tasks was to spend 15 minutes memorizing some stanzas from *The Rime of the Ancient Mariner* as well as they could within the time limit. After the memorizing was done, the children were tested at various times, some being tested at once, and others at intervals up to 7 days. After 1 day an average of 45.5% was remembered. After 2 days an average of 55.3% was remembered. This improvement, noted on the second day, was the greatest achieved, but the effect persisted throughout the period of the experiment. It is this improvement of memory after a time interval that is called "reminiscence."

Later investigations with persons of many different ages have confirmed the fact that reminiscence does take place. In one remarkable experiment with 1,500 college students, recognition rather than recall was studied, and the material used was meaningful prose. That is to say, the subjects learned prose passages, and then had to tell whether they could recognize items from those passages when presented along with similar material that they had not learned. It was found that the recognition scores of these subjects improved over an interval of two months without any intervening practice (166).

Various attempts have been made to explain this phenomenon of reminiscence or improved memory without practice over a period of time. One obvious possibility would be that the subjects might think over what they had learned even without overtly practicing it. Some subjects do, in fact, think over the learned material in the non-practice interval. Others, however, apparently do not, and with them also the reminiscence effect occurs. Furthermore, reminiscence does not seem to be affected by the massing or distribution of practice, or even by the degree of efficiency and thoroughness of the first learning. On the whole, older subjects seem to show more extensive reminiscence than younger subjects, but the difference is not great. The most decisive influence by far is the meaningfulness of the material. There is far less reminiscence effect from memorizing nonsense syllables than from memorizing prose and poetry (425, 426).

From the standpoint of our present discussion this last finding is very significant. To memorize material is not to store it in one's mind, but to prepare to meet a challenge—the challenge to repeat it under certain conditions. The challenge is met and the act of repeating is accomplished by relying on internal cues in the material, such as connections of ideas, turns of expression, rhythms, and so forth. Prose and poetry are rich in such internal cues. Lists of nonsense syllables are very poor in them. That is why prose and poetry are easier to memorize than nonsense syllables.

The original learning or memorizing by which one learns the material, in so far as it goes well, is a process of noticing the internal cues which will carry one through under the challenge of recall. The learning is a process of discovering *how* to recall the material when we are required to do so. Reminiscence itself is possible because during the time interval the internal cues clarify and rearrange themselves, and become less clogged with irrelevancies. During the time interval after practice, a better command of the material and a more efficient method of controlling it emerges. Reminiscence works better with sense material than with nonsense material because sense material offers far richer chances for a good memory technique than nonsense material.

Once again, experimental studies of problem-solving and thinking have shown that a temporary retreat or disengagement may be helpful. In one of these studies great emphasis has been placed on the necessity for what the investigator called a "participant attitude," a strong and definite self-engagement with the problem being attacked. But from time to time her subjects would find solutions by relaxing into a "spectator attitude" which meant the temporary discontinuance of focalized and positive endeavor (290).

Another famous investigation of problem-solving pointed in the same direction. In this case the problems to be solved were wire puzzles from each of which a movable key had to be detached. Success with these problems depended on finding a method of analyzing them, of seeing where and how the key had to be moved to get it off. There were always many positions, or many "variations" into and through which the key could be maneuvered, and the issue was to find the right one. Sometimes intense hard work and concentration would actually block a solution, because the subject would get the key into an impossible position, be unable to think of any alternative, and become frustrated. Then it often happened that a "take it easy" attitude, which meant almost playing with the puzzle for the time being rather than working at it, would evoke just the right variation (557).

These rest periods, or psychological withdrawals during the process of thinking through a problem, have been recognized in the experimental research, and are, of course, quite familiar in everyday experience. They are instances of learning—i.e., of the creation of new patterns of response—without overt practice; and once more the conclusion they clearly indicate is that learning itself is the discovery of a method of dealing with a situation.

Finally, it has been shown that problems that have been attacked but not solved are much better remembered than solved problems (397). In the series of experiments which led to this finding, problem tasks of many different kinds were set up—sketching objects, printing names, assembling puzzles, and so forth. Sometimes these tasks were interrupted before completion, and sometimes not. Then later on, the subjects in the experiment were tested to find how well they remembered the problems on which they had worked. Adults remembered uncompleted tasks 90% better than completed tasks, and children remembered uncompleted tasks almost exclusively. On the premise that learning is a quest, one can readily see how learning can go on after overt practice has stopped.

These varied lines of research which show that a great deal of learning both can and does go on apart from practice are full of practical implications for teaching. We should remember that children do not learn only when they are reciting or drilling in class or studying textbooks and working on written assignments at home or in study hall. To organize learning on the covert assumption that it takes place only during active practice is to slip into the fallacy of treating it as assimilation rather than discovery. This, in fact, is precisely the underlying assumption of the standard test-recitation-textbook-assignment routine. Such and such an amount of time required for assimilation, and then a test to see how much has been assimilated! This procedure, operating with sundry variations, seems inevitable to many teachers, partly because they do not see that it is based on a fallacy, and partly because they do not know how to do anything else. But a different basic procedure is quite possible.

What we want to produce is a process of *gestation*—a process in which learning will go on when pupils are not studying their textbooks, writing themes, working out mathematical problems. Unless learning does go on apart from practice, it will never be very good learning. Now clearly this process of gestation cannot be assigned in the conventional way. But it can be promoted and encouraged. We can organize situations which favor it.

For instance, class periods can be given to group discussions of methods of attacking mathematical problems without working through to final solutions. Out-of-class learning activity would be to find the solutions. But since we have set up unsolved problems, or rather half-solved problems which have a certain momentum, we have favored an inner process of gestation which is very likely to take place. Or a teacher can present in class some striking natural phenomenon, having to do with electricity, let us say, or with heat, or with the transmission of sound. The phenomenon needs understanding and explaining. The teacher gives hints about how to find an explanation, but leaves the finding to the pupils. Then she has set the learning up in such a way that there is a good chance that the pupils will not merely sit down at a stated time and try to work out the explanation, but that they will also turn the problem over in their minds.

Similar procedures are possible in any curricular field. Such procedures are not far-fetched or impractical, even though they are not conventional. The psychological principle back of them is to organize learning as the search for an answer to an intriguing question rather than as the assimilation of stated material. This is always the right and proper way to organize learning, as it favors the process of inner gestation through which solutions and answers are so often found.

MOTIVATION AND LEARNING

We have already seen that feeble motivation makes for feeble learning, that powerful motivation makes for good learning, and that the will to learn is essential in all learning. But why should this be so? This is the question to be considered now. What does motivation do to learning? If it is true that people learn best when they strongly want to learn, why is it true?

The answer is that motivation has a direct effect on the learning process itself. Strong motivation always tends to shape learning into the pattern of a quest for a solution, and to make that quest or search a more effective and assiduous quest or search. Two of the research studies to which reference has already been made deal at some length with the effects of motivation not only on the results of learning, but on the actual learning process itself. What I shall say here is largely based on the analysis presented in these two studies (290, 638).

1. A strongly motivated learner tends to analyze. He tends, that is to say, to seek for the essential issues in the situation, to look for key factors, to consider various possibilities, to scrutinize and criticize and clarify his own responses.

One can see this, perhaps on rather a low level, when competent candidates are studying for a very important examination. Such candidates do not usually rest content with assimilating a certain amount of material and hoping for the best. They try to find out exactly what the examination will demand, and to meet this demand. They look up previous examination papers. They search for tips and pointers. If they have a tutor they want him to give them useful hints and not merely to drill them. Quite possibly they care far less about mastering the subject than about developing a good examination-passing technique; and they develop this technique by seeking for essentials. The drive to pass the examination tends to compel the candidate to seek for the crucial features of the situation, because this is in part, at least, the right way to learn.

An educationally more desirable illustration of this effect of motivation is provided by a project in which a group of pupils undertook to make furniture polish. The teacher brought to class a recipe for a quart of the polish. Thirty-seven pupils wanted to make four-ounce samples for themselves. Therefore a total of 148 ounces in all had to be made. The crucial problem was to boost the amounts in the recipe by the required proportion. When the quart of polish was weighed it was found to come to 32.75 ounces. So the recipe had to be boosted 4.51 times. All these relationships, with the associated technique of using decimals, were arrived at by a process of discovery; and this process of discovery was not, and, indeed, could not have been taught by routine. It arose naturally out of the motivation (264).

When a child is given an assignment consisting of one chapter in a social studies textbook, he usually does not analyze, or consider various ways of attacking the job, or try to distinguish between essentials and nonessentials. He sits down with his book, spends a certain amount of time, and lets it go at that. But if he has been delegated by a group to bring in material to be used for a historical pageant, then his learning takes on the aspects of a quest. Where can good material be found? What material is or is not worth collecting? How can it best be reported? These become real and urgent questions, which control his learning activities.

2. Another effect that strong motivation has upon learning is that it acts as a challenge to work sufficiently to achieve desired standards. Here is an excellent illustration. A group of high-school students decided on their own initiative to put on a play which might be considered rather questionable and perhaps unsuitable for young people. The teacher in charge was doubtful and even a little alarmed; but the students were very eager and serious, and so she gave in. She warned them, however, that there might be criticism, and pointed out that in consequence the performance should be very good. The result was an almost overwhelming burst of tremendously hard and persistent work. No sacrifice was too great, no effort too fatiguing. Contrast the labor these young people put in on their play with the labor they probably devoted to their classroom assignments! The difference was due to motivation. There was a challenge to be met, a problem to be solved, and the challenge took charge of the learning.

Another illustration is a project in which a group of seventh-grade children undertook to prepare a history of their local community for display in the public library. As soon as the project took hold there was no need for the teacher to drive the pupils to greater endeavors. Pictures were collected, reminiscences of old residents were secured, printed sources were canvassed, explanatory items were written up. The children were not easily satisfied. The brochure and its accompanying display went through many anxious revisions. Was the material pertinent? Was it interesting? Was it clearly presented? Were grammar, spelling, and punctuation all that they should be? Such questions were very urgently considered, and the teacher functioned not as a taskmaster, but as a guide, a helper, and a critic whose criticisms were eagerly welcomed.

So, in general, when learning is strongly motivated—when there is a definite and desired objective to be attained, a definite and important challenge to be met—the learning process becomes a quest, and the quest tends to take charge. One of the greatest weaknesses of much conventional learning in school is that children study their assignments without any definite criterion of successful achievement, and without any clear-cut picture of a successful outcome that they wish to achieve.

3. Strong motivation in learning tends to overcome and break down antagonistic impulses. Every choice we make in life is a choice between attractions. Shall I work at my algebra or go out and play baseball? Shall I write my English theme or indulge in a nice chat? Always there is a competition between goals or motives. So if the algebra or the English theme is feebly motivated—that is to say, if there is little or no sense of an unsolved problem clamoring to be solved—the algebra or the English is almost sure to suffer in the competition. Even if, under very strong negative compulsions and threats, the algebra or the English is done, they still suffer competitively. For although the youngster who works because he fears not to work may do his work after a fashion, he will never do it as well as if he worked because he wanted to. Negative motivation may temporarily overcome antagonistic impulses, but the competing impulses are still effective, and the learner escapes from the task and abandons it as soon as he can.

The three points which have been made in this section indicate how motivation affects not merely the results of learning, but the actual process itself. The tendency of strong motivation is always to give learning its true character of a quest for a solution, a discovery of a method of meeting a challenge. This, as a matter of fact and of common experience, is how all of us tend to learn when we really want to learn.

FURTHER ISSUES

So far we have seen that a wide variety of experimental data and many facts of common experience support the claim that learning is essentially the discovery or emergence of method or technique in dealing with a challenging situation, and that improvement is essentially the improvement of method or technique. This interpretation will be still further confirmed and developed as additional aspects of the learning process are considered. But before passing on, there are certain questions that need clearing up.

1. How does our present interpretation of learning bear on habit formation? It is sometimes said that learning *is* habit formation, and that a teacher's main business is to see that her pupils form proper habits. Is this true, or is it false?

Habits are routine ways of behaving, routine ways of dealing with situations and problems. A child discovers that two things plus four things make six things, and then whenever he sees $2 + 4$ he thinks of 6. He discovers that one spells *radiance* with an *a* instead of an *e* in the last syllable, and then whenever he writes the word *radiance* he uses an *a* at that point. He discovers that if one is to avoid difficulties and mistakes in doing column addition, one should be careful to write down all the units, tens, hundreds, and so forth underneath each other; and then when he has a column of numbers to add, he writes them down in this way. He discovers that if he teases long enough his mother will let him go and play with the other children instead of doing his homework, and so he forms the habit of teasing. These are all instances of habits, and you can find many more of the same sort. From such instances we can gain certain insights which answer our question about the relation of habit formation to learning.

a) Habits are routine ways of responding, but they are not typically formed by routine repetition. On the contrary, they are typically formed by discovering ways of response that are, for the time-being, at least, satisfactory and successful. Some teachers of elementary-school music make a great point of teaching children what they call "correct habits of voice production." They often try to form these habits by repetition and drill, but the results are usually rather disappointing. It would be far better to encourage children to sing enjoyable songs, and to give them hints and pointers which would make the singing better and still more enjoyable. Other teachers try to insist on habits of neatness in arithmetic papers, but it often seems difficult to establish such habits. It would be much better to help the children to see that when an arithmetic problem is properly laid out on paper, it becomes much easier to solve.

Most teachers want to establish habits of good order in the classroom, and to some extent, no doubt, they succeed in doing so. But such habits often seem remarkably fragile. For instance, if the teacher happens to be absent when the time for starting class arrives (and this is a real test situation), the so-called "habits of good order" often evaporate. If, however, the classroom is made an arena of group projects, group enterprises, and group thinking, then there is at least an excellent chance that everyone will discover the necessity for order. So to generalize, there is no doubt that habits are products of learning and that they are important. But it almost seems as though they are by-products of learning.

b) The difference between bad habits and good habits is that bad habits are poor and inadequate ways of dealing with challenges, whereas good habits are excellent and effective ways of dealing with challenges. Lip movement during reading is a bad habit because it slows reading and impedes comprehension. Counting under one's breath is a bad habit in arithmetic, because it is slow, clumsy, and liable to error. Throwing temper tantrums to get one's way is a bad habit because it arouses dangerous antagonisms and oppositions in others. Still, these bad habits are not altogether unworkable techniques, for people undoubtedly manage to read, and to do sums, and to get their way after a fashion, by using these routine methods.

A bad habit, in fact, is usually the best way of responding or coping with a challenge that a person can find by his own efforts and without help and advice. So the proper policy is, not to try to root out bad habits, but to show the way to acquiring better habits. In almost any third grade there will be numerous children who always count up on their fingers or use some such clumsy device when they do sums; and a surprising number of these same children are still arithmetical finger-counters when they get to college. It would, however, be quite wrong for a teacher to try to devise some clever method of drilling and testing to *prevent* finger-counting. What the teacher ought to do is to show children how to use more efficient and reliable techniques. The case of the boy already mentioned, who was sullen, hostile, and antagonistic to teachers, school, and schoolwork is instructive here. To punish this boy because he was naughty and annoying would probably have been hopeless. What was actually done was to create a situation where he could find out how to fit constructively into the school life and activities; and when this discovery was made, the bad habits (which came from previous imperfect discoveries) melted away.

c) Habits—yes, even fairly good habits—can be dangerous. This is so because they can block further learning and improvement. Arithmetic, for instance, is often taught as a set of routine procedures for dealing with numbers and for getting "right answers." These routine habits are satisfactory up to a point, but they create an extremely difficult problem when algebra is introduced. A person can learn to typewrite fairly well with only two fingers, but although this technique is not unworkable, it will never let him improve beyond a certain level. If this person wants to be able to typewrite much faster than he now can, it will do him no good to try to polish up and refine his two-finger technique. He must remake his whole habit-set.

So, in general, improvement and learning do not depend on the formation and the refinement of sets of habits, but rather on the transcending of habits. *The formation of a habit is a symptom of satisfaction; and when habits form, learning and improvement stop.* So the practical conclusion is that teachers should think, not in terms of the formation of habits, but in terms of the discovery of ever more effective methods of dealing with challenges and problems.

2. My central argument in this chapter has been that the essence of learning is the discovery of method or technique. This seems to be what happens when we learn. But cannot one go further? Should not one go further? Is it not also necessary to ask what happens *in the nervous system* when we learn, and to find some kind of answer? Here is an issue important enough to deserve at least some comment.

No doubt a complete and final account of learning would include an objective account of what happens in the nervous system during the learning process. But at the present time all that can be said about these neural happenings is that we know virtually nothing about them. There is one neurological explanation of learning which is, or, at least, recently was, very popular. According to this explanation, whenever we learn anything, resistance is reduced in a pathway in the nervous system. The reduction of resistance is brought about by the repeated passage of impulses from the receptors, or sense organs, to the effectors, i.e. the muscles or glands. It would be quite possible to discuss this account of learning at considerable length; but to do so would be a waste of time, for it can be dismissed with the simple statement that there is not one scrap of objective evidence in its favor. No one has ever seen a neural pathway which has been formed by learning. No one has ever demonstrated that such pathways exist or could exist. The whole account is neither more nor less than a theoretical fabrication.

It is, however, quite true that many important psychologists prefer to think of learning in terms of the establishing of connections between stimulus and response. But when these psychologists talk about connections they do not necessarily mean actual physical connections, like the connections between telephones made through an exchange. Their interpretation of the word "connection" tends to be statistical, and to mean that what learning does is to increase the probability of a given response when a given stimulus occurs (201).

This is a plain statement of fact. There is not the slightest objection to it so long as certain precautions and qualifications are observed. Indeed, it may well be in some respects an advantageous and revealing way of thinking about the learning process. A boy in a workshop is more likely to make the right response in running a square cut with a saw if he has learned to handle the saw. A chess player confronted with an end game situation is more likely to make the right choice of a move if he has learned a great deal about chess. All this is perfectly true. We can agree to it without bringing in the nervous system at all. And it is in no way essentially inconsistent with the proposition that the essence of learning is the discovery of a method or technique.

3. Does the conception of learning as the discovery of method imply that learners should be left to flounder and to make their discoveries by whatever light their own reason may provide? Does this conception glorify trial and error as the ideal learning-teaching situation? Most certainly not. If a boy were left to his own devices in a workshop he would certainly waste hundreds of hours of time and hundreds of feet of wood, probably never acquire numerous techniques, any one of which he could be helped to discover in fifteen minutes by an expert, and still more probably give up in disgust and despair, and

rationalize his failure by saying that he was born without the necessary natural gift.

It is certainly not the proper function of the teacher to indicate, verbally or from a textbook, the right answers and the right solutions, and to insist on their being memorized. Such procedures are contrary to the essential nature of learning. The true function of the teacher is to create situations which facilitate discovery, to give hints, suggestions, guidance, and criticism. From all that we know of the learning process, the watchword of every effective teacher should be, not trial and error, but trial and success. Putting the matter otherwise, the great function of the teacher is *to reveal real and cogent problems and challenges, to bring these problems home to learners, and to help the learners to discover ways and means of dealing with them.*

QUESTIONS FOR DISCUSSION

1. A high-school boy was failing in mathematics. His teacher discovered that he had done a great deal of studying "on his own" on the ballistic problems of a .22 caliber rifle given him by his father. In this way the boy had learned a great deal of mathematics by his own efforts, and had done so very well. How would you account for his failure in one situation and his success in another? Can you see any practical implications for teaching?

2. This chapter has presented a number of concrete illustrations of the idea that when we learn, we always "learn how" to do something. Assemble and discuss a number of additional illustrations from your own experience, either in school or elsewhere.

3. A certain geometry teacher often introduces a new theorem with a class discussion which may last an entire period. He presents the idea of the theorem in informal language, and invites consideration of possible methods of proving it. Quite often no clear decision is reached by the end of the discussion. Is this teacher putting into operation any of the ideas about effective learning which have been presented in this chapter?

4. The central idea of this chapter is that when one learns, one

always learns "how to do" something. When pupils undertake to "cram" factual information in connection with their assignments, just what are they really learning to do? Should teachers be satisfied with this kind of learning?

5. One often hears a good deal of talk in educational circles about the importance of gaining a "real mastery" of such and such subjects. What do you think a real mastery of any subject actually means? Consider this question with reference to some specific subjects, such as science, French, history, English literature, mathematics, and so on.

6. A distinction is often drawn between "tool subjects" and "content subjects." Arithmetic and English composition would presumably be tool subjects and history and science would be content subjects. In the light of the discussions in this chapter the distinction is extremely questionable. Consider and review it carefully. From your examination of the general issue draw some practical inferences for the teaching of content subjects.

7. It is often said that pupils in school show very little initiative in finding effective and ingenious methods of working on their assignments. Yet when it comes to planning social events these same pupils may be very ingenious indeed. How do you account for the difference?

8. It is important for you to bring the conception of learning that has been presented here into relationship with the discussions in the four previous chapters. Review and re-think all the material presented in these pages so far in the light of this question: Why is it that one does not learn unless one really wants to learn?

9. As another and even more extensive exercise or challenge in tying together the pattern of ideas with which we are dealing, consider the bearing of this chapter on the proposition that the study of school subjects can be and should be a means of shaping personality.

SUGGESTED READINGS

Gates, Arthur I., "The Nature and Limit of Improvement Due to Training." *27th Yearbook*, National Society for the Study of Education (1928), 440–460.

Hill, L. B., "Quarter Century of Delayed Recall." *Pedagogical Seminary*, XLIV (1934), 376–377.

McConnell, T. R., "Discovery vs. Authoritative Identification in the Learning of Children." University of Iowa Studies in Education, IX (1934), No. 5.

Symonds, Percival M., and Chase, D. M., "Practice versus Motivation." *Journal of Educational Psychology*, XX (1929), 19–35.

6

How We Learn

ROLE OF INSIGHT

When we learn we discover a way of acting, a way of dealing with a challenge, a solution for a problem. This discovery we make by dint of insight. Here is the answer to the question, How do we learn?

Insight is a term much used in present-day psychology. In general, it means just what one would think it means—"seeing into" a situation or a problem. Of course the obvious way of discovering how to deal with any problem is to "see into it," to grasp its purport, its significance; and if learning is discovering how to deal with problematic and challenging situations, then clearly we learn by means of insight.

So far so good. But perhaps not quite far enough. The argument may seem sound, and yet perhaps the conclusion remains a little vague. In raising the question of how people learn, teachers want an answer which will show them what to do about learning when they have to try to control and organize it. The statement that people learn by dint of insight may be a good starting point for a helpful and practical answer. But it is necessary to go further. The meaning of the concept of insight needs to be particularized beyond its general sense of seeing into a situation. Its meaning needs to be filled in and made more specific. This filling in and particularization I shall undertake to do by setting up three statements about how we learn. First, we learn by *understanding.* Second, we learn by *thinking.* Third, we learn by *grasping organized relationships.* Understanding, thinking, and grasping organized relationships are not three different processes. They are different names for the same process as it appears under different sets of circumstances. That process is the process of insight; and all that I have done in setting up these three statements is to suggest that it is helpful and illuminating to look at the process of insight from three different perspectives or points of view.

LEARNING THROUGH UNDERSTANDING

You order a refrigerator from Sears Roebuck, and it arrives partly disassembled. In the package is a sheet of directions for putting it together. These directions are very complicated (or so it may seem to you) and very concise. You have to work through them line by line, finding each part of the refrigerator as it is mentioned, drawing conclusions, putting two and two together. In this way you learn to assemble your refrigerator from the directions. How do you learn to do this? Not by repeating the directions again and again. Not by memorizing them as if they were the proof of a geometrical theorem which you had to recite in class. You learn to assemble your refrigerator by *understanding* the directions.

A boy finds the following statement in his textbook: "The square of the sum of two numbers is the square of the first plus twice the product of the two plus the square of the second." This statement has two similarities to the directions for the refrigerator. First, it is complicated and compact. Second, it tells one what to do in various situations. What would be the best way for the boy to learn this statement? He might memorize it so that he could rattle it off. But then quite likely he would be unable to use it in situations to which it was supposed to apply. One could hardly say, in that case, that he had learned the statement at all. In fact one would suspect that he had merely learned to please a teacher. What he clearly ought to do, and what any good teacher ought to want him to do and to help him to do, is to try the statement out—in other words, to understand it.

Suppose we want children to "learn" the geography of the Mediterranean. Here are two contrasting ways of accomplishing this end. In one school the topic is set up as an assignment in a textbook. Pupils memorize the names of capes, bays, estuaries, continents, countries, islands, straits, and so forth, quite possibly without knowing just what these names mean. Perhaps they look at a little map. Perhaps they draw some outline maps. Then they are given a test, and most of them do fairly well on it—"fairly well" meaning that they give right answers to from forty to seventy per cent of a haphazard set of questions.

In another school the children are provided with a big sand tray. On it they construct a model of the Mediterranean, made as close to scale as possible. There is much discussion and research, much checking of sources, numerous rearrangements. Questions come up about how far it is from one place to another, and how long such and such a journey might take by boat or by airplane.

This is a much less tidy and compact procedure than the textbook procedure. It certainly consumes, and may sometimes seem to waste, more time. Quite probably, fewer facts are "covered." But which group of children is likely to come out with more worth-while knowledge of the Mediterranean? There can only be one answer. In fact, the difference in the amount of knowledge acquired is likely to be very great. Why the difference? Because everything has been done to encourage understanding in the one situation, whereas in the other situation very little has been done.

The only really good way of dealing with any of the problems of life, including the numerous life problems that constantly come up in classroom learning, is to deal with them by means of understanding. To understand a situation is to see how to cope with it. To understand an abstract statement or a general principle is to be able to use it for the solution of problems and the attainment of goals. "When a geometry student sees the usefulness of the Pythagorean theorem for laying off the corners of a tennis court, we may be sure that he has some understanding of that theorem. When a fifth-grade pupil, by means of his maps, discovers for himself a probable connection between the physical features of a region and the manner of life of its inhabitants, we may be sure that he, too, has some understanding of the geographic principles involved. And when a primary grade pupil translates the statement $5 + 2 = 7$ into a concrete representation by setting up one group of five and another of two objects, and then combining them into a new group of seven, we may be sure once again that he also has some understanding this time of the abstract relationships in the statement" (91, p. 27). The significance of all these illustrations can be summarized in the statement that *to understand is to learn and to learn is to understand.* Here is one way of answering the question: How do we learn? From this answer many important consequences follow.

1. Learning is greatly facilitated, and the results of learning are greatly improved, by doing everything possible to make understanding both possible and as complete as it can be. In general there is a very striking contrast between the learning of meaningful (understandable) and of virtually meaningless material. In one comparison it was found that as much of a passage of meaningful prose was remembered after a thirty-day interval, even though the prose had been read only a

single time, as was remembered after a one-day interval of a set of nonsense syllables perfectly learned (540).

Moreover, anything that is done to help comprehension is a direct help to better learning. This was shown, for instance, in an investigation of the use of questions as guides to the reading and remembering of prose passages. A total of 1,456 junior high-school pupils were given a 3,000-word passage in the field of social studies. Some of these students read the passage without any interpolated guide-questions at all. Some of them read versions in which questions about the material were placed at the beginning, or interpolated between paragraphs, or placed at the end. It was found that questions which came at the beginning of the passage were always the most helpful, and that students who read the material with the questions at the beginning knew forty per cent more of its content after one reading than did those who read it without any questions at all. The introductory guide-questions showed them how to read, how to interpret, how to understand (702).

Or again, it has been found that special instruction and help in outlining can have a very marked effect upon the learning processes of high-school students. Instruction and practice in outlining shows these students how to read material in general with better comprehension, and the influence of this instruction is definitely manifest in their achievement in many of their subjects (562).

Another example of a different kind still further emphasizes the importance of promoting understanding if we want good learning to take place. This is the case, already referred to, of the autocratic group leader who was converted to democratic practices. The conversion was brought about by a combination of general explanations of the nature and requirements of democratic behavior and of concrete applications through the pedagogical technique of role-playing. This may very well remind you of the assembling of the Sears Roebuck refrigerator, for in both cases verbal explanations and concrete applications are closely linked. Real understanding is promoted, and real learning takes place (37).

2. The effect of understanding is always to reduce the labor and toil of learning, to cut down the number of times one must go over material in order to learn it. When you have to go over the instructions on assembling the refrigerator twenty times, it simply indicates that you did not understand them well the first time. If a teacher finds it necessary to drill at great length on some principle of grammar, it simply indicates that the pupils are not understanding that principle any too well. If a guidance officer has to explain again and again to a boy that he must not trespass on other students' rights, this again means that the boy has a dim, imperfect, or perhaps quite wrong understanding of the social situation with which he has to deal.

There is an old saying that practice makes perfect. But practice with a minimum of understanding approaches perfection at a crawling pace, and indeed may very well never get there at all. So there would be considerable truth in saying that the less the practice, the better the learning, so long as the reduction of practice depends upon the deepening, strengthening, and clarifying of understanding.

A story is told, illustrating this idea, about the Irish statesman Eamon de Valera. In his youth de Valera was an accomplished mathematician. During the Irish rebellion of 1916, he was besieged, along with some of his colleagues, by the British troops. Fighting was not active. The besieged group was bored, and conversations rambled far and wide. Quite casually de Valera said to one of his companions, "What do you think of the Quaternary Theorem?" (This theorem, I should explain, occurs in the upper ranges of mathematics.) The man replied that he had never even heard of the Quaternary Theorem. "Dear me!" exclaimed de Valera, "then I must explain it to you." And within two days he had carried his companion completely through elementary mathematics, and well into the advanced level. This tour de force of teaching was possible because de Valera was an expert in the subject who also knew how to make it clear. It was possible because of the invocation of understanding!

Understanding, as we have already seen, is insight viewed from a certain perspective, or operating in certain types of situations. In many of the classic discussions of insight the point is often made that insight can be achieved very quickly and suddenly—that what is called a "flash of insight" is possible. Certainly this is true. A single drastic experience—for instance the experience of being laughed at because of one's costume—can establish a very persistent attitude. One sees in a single flash that it would be a good idea not to wear those clothes again! Or there may be a dramatic moment when a child realizes what long division is all about, or when an older student comes to the same realization about the binomial theorem.

These flashes of insight are possible precisely because we do learn by understanding, and when all circumstances are just right, understanding can come in a moment. But they are not, so to speak, standard and regular means of learning. Understanding and insight usually come somewhat slowly, like the dawn, rather than abruptly like a lightning flash. But even so, labor directed towards understanding is far more economical and far more effective in its ultimate results than routine toil centered only upon assimilation. Teachers may not be able to evoke many flashes of insight, but they should always seek to help pupils to achieve understanding as quickly and clearly as may be.

3. The proposition that we learn by understanding shows what ought to be done about errors that occur during learning. The occurrence of error in learning, and its proper treatment, is often supposed to be a considerable puzzle. Some teachers quite seriously believe that ideally, at least, children should *never* make any mistakes when they practice. When children learn a new song, it should be presented so slowly and carefully

that there will be no wrong notes. When they do sums, guidance should be so close and intensive that there will never be any wrong answers. There are two reasons for this belief: (*a*) that if children are allowed to make mistakes, these mistakes may become habitual; (*b*) that we always learn anything by doing it properly, or by succeeding with it. There is some truth in the first of these ideas, and a great deal of truth in the second. But the trouble is that when one tries to put the doctrine of errorless learning into practice, one finds that it cannot be done. Quantities of mistakes always occur even in the very best learning; and so we cannot deal with mistakes simply by eliminating them.

What then is the solution? Simply to let practice roll along more or less as it will, hoping that mistakes will take care of themselves somehow or other? Certainly this is not a very hopeful policy, for it is just when practice and learning are vaguely directed that mistakes are really likely to become habitual, and that achievement is likely to be thwarted because the learner never really succeeds at all. The true solution is to remember that learning is essentially a process of experimentation, of seeking for a solution, of trying to understand. Mistakes constantly occur in experimental research, but although they are inconvenient, they are not fatal. They are inevitable incidents in the course of transforming an imperfect understanding into a better understanding. Errors, in fact, are stupidities. They are stupidities both in the very high-level and complicated learning which we call original research, and also in the less complicated though not-so-simple learnings that occur in school.

The original-research worker has to find his own way through the maze, because there is no one who knows better and who is able to put him right. He must diagnose and overcome his own stupidities as best he can. But in dealing with learning in school, the diagnosis of the stupidities which we call mistakes becomes one of the most valuable functions of the teacher. A boy is doing quite well with subtraction sums up to a point, but beyond that point he makes innumerable mistakes. To indicate these mistakes, to urge him to try harder, and perhaps to penalize him would be most ineffective, yet this is just what is often done. There must be a reason for his errors. Can we find it? Often only a very little examination of what he is doing and failing to do will reveal the reason. So long as this boy is working sums like this

$$\begin{array}{r} 7\,9\,6\,3 \\ 2\,5\,1\,1 \\ \hline 5\,4\,5\,2 \end{array}$$

he is all right; but the moment he gets a sum like this

$$\begin{array}{r} 5\,1\,7\,2 \\ 3\,2\,8\,1 \\ \hline 1\,8\,9\,1 \end{array}$$

he seems quite helpless. This should immediately suggest where the trouble lies. Quite likely he has never really gotten into his head the process of "borrowing" which one must use in subtracting a bigger digit from a smaller one. Once he understands this process, and he can be enabled to understand it in a ten-minute conference, his troubles with subtraction are over.

Or again, there is the case of a girl in college who had great difficulties with her English themes. She was intelligent and a good student, but her ratings on English composition were always inexplicably low, although she tried hard enough. In the English courses she took, her themes were always returned to her with rather vague comments and criticisms, and with low grades. Finally, a teacher of much insight took an interest in her problem. He analyzed a number of her themes and found that the trouble was the steady recurrence of quite a small number of errors of the same kind. One of her most frequent mistakes was vagueness in pronoun reference. For instance, she would produce such sentences as, "A girl in college makes many friends which is good for them." As soon as these errors were identified and analyzed—as soon as her specific stupidities were recognized and diagnosed—there was an enormous immediate improvement in her English composition (531).

Teaching in which a special effort is made to diagnose specific errors is often called "diagnostic teaching." Beyond a doubt it is very effective teaching. Just as one instance of its value, we have the case of four elementary-school children whose arithmetic received this diagnostic attention. Instead of being allowed or compelled to practice on general principles and with a general hope of improvement, these children were shown how to deal with the precise errors that they were most apt to make. The four of them showed as much improvement under this regime in six weeks as would ordinarily be made in from one and a half to two and a half years (87). Here, clearly, is the way to deal with error and to teach not sometimes, but always. Indeed the very expression "diagnostic teaching" is objectionable, for all good teaching is diagnostic in the sense we have been discussing. All good teaching treats error as stupidity, and deals with it by seeking to establish better insight and understanding, in and through which learning goes on.

4. Failures in learning are failures in understanding, and should be treated as such. For instance, suppose an arithmetic problem is set up in the following terms: "A boy wants to buy a candy bar for each of a group of six friends. Each bar costs eight cents. How much will the boy have to spend in all?" Some of the children to whom this problem is given will be almost sure to answer, "fourteen cents," adding six and eight; others will probably answer, "two cents." What they see is that the two numbers in the problem must be combined somehow. But beyond this, understanding does not go. It is very unlikely, however, that anybody will say that the answer is six-eighths of a cent, or eight-sixths of a cent. Why should this

be so? Why is nobody as likely to divide as to add or subtract? Because in this case division does not "come out even," and for those who do not fully comprehend what they are doing this in itself is a sign to avoid division.

Now consider a problem exactly similar in principle and on just about the same level of difficulty, but differently worded. "A boy rides six times on a merry-go-round. Each ride costs him five cents. How much must he pay in all?" Very likely more children will get this one right than the former problem. That is, more children will see that the thing to do is to multiply. Why so? Because in the second problem as stated the word "times" appears, and for many children this word has been made a signal for multiplication. So understanding here is perhaps a little better, but still very limited.

The children to whom these two problems are given are quite likely to have a fair knowledge of the "multiplication facts," a fair verbal knowledge of the techniques of multiplication. But they do not really understand the process, because they do not know when to select and apply it, instead of addition or subtraction. Many failures in the face of such problems would have been avoided if the children had been shown just what multiplication really means. Then they would see at once that the first problem has to do with six groups of eight things, and the second with six groups of five things, and that in such combinations of groupings is the essence of multiplication.

The truth is that people, both young and old, always solve problems and reach goals by dint of the best understanding they have. But the trouble is that often such understanding is incomplete. In one investigation it was found that eight-year-old children thought that the word *muzzle* had something to do with the strength of one's arm (i.e. muscle), and that the word *ocher* meant something to put into soup (i.e. okra). High-school students might come through with the statement that the Crusaders fought in *Plasticine*. Also, the investigator found that when children draw copies of some figure, anything at all round tends to be reproduced as what was intended for a circle. Also, when children were asked how many pencils one would get for twenty cents if two pencils cost five cents, many of them answered "a hundred," the reason being that they found multiplication simpler and more intelligible than division. Errors of this kind constantly occur, and are made by adults as well as children. For instance, when a group of elementary-school teachers was asked to explain the functions of the U.S. minister to China, many of them revealed that they thought this diplomatic officer was a Methodist preacher. Such errors are not *merely* wrong, although they *are* wrong. Essentially they are failures of understanding, attempts to interpret in terms that are familiar or easy, but not relevant to the situation.

LEARNING THROUGH THINKING

Thinking, understanding, and insight are three terms for what is essentially the same process. Very often it is possible to use them interchangeably. Yet they do emphasize distinguishable aspects of the same process. In particular, the word "thinking" introduces a new shade of meaning, and for this reason it is helpful in clarifying our discussion.

The process of thinking can be very simply described. *Thinking takes place when a person becomes aware of a question and seeks for an answer.* Most of us, most of the time, go along through life without being conscious of questions, although as a matter of fact innumerable questions constantly stare us in the face. Before the time of Newton, innumerable millions of human beings had seen apples fall to the ground; but the sight suggested no question to them, and so they learned nothing from it. But to Newton the falling apple posed a question, and his search for an answer was a process of learning, the outcome of which was a complete new system of physics.

Children who attend a country school that I happen to know

enter the school grounds by walking alongside a small brook. To them it is just a brook and nothing more. Yet that brook is a treasure house of potential questions, all of them fascinating—questions having to do with the direction and velocity of flow, the determination of the course, the sequence of the water cycle, the plant life, insect life, and animal life along the banks and in the water. It would be quite possible for the teachers to bring the children to realize some of these questions; and in seeking for the answers both teachers and children would certainly learn a great deal of science, and would learn it in a most effective fashion. The recognition of a question, the quest for an answer—this is the process of thinking, and also the process of learning.

A certain experimental course in geometry is a splendid instance of organizing the process of learning by thinking in a school setting (171). Twenty-five ninth-, tenth-, and eleventh-grade pupils were enrolled in the course, this being a convenient number for what was to be done. The key idea was to enable these students to reason about geometry in their own way, rather than in ways determined by the teacher or textbook.

The first four weeks of the course were devoted to non-geometrical topics, the purpose being to show the students what thinking involves, and more particularly to show them that conclusions will often depend on assumptions that are not clearly recognized. For instance, there was considerable debate on the proposition that "awards should be granted for outstanding performance in school." This led to many questions. What was "outstanding performance"? Did it include good teaching? Did it include orderly behavior? What was an award? Did it include a teacher's salary? What, indeed, was "school"? A building, an area, or what? Other similar propositions led to definitions of the concept "aristocrat," and of the concept "one-hundred-per cent American." Thus it was shown that conclusions depend on assumptions, and that it is often hard to agree on assumptions when a situation is exciting and intriguing.

After four weeks spent on thus establishing certain aspects of thinking, the students were brought face to face with space concepts. The proposal was to build a theory of the space we live in. The first step was to challenge the students to give a general account of the nature of the space in the classroom. This challenge brought forth various vague suggestions. Space somehow involves distances. One might think of space as all filled up with cubes. One might think of the space in the room as made up of a pile of plane surfaces, one on top of another. These were some of the ideas that emerged. Finally it was agreed that the best way to begin would be to define certain "primitive concepts," among which was the concept "straight line." What made a line straight? That was the question. At about this stage each student began to keep a notebook of his own, with the title "A Theory of Space," in which he put down the various concepts on which agreement was reached. Satisfactory meanings for such concepts as "point" and "line" were worked out. Then the idea of distance emerged, defined as part of a line between two points, or part of a line, or a line segment.

Next, relationships between lines were considered, and meanings were clarified in saying that lines could be parallel, intersecting, perpendicular, or skewed. Covert assumptions were discovered and brought to explicit statement. For instance, the students found themselves unconsciously assuming that one and only one plane could be passed through two parallel lines, and that two parallel lines determine one and only one plane, and these assumptions were explicitly formulated and discussed.

The concept "angle" emerged as an undefined term, and properties of angles were explained by using the concept of rotation, so that angles could be acute, obtuse, adjacent, and so forth. There was further discussion of the idea of rotating a line about a point, which led to a clarification of the properties of parallels and of the angles formed by a transversal cutting parallel lines. A typical development of thinking had to do with the concept "triangle." At first the students were satisfied to say that a triangle was a figure with three sides; but they came to see that a further qualification was necessary, and that a triangle was also a closed figure.

The group as a whole developed twenty-one geometrical theorems in common in this way. But each student also worked independently, and the total number of different theorems developed by everybody was thirty-three. This was somewhat less material than would be "covered" in the ordinary course, and there was no systematic comparison with the results of conventional teaching. However, the use of a standard test showed that geometry was, in fact, very well learned. And really, one hardly needs research evidence to feel convinced that this was an admirable and effective procedure.

Another instance of learning by thinking is a highly developed plan for teaching competence with the English language. The ordinary way of teaching, or trying to teach "English expression" is by drill on grammar and "good English usage," and by not very closely directed practice in writing English themes—the results usually being most discouraging. The plan to which I now refer centered on reflection about precise English meanings (536). Thinking about meanings in English expression is organized in a number of different ways under this plan. A good illustration of one such way of organizing thinking is the treatment of abstractions.

Abstractions, it is pointed out by the authors of the plan, are in a sense "fictions." We can talk about them, but we cannot actually point to them. So various analytic studies of the use of abstract terms were set up, of which the following is a typical example.

Directions—expand each of the following passages quoted in one of your history reference books, into paragraphs of about forty or fifty words. In your expansion do not use any of the underlined words or phrases. Your expansions should be aimed toward making the meaning of the passage clear and "operational." The passage should be completely re-written; do not merely substitute a synonym which includes the same abstractions as the underlined word. For instance, in passage 5, do not simply put for "America" an easy phrase like "this country," or "this land," but expand it until it becomes clear exactly what is meant by "America."

1. If the proper object of society is to produce and maintain an aristocracy Virginia had achieved it. But if it be to maintain a high general level of comfort and intelligence, she had not.
2. The plantation system never obtained a strong foothold in North Carolina; the state remained a farming democracy, aided rather than based on chattel slavery.
3. The Americans should be an example of political, religious, commercial and industrial liberty.
4. There was one dominant force in American history that none foresaw in 1785; the expansive force.
5. The frontier vanished with the wild Indian, and America's youth is waning fast.
6. Jefferson's political theories had more validity for future America than for the simple society with whose common mind and condition Jefferson's theories agreed (536, p. 182).

I shall have several comments later on about this and other illustrations. But in passing it may be remarked that this looks very much like a systematization of the way in which a practical author improves his style. Very few authors, so far as I know, try to learn to write better by drilling on grammar and usage and writing short themes on trivial subjects.

A more limited but still interesting and significant experiment on learning by thinking was one in which the investigator undertook to teach pupils to deal with "originals" in geometry essentially by guided group discussion (347). The original or problem would be set up, and plenty of time would then be given to talking it over. The points which were stressed in the group discussion were the need for sensing the central difficulty of the problem, the need to suggest as many possible solutions as people could think of, the need to test out such suggestions and to experiment on the basis of the answers that seemed to appear, the need to find out if a method which would give a solution for one problem or original would also apply to other problems. In this case a systematic comparison was made between the students who had been taught in this way, and others who had taken the conventional geometry course. When the experiment was over, a test was given which consisted of new originals. The members of the experimental group persisted much longer in working on these problems than did the members of the conventional class. They made twice as many suggestions for solving the new originals in the test. At the end of the course, their final grades in geometry were much higher.

No one would be likely to deny that the above instances are genuine illustrations of learning by thinking. But perhaps they seem to be specially selected, or biased, or favorable instances. Learning by thinking might seem quite possible and reasonable in mathematics, or in using English, because intellectual processes in general, and thinking in particular, are obviously involved. But is this kind of learning possible elsewhere? Is it possible in other curricular fields? To suggest, at least, an answer to this question I will take a field of learning where thinking might seem to play very little part if any, namely, the learning of a motor skill.

Three groups of boys and young men, from junior high school, senior high school, and college practiced throwing darts at a target and shooting basketballs at a basket. All the subjects of all ages were given a few days preliminary practice at these two performances. Then they were subdivided and given different treatments. (*a*) Some were dismissed and did no more practicing. (*b*) Some went on with physical practice, which consisted of making 25 dart shots at the target or 35 ball shots at the basket each day. (*c*) Still others carried on what the investigators called "mental practice." They would sit comfortably and *imagine* throwing the dart or tossing the ball. In this imagining they spent thirty minutes each day, with a one minute break for rest. These different conditions continued for eighteen days. At the end of the eighteen days, the subjects who had practiced physically were much better than those who had not practiced at all. But those who had just sat and thought were almost as good as those who had practiced physically (693). So even where a physical skill is involved it is not true to say that we learn only by doing. It is possible, under certain conditions which I shall discuss later, to learn a great deal by thinking, even in learning a motor skill.

Notice that in each of the instances I have described, a *question* is raised. How can one think about and understand space? How can one convey the meaning of abstract words and phrases? How can one attack an "original"? How does one go about throwing darts or basketballs? In most of these cases, and indeed perhaps in all of them, the questions would never have occurred to the pupils without the intervention of the teacher. The phenomena would be there, waiting to be explained, but in and of themselves they would not have challenged thinking. Children deal with space all the time every day, but it rarely presents itself to them as a problem. Some of these children, probably in the tenth grade, study geometry, which is the theory of space. But still they do not think about space, do not feel any question mark attaching to it. Boys throw darts and basketballs, but they rarely ask themselves just how they do it.

The process of learning by thinking, as it manifests itself in this last instance, is specially instructive. You will remember that the subjects in the experiment, who improved their motor skills by sitting and imagining their own performance, had a few days of practice before they were invited to think about what they did. The point of this practice was to give them something to think about when they sat comfortably relaxed and learned by reflection. The situation was specially arranged to play up or high light the crucial question. In the case of the motor skill this playing up of the question was very conspicuous and very essential. But the same thing happened in all the other instances as well.

Thus, the first necessary task of a teacher who wishes her pupils to learn by thinking is to establish a question in their minds, and to define and delimit it. Then, following on this, she must help them to find out how to deal with it.

Dollard and Miller (147, Chaps. 18, 19, 20) have shown at length that this process of learning by thinking is the process by which the psychotherapist deals with disturbed and neurotic patients. Such a patient may display a range of unfortunate symptoms, such as fears, obsessions, compulsions, and so forth, which he seems unable to control. Moreover, he does not know the origin of these symptoms. He does not know "what makes him act that way" even apparently against his will, judgment, and preferences. The therapist, by various techniques, one of which might be free association, discovers that these symptoms go back, perhaps, to a disastrous sexual experience early in life, which has been so profoundly damaging that the patient has repressed it, i.e. has unconsciously decided not to face it. Treatment then consists in helping the patient to recognize the cause of his unfortunate symptoms, these symptoms being ways which he has learned for dealing with the underlying problem-cause as well as he can, and also in helping him to see that these really frustrating methods of dealing with his problem are not inevitable and to learn better and more constructive behavior patterns.

How learning by thinking works in such psychotherapeutic situations can be seen from a simple everyday application. A person finds, as he goes about his business for the day, that he is very cross. He blames those around him for the most trivial actions. He cherishes a sense of grievance. He has a "chip on his shoulder." If he is wise, he does not simply accept all this emotional disturbance. He confronts it as a question. "Why am I acting in this way?" he asks himself. He finds, perhaps, a very simple answer. He has worked extremely hard on the previous day and is overtired. Once the question has been set up and the answer has emerged, he can see that there are far better ways of handling the matter than becoming furious at his wife because she burns the breakfast toast, or threatening to fire his stenographer for a short delay in producing a letter from the files. This is a very minor and superficial disturbance compared with those with which psychotherapists and guidance officers have to deal. But its rationale is the same. Moreover, the process of thinking, out of which come more successful ways of behavior, is precisely that by which the children in our previous instances learned geometry, English style, and dart throwing. It involves the sense of a question, and the development of a rational answer.

Dollard and Miller carefully point out that while many psychotherapeutic cures depend on learning by thinking, this does not imply that the patient goes through a purely intellectual experience. The patient must have a genuine and substantial emotional experience in his dealings with the therapist. It is not enough for the therapist to explain what is wrong, and to show in rational terms how to put it right. The patient must feel in his own person the force of the explanation, and the saving power of the new thoughts and interpretations. But neither is learning geometry, or English style, or the throwing of basketballs a purely intellectual affair. Thinking always stems from emotion, and always channels emotion. The experimental course in geometry was *exciting* to the pupils. It appealed to their feelings as well as their intellects. They found themselves looking at the world with different eyes, coping with it in different terms. Needs were being satisfied. The shaping of personality was going on. This is always true in thinking and in learning by thinking.

LEARNING THROUGH STRUCTURALIZATION

Learning takes place by grasping the relationships, the organized structure of a situation. This is a process often called *structuralization.* Structuralization is not a different process from understanding and thinking. It is, in fact, another name for the same process which can be called either understanding or thinking. But it involves a somewhat different way of looking at that process, and introduces a new shade of meaning which is helpful and clarifying.

There have been a considerable number of investigations on the relationship of structuralization to learning. In one of these investigations the subjects were required to memorize sets of digits. These sets or series of digests were of three types: (*a*) with digits arbitrarily arranged; (*b*) with digits arranged according to some principle, but with no indication to the experimental subjects that there was any principle; (*c*) with digits arranged according to some principle, and with the subjects told that there was a principle involved. It took an average of 3.2 repetitions to memorize series of the first type, and as many or more repetitions to memorize series of the second and third types when the subjects did not grasp the organizing principle or form of these series. But when the form or organizing principle was grasped, an average of less than two repetitions were needed for memorization, and often only one repetition was necessary. That is to say, where structure was grasped immediately, learning took place immediately (256).

A later investigation of structuralization was much more extensive. It included a number of different experiments. In one of these experiments the subjects were again required to memorize series of digits. One such series was as follows:

1 4 9 1 6 2 5 3 6 4 9 6 4 8 1

This and similar series were presented for memorization in four different ways. (*a*) The class was told that the series was con-structured on a principle, but were not told what the principle was. (*b*) The digits were presented as three-place numbers, i.e. 149, 162, 536, 496, etc.; and these three-place numbers were to be read rhythmically five times. (*c*) The class was told that these digits in new combinations stood for government expenditures, e.g. $1,491 millions in such and such a year. (*d*) The class was given a general lecture on government expenditures with such numbers as $1,491 millions, $6,253 millions, etc. displayed on the blackboard.

A memory test was given half an hour after the learning, and another memory test was given three weeks later. In both tests the first of the four modes of presentation proved the best for memorization. Half an hour later 38% of the individuals who had learned the series when presented in this way were able to make perfect scores. Three weeks later 23% could make perfect scores. When the second mode of presentation was used, 33% made perfect scores in the half-hour test, and nobody made a perfect score after three weeks. With method three, 20% made perfect scores in half an hour, and nobody did in three weeks. With method four nobody made a perfect score in either test.*

Other experiments in this same investigation had to do with learning to manipulate space-relationships. Certain match "tasks" or problems were set up. For instance, sixteen matches were arranged to make five squares, like this:

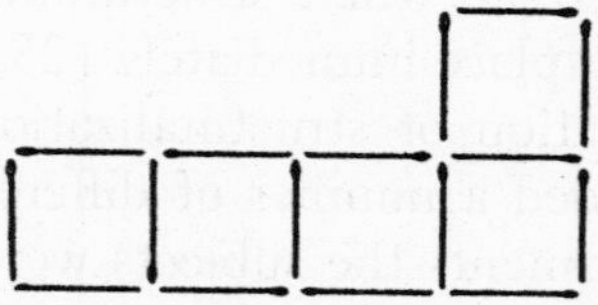

and the problem was to rearrange them into four squares, still using all the matches, and moving only three of them.

* The digits of the sample series above are made up of the squares of the series of integral numbers beginning with 1, i.e. the squares of 1, 2, 3, 4, etc., which are 1, 4, 9, 16, etc.

One way of making such a rearrangement would be like this:

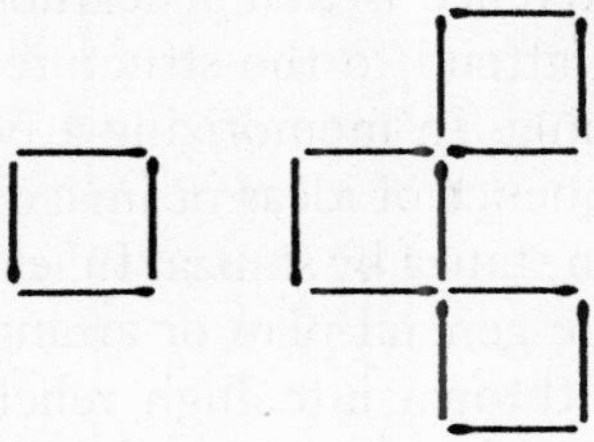

Another way would be like this.

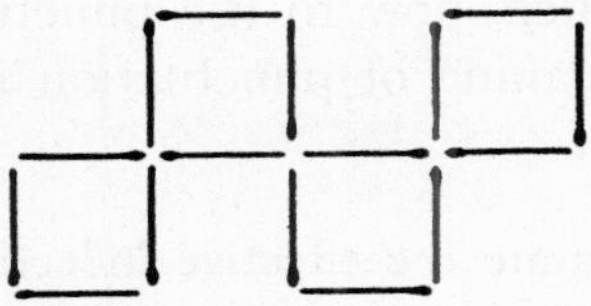

The problem was set up somewhat as it has been here. Two different plans were used for having the subjects learn how to handle this situation. Sometimes a number of specific demonstrations were given, like those above. Sometimes the general principle by which a solution can be reached was shown, this principle being always to arrange the sixteen matches so that none of the squares have any side in common. When the subjects became able to handle the problem in the form in which it appears above, new forms of the problem were set up, one of them being the following:

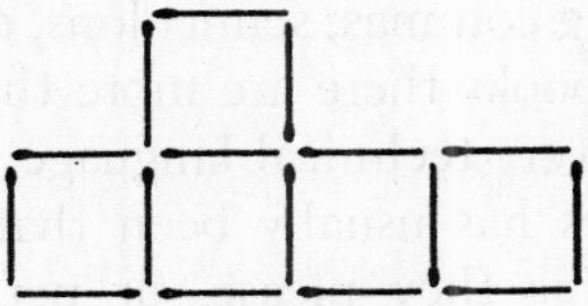

It was always found that presenting the organizing principle yielded better learning than using the demonstrations. The learning went faster. The subjects could handle new problem-situations better. They retained the ability to deal with such problems better (360).

The practical inference is that if learners are to learn well they should always attend to the structure or organization of what they are learning. In memorizing a poem it is far better to attend to the sequence of ideas or images than to memorize it line by line or even stanza by stanza. In learning a sequence of historical events, the general plan or arrangement of the happenings should be thrown into high relief. The Gregg Publishing Company has a brochure entitled *Pictured Punctuation* which utilizes the psychological process of structuralization in teaching stenographers how to use punctuation marks. The importance and meaning of punctuation is explained in the brochure as follows:

> Punctuation marks are the effective inflections and gestures of your written language, not simply a number of out-of-date and useless annoyances. You can conquer every one of them, and they will serve you. For this purpose, "Pictured Punctuation" has been written. Each page is really a word picture into which have been sketched the chief uses of punctuation marks. Use sentences of your own to change the scenes. By doing this, you will be able both to "see" and to "hear" punctuation and thus punctuate with ease.

One of the pages on the use of the comma is reproduced below (page 173).

It is interesting to compare this way of teaching people to punctuate with the old-fashioned conventional way of formulating rules for using commas, semicolons, colons, periods, and so forth. In some books there are more than a hundred such rules, expressed in very technical language. The net upshot of studying these rules has usually been that learners continue to punctuate just as they please, or perhaps hardly at all (561).

The learning and teaching of mathematics is full of opportunities for emphasis on structure or organization. For instance,

THE COMMA

Dear Students:

Every one of you who would be successful as a stenographer or a secretary must be able to read shorthand notes, transcribe letters, and punctuate correctly. If, however, you will take time to consider, you will soon realize that you can, by earnest effort, become proficient in these abilities.

The excellent course, "Business English and Letter Writing," is one you will especially enjoy, students. It is both simple and complete, and you can fully appreciate its value only after having completed the work.

The entire scope of this course, which represents every phase of the subject needed by those in office positions, is unique and original. The first object has been to present the subject in an interesting way; the second, to make it as profitable as possible for you.

A prominent businessman and editor has said, "The art of punctuating properly is indeed a prize well worth the effort required." One who knows gives only good advice.

Ability and confidence, speed and accuracy, are what you must have in punctuation. Your punctuation is the necessary signal light system regulating the traffic of thought in your written composition, not merely a number of uninteresting and misunderstood marks.

Sincerely yours.

Your Teacher

From Pictured Punctuation (*Gregg Publishing Co.*)

the nine-times table is usually said to be one of the most difficult of the multiplication tables. But if one looks at it, one can see that it has many internal relationships, the grasp of which helps one to learn it quickly and surely and remember it permanently. Here is part of the nine-times table:

$$9 \times 1 = 9$$
$$9 \times 2 = 18$$
$$9 \times 3 = 27$$
$$9 \times 4 = 36$$
$$9 \times 5 = 45$$

If you look at this table you will see that the units column of the products runs 9, 8, 7, 6, 5, etc.; that the tens column of the products runs 0, 1, 2, 3, 4, etc., and that the sum of the digits of all products is always 9.

Structuralization is very clearly involved in motor learning. If we analyze any skilled act, such as hitting a golf ball with a club, hitting a tennis ball with a racket, running a typewriter, and so forth, such an act always turns out to be a complicated pattern of interdependent movements. The touch-system typist establishes anchor points for his little fingers, and orients himself on the keyboard about these anchor, or reference, points. Golf professionals tell their pupils to keep their eyes on the ball. The importance of keeping one's eye on the ball when playing golf is not so much because one needs to see the club head hit the ball as it is because looking down at the ball will keep the head and neck steady and furnish an axis for the swing. I have already referred to the series of experiments on motor learning in which the subjects were required to learn to trace a six-pointed star which they could only see in a mirror. This quite difficult and frustrating task is not learned by learning to trace the star a bit at a time. A complicated new organized pattern of co-ordination between the eyes and the hands has to be established. A new set of relationships, a new structure, has to be learned (606, 607).

So it would seem that learning depends on structuralization, and that one of the functions of a good teacher or a good coach is to help learners to analyze what they are trying to learn, so that its internal relationships or organization can be clearly noticed. Yet if you have been careful in reading the reports of the investigations here presented, a certain question may suggest itself. One can learn series of digits *better* if those series have a logical structure, and if one knows what that structure is. But one can still learn series without any logical structure at all. Children may find the nine-times table easier to learn and remember if the teacher helps them to see its internal relationships. But millions of children have, in fact, learned that table without having the least idea of these relationships. A first-rate golf coach can help his pupil a great deal by showing him how to analyze his golf swing; but a great many people have learned to play golf with a bare minimum of conscious analysis, and perhaps without any at all. Would it not, then, be better to say that structuralization helps learning, instead of saying that we learn by structuralization?

The answer to this question is that every learner structuralizes up to a point and as far as he can, and that if he does not structuralize at all, he does not learn. This is true even with memorizing nonsense syllables, which have as little structure or logical organization as can possibly be contrived. "One thinks . . . of innumerable experiments in learning and remembering nonsense syllables, a material expressly chosen for its meaningless character. But although the meaning we usually attribute to verbal forms is lacking in nonsense syllables, it does not follow that such a series has no significance at all. On the contrary, what these experiments have shown is that, in the absence of a representative significance, the learner must devise a pattern of rhythms, or positional references, such as are possible with the graphic, articulatory, and auditory features of the series before he can learn the series at all. If the instruction be such that the learner can make no use of these aids, he can repeat the series indefinitely without ever committing it to memory" (497, pp. 187–188).

If this general statement seems a little difficult and technical, a very simple example will make the point clear. The nine-times table is usually taught and learned without any emphasis on its inner structure. It is usually taught and learned by routine drill, and with very little insight on the part of the learners. But children who learn the nine-times table routinewise, are very likely to drill on it in a sort of sing-song, or crooning, or rhythm. What they are doing then is *to impose a structure upon the table.* This arbitrary, external structuralization is very common indeed. It is used very often in learning history dates, or the spelling of words, or grammar rules, or English equivalents of foreign words. The jingle about the number of days in each month is an imposed structuralization of the material. And even when there is no such conscious and deliberate invention, structuralization still takes place. No structure, no learning! That is the rule. The point for teachers is to see to it that the structure, the grasp of relationships in and through which children learn, shall be as meaningful and efficient as possible.

ROLE OF REPETITION

Most people, if asked how we learn, would be likely to answer: "By repetition." The idea that learning is caused by repetition is deeply ingrained in many minds, and it greatly affects the organization of learning in school. The Jesuits had a pedagogical proverb: *Repetitio mater studiorum*—repetition is the mother of studies. And many an elementary-school teacher who may have never heard of this saying acts as though it were true when she teaches arithmetic, or spelling, or grammar, or historical facts, or indeed almost anything else. So the belief or claim that we learn by repetition requires careful scrutiny.

The first thing that strikes one as one considers this belief is that the word "repetition" is ambiguous. It may mean going over exactly the same performance in exactly the same way a number of times. Or it may mean making a number of attacks (which of course might vary in many of their details) on the same problem. If repetition is understood in the first sense, it is certainly not a cause of learning. If it is understood in the second sense, then repetition establishes a condition usually necessary for learning, although it is not in itself a cause of learning. These two statements must now be justified and explained.

1. Forty years ago there was undoubtedly a widespread, though not universal, belief among American psychologists that repetition in the sense of going over and over exactly the same performance did cause learning. The best known formulation of that belief was made by E. L. Thorndike in what he called the "law of use." The law of use was a statement that when a given response to a given stimulus was repeated, the connection between the stimulus and the response became stronger. At that time, Thorndike, along with many other psychologists, believed that the strengthening of the connection took place in the nervous system. But one could leave out the nervous system, and say that the repetition of a given response to a given stimulus increases the probability of the response happening when the stimulus occurs; and one would still have the law of use.

But after carrying on a great many experiments on learning, Thorndike revised his views and abandoned the law of use (658). A typical sample of these later experiments was one in which Thorndike had his subjects make ten repetitions of such statements as "Alfred Dukes and his sister worked sadly. Edward Davis and his brother argued rarely. Francis Bragg and his cousin played hard," and so forth. Thorndike found that, after ten repetitions, his subjects were far better able to tell how Alfred and his sister worked, or how Edward and his brother argued, or how Francis and his cousin played, than to tell what word came after Alfred in the first statement, or what word came after "his" in the third statement. Yet the subjects had repeated all these words the same number of times. The reason seemed to be that the subjects were aware of some sort of logical connection between Alfred Dukes and his sad working, or between Francis Bragg and his hard playing, but that they were not aware of any such logical connection between the separate words of the statement. Thorndike's conclusion from this and many other experiments was that learning depends, not on repetition, but on *belongingness.* Perhaps one might not perceive the belongingness without going over the statements several times. But it was the belongingness that caused the learning, rather than the repetition of the statements in the sense of repeating precisely the same response again and again.

2. A great and, indeed, a fatal difficulty with the belief that we learn by going over and over exactly the same response is that whenever we learn at all, we *change* our responses. Everyone makes a great many mistakes in almost all the learning he ever does. This fact is so obvious that it hardly needs proving. But it was dramatized in an experiment in which the subjects had to learn to trace a maze, using a pencil. The maze was devised so that there would be only one way of going right compared to a total of 1,200 possible ways of going wrong. Of course the subjects went wrong far more often than they went right. Yet all of them learned to solve the maze. This completely cuts the ground away from under the law of use; for if it is the exact and literal repetition of a performance that makes us learn, then these subjects would obviously have learned the mistakes instead of the correct solution (519).

When we ourselves learn anything, or when we try to get children to learn anything, we hope to bring about a change, an improvement of response. But this change and improvement cannot happen if we insist on having the same response exactly repeated again and again. This is why an attempt to insist on repetition actually hinders rather than helps learning.

For instance, we want children to learn that $7 + 5 = 12$, which is one of the addition facts. One widely accepted way of trying to get children to learn this fact is to begin by telling them that seven plus five is twelve, and then to have them repeat the statement for themselves several times, orally and in writing. Later on we find that some of the children who seemed to have learned this fact at first, have forgotten it. What to do then? According to the practice I am describing, the teacher should be careful not to let the children guess the sum of five and seven, because the guess might be wrong, and because they might learn the mistake. No! The children should be told once again that seven plus five is twelve, and drilled some more.

This perhaps looks like a sensible and practical procedure—until we find out what is really going on in the children's minds, a discovery that has been made. The challenge to the children is to get an answer to the question, "What are seven and five?" that will satisfy the teacher. Some of the children will try to get this satisfactory answer by secretly counting as fast as they can. Others will use peculiar and roundabout methods, such as saying to themselves: "5 is $2 + 3$, so $5 + 7$ is $7 + 3$, which is 10, and then 2 more," and so on. Others will try again to get the answer by blind memorization. The point is that the children are not really repeating. They are not all doing the same thing in the same way. They are wrestling with a problem as best they can, and without any help from the teacher.

What, then, ought to be done? When a child has difficulty with the statement $5 + 7 = 12$, the trouble is that he has not understood properly, he has not grasped the meanings and relationships involved. The child may have to come back to the statement several times before the light breaks through. In this broad sense he may have to repeat. But each time he attacks the statement he should be seeking, experimenting, and the teacher's business is to help him to learn the statement by understanding what adding seven and five really means (81).

3. It has been demonstrated that under certain circum-

stances a person can learn by what has been called "negative practice." This directly contradicts the idea that we learn only by repetition.

The investigator who first called attention to negative practice used himself as his own experimental subject in his earliest experiment. He was an amateur typist, and he found himself constantly writing *hte* when he wanted to write *the*. Like a sensible and serious person, he isolated the problem and drilled himself severely on writing the letters of the word *the* in the proper order. But the drill did no good, and he still transposed the letters when he wrote at speed on his machine. As a sort of afterthought, he deliberately drilled himself on writing the letters in the wrong order, i.e. as *hte*; and immediately the difficulty was cleared up (152, 153).

The experiments on negative practice certainly knock out the idea of repetition as the necessary cause of learning. But the question remains as to why negative practice works. Why can we learn to do something by deliberately doing the opposite? The answer seems to be that negative practice forces very keen concentration. Analytic and conscious attention comes to a focus on the mistake. Negative practice tends to high light the faulty habit-set that is causing the mistake, and leads to the recognition and discovery of a better and more successful co-ordination. To use an illustration, a person being led through the woods by a guide might persist in taking a wrong turning even though the guide told him that the turning was wrong. Finally the guide might say, "Very well, go that way and see for yourself."

Negative practice undoubtedly has possibilities in the way of application. Something may very well be learned from consciously doing a sum in the wrong way, from consciously writing ungrammatical sentences, from consciously misspelling words, from finding wrong instances of concepts, from hitting golf balls or tennis balls with a consciously wrong co-ordination. Practices of this kind should not be the staple fare of learning, but under certain conditions, and used with discretion, they can help (153). However, what brings about the learning is not the wrong response in and of itself, but the exploration and discovery touched off by the wrong response.

4. A great deal of learning takes place without repetition. That is to say, there is a great deal of "first time" learning. One single try is often enough to convince a child that he can get his way by throwing a tantrum. In this case it is very evident that the child learns simply by "getting the point." Moreover, investigations of the study practices of students have shown that a great many high-school boys and girls give only one reading to their content assignments. Yet these boys and girls learn, if not everything in the assignment, at least something. As a matter of fact, certain experiments have indicated that a high-school student may get from a third to a half of what the investigators thought were the "essential ideas" in social studies assignments, with only one reading (145, 229, 755). These same experiments also showed that when the students went over their assignments a second time, they did not seem to learn a great deal more.

As a matter of fact, the most promising way to bring about better learning is decidedly not to increase the sheer number of repetitions. This can be inferred from experiments on overlearning. In the psychological laboratory, overlearning means the continuation of repetitions beyond the point at which the material the subjects are dealing with has been perfectly learned. There have been many investigations of the subject. Three of the best of these investigations have shown that retention is likely to be somewhat improved by overlearning, but not in direct proportion to the number of additional repetitions (134, 379, 380). So it would seem that if a person wants to strengthen his grasp on a body of material, the effects of merely going over it again and again in more or less the same way are likely to be doubtful and disappointing, and that such repetitions of the material will yield diminishing returns.

There is an interesting report on the significance of overlearning in a practical school situation. A group of eighth-grade pupils were given a reading assignment in social science material. This material was read once, and then the pupils took a multiple choice test on the content of the reading. The 25% of the pupils who scored highest on the test, and the 25% who scored lowest were separated for special study. It took three additional readings of the assignment for the lowest 25% to equal the test performance of the best 25% (621). As a comment on this investigation the point has been made that there simply would not be time enough in the day for the lowest-rating pupils in a class to bring their achievement up to that of the highest-rating pupils, because to do so the lowest-rating pupils would need from 300–400% more work than the highest-rating pupils.

This comment is an interesting one, but it is based on an unsound assumption. The way to get students to learn better is not by dint of "more of the same"—more grind, more drill, more time spent on the same basic routines. Repetition, in the sense of doing the same thing in the same way time after time, is precisely not a cause of learning. Indeed, strictly speaking, repetition in this sense never takes place, even in the laboratory where conditions are controlled and tasks are routine and trivial. A person in a laboratory experiment who repeats a list of nonsense syllables ten times may seem to be doing exactly the same thing ten times; but as a matter of fact his attitudes and impulses will change to some extent with every repetition. In another experiment a person may throw ten darts at a target. The darts are all the same weight and size and the target is constant. But each time the person throws, his muscular coordinations will change. The learner of nonsense syllables and the dart-thrower both improve during their ten tries. But how could they improve if their muscular and mental reactions did not change? And if their reactions change, they are not really repeating, although they seem to be (123).

When we try to get pupils in school to learn better, we should not try to have them do more practice and study of exactly the kind they have been doing. We should try to show them how to practice and study more intelligently and discriminatively. When we suggest to a high-school student that he might read his social science assignment three times instead of just once, we do not want his second and third readings to be mere repetitions of his first reading. We want them to be different and better. Undoubtedly one main reason why students do not read their assignments more than once is that they do not know how to read them differently and better a second or a third time. This is precisely the kind of thing that a good teacher will try to help students to do, for learning does not depend on the amount of time spent, or the number of practice periods, still less upon literal repetition in the narrow sense. Learning is always a quest for a workable solution, and it depends upon understanding, thinking, and structuralization—in a word, upon insight.

THEORIES OF LEARNING

The research literature on learning is enormous. That literature includes not only reports of many thousands of experimental investigations, but also numerous attempts to formulate comprehensive theoretical accounts of learning. While general and inclusive theories of learning are of interest chiefly to specialists, the relationship of these theories to what is said about learning in this book needs to be indicated.

There are two main types of learning theory. The first of these is associationism, or, as it is often called nowadays, connectionism.* The central doctrine of associationism, or connectionism, is that learning consists of the establishment of

* Associationism is the older and, indeed, the classic name for this type of learning theory. It is a viewpoint that has existed at least since the days of the ancient Greeks. For this reason the word associationism seems preferable to connectionism.

connections or associations between experiences, or between stimuli and responses. The second main type of learning theory, unlike the first, has no single, definite name that is universally recognized and used. It is often called the organismic, or Gestalt, or holistic point of view. Its key doctrine is that learning essentially consists of the apprehension of meaning, or of organized pattern, and that it depends upon insight. Within these two great divisions of theory there are many subdivisions, or subsects, just as there are many subdivisions of Catholics and Protestants. But all learning theories belong, in a general way, either to the associationist or the organismic persuasion (309).

If one reads the writings of upholders of different learning theories, one is impressed, at first sight, with the differences in their terminology and in their methods of explanation and analysis. But if one takes the trouble to try to understand what these various writers are saying, the apparent divergencies between them begin to seem surprisingly unimportant. They do not seem to differ very much in their total conception of learning; and I would hazard a guess that most of them would substantially agree about what makes good teaching good and bad teaching bad.

At least two careful attempts have been made to list points of essential agreement among present-day theories of learning. The chief of these points of agreement are as follows. (*a*) Learning must be motivated. (*b*) Learning occurs in the presence of a challenge or an obstruction. (*c*) Such a challenge or obstruction tends to produce more intense activity in the subject. (*d*) Learning always involves variation and change of response. (*e*) In learning, the learner always responds to patterns of relationships in the stimulating situation. (*f*) Learning is always an adaptation of means to ends (or, as we would say, a discovery of how to deal with a challenge). (*g*) The learner will always tend to learn the easiest (or the most apparently reasonable) response. This is often called the principle of "least action," i.e. the principle of getting a result with the least trouble. (*h*) In learning, the effects of the achieved response are crucial. Some psychologists would say that these effects are pleasantness and unpleasantness; others that they are success or failure. But all agree as to their importance (137, 421).

Now, you may very well ask, if there is all this agreement, why the various theories? One chief reason, and perhaps indeed the main reason for the variety of theories of learning is a preference for certain methods of analysis and certain ways of explaining phenomena. Associationists on the whole would tend to think that an analysis of learning in terms of stimulus, response, and connection gives us our best chance for a clear and precise explanation and account of what happens. Some of them, for example, would say that what are often called physiological needs are best understood as the operation of internal stimuli, and that the concept of internal stimulation is better than the concept of physiological need because one can really identify the operating stimuli, or at least try to do so. Organismic psychologists, on the other hand, would insist that the apparent clarity of analysis via stimulus, response, and connection is really spurious, and that it cannot do justice to the facts of learning and behavior. So the differences between the various learning theories turn largely on questions of method rather than of fact. And the value of these theories is that they suggest avenues of experimental research.

Ultimately, however, the reason why there are so many different theories of learning can be summarized in one single painful word—*ignorance*. In spite of all the facts that have been collected, our understanding of the learning process is quite limited; and above all, it does not get down to the root of the matter. Presumably something happens in the nervous system when a person learns. But nobody knows what that something is. If we did know what happens in the organism when learning takes place, what causes this happening and what prevents it, then probably there would be general agreement rather than conflicting theories.

Must we then conclude that learning theories are futile, and the making of them a waste of time? Certainly not. Psychologists who develop theories of learning are themselves learners, and they can only learn by striving to understand phenomena as well as they are able.

Again, if it is true that we simply do not understand the ultimate nature of learning, must we conclude that there is nothing sound or solid or worth heeding in the whole psychology of learning? By no means. What psychology can present, and does present, is a good descriptive picture of the learning process, and although this picture is not an ultimate explanation, it is extremely useful and helpful. When we find that, in spite of all differences of terminology, method, and outlook, there is a wide area of agreement among all students of learning, we may be sure that here is something very well worth knowing, something that can save us from stupid errors, disastrous misconceptions and mistakes, something that can point the way towards improved practice, as we try to direct and organize learning in ourselves and others. Such a constructive account of learning is what I am trying to present in these pages, and I think you will find that most of what I have to say on the subject falls well within the wide area of agreement among learning theories.

QUESTIONS FOR DISCUSSION

1. A very distinguished public man said recently that it was important for students in high school and college to have a better grasp of natural science. To bring this about he recommended devoting more time to science teaching. Does this seem to you the best way to achieve the indicated result?

2. It sometimes happens that after much seemingly fruitless effort one learns some skill or achieves some insight very suddenly.

In the light of the last two chapters consider the conditions under which these "flashes of insight" are likely to occur. Could a teacher do anything to encourage them? What do you think happens during the apparently fruitless efforts previous to the flash of insight?

3. A child transfers into a new school and manifests hostile and aggressive attitudes, so that he is earmarked as a "problem pupil." If he is to achieve more constructive behavior he must somehow or other learn new attitudes and tendencies. What suggestions can you make about how such learning might be encouraged?

4. A freshman girl in college was doing quite well in all her subjects except mathematics. In this subject she was a complete failure in spite of her most earnest efforts. Could you derive from our discussions of learning any suggestions that might be helpful in such a case?

5. Assemble from your own experience instances of repeating some action without any learning taking place. Under what conditions is repetition likely not to produce learning? What practical inferences can you draw from this to practicing a motor skill, memorizing a poem, or studying a history assignment?

6. The term "diagnostic teaching" has been used in this chapter. It is a term widely used in modern education, so you should be sure to understand it clearly. As ordinarily used, it stands for a rather special type of teaching. Consider, however, whether all teaching should not be diagnostic. Also consider to what extent ordinary classroom teaching is not diagnostic and whether this is not a very serious defect.

7. Think of a possible course unit on the history of the American Revolution. The unit will contain many specific facts, so that it might seem chiefly a challenge to rote memory. Map out as many ways as you can in which one might "master" this unit by understanding it rather than merely by memorizing its detailed content.

8. In our discussion of theories of learning you will find a considerable list of points in which all modern representative theories are in agreement. Use this list for the sake of reviewing, reconsidering, and re-thinking the treatment of learning in the present and the previous chapter. How many of the points listed have been brought out in the two chapters? Have any been omitted? Are any of the points in the list dealt with in different words in our two chapters?

SUGGESTED READINGS

Hartmann, George W., "The Field Theory of Learning and Its Educational Consequences." *41st Yearbook*, National Society for the Study of Education (1942), Chap. 5, 164–214.

Hilgard, Ernest R., *Theories of Learning*. Appleton-Century-Crofts, Inc., New York, 1948, Chaps. 1, 12.

McConnell, T. R., "Reconciliation of Learning Theories." *41st Yearbook*, National Society for the Study of Education (1942), Chap. 7, 243–286.

Reed, H. B., "Meaning as a Factor in Learning." *Journal of Educational Psychology*, XXIX (1938), 419–430.

Vandell, R. R., Davis, R. A., and Clugston, H. A., "The Function of Mental Practice in the Acquisition of Motor Skills." *Journal of General Psychology*, XXIX (1943), 243–250.

7

The Course of Learning

TWO PHASES

ANY AND every learning undertaking, as it occurs in time, moves through two phases—a phase of advance and a phase of retreat, a phase of improvement and a phase of deterioration. A person learns to drive a car, to solve problems involving the binomial theorem, to play golf. In this learning he makes progress until his achievement reaches a peak. Then, unless he continues to use his ability, that ability declines. We improve, we achieve, we forget. This, in outline, maps the course of learning. Learning, we might say, goes through a phase of crescendo and a phase of diminuendo.

It is most important to think of both the improvement and the deterioration, both the crescendo and the diminuendo, as phases of the same process instead of as two distinct and more or less independent processes. Yet much in the language and even in the thinking of psychologists seems to suggest, if not actually to imply or affirm, that improvement and deterioration are separate processes. There are hundreds, if not thousands, of research investigations of learning which are almost entirely limited to dealing with the upward part of the course, that is to say, with improvement, its speed, and its upper limits. Then on the other hand there are important, though by no means so numerous, studies dealing with forgetting, i.e. with the downward phase of the course of learning. So there is at least a tacit suggestion that improvement and deterioration are two separate and different processes, instead of two phases of the total course of the process of learning.

No doubt this separation between improvement (a word often used interchangeably with the word learning) on the one hand, and deterioration or forgetting on the other is partly due to the specialization always necessary in research work. Any experimental investigator has to isolate a certain aspect of a process and deal intensively with that aspect, even though he knows very well that he is omitting a great deal. So when psychologists single out either the rising or the falling part of the total course of learning for special experimental study, they are perfectly justified.

But these very investigations show clearly that it is perfectly unjustifiable to consider improvement and deterioration as two separate and more or less unrelated processes. It has been shown again and again that the permanence and completeness with which any knowledge or skill is retained depends very much on how that knowledge or skill has been acquired. We know, for instance, that a given ration of practice will bring about more improvement, i.e. a more extensive crescendo, if the practice is distributed than it will if the practice is concentrated or massed. But also we know that distributed practice tends to bring about longer retention, i.e. a slower decrescendo, than massed practice.

Or again, we know that when almost meaningless material like nonsense syllables is being learned, the improvement or crescendo starts very fast and then slows down, whereas when meaningful material is being learned the crescendo may start quite slowly and then speed up. So the factor of meaningfulness affects the upward part of the course of learning. But this same factor also affects the downward part of the course of learning just as much. When practice on a set of nonsense syllables stops, most of the material is forgotten very fast, and a little lingers on for a long time; but when a body of meaningful material has been grasped, deterioration or forgetting is very slow, and there is often no sudden drop anywhere or at any time. Once again, an intense will to learn brings about faster improvement and higher achievement, and it also tends to bring about slower forgetting. Clearly then, on psychological grounds, improvement and deterioration are not two processes, but phases of one and the same process, and if we wish to get a sound understanding of the total course of learning, we must take into consideration both its upward and its downward phase, both crescendo and diminuendo.

If it is necessary for the psychologist to recognize that both improvement and deterioration are phases of the same process, it is even more obviously necessary for the teacher to recognize that this is so. No teacher who applies the most ordinary common sense to her work can be perfectly satisfied to have pupils learn anything at all without at least wondering how much of it they will remember later on. Surely every teacher must at least hope to produce, not merely a stated result, but also a lasting effect. Standards which simply contemplated a given level of achievement on a certain calendar date, and which disregarded everything beyond that date would be unrealistic to the point of absurdity. And if we agree that the great business of the teacher is to help to shape the personalities of her pupils, then long-term effects become even more important than immediate levels of achievement. Mathematics, science, literature, history, and the arts can and should be agencies for more enlightened living, and for the more complete and constructive satisfaction of basic human needs. The subjects of the curriculum can be made to serve these values, and they must be made to serve them if they are to be justified at all. But what possible profit is there in any and all such subjects if they are consigned to oblivion two weeks after the final test? So the intelligent teacher is bound to recognize that forgetting as well as improvement is an essential phase in the total course of learning, and to provide for both phases in her planning and procedure.

It is my impression that most teachers are very reluctant to face the formidable fact, and problem, of forgetting, and I think one can see why. To bring most of the youngsters in a class up to at least a nominal level of achievement in a given time does seem practical. Drills, recitations, specific assignments, tryout tests, and a combination of pressure and helpfulness can perhaps do this much; and then there is a sense that something tangible has been accomplished. But the question, How much will remain in the youngsters' minds in a year or in twenty years? is exceedingly disturbing. Moreover, what can be done about these long-term effects?

On this last question the whole issue hinges. Nothing that we can do can prevent forgetting. Forgetting is an essential part of the economy of mental life and of personality adjustment. It is not merely a misfortune. As a human being passes on to new challenges he must do some forgetting, or his power to cope with new issues will be hopelessly clogged. But although we cannot prevent forgetting, we can in large measure control, influence, and shape it. We cannot prevent forgetting from happening; but we can prevent it from stultifying our efforts when we teach. We can teach for the long future and for the lasting effect. We can make our teaching *memorable*, which all good and vital teaching must be. And the way to understand how this can be done is to reach some understanding of the total course of learning, in its two phases of improvement and deterioration, ascent and descent, crescendo and diminuendo.

FROM ORIENTATION TO DETAIL

The natural sequence of improvement—of the process which takes place during the ascending phase of the course of learning—is from orientation to detail. Remember that all learning centers upon discovering a way of dealing with a problem or challenge. In this process of discovery the general direction emerges, and the details declare themselves as the process goes on.

Elsewhere I have given what seems to me a very good illustration of this sequence from the writings of the explorer Stefansson. There is a passage ". . . in which he gives an account of what he does when he has to find his way through an unknown and unmapped territory. Always, he says, he follows a deliberate and definite plan. His procedure is the very opposite of relying upon a general, vague sense of direction. He hunts about until he finds a good lookout with a wide view ahead. It may be the bare top of a rocky hill; or if there is nothing of the sort available, he climbs high into a tall tree. When he has found his outlook, he does not satisfy himself with a few cursory glances and then go on. He settles down as comfortably as possible for a long stay and for relaxed and careful study. He takes out his field glasses deliberately and proceeds to examine the terrain at his leisure. He spends just as much time as he needs to get a complete picture in his mind of the ridges, the valleys, the forests, the open tracts, the thickets, the run of the streams. All this may consume as much as half a day, but until he has the whole picture before him, he stays where he is. When everything he can see is coordinated in his mind, then and not till then he is ready to move forward. There may still be surprises. A stream may be deeper or swifter than he had expected, a valley more precipitous and winding, a forest denser. But these are matters of detail. He will always be aware of the relationship of one thing to another. Above all, the mental picture he has formed will enable him to know where he is going and in a general way where to go" (474, p. 40).

This account is more than a parable. It is a direct and literal description of learning, and very efficiently organized learning too. Stefansson on his high outlook is a learner; and like all learners, he is learning *to find his way*. And the process of improvement, from the first sensing of the problem to its final solution, is a movement from orientation to the mastery and control of detail.

In one sense this illustration (which might really be called a case study of learning) can be a little misleading. It might suggest that the achievement of orientation and the mastery and control of detail are two separable stages on the path of improvement. This is not so at all. Orientation grows clearer and more certain as details accumulate and errors are eliminated. Detail supports and focalizes orientation, and orientation makes details meaningful.

This possible mistake of separating orientation from the mastery of detail can perhaps be avoided if one thinks of the course of improvement as a rhythm of synthesis, analysis, and re-synthesis. One has, let us say, an assignment in a social studies textbook. One glances it over to get the content and general drift. This is the preliminary synthesis, the first orientation. Then one pays particular attention to this or that specific aspect of the material. This is a phase of analysis. As a result, the picture of the whole becomes a little clearer; or to put it otherwise, a better synthesis and a more adequate orientation emerge. But as the picture clarifies, still further aspects and details demand attention, so the rhythm shifts to more analysis. So the process of improvement goes on, with orientation becoming clearer, and with details becoming more controlled and organized, until one has satisfactorily "learned" the chapter, which means that one can use it for whatever purpose one had in mind in undertaking to learn it.

This rhythm of synthesis-analysis-re-synthesis appears in

problem-solving, for one searches for promising leads, tries them out in detailed applications, revises them, tries them out again, and so on till the solution is developed. The same rhythm appears also in motor learning, as, for instance, when a man practicing his golf swing begins with a few preliminary swings (the first synthesis), attends to this or that weakness (analysis), tries out the swing as a whole again (re-synthesis), attacks other weaknesses (more analysis), goes back to the total swing (more re-synthesis), and so on. Always we have orientation and the control of detail, not as separate but as distinguishable phases of learning; and it is their interaction that brings about improvement.*

WHOLE AND PART LEARNING

The experimental work which bears most closely on this conception of a rhythm or sequence through orientation towards detail is the work that has been done on learning by parts and learning by wholes. In the research literature the whole-part issue has been set up as follows. We give our experimental subjects a certain learning task—memorizing nonsense syllables, selections from poetry or prose, acquiring the ability to recognize geometrical figures, and suchlike. In general, any such learning task can be attacked in two quite different ways. Our subjects can go right through the list of syllables, or the selection of poetry or prose, or the set of geometrical figures again and again as a whole. Or they can take each separate syllable, or each line of the poem, or each prose sentence, or each single geometrical figure, and try to learn each item perfectly before passing on to the next. The first mode of attack would be learning by the whole method. The second mode of attack would be learning by the part method. Minor variations and combinations of these two

* I have carried the application of the idea of synthesis-analysis-re-synthesis as the basic learning pattern a good deal further elsewhere. See bibliography item 473.

methods have been investigated. For instance, one might memorize the first line of a poem, then memorize the second, then go back to the first and be sure one could combine it with the second, then go on to the third, and so on. This is sometimes called the progressive part method of learning, and there are other variants too. But these minor variations need not concern us here, although numerous studies have dealt with them, for we are interested merely in the broad distinction between learning by wholes and learning by parts.

The relative value of whole and part learning has been a subject of psychological investigation for many years. Not so long ago it seemed to be fashionable to say that the issue was settled, and that a clear-cut superiority for the whole method had been established beyond question. But no such flat statement is tenable. It is quite true that many of the earlier studies did come out with the finding that people learn quicker and better by the whole method than by the part method. But on analysis many of these studies turn out to be technically defective, which casts doubt on their results.

Moreover, they are offset by other studies which do not show any decisive superiority for whole-wise learning, and which even indicate that some variant of the part-wise method may be better. If one were to count up the experimental investigations on the problem, as if one were taking a public opinion poll, the whole-wise method would have a considerable majority. But a question of scientific interpretation can hardly be decided in this way; and the outcome of the debate about the two methods of learning is by no means clear-cut; at least so far as most of the experimental evidence is concerned (428, 429). It has not been established that either one has a flat and indubitable superiority under all circumstances.

But in more recent experimental work there has been a shift of ground. The issue has ceased to be one of *either-or—either* the part method is better, *or* the whole method is better—and several very far-reaching questions have been raised.

1. To what extent is what may seem to be a part-wise method of learning really a part-wise method? I propose, let us say, to memorize a poem by the part method. I cover up everything but the first line, and go over that until I can repeat it perfectly. Then I cover up the first line and slip my paper down until I can see the second line and memorize that. Then I go on in the same way to the rest of the lines, taking each one separately. This looks like a strict part-wise method of learning the poem. Well and good! But how many lines will I have memorized until I begin to have a pretty clear idea of what the whole poem is about? Surely not so very many. And when this idea arrives, has not the poem as a whole crept into my mental operations, and ruined the integrity of my part-wise learning?

There is an experiment in which this covert introduction of the idea of the whole actually took place, apparently without the experimenter realizing what had happened. A class of children were set to work to memorize several poems. Sometimes they learned these poems by going right through them again and again from beginning to end—the classic whole-wise method. Sometimes they learned the poems single line by single line. *But always the experimenter summarized the poem that was to be memorized in advance, and discussed it with the children before they set to work to memorize it.* As a result of her experiment, this investigator reports that children learn best and quickest by the part-wise method. But she had already established an orientation, and given them an excellent working idea of the poem as a whole before it was learned (732). Quite possibly just such an orientation may have established itself, although less obviously and completely, and more secretly, in many experiments which indicate a superiority for part-wise learning.

2. Does the intelligence of the subjects affect the relative value of the whole and the part methods of learning? This question was ignored in the earlier studies; but it has now been attacked, and an answer is at least indicated. It has been shown

that whole-wise learning, as compared to part-wise learning, is particularly advantageous for brighter children and for older children, and that it is much less advantageous as compared to part-wise learning for younger children and for dull children. In the experiment from which this general finding is reported, the children had to memorize paired English-foreign-language vocabularies and also poems. Now these are just the sort of tasks which children who rate high on a verbal intelligence test are likely to do well. High standing on a verbal intelligence test means that a child is well equipped to cope with a challenge to manipulate and deal with language. So the brighter children (those with higher I.Q.'s) and the older children (who would of course have a higher mental age than the younger and the duller ones), would tend to have a better orientation when they had to cope with a vocabulary list of a poem. They would be likely to deal with the list or the poem more or less patternwise; and so they would handle it more competently (427).

3. The first point that was made above might be rephrased by saying that a part is not always a part. A single line of a poem may *look* like a separate part. But it may contain a pregnant hint as to what the whole poem is about, and then it is a great deal more than a separate part. And just as what seems like a part may not always be really a part, so what seems like a whole may not always really be a whole. We say that learning by wholes is very effective; and by whole-wise learning we mean going right through the "whole" from beginning to end again and again. But just what is this whole? One speech from one scene of *Hamlet?* The entire scene? The entire play? One sentence from *Paradise Lost?* One book from *Paradise Lost?* Or all of *Paradise Lost?* One section from a chapter in a textbook, or the entire chapter, or the entire book? These are awkward questions, and exceedingly important and practical ones too. Some teachers who have heard of the advantages of whole-wise learning try to put the idea into practice by assigning long blocks of material, or setting up large and long units.

But mere size or length cannot constitute a true whole, and our problem is not to find out whether learning by large gulps is better than learning by small ones. A true whole must have some kind of internal belongingness, some kind of inner logical constitution, and a logical differentiation from anything else.

This issue of logical or "qualitative" wholeness has also been experimentally attacked. The investigator attempted to set up learning tasks, in which there were differing degrees of wholeness, that is, of internal belongingness and self-completeness. The material she used consisted of a number of block designs, each of which was cut up into a sixteen-piece jigsaw puzzle, the task being to assemble the puzzle. Sometimes the design was planned so that the total meaning it embodied was emphasized, sometimes it was planned with emphasis on the parts. She reported that where there was a highly organized qualitative unity, the whole method of procedure worked better than the part method, and that where there was no such highly organized qualitative unity, the part-wise procedure worked better. That is, if the sixteen pieces of the puzzle were all related as elements in a very definite and meaningful figure, the subjects would do better if they always looked for the figure, but if there were no meaningful design conspicuously embodied in the pieces of the puzzle, the subjects would do better if they tried to manipulate the pieces one by one (574, 575, 576).

The clear suggestion for the teacher is that whole-wise learning is by no manner of means a matter of mere length, and that the problem of organizing such learning cannot be solved just by setting up large units, long assignments, or comprehensive courses. To give children a block of material without any particular internal coherence—without a "beginning, middle, and end" to quote a very famous dictum—and then to expect them to handle it advantageously by the whole-wise method, is very foolish. We must organize material so that it contains a coherent clue if we want children to look for that clue. We must organize units that have an internal logic, instead of being hit-or-miss collections of facts labeled with some sort of makeshift title, if we expect children to deal with our units via understanding and insight. Mere quantity does not constitute wholeness; and wholeness in the material is a prerequisite for effective whole-wise learning.

4. Now that we have gotten together a good deal of representative data on whole and part learning, we must try to make an over-all interpretation of the material and to look for practical conclusions. An interpretation of the findings on whole and part learning is very necessary, because these findings were obtained in the very special situation of laboratory experiments. Outside of a laboratory it is not very likely that anyone would use the whole method of learning in all its strictness. To memorize a ten-stanza poem, or a twenty-item French-English vocabulary list by going through the entire poem or the entire list again and again, and doing nothing else, would seem a peculiar and improbable procedure. On the other hand, pure, or strict, part-wise learning does not often happen in normal or non-laboratory situations. Investigators find that children tend to break assignments into little segments to be memorized bit by bit—certainly not a wise or efficient proceeding. But usually the children have at least some overview, and the bit-by-bit study of a school assignment is by no means identical with the pure part method in a laboratory.

So the practical outcome of the investigations on whole and part methods of learning is not that a person should always use one or the other, or even any stated combination of both methods. The practical outcome is that these investigations show us *how any learning undertaking should be approached.* Overview, orientation, or a general comprehension of what is to be learned should always be established in order to coordinate and guide the learner as he attacks the details. It is, no doubt, very true that children in school, and probably learners in general, have an unfortunate and self-defeating tendency to break up learning tasks into small segments, and to deal with these segments one by one. The proper corrective, however, is not to try to get these learners to use a pure whole-wise attack, i.e. to learn material by always going through it from start to finish. What learners need to do is to make quite sure that they see the wood before they begin to count the trees, and to keep the shape of the wood always in mind while they are busy counting the trees. The practical issue is not to choose between whole-wise learning and part-wise learning as mutually exclusive alternatives, but to maintain always the view of the whole while dealing with the parts.

This question of the proper approach to any learning task, which is the central question involved in the whole lengthy discussion of whole and part methods of learning, has itself been directly investigated. It was found that the best approach is always one that "structuralizes" the field, that enables one to *understand* details as one comes to deal with them, that makes it possible to *think through* details and to see their interrelationships. The best approach is always to begin by evoking *insight* into what is to be learned (361).

This is why the children in the investigation already cited (732) were able to memorize poems very well when those poems had been explained and discussed in advance, even though what seems like a very mechanical, part-wise method of memorizing was used. It is also the reason why content questions set up in advance of the actual reading of a passage have more effect on comprehension than questions placed elsewhere (702). In both these cases an orientation had been established. The subjects were given an understanding of what they were to try to learn in detail, and so they were able to deal with detail in terms of insight.

This working principle of establishing an intelligent orientation, or of evoking and applying insight as the essential effective approach to any learning task, has innumerable applications. For instance, it has been shown that students will often get as much comprehension and grasp of content from reading a digest of an article as from reading the article itself (418). The reason is that the digest presents the essential points on which a competent reader will concentrate, and that the elimination of detail makes these essential points easier to identify and grasp.

Or again, as another instance, the principle of approaching learning through insight has been applied to the learning of a foreign language. Ten or fifteen years ago the so-called "direct method" of teaching foreign languages was very popular and highly regarded. This direct method meant the use of nothing at all but the foreign language itself from the very start. The names of common objects in the classroom and simple statements about them were made clear to the learners, not by using English as an intermediary, but by a system of hints and gestures associated with the foreign-language expressions. It was said that this is how we all learn our mother tongue; and there was some truth in the statement, although of course children are in contact with their native language most of their waking hours instead of for a few class periods a week.

But the fact that we do really learn English by a direct method is in itself no argument for learning other languages in the same way. A person who has learned English has a great many language-patterns which can help him very much in dealing with a new language. He has, for instance, a working concept of "sentence"; and in present-day instruction in foreign language these existing patterns are utilized to make the new language more intelligible and manageable from the start (610). Hence there are good reasons for the utilization of one's mother tongue when learning a new language. The direct method is no doubt the method by which a little child learns language for the first time, but this does not mean that it is the best method for acquiring another language later on.

The approach to any new learning task via insight or structuralization also proves to be desirable, and sometimes almost essential in motor learning. I have already several times mentioned the investigations in which the task was the mirror tracing of a six-point star, and here I must refer to them again, for they are among the most significant studies of motor learning ever made. It was found to be quite necessary for the subjects in these experiments to establish a definite orientation, a feeling for the total structure or pattern of the reaction they were learning, before any real progress was possible. This orientation was achieved by taking plenty of time, by relaxing and working slowly, by trying, above all, to get the "feel" of tracing the star when guided only by the confusing mirror-image. Here is the counterpart of the introductory discussion of the poems that were to be memorized, of the preliminary questions at the top of the passage that was to be read. One might say that the preliminary orientation was by way of being a bird's-eye view, or conspectus of the motor problem to be mastered (606).

This whole discussion of the upward phase of the course of learning can now be brought to a head in a few summary statements.

1. Learning always originates in a challenge—in an unsolved problem whose solution is desired. The more insight into the problem that can be evoked from the very start, the better the learning will go, and the faster the solution will arrive. This has been directly shown by comparing the course of learning when material is easy and manageable on the one hand, and difficult and baffling on the other. With easy material the curve of learning rises very fast at first and then slows down. With difficult and baffling material the curve rises slowly at first and much more rapidly later on. The slow early rise of the curve in this second set of circumstances is due to the fact that there is very little insight or understanding or structuralization at first. But when some co-ordinated grasp of the previously baffling material has been achieved, learning progresses very fast (381).

So a part of the task of every skillful teacher is to make learning as easy and rapid as possible, not by denaturing the content of what is to be learned, but by trying to make it understandable to the learner. When understanding arrives at once, the way of dealing with the problem from which learning stems is found at once, and a person learns completely without any repetition. When understanding comes slowly, many trials, much fumbling, and a great deal of time may be necessary. When understanding never dawns at all, there will be no satisfactory learning.

2. The character of learning tends to change as learning progresses and as the curve rises. Learning begins with orientation and insight; and insight and orientation cannot be hurried and cannot be pushed. This is why, in the early stages of a learning process a learner may not seem to be covering ground, or assimilating anything tangible. Very probably a learner, in the early stages, ought not even to try to cover ground or to assimilate small details. On the contrary, he ought to be feeling his way, trying to sense the "whole" and its broad significance.

Many teachers, in their zeal for tangible results, never clearly see that good learning must start with nothing more tangible than a general orientation to the problem to be mastered, a general and perhaps quite cloudy and limited insight into its significance. They undertake to teach children what are called the "fundamentals" of grammar, or arithmetic, or music, or what not. These fundamentals actually consist of an array of detailed facts or statements or principles, and the mastery of them is supposed to be essential for progress with the subject itself. Psychologically speaking, this is an absolutely false approach. What a teacher should convey to children first of all is a feeling for English expression, or for relational thinking, or for musical values. All that we know indicates that these are far sounder starting points for effective learning and rapid improvement than any body of specific details, whether these details are labeled "essentials" or "fundamentals" or anything else.

As learning progresses, as improvement advances, details come more and more into the focus of the picture. Then is the time for tangible results, for specific outcomes, for drill and, indeed, for pressure looking towards the final polish. What can be quite destructive and fatal in the earlier stages of learning becomes natural and desirable in the later stages. For as learning advances, the learner can more and more deal with the details of the trees without losing his informing and absolutely essential awareness of the configuration of the forest.

3. In all this we see once more how remarkably little sheer repetition has to do with learning. How many repetitions does one need to see the focal point in the proof of a theorem, the general drift and significance of a poem, the clue to the solution of a problem, or to grasp the right "feel" of a motor reaction? There is no possible answer to such a question; yet these evocations of insight are the essentials of improvement. One of the great weaknesses of nearly all the studies on whole and part learning has been that the method of learning imposed on the subjects was always to repeat either by wholes or by parts or by some combination of wholes and parts, and also that one of the criteria of good learning was the fewness of the repetitions needed to get a given result. But to try to learn simply by going over material again and again is certainly a stupid and wasteful proceeding. One learns by striving to understand, and the whole-wise method is superior only in so far as it facilitates understanding. For it is the understanding, and not the whole-wise repetition, that brings about the learning.

Learning, let us remind ourselves once more, is discovering how to deal with a problem or a challenge. The prototype of learning is Stefansson on his high outlook, with his mental processes moving in a crescendo from vagueness and doubt towards accurate and certain comprehension of the terrain before him. If teachers want learning to go well, the more closely they model their organization on this prototype, the more rapid and assured will be the crescendo they secure.

FORGETTING

Learning in its ascending phase moves forward from an orientation that is probably vague, partial, and imperfect towards a given level of specific and detailed achievement. Clearly this is not a process of addition. It is a process of *organization*. So, too, the phase of decline is not a process of subtraction, but of disorganization. The descending phase of the course of learning is in many ways a counterpart of the ascending phase. And the entire course of learning in both its ascending and descending phases must be considered if we are to be effective in our teaching.

Early experiments on memory and forgetting tended to treat memorizing as addition and forgetting as subtraction. The material consisted of nonsense syllables, digits, and so forth. The crucial question usually was what percentage of these nonsense syllables or digits would be lost after different periods of time. Various percentages and rates of loss were reported by various investigators. But there was general agreement that forgetting goes very fast at first, and then slows down.

It is now generally recognized that these early experiments were very limited in their significance, and that one cannot draw any sweeping conclusions from them. The material used was as meaningless as it could possibly be. It consisted of lists of separate items, each one of which would be either perfectly known or wholly forgotten, for there could be no half-remembering of a digit or nonsense syllable, although half-remembering constantly occurs in actual experience. And the only measure of the amount of remembering and forgetting was the number of separate items perfectly remembered or completely lost. So this early experimental work was very artificial and had no practical value. Any suggestions about the proper management of reviews, for instance, that might be based upon this work would have no sound foundation at all.

Later experimental work on memorizing and forgetting has corrected most of these deficiencies. This has been done by centering upon the forgetting of meaningful material. A number of vitally important findings have come from the investigation of forgetting as the descending curve of meaningful learning.

1. Meaningful material is forgotten far more slowly than relatively meaningless material. This has been shown in a great many studies, of which a few samples are summarized here.

In one important investigation the subjects learned passages of difficult but meaningful prose. They went through each of these passages four times. Then they took true-false tests, some of which were on the exact wording of the passages, while others were on their content. Memory for exact wording showed a rapid and very marked decline. But memory for content that had been understood did not decline at all for as long as seventy days. This is a very dramatic contrast; and the investigators make severe but quite justifiable comments on the folly of testing for verbal knowledge for the sake of revealing understanding (165).

A later investigation of the same general type used another kind of meaningful material. The subjects studied sets of cards in which each card pictured an office scene. Then three sets of eleven questions were given at different intervals, dealing with what was shown in the pictures. Forgetting was measured by the number of items a subject could mention when he was questioned. This, to be sure, was a somewhat artificial and arbitrary proceeding, but the results were very suggestive. There was some falling off in retention, but the downward curve was entirely different from the curve of forgetting nonsense syllables. For instance, after 48 hours one group of subjects could mention 85% of the items they had noticed (224).

Yet another experiment dealt with the learning and retention of concepts. The set up in the laboratory was rather remote from the kind of learning that goes on in school, but again the findings were highly suggestive. The concepts were somewhat similar to grammatical concepts, such as "noun," "adjective," and so forth. They were studied not merely as verbal definitions, but in relationship to concrete examples and illustrations. When the illustrations were difficult and complicated, the learning was delayed and confused, and retention was diminished, the reason being that under these circumstances the subjects did not understand the concepts so well as when they were given simple illustrative material (539).

These studies of the forgetting of meaningful material have a very direct bearing upon school work, as no doubt can be easily seen. The connection has been directly brought out in an important project carried out some years ago, which undertook to improve examinations in biology and zoology at Ohio State University. One question raised in this project was how different kinds of material are remembered after a lapse of time. It was found that 15 months after the end of the courses which were under scrutiny 76.8% of the ability to name animal structures from diagrams was lost, 26.2% of the ability to identify technical terms was lost, and 20.7% of the general information in the courses was lost. But over the 15-month period there was an actual gain of 0.7% in the ability to apply biological principles to new situations, and a gain of 24.8% in the ability to interpret new and previously unfamiliar experiments. Any teacher might surely think these gains very startling indeed. In all probability they are not gains without practice. The likelihood is that they happen because, when a person has achieved some genuine insight or understanding, he tends to use it and apply it, and so to strengthen it (689).

From these and many similar experiments it is perfectly

clear that anything really understood tends to be remembered well and long, and to be forgotten slowly and partially. This is a most important and far-reaching finding. There is no psychological strategy whatsoever for getting people to remember masses of unrelated details for any considerable length of time. Nevertheless, there is a most effective and reliable answer to the great problem of forgetting. That answer is to try in every possible way to see that children and young people really understand what they learn and, indeed, learn by understanding.

2. Another very interesting and significant point that comes from the later studies of memorizing and forgetting—studies in which meaningful material is used—is that forgetting is largely a process of distortion or disorganization.

Children of three different age groups were set to work to memorize four poems whose thought-content was increasingly difficult. It was found that as the material to be learned increased in difficulty, the children came out with more and more striking distortions and inventions when they tried to recall it. The fourth and most difficult of the poems was as follows:

> I leant upon a coppice gate
>   When frost was silver gray;
> And winter's dregs made desolate
>   The weakening eye of day.
> The tangled vine stems scored the sky
>   Like strings of broken lyres,
> And all mankind that haunted nigh
>   Had sought their household fires.

This poem, like the other three, was memorized by the children. Then they were asked, "What is the poem all about?" Here are some of the answers made by the group of children whose average mental age was 140 months (11 years, 8 months).

"He lent a copper gate to somebody."

"A woman who walked a long way up hill. She rested on a gate and a far came out and hit her."

"A little girl leaning against a gate, looking out over the lake and listening to the birds."

"I leant against a coppice gate and heard a shoemaker singing."

Notice the sheer invention that goes on here. The author has called this process "creative memory." Some meaning is vaguely caught, but it is never clarified; and when the children are called upon to recall, they fill in the outlines more or less at their own sweet will and by free association, so as to make some kind of sense (491).

This shifting, and recombining, and muddling, and omitting, and inventing constantly goes on when we forget. Because of this process two perfectly honest witnesses will tell actually contradictory stories of an automobile accident that happened before their very eyes. Because of it two people who have listened to a debate will give quite different accounts of what was said, when it was said, and who said it. For forgetting is not a process of mere loss or subtraction, but of disorganization.

One investigator has presented an impressive list of the changes that take place when we forget. There may be *typification,* as when one or two details take on far more than their original importance, so that they come to stand for the entire original experience. There may be *analysis,* in which there is a shifting of clearness from one detail to another as time passes on. There may be *condensation,* in which items or events run together and combine. There may be *displacement,* in which the arrangement or order of items is altered. There may be *dramatization,* in which certain items are remembered as far more striking than they originally were. And there may be *secondary elaboration,* in which items are simply concocted or invented (132).

I would not wish to insist upon this listing of the kinds of change that occur in forgetting, or upon the names which the investigator has given them. But the essential point is that forgetting is the deterioration of meaning rather than mere loss of content. Outlines become blurred, interrelationships grow cloudy and shift about, mirages form, often in queer positions. Yet when we try to recall, we always try to make a response that will be as meaningful as possible. We always try to make some kind of sense. It may be a crazy and flimsy sort of sense that we make—a sense that could easily be blown to bits by a few well-directed questions. But our response always tends to have a certain coherence, and it is never entirely unrelated to the true sense of what we learned in the first place.

3. The third point that emerges from the studies of the forgetting of meaningful material can best be put in the form of a question. When anything has been truly understood, is it ever completely forgotten? This is a very interesting and challenging question, but it is a question that cannot be definitively answered. It cannot be proved experimentally that a person *never* completely forgets *anything* that he has learned via insight, simply because one learns a great many things and because "never" is a very long time. But it is most certainly true that meaningful learning is astonishingly permanent. This becomes very evident if, instead of considering a person's ability to recall what he has learned, one considers what happens when he undertakes to relearn what he has previously learned.

In one very striking experiment on the relearning of memorized material, the investigator served as his own subject. In 1915 this investigator memorized 21 items of material, each of which ran to about 100 words. After he had memorized these items so that he could repeat them perfectly, he put them away in a folder. Five years later, during which time he had not looked at or tried to recall these items, he had a friend take them out of the folder, and combine them with 21 very similar items. The investigator then tried to recite or reproduce the items he had learned. He was completely unable to do so. Then he looked over the 21 items previously learned mixed in with the 21 new items which his friend had added. Only in a very few cases did he have a vague notion which the old and previously learned ones were. Then he set to work to memorize all 42 items (21 old, 21 new), using the same memory technique that he had previously used. He saved 44% of time on relearning the old items over the time required to learn new items of the same type. So it is very clear that although he could not recall and could not recognize, something remained from the original learning over all these five years (747).

This case is exactly comparable to the instance of the investigator who relearned typewriting, and found that the relearning went much faster than the original learning after an interval of twenty-five years without any practice at all (310).

Considered by themselves these two experiments are slender evidence. But they correspond so well with what might be expected, and they have so much indirect confirmation, that their indications deserve to be taken very seriously. When a person has achieved a genuine insight, when he has established an intelligible way of dealing with and thinking about a situation or a challenge, that person is never quite the same again.

Consider, for instance, the students who took the experimental course in geometry which I have already described at some length. Very likely these students will, in future years, forget many details. Very likely certain confusions will build up in their minds. If ten years hence one of these students were asked to produce, at a moment's notice, a formal proof for the theorem of Pythagoras, he might not be able to do so. But still he will have established a way of understanding and of thinking about space relationships which, in all probability, he will never lose, which he could very soon bring to bear on any specific problem if he wanted to do so.

A child in school is taught how to make music with his voice or with an instrument, not as a painful spelling out of notes, but as the delivery of a meaningful and expressive pattern of sound. Later on he may seem to lose whatever technical skill he may have acquired. But his understanding of music, his ability to deal with and use it as it should be dealt with and used, and his capacity to take it up again whenever he likes will not be lost.

Students in high school come to a genuine realization of the momentous issues of the American Civil War, or of the influence of geography in shaping the destinies of our country. Names, dates, distances, the details of legal enactments may fade into a seeming oblivion, at least to the extent that they cannot be produced instantly on any and every occasion. But a way of thinking about, of feeling about, and of reacting to our national life will have been established which is probably inescapable for them.

All this shows very clearly what any teacher must emphasize if she wants to reckon realistically with the plain facts of learning. To stress details simply for the sake of remembering details is simply to assure rapid forgetting. As a matter of fact, details in isolation are never learned simply for the sake of keeping them in mind. When students, for example, prepare for a long objective test calling for scores or hundreds of purely factual items, they do not learn these items for the sake of storing them up indefinitely. *They learn the items for the sake of passing the test,* which is a perfectly reasonable and intelligible solution of the actual challenge before them.

Does this mean, then, that specific facts, precise information, exact techniques should receive no emphasis and no attention at all? Certainly not! The upward phase of the course of learning is from orientation towards the control of detail; but the control of detail confirms and defines the orientation. No insight, no explanation is adequate unless one sees how it works out in detail. If I am to understand how a navigator lays out a great circle course across the ocean, I must know how to solve spherical triangles; and to know how to solve spherical triangles I must work at using the proper formulae, and at developing skill in using the trigonometrical tables. Without a grasp of these details I do not really understand spherical triangles.

But it is one thing to try to memorize these details of procedure for the sake of passing a test, and quite another to study them in order to get clarity on a set of mathematical and physical relationships. In order to have even a glimmer of understanding of the social and political and strategic and economic problems of the Mediterranean I must have in my mind a rational and intelligible picture of the Mediterranean and its coasts. To create such a picture I must bring together many facts. But it is one thing to learn these facts as listed in a geography textbook, and quite another thing to learn them in the process of making a scale model of the Mediterranean basin on a sand table. Details, then, are necessary. But they are necessary, not in their own right, but because they are required to clarify and define understanding and insight, on which the permanence of learning depends.

4. Retroactive inhibition is a factor that is thought to account for a good deal of forgetting. For instance, a music teacher visits an elementary-school class on Monday, and drills them on how to find "do" in a certain key. Then she goes elsewhere for the rest of the week, and comes back to the class on Friday. On the previous Monday most of the children seemed to have learned the trick or formula for finding "do." But on Friday most of them have forgotten it. One important reason for this forgetting may be that the children have been learning a great many other things between the two visits of the music teacher. The effect of these interpolated learnings upon what the children learned from the music teacher on the Monday is what is called retroactive inhibition. So, to give a general definition, retroactive inhibition is the effect of new learnings interpolated between the original learning and its recall.

There has been considerable experimental work on retroactive inhibition, but the details of this work are of very limited significance for us. Beyond question there is such a thing as retroactive inhibition. If one wants to recall something an hour after one has learned it, one would do well to avoid filling the hour with various and sundry new learning tasks. There is reason to believe that if one can go to sleep immediately after learning something, one will remember it better when one wakes up than if one filled the time with all sorts of other doings. So the general fact itself cannot be questioned. Any new experience or learning task does have a tendency to work backwards, and to obliterate or at least haze over what was learned just previously.

Various rather futile attempts have been made to apply the experimental findings on retroactive inhibition to the organization of schoolwork. We teach a lesson in arithmetic, and then we pass on to spelling. We would like the arithmetic to stay learned, but there will be a tendency for the spelling to blot it out. Can psychology suggest any means or measures for eliminating or at least reducing this backward inhibition produced by any new learning? Would some rearrangement of the daily schedule help? Questions of this kind are often brought up and discussed at some length.

The answer to such questions is, in a sense, disappointing. At least it is disappointing to those who are looking for some quick, easy, and certain specific which will solve the practical problems of teaching. No superficial manipulation or rearrangement of the schedule will do anything worth-while to overcome what are supposed to be the baneful influences of retroactive inhibition. For retroactive inhibition is one of the most basic phenomena of all learning. We learn in response to a challenge. Learning consists in finding a way of dealing with that challenge by dint of whatever insight we can muster. At the moment when the way is effectively found, we have control of whatever details and minutiae are necessary; and we control these details and minutiae by understanding their relationship to the problem before us, and so being able to use them. But then we pass on to new situations, new problems, new challenges. In the very nature of things our previous learning cannot remain at concert pitch, although much of it may remain permanent, and although it may be readily recoverable. But the details and minutiae are sure to degenerate; and nothing can be done to prevent this because it is, after all, essential to the economy of learning and adjustment, because it frees us for the new challenges we must continually face.

If, then, a teacher emphasizes facts and skills in isolation and simply with the thought that they will be assimilated and retained, retroactive inhibition becomes an unavoidable nemesis. Our visiting music teacher perhaps teaches the finding of "do" in a given key as a purely routine act of skill. Then no conceivable rearrangement of the daily or weekly schedule will make the children remember more of this Monday lesson when Friday comes round. The children, in the Monday lesson, responded to the challenge of the teacher's pressure, and met it in a reasonable way. But once that challenge was removed, the later learnings obliterated practically all of the effects of the previous learning, or, at least, practically all of the effects that the teacher herself hoped might endure.

But let us suppose that our music teacher tries to enable children to get a better insight into key-relationships in music, as an important means for making their singing sound better and for making music itself more pleasurable and successful. Let us suppose, furthermore, that she introduces the specific problem of finding "do" as one particular and perhaps revealing application or illustration of the meaning of key-relationships in music. Then there is very good reason to expect that although the details of the trick of finding "do" may escape, the underlying principle (which is one of the operative principles of the musical art) will be clarified in the learners' minds, and that this clarification will resist the effects of interpolated learnings, which effects we call retroactive inhibition.

So long as we think of a lesson as a little clutch of more or less meaningless details, bound together by no interpretive idea or rationalizing principle, nothing can stop quick forgetting and the erosions of retroactive inhibition. But if we think of and plan lessons and units as organized activities in which children are helped to achieve understanding and insight, then the details and minutiae which are indeed necessary instrumentalities for understanding, but merely instrumentalities none the less, may fade away. But much will still remain.

EFFECTIVE LEARNING

The whole discussion in this chapter comes to a head in the question of how to make learning in school as effective as possible. Just what do we mean by "effective"? Our analysis of the course of learning makes a very clear answer possible. Effective learning is learning whose ascending phase rises as fast and as far as possible, and learning in which there is a minimum of vital loss during the downward phase of the course.

There can be no doubt that a great deal of learning in school is, in this sense, extremely ineffective. It goes far more slowly than it ought to go. It reaches far lower levels than it ought to reach and than it can reach, as is clearly shown by what can be accomplished by expert diagnostic teaching. And it fades away far more rapidly and completely than it should.

There are two general reasons for the ineffectiveness of school learning. (*a*) The first of these reasons is feeble and misdirected motivation. So long as the operative challenges before children turn on getting satisfactory marks on memory quizzes, it is futile to expect them to go far or fast in mastering the actual material with which they are dealing. Subject matter is effectively learned only when it is brought into contact with the challenges and problems of life, and when it is recognized as a means of reaching satisfactory solutions for those challenges and problems. (*b*) The second reason for ineffective school learning is inveterate emphasis on the wrong factors in the learning process. Unrelated facts and purely routine and unintelligible skills are never likely to be well and quickly learned and long retained. Teaching whose primary emphasis is on unrelated facts and uncomprehended skills is heading straight towards futility. It is worth-while noticing that these two defects interweave and interact, for a test-passing motivation makes directly for the unintelligent assimilation and the quick forgetting of details, whereas the study of material for the sake of finding significant solutions for vital problems has a strong tendency to give learning its true character of a quest and a discovery carried on by dint of insight.

There is no reason why these twin weaknesses of off-center motivation and emphasis on unrelated detail cannot be overcome. Nor is there any great mystery about what must be done to overcome them. Several instances of what must be done have already been given in this book. One of them is the instance of the children who were put in a situation where they came to want to sing, and who were helped by appropriate guidance to discover how to sing. Another is the instance of the college girl who wanted to write better English, and who became able to do so very quickly when she was helped to discover the chief source of her own difficulties. I will offer here two further examples from elementary-school work.

In a group of children whose ages ran from 5.5 to 9 years, 10 were rated "inartistic" and 4 were rated "artistic," the rating being made on tests of artistic performance and on the judgment of their teachers. All 10 "inartistic" children were given two years of special stimulation in the field of the visual arts. There were group activities and joint art projects. Free individual art expression was encouraged. When the children drew or painted they were given mild and helpful, positive criticism. They were given special help in the visual analysis of objects when they seemed to need it. They were taken on visits to art exhibitions. There were exhibitions of their own work. Arrangements were made for them to possess their own art materials, and to have those materials in their homes. The work of these children was carefully evaluated by expert judges, both before, during, and after the specially organized period of experience. These judges agreed that beyond all doubt profound and radical changes were produced in the "inartistic" children's capacity to draw and paint and otherwise express themselves in visual media, in their insight into and interest in art, and in their personal adjustment to school. The limiting factor in the case of the ten children who were rated "inartistic" did not seem to be heredity or lack of natural gift, for as a matter of fact the capacity of these children to deal with art problems was raised much above the average level. Inhibiting influences were inartistic and insensitive home environments, inexperience with drawing or experience of failure with drawing, and the use of improper and unfeasible materials which led to failure (566).

Again, the organization of work particularly in reading at the Speyer Experimental School (P.S. 500) in New York City, is an excellent instance of effective teaching and learning. A co-ordinated program was set up in this school, with a minimum of barriers between various subjects. There was a special concentration on reading, which was treated not merely as a special subject, but as one of the central concerns of all teachers working with the co-ordinated program. A wide variety of reading experiences was organized, many, if not most, of them more or less informal. The reading material was chosen so as to be interesting to the children—that is to say, it dealt with topics that were of concern to them, and treated those topics in a way that they could readily understand. At the same time, the reading experiences were not merely sporadic, but were related to the central-core ideas underrunning the whole curricular program. There was very little isolated reading material specifically chosen for the teaching of reading skills as such. The children were given instruction in proper methods of reading, but such instruction was not extensive or heavily emphasized.

Under this plan six groups of dull-normal children, with I.Q.'s running from 75 to 90, made from 8 to 13 months normal progress in 3 months, and a reading-disability group made 13 months normal progress in 3 months. Most of these children had transferred in from other public schools. Since they were below average ability, they had experienced much frustration and humiliation, as often happens. The teaching at most of the schools from which they came was routine in character and poorly organized, and had produced a whole array of bad attitudes. Under the new regime the children not only made very rapid improvement in reading ability, but also their attitudes towards school and learning were transformed (207).

In these instances the following conditions are present. (*a*) A strong positive motivation is established. The children are led to set up goals in which they can find real satisfactions, and the fulfillment of genuine personal needs. (*b*) These goals are defined and underlined by bringing to the children the genuine prospect and the early experience of success. (*c*) The emphasis of the teaching is not upon routine drill, the accumulation of detailed facts, or the acquisition of routine skills, but upon helping the children to discover how to achieve the goals that they desire to achieve.

The effect of such teaching upon the ascending phase of the course of learning is clear and evident. Improvement goes much faster and much further than under standard, routine teaching. What happens afterwards is a matter of guesswork, but it is hard to believe that forgetting, loss, and decline would not be minimized. Notice that in such teaching, specifics are not ignored or slighted, but are treated as means for the attainment of ends, which is how specifics always should be treated. Notice, too, that when the material of the curriculum is learned as it was in these instances, it has a profound transforming effect on the whole personality.

QUESTIONS FOR DISCUSSION

1. A certain teacher of English was to organize the study of Shakespeare's *Hamlet*. He began with some very general discussions of the play, read various excerpts, and worked to give the class a

general impression of the whole. This phase of the teaching lasted for three class periods, during which the teacher did not seem interested in having any specific items or details clearly grasped or remembered. Was this a good way to begin? Why? Was this approach similar in a psychological sense to that of the geometry teacher described in the third discussion question for Chapter 5?

2. Here are four actual lesson and assignment topics. (*a*) Chapter nine of the textbook. (*b*) Problems 1–10 on page 96 of the algebra textbook. (*c*) The chief results of the American Civil War. (*d*) How men of past ages told the time. Do any of the four seem to you to be true "qualitative wholes"? If so, which? Also why?

3. A teacher is presenting a lesson in history. During the lesson she reflects that the pupils are sure to forget a good deal of it quite soon. Should she ignore the thought? Should she entertain the private conviction that the lesson is not worth teaching? Should she try to do something about the prospective forgetting, and if so, what?

4. Whenever one has a great deal of material to learn, there is always a temptation to learn it bit by bit, mastering each "bit" as thoroughly as possible before passing on to the next. Is this a good plan or a bad one? Why? What might be an alternative plan?

5. It is often claimed that slow-learning pupils must learn by sheer routine drill, without being encouraged or helped to understand. One reason given for this claim is that in numerous experiments, the brighter subjects have been found to learn better by the "whole method" while the duller subjects learn better by the "part method." Is the rather sweeping inference drawn from these experimentally ascertained data really legitimate?

6. Some psychologists have asserted that once we have really learned anything, we never forget it, even though we may not be able to recall it completely at any given moment. Discuss this idea.

7. In this chapter it is argued that the natural sequence of learning is from orientation to detail. Is there any relationship between this idea and the claim made in the preceding chapter that we learn by insight?

8. Most courses in school and college are pointed very definitely towards tests and examinations. Do you find in this any suggestion

which might help to explain why so much of the content of these courses is forgotten?

9. How might one go about "structuralizing the field" in connection with (*a*) a lesson on specific gravity (*b*) a lesson on quadratic equations (*c*) a lesson on the Missouri Compromise (*d*) starting a child on piano study (*e*) trying to get an aggressive child to learn a better adjustment to the school?

SUGGESTED READINGS

Crossland, H. R., *A Qualitative Analysis of the Process of Forgetting.* Psychological Monographs, XXIX (1921), No. 1, Whole No. 130.

Katona, G., "The Role of Order of Presentation in Learning." *American Journal of Psychology*, LV (1942), 328–353.

Mursell, James L., and Glenn, Mabelle, *The Psychology of School Music Teaching*, 2nd ed. Silver Burdett Company, New York, 1936, Chap. 4.

Tyler, Ralph W., "The Relation between Recall and the Higher Mental Processes," in C. H. Judd, *Education as Cultivation of the Higher Mental Processes*, Harcourt, Brace and Company, New York, 1934, 12–16.

8

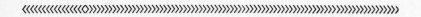

Intellectual, Motor, and Social Learning

KINDS OF LEARNING

ARE THERE different kinds of learning? In one sense, yes! There are obvious differences between learning the binomial theorem and learning to swim, or between learning how to behave in a social situation and studying a history assignment. But how deep do these differences go? Are they only on the surface, or do they amount to actual differences in the learning process itself? That is how the problem defines itself.

It is a very practical problem. When we ask whether there are fundamentally different kinds of learning we are also, in effect, asking whether there are fundamentally different kinds of good teaching, since "teaching" is the business of helping people to learn better than they would or could by themselves. If there are different kinds of learning, then there are basic differences in principle between the best way of coaching a football squad, teaching art appreciation, teaching Latin, teaching woodworking, and teaching a bewildered and refractory youngster how to deal constructively with the demands of the school. But if the learning process is always fundamentally the same, and if the differences are only superficial, then the basic principles of good teaching are also always the same in all situations. This is how the issue needs to be understood.

The general answer has already been anticipated in previous chapters, but now we are to develop it explicitly and in more detail. We shall see that the learning process is always the same in all situations, that there is only one kind of learning in the ultimate sense, that we always learn in one way. In this chapter I shall develop the above proposition in connection with intellectual learning, which includes memorizing and rational learning, and in connection with motor learning and social learning. In the next chapter I shall discuss emotional learning. Emotional learning needs a chapter to itself for three reasons. First, it is very important; second, it is not usually well understood; third, it is the crucial point of the whole issue about kinds of learning.

MEMORIZING

Let us begin by considering memorizing. "Memorizing" is a loose and inexact term. Sometimes it is stretched to mean almost the same thing as "learning" itself. But operationally the term "memorizing" is used for what is often supposed to be a special and distinct type of learning, and particularly a type of learning set off against what is often called "rational learning." One memorizes the exact words of a prose passage in contrast to learning to understand its content. One memorizes the "multiplication facts" in contrast to learning to understand the process of multiplication. One memorizes the symbols of chemical formulae or the postulates of geometry in contrast to acquiring an insight into what the formulae or the postulates mean. Even here the distinction is none too clear. One cannot quite keep memorizing on one side of a fence and rational learning on the other, for even when one memorizes rather mechanically, one usually understands more or less. But still there is often supposed to be a fundamental difference between memorizing and rational learning.

Moreover, it has been shown very incisively and impressively that memorizing and rational learning do not by any means always go together in schoolwork. In an investigation at Ohio State University and the University of Arkansas, tests of various kinds were developed in connection with a number of subjects. Agricultural engineering, botany, business organization, chemistry, economics, geography, history, home economics, statistics, and zoology were the curricular fields considered. The tests were of three types, and were intended to reveal (*a*) the student's knowledge of the facts presented in the courses (*b*) the student's knowledge of the facts together with his understanding of how those facts would apply to new situations (*c*) the student's ability to draw inferences from the facts presented in the courses. Several hundred students were involved in the study, and the general outcome was to show a fairly slender relationship between these three types of ability. (The actual correlations ran from .20 to .51.) The inference was that the memorizing of facts is a different process from the understanding of facts, or more generally, that the "lower" or routine mental processes are essentially different from the "higher" mental processes (357).

The actual findings of this study were, of course, exactly as reported. But the inferences drawn from these findings, and the interpretations put upon them are open to a great deal of question.

1. It is quite true that there were low correlations between being able to reproduce facts on call, and being able to apply those facts or to draw inferences from them (which is tantamount, of course, to understanding them). But still, all the correlations were positive and significant. There was what one commentator calls a "distressingly low" relationship between these abilities (690, p. 200–201). Yet the relationship existed,

whether it distresses us or not. An outcome of the investigation which bears directly on this point was that students might often know a great many facts without seeming to understand them very well. This in itself could account for the low correlations. What the investigation does *not* show is that students who understood very well knew very little. A person might be a mine of *memoriter* information and yet have very little insight. Possibly! But could he have much genuine insight with very little information? That was not established, and on general principles it seems very doubtful.

2. The investigators thought that students who were able to reel off many facts from their courses, but who were not able to interpret or apply those facts were not using their "higher mental processes." But this does not follow at all. There can be a great deal of skill and cleverness in memorizing a body of material without pondering much about its deeper and wider significance. Every commercial memory system is founded on this truth. Every experienced actor knows that there are numerous tricks, some of them obvious, some of them subtle, which help to make a person what is called a "quick study." Many students who came out with an excellent memory knowledge of facts, but with little insight may have been very smart indeed in their ways of memorizing those facts. They may, for instance, have had the advantage of intensive coaching sessions in fraternity houses. Such measures and devices are certainly not profound intellectual processes. But they *are* intellectual processes nevertheless. Students who used clever methods of memorization were not using their "higher mental processes" as their teachers no doubt hoped they would. But they were using higher mental processes just the same. No one can be sure that such things happened, for the investigators made no inquiries about them. But the probability is that they did happen in a good many cases.

3. The investigators who made the study never seemed to ask *why* so many students were able to recall numerous facts

without understanding those facts. But this is an absolutely vital question, for learning always takes place in response to a challenge. What, then, was the challenge? Here again one has to guess, but guessing is not very difficult. Surely the challenge which produced so much purely factual learning was the desire to get a good mark, which could be had by parrot-like reproduction and a minimum of insight. Perhaps it is not necessary to demonstrate that this is exactly the sort of challenge projected by a great deal of teaching, whether the teacher means to project such a challenge or not. Yet demonstration is available. Twenty-five years ago an extensive study of history examinations set by teachers revealed a tremendous emphasis on sheer factual knowledge. In this study over 56,000 teacher-made examination questions in history were examined, and by far the greatest number of these questions had to do with information pure and simple (503).

Now the securing of a good or, at least, a passing mark is a very cogent goal which stems from deep and powerful basic needs. If we define the method of attaining such a goal as the temporary memorizing of masses of facts, what else can we expect students to do? In terms of such a goal, meditation and reflection become a waste of time. In fact, meditation and reflection might even be considered stupid, as, indeed, they are considered at certain cramming schools. Thus students who build up a big *memoriter* knowledge of facts may be using their higher mental processes very well, and displaying a ruthless and effective cleverness. And if teachers find the outcome disconcerting, whose fault is that?

There is nothing new in the discovery that students may do well in school tests, and yet be unable to bring what they have learned to bear on the life situations to which it is supposed to apply. In fact, this was strikingly revealed in one of the earliest educational research studies ever undertaken. Practices in the teaching of spelling were investigated in a very large number of schools, involving more than 33,000 pupils. The time devoted to spelling ranged from 10–15 minutes daily in some schools, and up to 40–50 minutes daily in others. But when dictation and composition tests were given—that is, when the children were called upon to *use* their spelling in a normal way—there was no discernible difference at all, in spite of the great differences in time spent (543). However, it is very likely that the children who were drilled more intensively and longer did better on the formal school tests in spelling, although the study does not bring this out.

Let us now pull the threads of this discussion together in a general summary statement. Memorizing is not a special kind of learning. It has the same basic characteristics as all learning.

a) We memorize in order to deal with a challenge. We do not memorize "in general," or simply to store the mind with information. We memorize a telephone number when we look it up so that we can dial the number without looking at the telephone book while we do so. We memorize a street address so that we can go there without referring to something jotted on a card. An actor memorizes a part in a play so that he can carry it through on the stage in a seemingly natural manner. A research worker memorizes his own data and the data of other investigators (though he usually does so in an informal, but still effective way) so that he can have the material in mind to think about. A man who is writing a section of a book on history half-memorizes masses of facts, although he still relies greatly on his notes, so that he can co-ordinate everything in an organized statement. So, too, children in school do not memorize for the sake of memorizing. They *ought* to memorize in order to solve problems, or to reach conclusions, or to think through a body of evidence, or for some such reason. The trouble is that their work is often set up so that they memorize primarily to pass tests.

b) The actual process of memorization depends just as much on insight as does any other type of learning. The best way to memorize material is always to understand that material, or to think about it, or to structuralize it, whichever expression seems most suitable. The worst way to memorize material is to go over and over it with a minimum of insight. Indeed, if there is no insight, no structuralization at all, it is likely that there is no memorization. Preparing for a conventional memory test does not make for the most efficient memorizing, although it does not wholly rule out the use of clever devices and the application of skill. But usually when students prepare for such a test, organization and structuralization are at a minimum, and the students are not encouraged or helped to think the material through, to co-ordinate it clearly in their minds, or to structuralize it effectively. That is why preparation for such tests seems to involve "lower" rather than "higher" mental processes, whereas what it really involves is apt to be nothing more nor less than inefficient learning. For memory itself does not belong in a special class of "lower," or merely routine, mental processes.

RATIONAL LEARNING

Now let us turn to another type of learning, namely rational learning. The term "rational learning" is very widely used, but it is not too exactly defined, and perhaps, indeed, it cannot be. To say that rational learning means *learning to think* is a sufficiently accurate description. At first sight, learning to think seems a fundamentally different affair from memorizing. But what has already been said about memorizing indicates that the difference does not go right down to the root of the matter. That this is certainly true we shall see clearly as we consider the nature and management of rational learning.

The importance of rational learning lies in the fact that it makes behavior flexible and efficient.

If you put a hungry hen on one side of a fifteen-foot length of wire fence and scatter corn on the other side, the hen will dash at the fence, beat her wings against it, rush back and forth for short distances, but it will be a long time before she finds her way around it. If you continue to do this every day, using the same fence in the same place, after a time the hen will learn to run around the fence very quickly when she sees the corn. But now if you put her in a new place and substitute a wooden picket fence for the wire fence, her previous experience will not help her much. She will go through the same old round of fluttering her wings against the fence, dashing against it, running back and forth along it until finally she happens to find her way around. Each new fence in a new place is a completely new experience for her because she is responding only to the individual items—the particular fence, the particular place. But to a human being, even to a child, the two situations would have so much in common with each other and with other previous experiences of a like nature that they would present but few difficulties. A child of three or an ape will pile boxes one on another in order to secure an object that is beyond his reach, but a goat sees no relationship between a box that he could easily push into position and food that is too high for him to secure (232, pp. 358–359).

The ability to think about a situation, or to understand it, or to grasp its general aspects is, of course, basically inborn. Hens and goats can generalize to some extent, but only to a very limited extent. Apes can generalize more extensively, and human beings can generalize enormously more extensively. But even the most brilliant and gifted of human beings will not generalize and think nearly as extensively or as well as they could unless they learn to do so; and they will not get very far with such learning unless they are taught. So one of the supreme functions of the school is to teach people to think; or to put the idea in somewhat more formal language, one of the supreme functions of the school is to organize and guide the process of rational learning.

Imagine a primitive savage who had the inborn mental ability of a genius, but who could not read, or write, or use arithmetic. In spite of his great natural ability this man would seem to us a very limited and even stupid person. He would not be able to plan his day because he could not tell the time. He would not be able to plan a journey very well because he would have very vague ideas about distance. He would not be able to make well-considered and intelligent business agreements because he could not keep records. If some difficult problem came up in the life of his tribe, he would not be able to deal with it in the light of past experience, because he would have none of that grasp of past experience which we call a knowledge of history or of social development and practice. He would have no definite standards of economic value, because he would have no monetary system with which to measure value. If you tried to convince him that mosquitoes cause malaria, he would probably refuse to believe you, because any notions he might have about the causes of sickness would be quite fantastic. Potentially this man might be able to live a very intelligent life. But actually he would live a very stupid life, because although he had the innate ability to think well, he did not possess the tools and implements which we need for thinking.

Now the school curriculum is a storehouse of tools and implements for thinking, and the school itself is a workshop where young people learn to use these tools. That, at least, is what the school ought to be, and what it is really intended to be, although it does not function in this way as well as it should. It is quite true that we tend very strongly to think that school subjects ought to be learned "for their own sake." In actual practice this means learning school subjects in order to pass tests. Of course, if we sit down and really face the question in our own minds, we are not likely to say to ourselves that children should learn subjects in school merely to pass tests in those subjects; but we tend to act as though we thought so, which is the important thing.

Obviously the idea is completely wrong. To "know" mathematics means to understand mathematics; and to understand mathematics means being able to use mathematics when one buys on the installment plan, or places a mortgage, or reads advertising claims about averages and percentages, and in countless other situations. To know the history of the United

States means to understand the history of the United States, so that one has a personal point of view, an informed and intelligent personal "philosophy" when one makes up one's mind about political, or social, or economic issues. To know a foreign language means to understand that language, so that one can use it for one's own enjoyment or instruction, or to communicate with others.

So, in general, one knows a subject only in so far as one understands it, which means being able to use it as a tool for living. To return for a moment to our uninstructed primitive savage, the great thing that the school could do for him would not be to stuff him with conventional information so that he could get passing marks in his courses and a diploma at the end of them, but to equip him with the means of thinking, so that he could live a more intelligent life. One learns a subject only by thinking about it. One knows a subject only by understanding it. And when one understands a subject it ceases to be an end in itself, and becomes a means of making personality more flexible and behavior more effective. Hence the enormous importance of rational learning and the teaching of rational learning.

Rational learning is often subdivided into the learning of problem-solving and the learning or acquisition of concepts, and I shall follow along with this classification. However, in dealing with problem-solving and the acquisition of concepts we are simply looking at the same process from two different perspectives. So most of what is to be said about problem-solving applies also to the acquisition of concepts.

Problem-solving

From what has already been said it is clear that the process of problem-solving is of the utmost importance in education. We want to develop *thinking people*—people who deal with the problems and issues of life by means of reflection and understanding. Moreover, the central value of subject matter is that it provides the necessary tools for dealing with the problems and issues of life. It follows, therefore, that subjects should be taught and learned in and through their bearing upon problems which require solution. Problem-solving is not one special phase of mathematics, set off against the memorization of formulae and proofs. It is the very heart of mathematics. History should not be taught as a body of facts to be learned by heart, but as a body of insights and interpretations which bear upon issues of personal feeling and action and of social policy. So the intelligent promotion of rational learning in general, and of problem-solving in particular, is one of the school's most crucial tasks.

Yet this crucial task is ill-handled. So much is all too clear from a great many investigations. One typical investigation dealt with the question of how pupils solve problems in arithmetic. Twelve problems were taken from a number of seventh-grade arithmetic textbooks, and were restated in various forms. Sometimes a problem would be put in simple everyday language, sometimes in technical language. Sometimes the statement of the problem would contain all the data needed for its solution and no more. Sometimes additional irrelevant data were included.

These problems in their various forms were given to 9,256 pupils in grades six and eight. The language in which the problem was expressed made some difference in achievement, but not a great deal. In general, the pupils did best when problems were stated in the language of the textbook. Irrelevant data were very confusing. Enormous numbers of wrong and futile responses were made. Moreover, most of these wrong responses were "stupid" errors, i.e. they were responses which showed no gleam of understanding as to how to attack the problem or what was involved in it. The investigator goes so far as to say that very few of these children seemed to reason about the problems at all. "Indeed many of them appear to perform almost random calculations upon the numbers given. Where they do solve a problem correctly, the response seems to be attained largely by habit" (459).

This is a familiar story in all courses where problems are set up to be solved. In geometry, for instance, tests are usually organized so that they can be passed by means of *memoriter* knowledge, although geometry can only be learned by thinking, and is only useful when it is understood. Once again, a distinguished commentator has remarked that while a great deal of talk goes on about the importance of thinking in the teaching of science, most science textbooks are classified compendia of facts (357). There is no need to go further in demonstrating what is all too obvious, namely that problem-solving, in spite of its vital importance, is poorly taught and poorly learned.

How can these weaknesses be corrected, if they can be corrected at all? How can problem-solving be taught and learned effectively? There are two major points to be kept in mind.

1. *Problem-solving starts with a problem!* This may seem a superlatively obvious statement. Yet as things go in school work, it is a statement that needs to be made, understood, and kept continually in mind.

What is a problem? "A problem exists for an individual when he has a definite goal that he cannot reach by the behavior patterns which he already has available. Problem solving occurs when there is an obstruction of some sort to the attainment of an objective" (208, p. 467). This answers our question as well as need be. Now let us see how the reply bears on the kind of problems presented to children in school. Here is an instance. "Find the amount of a bill for 3½ yards of material at 40¢ a yard, and for 10 yards at 80¢ per yard." This is one of the problems used in the study of problem-solving in arithmetic which was mentioned above. The children who attempted it dealt with it in no fewer than 80 different ways, only 18 of which showed any comprehension of how the numbers ought to be combined to get a solution (459).

The thing that instantly impresses one about this instance is that the so-called "problem" was not really a problem at all for most of the children who attempted it. What was the "goal" which these children could not "reach by the behavior patterns which" they "had available"—the "objective" the attainment of which they found obstructed? They were not buying "material" or spending their own money. Fundamentally they did not care about the outcome. These children were simply put in a situation where they found themselves coerced to manipulate numbers. The adventure in problem-solving was a hopeless failure for the very simple reason that there was no real problem to solve.

For many years psychologists have insisted that problems must have the quality of *genuineness* if they are to be of value in teaching problem-solving. Those problems, in other words, must be related to impelling goals and basic needs. They must be personal problems, not mere empty jugglings. This instantly rules out an enormous amount of the material found in conventional textbooks—clock problems, bathtub-filling problems, train-collision problems, angle problems, and the like. To speak very bluntly, a great deal of this material is sheer pedagogical trash. Pupils will certainly not learn problem-solving from using it, for the reason that it consists of spurious and unreal problems (666).

Yet genuine and impelling problems certainly can be found, unless indeed we are prepared to believe that subject matter has no reference beyond itself and no meaning that is not limited to the textbook. For instance, in one school situation the use of decimals was taught in connection with school banking, the keeping of spelling records, the making of tooth powder, the planning of gardens, and a number of similar activities (264). Just such genuinely problematic situations and opportunities can be found in great profusion in connection with the teaching of natural science, of the social studies, and indeed in relation to all the subjects of the curriculum. The daily press, magazine articles, advertising displays, automobiles (with their gasoline consumption), bicycles (with their gear ratios), electric fixtures, heating plants, ventilating systems, and so on without end, provide endless challenges to problematic thinking. It has been very well said that one need only turn over a rotten log or look at a running brook to find enough scientific problems to keep one thinking and learning indefinitely.

Genuine problems stare at us from every side, and the material of the curriculum is the array of instrumentalities devised by man for the intelligent solution of these problems. To the psychologist, who perhaps must always remain a little naïve, it seems astonishing that in a world so crammed with interest and challenge, pedagogs can think of nothing better than empty and trivial verbal manipulations when they propose to inculcate problem-solving. If we propose to take the teaching of problem-solving seriously, the first step is to recognize the myriad genuine problems that surround us clamoring for recognition, and to reveal them to the children as things worth thinking about and comprehending.

2. *Problem-solving is experimentation.* The first, and by far the biggest, step in teaching problem-solving is to set up genuine problems. But also it is necessary to understand the process of solution, and to guide that process properly. All the investigations on this subject go to show that the solution of a genuine problem is not usually very systematic, or focalized, or even in a sense very logical. Solutions are found by accumulating material in one's mind and molding and shaping that material, by a search which may take us up many a blind alley, by picking up a hint here and an intimation there, and following these hints and intimations to see where they lead. In a word, problem-solving is an adventure in experimentation, in search and research, and it must be so understood and treated if it is to go aright (290, 517).

Thus problem-solving may take time, perhaps much time, for it requires accumulation, structuralization, meditation, and the emergence of insight. For this reason the pressure of a close schedule can ruin the whole process. Anything one can do to clarify essential issues and to help learners to discover crucial elements—and this means using such measures and devices as graphs, concrete applications, outlining, tabulating, note-making, prediscussion, and so forth—can very well help. At the same time there is a very great danger of oversystematization when we try to teach pupils how to solve problems. Some well-intentioned persons have drawn up quite elaborate schedules of questions which a child is supposed always to ask himself and to answer when he attacks a new problem. What is given? What is to be proved? What information do I already have? What more information do I need? What is the central point of the demonstration? These are some of the typical questions included in such schedules. There are two troubles with many devices of this sort: (*a*) they are far too rigid (*b*) they tend to place the emphasis on the process of solution without considering the far more vital issue of the genuineness and cogency of the problem itself.

As a matter of fact, the essential conditions for the effective teaching of problem-solving can be very simply put. *Have a genuine problem, and do everything possible to help the children to experiment with it.* That this is sound psychological doctrine there can be no doubt at all. Also, there is no doubt that under the organized conditions of conventional school work the precept is difficult to apply. Tight schedules, routine drills, and the demand to cover a stated amount of ground in a stated time are the deadly enemies of problem-solving in particular and of rational learning and thinking in general. Yet it must be remembered that one genuine problem solved by genuine experimentation will do far more to teach the realities of problem-solving than a hundred verbalistic trivialities.

Formation of concepts

The acquisition of concepts is another aspect of rational learning. When we deal with a problem, we find a solution for a specific difficulty or puzzle. When we acquire a concept, we learn a general idea which can be brought to bear on many situations. Problems are solved by selecting and applying the right concepts, and concepts are acquired and understood largely in connection with problem-solving. So problem-solving and the acquisition of concepts are very closely interrelated, although they are sufficiently different to call for separate consideration. Both of them, to repeat, are aspects of rational learning. In the one case we deal with rational learning as the process of coping with a challenge; in the other case we deal with rational learning as the process of establishing general interpretations, or constellations of ideas. It follows that a great deal of what was said about problem-solving holds true also of the acquisition of concepts (282–289, 325, 605).

1. A concept is a tool of thought and a guide for action and behavior. In order to see that this is so, all one has to do is to name a few concepts. Multiplication, fair play, conservation of natural resources, the industrial revolution, and so forth are essentially insights, interpretations of a great wealth and variety of specific experience. They help us by establishing ways of thinking and by showing us what to choose and what to do.

A person is planning a camping trip which will take him away from civilization for a week. How much food must he take along? If his mentality were on the level of a primitive savage, this would probably be a difficult question. He might have to solve it by actually piling up his supplies and estimating from the size of the pile whether he had enough. But since he has no doubt been well taught in an elementary school, he can jot down how much he needs for each meal, remember that he will need twenty-one meals, and bring the concept of multiplication to bear. Another person sees an advertisement saying that one brand of cigarette has a slightly lower percentage of nicotine than another, and if his concept of percentage is in good working order he can interpret the statement for what it is worth and draw his own conclusions. Yet another person is approached by certain interests who want to put up a dam in one of the national parks. The intelligence of his response—and please notice that his response involves feeling and action as well as intellectual understanding—will depend a good deal on how just and adequate his concept of conservation happens to be.

I could easily go on with innumerable similar illustrations, but there is no need to do so, for you can readily find them for yourself. The point is that a concept is not just an intellectual abstraction, but a working tool. This is why the acquisition of concepts is so important in anybody's education, and why the concepts in terms of which anybody operates have so much to do with the shaping of his personality.

2. The formation of concepts is a dynamic process. In this respect it is exactly like problem-solving. No one learns problem-solving unless he deals with genuine problems. No one really forms concepts unless he is dealing with situations that he wants to interpret and understand. We do not learn meanings by memorizing definitions. Nor do we learn meanings by just being "exposed" to experiences. The street cleaners in Williamsburg, Virginia are exposed to many fine examples of Georgian architecture, but it is pretty certain that some of them, at least, never establish the concept of Georgian architecture.

From this piece of analysis we can derive several important working principles for teachers to use.

a) The only way children (and older people, too) ever really acquire concepts is by dealing with situations which they want to deal with, and trying to find out how to manage those situations better. An elementary-school chorus was preparing for a public performance. The children knew, and the teacher also knew, that the songs were not sounding any too well, in spite of a good deal of rehearsal. The music supervisor was called in to help, and introduced just one working concept, the concept of the musical phrase. The concept acted as a guideline, as properly understood concepts always do, and although perfection was not achieved there was a very prompt, very marked, and very gratifying improvement.

b) To understand a concept is to be able to use it. In a certain social studies textbook there is quite an interesting and well-written passage describing the interior of a typical log cabin of the Colonial period. One thing the author mentions is the crane which stood over the fireplace to hold the cooking pot (the pot, however, is not mentioned). A number of high-school students were asked to make sketches of the interior scene from the description; and in many of these sketches the crane turned out to be a bird (320). You should always, therefore, remember that *words are very deceptive.* A person may be able to use the right language for a concept, and yet not really understand it at all.

c) It has been shown that people grasp the meaning of concepts best when they are able to work with numerous simple illustrations and applications. This has been shown very convincingly in several experiments. In one of these experiments the subjects were set to work to learn a number of concepts which consisted of various patterns of Chinese word-symbols. The subjects learned these concepts by identifying each of the symbol-patterns when it was combined with other irrelevant symbols. It was found that the concept was always grasped most quickly and most surely when the application material itself was made as simple as possible (325). Much of the art of effective teaching turns on organizing and presenting simple, concrete, interesting material by working with which children can come to acquire clear and adequate general meanings or concepts.

d) We do not learn concepts by verbalization, yet verbalization is important. It has been pointed out that many of the social concepts that children are expected to acquire in certain schools are definitely too difficult for them. Two of the concepts I have already mentioned are among those probably beyond the range of elementary-school children, according to this study. These are the concepts of conservation and of the industrial revolution (448). When teachers, with the best of intentions, try to get children to learn such concepts, all that happens is that the children verbalize and recite, without really knowing what they are talking about.

From such experiences has come an idea that verbalization is a bad thing in itself. This is by no manner of means the case. To be sure, a mere knowledge of words will not help one to think well or to act intelligently. But words define and fix meanings, and enable one to manipulate meanings, once those meanings have been acquired. You can see the importance and the function of words from a very simple and common experience. You are driving across the country, and you see before you a range of mountains. "What are those mountains?" you ask. You want to know their name. The mountains, of course, would be just the same whatever their name might be, or even if they had no name. But your reaction to them is not the same when you do and do not know what their name is. Monsieur Jourdain in the French play was delighted when he discovered that he was speaking *prose*. He had been talking prose all his life; but he felt that he had made quite a discovery when he found out what it was that he had been talking.

e) The acquisition of concepts is of central importance in all teaching and all learning. A date in history is a concept. The "passive voice" in grammar is a concept. "Mortise and tenon joint" is a concept. Addition is in one sense a concept. The "French Revolution" is a concept. So it goes. Much, and perhaps even most, of the real stuff that children ought to get out of their studies is made up of concepts. When we say that teachers should always be trying to help children acquire well-understood, helpful, operating concepts from the subjects those children study, we are calling for something very different from the *memoriter* learning of the words of a textbook. The teaching of concepts calls for something quite different from conventional drills and recitations; yet it can be accomplished.

And the importance of the acquisition of concepts lies in the two facts that concepts tend to be lasting, and that they are guidelines for thought and action and tools for living.

MOTOR LEARNING

Such undertakings as the learning of handwriting, or typewriting, or tennis, or swimming seem very different from the learning of arithmetic, or English composition, or history. So a sharp distinction is often drawn between motor learning and intellectual learning. This distinction seems so obvious and inevitable that it is a test case for our proposition that the actual process of learning is always the same, however different its external appearances are in different situations. Moreover, the practical issues stand out very clearly; for if motor learning is fundamentally different from intellectual learning, then the effective coaching of a motor skill involves basically different procedures from the procedures in effectively teaching such school subjects as mathematics, language, or the social studies. If, on the other hand, the contrast between motor and intellectual learning is only apparent and not real, then a good tennis coach should use the same working principles as a good science teacher. From everything we know, it would seem that this second alternative is the true one.

1. The key to all motor learning is the establishment of co-ordinated or organized movement. This has been shown again and again, and it was brought out very clearly in some of the earliest studies of motor learning. More than fifty years ago a brilliant and illuminating investigation was made of the acquisition of the "telegraphic language," i.e. the sending and receiving of the Morse code on the telegraph key. The outstanding result of this investigation was that a person who is learning the "telegraphic language" goes through a number of stages of efficiency in his co-ordinations. First of all, he has to learn the twenty-six separate letters as patterns of dots and dashes. This takes a great deal of practice, and for a long time

he has to think of each letter and to spell out each word when he uses the key. Then a time arrives when he finds quite suddenly that he can form whole words without thinking of the separate letters. This wordwise telegraphic sending improves for a while, and may persist for a good many weeks. But sooner or later a better co-ordination takes its place, and again is likely to do so quite suddenly. Now the learner is able to form whole phrases without attending to the separate words, just as he could previously form words without attending to the separate letters. So the investigation identified three levels of efficiency in co-ordination, the *letter* level, the *word* level, and the *phrase* level. So long as the learner is on the letter level, he can only improve to a limited extent, and any great advance in speed and accuracy depends on his getting to the word level. So long as he is on the word level he is limited once again, and he must get onto the phrase level to make any very marked advance (98, 99).

The authors of this investigation called the three levels of efficiency a "habit hierarchy," and believed that the very essence of motor learning was the achievement of superior levels in a "hierarchy," or graded sequence, of increasingly efficient "habits," or co-ordinations. As motor learning has come to be better understood, the notion of a series of definite levels, i.e. a hierarchy of co-ordinations has been more or less abandoned. But the basic idea has never been changed. When a person learns to typewrite, or to play tennis, or to swim, or indeed to perform any skilled physical action, his improvement depends on his establishment of a better and better focalized and organized pattern of action, even though he does not go through any such definite and separated stages as were indicated in the learning of the Morse code.

This idea of improvement as dependent on better centered and co-ordinated action lies at the very heart of all really expert coaching of physical skills. For instance, the modern teaching of penmanship does not center upon drill on imitating letter forms from a copybook model, or even the exact position of the arm, the wrist, the hand, and the fingers. Instead, the stress is put on acquiring an easy, fluent, economical pattern of action (304, Chap. 19). Penmanship, of course, is what might be called a small-scale motor skill. But the same principle of trying to help the learner to acquire a well-centered, easy, economical flow of action applies to the coaching of any and every motor skill, such as golf, tennis, tackling at football, swimming, and so forth.

One cannot say that the learner goes through a series of self-contained stages arranged in an ascending order, or hierarchy, of efficiency. But his improvement certainly depends on "rationalizing" the pattern of action, or, to use a term already familiar to us, on better and better structuralization. It has, in fact, been very truly pointed out that what we call a motor skill is really intelligence expressing itself in physical action. From this it follows that improvement in the learning of a motor skill does not depend primarily on polishing up and perfecting separate details, but on shaping up the whole pattern of movement so that it achieves the desired end with a minimum of wastefulness and a maximum of well-centered control (236).

2. Thus the actual process by which a motor skill is acquired is a process of discovering a better and better method of doing what one is trying to do. There are many ways in which the process of discovery can take place.

a) Sometimes a learner will discover an improved method, and thus achieve an improvement simply by repeated, strongly motivated trials. This is exactly what happened with the subjects in the investigation on learning the telegraphic language to which I have already referred. First the subjects learned the Morse code letters. Then they practiced for days and weeks spelling out words on the key, letter by letter. Quite suddenly a new co-ordination came in, a new way of handling the key was discovered, for within the course of just a few practice periods these subjects found themselves able to deal with material wordwise instead of letterwise.

The authors of the investigation believed and maintained that such long plodding with a relatively inferior co-ordination was the only way of discovering a better action-pattern, but later studies have shown that there are usually other and better ways of making this essential discovery. For instance, the dot-dash patterns of the Morse letters have been learned as musical rhythms with fragments of tunes attached to them, and this procedure helps a learner to establish control and co-ordination wordwise, and even phrasewise, far faster than he could by almost endless repetitive drill on the separate letters in the ordinary manner.

Notice that the subjects who did in fact discover the "word method" of handling the Morse code by sheer drill on the letters were highly motivated. It is a reasonable certainty that such drill without the motivation will never lead to the discovery of a better method and so will never produce much improvement. If the material is so nearly meaningless that nothing better is possible, and if the learner wants very much to improve and does not lose heart and confidence, then repetitive drill on a clumsy co-ordination may at last bring about improvement. But as a basic procedure it is always slow and wasteful, and very often gets nowhere at all.

b) Verbal guidance can definitely help in the learning of a motor skill, if such guidance is brought to bear judiciously and expertly. One can analyze the problem of the golf swing, or the tennis swing, or the problem of parking a car against the sidewalk by backing it into an empty space, or indeed (theoretically at least) any other motor problem. Then the learner can partially understand what he is trying to do and how he must go about doing it. When such analysis is really expert and correct, it can help the learner to improve very fast and to build up self-confidence. For instance, airplane pilots in training are told how to look for and react to certain definite check points as they come in for a landing. Such instruction enables them to establish an efficient control, and a working skill far faster and with far less risk than they would if they simply hammered away at less efficient methods until they found a better method by the light of nature.

However, verbal guidance seems to be valuable only after the learner has had a tryout period on his own account, because until then he has nothing specific and concrete to which to apply the advice and analysis of his teacher. One might give a boy in a woodworking shop considerable preliminary advice about how to cut a square straight-line cut with a handsaw; but he would need to do some fumbling and experimenting with the saw before he could see just what the advice actually meant. Moreover, in this case, as in every other similar case, the advice would need to come from a practical expert who really knew how to do the trick himself, and who was able to tell others how to do it (514).

c) Sometimes a high level of efficiency in co-ordination can be attained by pushing directly for it, and ignoring the errors that the learner is sure to make under this procedure. One widely used and successful plan for teaching people to receive Morse code is based on this idea. The code material is dictated by phonograph recordings and the subjects get it through earphones. So speed can always be exactly controlled. At first the code is given very slowly, letter by letter, until the learners become accustomed to the situation. Then the dictation is speeded up much beyond their ability to receive accurately. There is great confusion and uncertainty, and very many errors are made. But the learners are told to get what they can. In a surprisingly short time confusion decreases, the bewildering flow of dots and dashes starts to make sense, and the learners begin to establish quite an efficient co-ordination or structuralization of the material.

Something of the same kind happens when a person goes to a foreign country and puts himself in a position where he hears absolutely nothing but the foreign language. For quite a while he is bewildered and exhausted. But sooner than one might expect, the outlandish sounds begin to fall into place and to make a structured order.

In the expert teaching of typewriting, too, there is no long drilling on the separate characters. On the contrary, the learner is helped to orient himself quickly to the layout of the keyboard, to establish anchor points with his two little fingers, to co-ordinate the movements of his thumbs and of the fingers of the two hands, and instead of perfecting each stage before going on to the next, to work as soon as possible for the highest-level co-ordinations (65, 66).

There are many other procedures in the teaching of motor skills besides the three I have just discussed. But these three have been mentioned because they very clearly illustrate the statement that improvement in a motor skill depends on discovering a better and more "rationalized" method of dealing with a situation or problem, and that the teaching of a motor skill turns very largely on helping the learner to make this discovery.

3. The fact that motor skills seem to be much better and longer retained than the outcomes of intellectual learning has already been discussed elsewhere, but a few additional comments are in order here. The superior retention of motor skills is very far from indicating that motor learning is a special or unique kind of learning. When a person has become able to write with a pen, or to use a typewriter, or to swim, or to play tennis fairly well, he really has found a way of dealing with certain situations. Moreover, he has established a co-ordinated, organized, structured pattern of response. So the skill he has acquired tends to be permanent; and even if its fine details disintegrate with disuse, they can be recaptured without very much difficulty.

But when a child in school studies an assignment in history or arithmetic well enough to get a passing mark or even a very good mark, he may only have memorized some material well enough to meet recitation and test requirements. If this is all he has done, he has not created a working tool which he can use in dealing with the situations and problems of living, and which influences his ways of thinking, feeling, and acting. So when the recitations and tests on the assignment are over, the learning disintegrates very fast, and perhaps all that remains is some increase in the ability to cope successfully with other recitations and tests.

When intellectual learning is as effective and realistic as motor learning, intellectual learning also seems to be very permanent. Once a person *understands* how to find his way in the woods, how to use the binomial theorem, how to work with committee groups, once he has established *ways of thinking* about social and economic problems, these understandings and ways of thinking are not soon or easily lost; and even though supporting details and fine points of application may grow hazy and confused, the pattern can quite readily be refurbished and brought back again to at least its previous efficiency.

SOCIAL LEARNING

Social learning will have to be treated here more briefly than intellectual and motor learning, in spite of its great and obvious importance. All that I shall do is to make one crucial point about it, without developing its innumerable implications or following it into detail.

In a broad sense all learning is social learning. Whenever we learn anything at all, a change takes place in our behavior. We come to deal differently with the world around us and with the people in that world. If a person has learned to typewrite, he is able to enter into social relationships which are not available to a person who cannot typewrite. If a person has learned some history, it affects his thoughts, his feelings, his conversation, and probably to some extent his actions. All learning is social because its outcomes are always in terms of social behavior.

But the term *social learning* is used here in a narrower sense. A little child is surrounded by an immensely complicated culture which poses endless problems and which also indicates various solutions for these problems. He must become able to sit, to feed himself, to dress himself, to use certain forms of conversation, to be polite to the right people at the right time, to decide when to conform to the demands of some special group and when to resist those demands, and so on without end. A human being has to become able to deal with a vast complex of social conventions and expectations; and he becomes able to do so by a process for which the general name is social learning.

One of the curious features of social learning is that although we are engaged in the process all the time, we are often quite unaware that any learning is going on. We say that a person from another part of the country has "an accent," but it is often quite a surprise to be told that we have one too. A foreigner's table manners may strike us as "bad" or at least as "queer," but we do not easily recognize that our own table manners are no less queer. Social learning is so effective in making us into the kind of people that we are that we tend to consider our ways of acting and feeling as perfectly "natural," without realizing that all of them are, in fact, acquired. This "naturalness" and relative unconsciousness of a great deal of social learning has led to the idea that it must be quite a different kind of process from the conscious learning of insights or physical skills. Specifically, the acquisition of our innumerable conventional ways of acting and feeling is often supposed to be brought about by conditioning, that is to say, by sheer contact with other people around us, and by nothing else.

It is difficult, however, to accept this view. For one thing, if we acquired our conventions simply by contact or conditioning, it would seem that a person would change all his conventional ways of acting when he came in touch with a new social group with different expectations and standards. This, however, does not happen, at least on a wholesale scale. A boy brought up in Scotland may never lose all traces of his Scotch accent. A child brought up in the United States may never come to feel perfectly at ease with the table manners that are expected and considered right and proper in England. Yet surely if these patterns of behavior were acquired by nothing but conditioning, they could and would be changed by conditioning too.

Moreover, long-established patterns of behavior *can* be changed, but not simply by conditioning. For instance, a person *can* learn to speak with a perfect foreign accent. But if he is to do so he usually needs expert teaching. He must be given precise models of the new accent. He must become able to criticize and scrutinize his own vocal efforts. Insight must be brought to bear on the problem, and the focus must be exceedingly sharp. Insight properly applied can bring about a change in a person's accent which cannot be accomplished by many years of contact with other people who use that accent. Probably the same is true with many other conventional patterns of behavior.

The fact that the relearning or modification of conventional behavior seems to depend on insight at least suggests that insight has a good deal to do with the original or first learning of such conventional behavior. This seems to be the case. According to a very excellent analysis, insight operates in the social learning of conventional behavior in the form of imitation. Imitation, it should be understood, is by no means to be regarded as an instinct. It stems ultimately from the human tendency to behave as others behave, and it affects social learning as what has been called "matched dependent behavior" (457).

Here is an instance to show what "matched dependent behavior" means and how it affects our social actions. A visitor in England went to the west end of London hoping to see the King drive along one of the streets. He found himself in a large crowd of like-intentioned people. Everyone waited patiently for a long time without anything happening, and then far away down a lengthy vista came the faint sound of a bugle call. Immediately the whole crowd began to run. The visitor had no idea what the bugle call meant or what was best to do, but he took his cue from everybody else, and ran too. In company with a multitude of others he just managed to get around a corner when the carriages of the royal procession drove past. His behavior *depended* on the behavior of others around him; and it was determined by *matching* or copying the behavior of these others. So it was by this *matched dependent behavior* that he achieved his purpose.

Matched dependent behavior has an enormous influence on the lives of all human beings, young and old. A child is confronted by the problem of finding a seat in a classroom, or of leaving the classroom in a mannerly and accepted way at recess. He himself does not know the solution, so he takes his cue from others who do know the solution, and acts as they act. Matched dependent behavior is often the explanation of why a child will be orderly and co-operative with one teacher and obstreperous with another. Just as an individual he may not know how to act in the two situations; but again he tends to take his cue from others, and to accept their solution of the problem of how to behave as his own solution.

Thus the basis of a great deal of social learning is not mere conditioning or contact, but the acceptance of models which seem to indicate reasonable and probably successful and acceptable ways of behaving. However, children and older people do not choose models indiscriminately. Matched dependent behavior itself depends very much on the prestige of the model. Older pupils are likely to have a great deal of influence in setting the general social tone of a classroom or a school. The younger pupils tend to feel that the older ones know how to act, and that matching their behavior will lead to good working solutions. Persons of superior social status also tend to have a prestige-value which greatly influences the behavior of others. Persons of superior intelligence or superior skill are also likely to become models for the behavior of others, because it is recognized that these abler individuals "know how to act."

This analysis of social learning leads to inferences that are both theoretical and practical. On the theoretical side, it is clear that social training is like all other learning. Social learning starts with a challenge or a problem for which there is no immediate, ready-made solution. The actions of other persons, and particularly the actions of prestige-endowed persons, indicate solutions that are likely to be successful and, in that sense, reasonable. So a way of dealing with the problem or the challenge establishes itself, and this way of acting is likely to be retained until a better way is found. Hence the persistence of accents and table manners, and also the possibility of changing accents and table manners by the use of sharply focused models of alternative behavior.

On the practical side, the implication is that the best way of controlling social learning in a school is to tie in the natural leaders of the group to the desired ways of behaving. This technique has long been used with masterly skill in the monitorial system of the great boarding schools of England. The older and abler boys, who have a strong natural prestige, are appointed as monitors or prefects, and given responsibility for much of the minor discipline. Over the years there can be no doubt that the monitors in these English schools have wielded a profound and pervasive influence, and have done much to develop those conventions of social behavior which are supposed to be the characteristics of that type of personality known as the "English gentleman." Whether or not these are the behavior patterns that we wish to establish, it is certain that this is the way to establish whatever social conventions we think desirable.

QUESTIONS FOR DISCUSSION

1. When a person serves as a subject in a conventional memory experiment, he usually is required to go over a list of nonsense syllables or similar material a given number of times. Thus he cannot vary his procedures, exercise choice, or, in general, make free use of his higher mental processes. When this same person prepares for a purely factual objective test, he has a great deal of choice. What are some of the "clever" methods he may use in the second situation? To what extent will higher mental processes actually be brought into play even in the first situation?

2. Examine a number of school textbooks in arithmetic, algebra, geometry, science, etc. To what extent would you consider the problems set up in these books to be "real-life problems"? Make a list of real-life problems to which the content of these books would apply, and which could be used in teaching.

3. A class is given a topical assignment in history. Most of them will devote some time to studying it. What, in a realistic sense, would you say that they are trying to do? What is the real motivation? What is the actual problem with which they are trying to deal? Does your answer to these questions give you any clue to what they do when they study, and to the learning outcomes of their work?

4. Consider the work of any teacher of a physical skill—a tennis coach, a manual arts instructor, a swimming coach, etc. Would such a teacher be wise to try to get learners to understand what they are attempting to learn to do, i.e. to learn by insight?

5. In the classrooms of certain teachers there seems to be a tradition of bad discipline and bad behavior. Newcomers seem to be quickly infected, and to learn to behave like all the rest of the class. Analyze the process of this social learning. Would you say that a decorous newcomer who quickly begins to misbehave in such a classroom is coming to behave in an "insightful" manner, granted the situation?

6. In many courses in mathematics there is a great deal of emphasis on memorizing proofs, formulae, tables, etc., and it is usually possible to pass the course if one does this memorizing fairly well.

Problems, or "originals," on the other hand, are set up more or less outside of these memory tasks, and treated almost as "extras." Do you consider this organization psychologically sound? If not, how would you correct it?

7. Consider certain concepts. "Average," "multiplication," "verb," "thirteenth century," are concepts. Take any or all of these, or others if you wish, and indicate how you would organize teaching so that pupils would come to understand them. How could you tell whether such concepts really were understood?

8. In this chapter the statement is made that in a real sense all learning is social learning. Discuss and explain this statement.

SUGGESTED READINGS

Heidbreder, Edna, "Problem Solving in Children and Adults." *Journal of Genetic Psychology*, XXXV (1928), 522–545.

———, "A Study in the Evolution of Concepts." *Psychological Bulletin*, XXXI (1934), 673.

Hull, Clark L., *Quantitative Aspects of the Evolution of Concepts*. Psychological Monographs, XXVIII (1920), No. 1, Whole No. 123.

Judd, Charles H., *Education as Cultivation of the Higher Mental Processes*. The Macmillan Company, New York, 1936, Chap. 1.

9

Emotional Learning

THE PROBLEM

How do we acquire our emotional responses? This is a momentous question, and an inescapable one. It has far-reaching ramifications, both for theory and practice.

The problem cannot be shirked if we hope to understand the learning process itself. Very clearly, we *learn* our emotional responses. Somehow or other we *learn* to love our parents, to feel affection for our friends, to be jealous of our rivals, to take pride in good work, to be kindly towards strangers, to be loyal to our country. An account of learning which cannot explain, at least in general, how these responses are acquired leaves out a major part of human life, and is so limited that all its applications are open to suspicion.

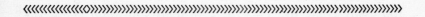

Furthermore, the problem of emotional learning cannot be shirked by teachers who wish to do their duty, or by administrators, or guidance officers, or, indeed, by anyone who is responsible for the education of young people. Emotional development and emotional learning must be taken into consideration and rightly directed if personality is to be shaped towards constructive ends. We want young people to develop not only desirable and proper insights, but also proper and desirable ways of feeling; and if we are to be intelligent in achieving this end, it is necessary to see as clearly as may be how emotions are learned.

Yet clarity about the nature of emotional learning is none too easily come by. There is enormous confusion about the whole subject of emotion, both in popular thinking and in technical psychological literature. But if we are to reach any understanding at all of what education can and should do about the vital issue of emotional life, we must try our best to cut through the confusion and to reach some kind of clarity. This is perhaps best done by raising a number of specific questions and answering them briefly and definitely, if rather dogmatically.

THE NATURE OF EMOTION

This is obviously the very first thing to be considered. Yet the moment we start to consider it we seem embarked on a sea of troubles. A great many different and often inconsistent definitions of emotion have been put forward by various authoritative writers. Of course these definitions are of importance for anyone who wants to familiarize himself with the vast literature on the subject, and to orient himself among the various theories of emotion. But if we are interested in practical issues—if we want chiefly to know what to do about emotional learning and the emotional side of education—then a discussion of theories and formal definitions pays remarkably meager dividends.

Still, it is important to know as clearly as possible what we are talking about. Probably the very best way of accomplishing this is to define emotion by what has been called the "pointing method" (393). We can say that when we talk about emotion we mean such psychological phenomena as fear, anger, grief, exultation, love, affection, pride in good work, humiliation at failure, pleasure in beautiful music or poetry, excitement in reading a novel or seeing a movie, enjoyment of companionship. This "pointing method," by which we indicate certain phenomena and say in effect, "Those are the things we mean," does not give us a formal, neat, self-contained definition, but it does give us a working and workable description of what we mean. The "pointing method" of defining emotion may seem disappointing and superficial, but it is about the best that can be managed. It would no doubt be splendid if we could capture and put into words the universal inner essence that makes any and every emotion different from any and every other psychological state or process. But at present, at least, this simply cannot be done. To be sure, many attempts have been made to construct definitions of emotion which would express its inner and essential quality; but all such definitions are debatable and seem to lead to theoretical arguments rather than to practical enlightenment and helpfulness. So we had better stick closely to our modest "pointing method" of definition.

As a matter of fact this "pointing method" clears up quite a few confusions. For instance, it breaks down the alleged distinctions between emotions and feelings. The difference is supposed to be that emotions are relatively strong and definite, while feelings are relatively mild and vague. But if we simply look at the phenomena before us, it certainly seems that emotions can be either strong or mild and still belong to the single general class of things we are talking about. So the distinction between emotion and feeling, which can cause endless debate and hair-splitting, can just be put aside, which is a great advantage.

Again, if we stick to the "pointing method," there seems to be no essential distinction, no difference in kind, between emotions and moods. Moods are simply emotional states which tend to be lasting, and which usually do not have any very definite point of contact with some specific experience or event.

Once again, if we try merely to look at and to indicate the

phenomena we are talking about, there will be no essential distinction between emotions and attitudes. An attitude is a way of feeling that is usually still more lasting than a mood, and also usually more definite than a mood. So if we undertake to define our phenomena by pointing at them, some of the things at which we will point will certainly be what are ordinarily called attitudes.

Furthermore, the "pointing method" does away with the sharp distinction between pleasant and unpleasant emotions, and with what is often supposed to be the importance of this distinction. Much has been made of this classification of emotions into pleasant and unpleasant. Pleasant and unpleasant emotions are supposed to arise out of different patterns of response in the nervous system.* Pleasant emotions are supposed to be benign and desirable. Unpleasant emotions are supposed to be disintegrating and harmful. All this, however, is a matter of theory, and dubious theory at that. The "pointing method" makes nothing of such distinctions and implications. People can certainly *enjoy* hate and anger, yet hate and anger may be the very opposite of benign. Under certain circumstances, again, people may find love very distressing; and yet love is highly thought of as a very desirable emotional condition. The truth is that emotions are so shifting, so subtle, so intermingled with one another, that neat classifications and theories based on such classifications are almost certain to be misleading and confusing. This is the reason why the "pointing method," humble and superficial as it may be, will give us a better working idea of what we are talking about than definitions that try to capture the inner essence of all emotion and far-reaching theories of emotion.

What is the place of emotion in human behavior?

In trying to answer this question as clearly as possible I shall make two general statements, and then point out an inter-

* To be more specific, the two classes of emotions have been thought to be due to contrasting responses of the autonomic nervous system.

pretation of great and far-reaching educational importance.

1. Emotion enters into every significant human response. By a "significant" human response I mean a response which involves some measure of choice and decision. This statement seems to be backed by normal experience. Think, for instance, of hitting a golf ball, solving an arithmetic problem, doing homework, going for a walk, hammering in a nail, and so on and so on. In all such doings there always seems to be an emotional component. It may be strong and violent. It may be quite slight. It may be variable. Its precise relationship to the total response may not always be very clear. But it always seems to be there. As to purely automatic responses, such as picking up one's fork at table, buttoning one's clothes, signing one's name, and suchlike, the case is at least more doubtful. Perhaps no emotion at all is involved in such responses unless they too call for decision and choice, so that they cease for the time-being to be purely automatic and become significant. All this, as I say, seems to be well supported by general experience.

But also, the statement that emotion enters into every significant human response is backed by sufficient research evidence. It is known that emotion involves certain bodily changes. When men and animals respond emotionally, the blood pressure is altered, the heartbeat is altered, the digestive processes are affected, the action of the ductless glands is altered, the chemistry of the blood is altered. When emotion is experienced, such bodily changes always seem to take place. But they do not take place independently. They are part and parcel of a total response to something or to somebody or to some situation—to an enemy whom one prepares to fight, to a beloved person whose company one prepares to enjoy, to a golf ball which one prepares to hit, to a wild animal from which one prepares to flee.

It is not true to say (although this very thing has been said) that these bodily changes, or at least our consciousness of them, actually *are* the emotion. Many of these bodily changes can be produced artificially, for instance, by giving a person an injection of adrenalin. But when they are produced artificially, the person does not experience emotion. He merely becomes tense, keyed-up, unstable, ready to explode in any direction at a moment's notice. The true interpretation is that these bodily changes are part and parcel of every significant response, so that the emotional state is not an independent something, but is woven inextricably into the total response.

This is why many emotions are so hard to classify and even to name correctly. They do not have any independent existence. Love, for instance! We talk about loving parents, children, brothers, and sisters, boy and girl friends, food, jazz, classical music, mountain scenery, surf bathing, money, and so on. Are we talking about varieties of the same emotion, or a number of different emotions? It is impossible to say. The point is that the emotional state which we try to name as well as we can (and usually none too well or clearly) is essentially a component part of a total response, and that it has no existence or meaning apart from that total response.

2. There are emotional states which are not specifically tied up to any one specific response. This seems to be true of moods, such as melancholy or enthusiasm. It is even more evidently true of attitudes such as optimism, or race prejudice, or respect for authority. Even so, moods and attitudes are not independent entities, existing purely in their own right and having no effect beyond themselves. They are not psychological floaters, so to speak. Moods and attitudes may not be tied up as component elements arising in connection with this or that response, but they certainly affect behavior in general. A mood or an attitude which did not influence a person's behavior in the slightest would be almost inconceivable. It would have no substance, no reality. Indeed, one would have to say that such a mood or attitude did not exist at all in any sense. If a person said he felt melancholy and yet behaved with wholehearted cheerfulness, or if he protested that he was full of

race prejudice and yet made many free and equal friendships with persons of other races, one could only conclude that he was a liar, though of a very peculiar kind.

So once more the point to grasp is that emotion is not an independent entity in our human psychological make-up. Emotion is always woven into the warp and woof of total behavior, and cannot be separated out from the complex texture of our total responses.

3. The two general statements that I have made and discussed lead to a far-reaching interpretation. They indicate what the true aim of emotional education ought to be, and this is certainly something that needs to be clearly understood.

Our analysis of the place of emotion in human behavior disposes of the very influential idea that emotional education should bring about the *control* or *reduction* of emotion, and should develop people who tend to act on a basis of cool, dispassionate reason instead of on a basis of feeling. This idea does not seem defensible, and yet it has been maintained by some very eminent authorities. For instance, the distinguished psychologist R. S. Woodworth says: "The difference between emotional and unemotional activity . . . depends on the degree to which the individual keeps his head, that is, on the degree to which the brainy life of relation dominates his whole activity. The degree of emotionality depends on how free the lower centers [of the nervous system] are from domination by the cerebral cortex. Or, if we do not pin our faith to any particular theory of the brain action, we can say that activity is unemotional in proportion as it consists in observing and managing the situation. Emotion is . . . a stirred-up state of feeling—that is the way it appears to the individual himself. It is a disturbed muscular and glandular condition—that is the way it appears to the external observer" (quoted in bibliography item 393).

Two immediate comments on this passage are necessary before we pass on.

a) Notice that Woodworth virtually defines emotion in terms of what he considers its essence. Emotion is a "stirred up state of feeling," or a "disturbed muscular and glandular activity." The idea of disturbance as he uses it indicates heat, turmoil, lack of control. No doubt some emotions do have these characteristics. But others do not. What about calm happiness, for instance? Woodworth might say that calm happiness is not an emotion but only a feeling, but if he did say so he would be imposing a verbal definition on reality in order to support his own theory.

b) In a wider and more general sense, no one thinks a thought, or performs an action, or indeed learns or does anything at all without being in some measure "disturbed" or "stirred up." Being "stirred up" or "disturbed" is only bad under certain quite special and fortunately rather unusual conditions; and it seems a little unfair to attach the name of emotion simply to the occasional pernicious "stirrings up" and "disturbances" to which we are subject.

The position taken by Woodworth in the passage quoted above represents a widely held theory of the psychology of emotion. Having stated it, he goes on to point out its broad practical consequences as follows: "The practical life of relation dominates more and more over the emotional life, so that the child's behavior becomes less emotional as he grows older. A scale for emotional age, after the analogy of Binet's scale for mental age, would consist in large part of tests for *not* being afraid or angry or grieved or inquisitive over things which regularly arouse these emotions in the younger child" (quoted in the bibliography, item 393). Emotion, that is to say, belongs among our childish misfortunes, like measles, mumps, and whooping cough. If these ailments afflict us in later life, the consequences may be disastrous. So the ideal personality which emotional education should strive to produce would be one which makes all decisions with the utter calm of a calculating machine, and whose behavior is as dispassionate as the motions of the solar system.

The position, of course, is utterly untenable. Emotion, as we have seen, is woven into the warp and woof of all our living; and while its effects may be evil, they can also be highly beneficial. No football coach, for instance, would be likely to believe that his players would do their best if they went into a game in a state of supernal calm. Descartes, in a wonderful and revealing passage, has told us of the intense and profound excitement that gripped him when the underlying principle of analytical geometry first dawned upon his mind. Handel composed *The Messiah* in a condition of the highest ecstasy, which was most certainly "disturbing" since it disrupted his meals and his sleep. Cardinal Newman wrote his *Apologia pro Vita Sua* while shedding floods of tears and uttering cries of anguish—and the *Apologia* is one of the world's masterpieces. Very occasionally one comes across a psychopathic individual who seems to feel no emotion at all, and such an individual is miserable and ineffective. It is, in any case, quite impossible to banish emotion from normal human life, and the very idea of doing so would suggest a psychological horror story which would be a farcical perversion of the constructive aims of emotional education.

Emotions, to repeat, are by no means always disintegrating or disturbing in a pernicious sense. An emotional state is not typically one in which we "fly to pieces," and cannot act or think effectively. Enthusiasm, for instance, can be very valuable. Love is usually helpful rather than shattering. Fear is one of the great human safeguards against disastrous choices. Even hate and envy have made people work harder. A person, young or old, whose emotions are reduced to a minimum, and who seems to have no strong feelings about anything, is to be pitied rather than emulated. Such a person is a problem to himself and to everyone who has to deal with him, as every teacher knows who has tried to cope with a completely bored and blasé youngster. For emotions are part and parcel of those behavior patterns by means of which we deal with the problems of living; and without an emotional component, those patterns of action would be denatured and feeble. So the educational problem is not to control or limit or negate emotion, which is impossible in any case—not to bring children up so that they will enthuse, and love, and hope, and fear, and even hate less and less urgently. The problem is to have them learn to enthuse, and love, and hope, and fear, and hate in ways that are related to constructive and satisfying goals.

ACQUIRING EMOTIONAL RESPONSES

The question of how we acquire emotional responses arises very directly from what has just been said, and, indeed, the whole of the foregoing discussion leads up to it.

1. One answer to the question that has been made is that *emotions are learned by conditioning*. According to this account, we do not acquire emotions in at all the same way that we learn to solve problems, or to comprehend concepts, or to master physical skills. These latter are said to be instances of what is sometimes called "discursive learning," which depends upon understanding, or thinking, or structuralization, or, more generally, upon insight. Emotions, on the other hand, are acquired by the impact of pleasantness and unpleasantness. A child comes to hate arithmetic because, for one reason or another, he finds the study of arithmetic disagreeable. He comes to like school because he finds being at school pleasant. Reason and insight have no essential part in shaping and determining his feelings about arithmetic, or school, or anything else. His feelings are determined simply by the conditioning effect of pleasantness and unpleasantness (688).

At first sight there seems to be a good deal to say for this view. Certainly it does not usually prove very promising to try to change a person's feelings by argument. This is a fairly obvious common-sense notion, and it has been validated and supported by a certain amount of research evidence. In 1940 a group of ninth- and tenth-grade students in New York City were tested to ascertain their information about the war and their feelings about it. All these students were very much aware of the war (although at that time the United States was not involved); but their information about it was scanty and inexact. Thus 62% of the group did not know that the British navy was larger than the German navy, or that the German air force was larger than the British air force. Their attitudes and feelings were often very strong and definite, but there seemed to be no relationship between such attitudes and feelings on the one hand and information on the other (533).

Various attempts have also been made to get at the same issue with older people, and the outcomes point in the same direction. An investigation was made using three groups of college students, one group being favorable to the New Deal, another group being unfavorable to it, and yet another group neutral towards it. A ten-minute address about the New Deal was read to all three groups, and afterwards the students were tested on the content of the address. The test consisted of items which allowed three choices in making a response. An answer could be true (i.e. correctly represent what had been said in the address); or it could be false; or it could involve a reinterpretation of what had been said in the address to make the material conform to one's own prejudices. It was found that there was a strong tendency to give rationalized or prejudiced answers, so that very often the students, in listening to the address, thought what they wanted to think about it rather than taking it objectively (159).

Another group of college students was given a number of photographs of people's faces and asked to examine them. Then they rated these pictures on the basis of preference. When they had done this, the students were asked to identify as well as they could the nationality of the persons whose pictures they had seen. It was found that they tended to choose or assign nationality largely on a basis of preference, i.e. a face that was liked would be assigned to a preferred nationality, and vice versa (248).

The general inference suggested is a formidable one. Information and logic are the staples of the school curriculum. Yet information and logic seem to have little effect on people's feelings. In fact, one might go further and say that a person will twist logic to suit his feelings, and will tend to reject information that conflicts with his feelings. So there seems to be a genuine reason for thinking that the only way to get a person to like any experience or activity is to make the conditions surrounding it pleasant, and that the cause of disliking any experience or activity is its unpleasantness. To put the matter more generally, this would amount to saying that we learn our emotions through a process of conditioning, or by the action of the law of effect, and that insight has nothing to do with the process.

The great weakness of the position, however, is that it makes emotion perfectly arbitrary and irrational. A child might come to love arithmetic even if he utterly failed to master it. He might come to love school even if he was disastrously unable to get along with teachers and fellow pupils or to manage his work. He might detest music even though his musical activities showed the highest competence and aroused great admiration. Indeed, one of the defenders of the theory that we learn our emotions by sheer conditioning has actually said that if we could make the experience of being charged by a tiger pleasant, people would enjoy the experience instead of being frightened by it.

2. The instances I have just given all point to the great *systematic* fallacy in the theory of emotional conditioning. As you will see, the assumption underlying all of them is that emotion is an independent element in behavior, a psychological floater, and that it is possible to mold and shape emotion without changing anything else in behavior. This, however, is certainly not true, and it is the great and central reason why the idea that emotional learning is brought about by independent conditioning will not hold water. The alternative view

is that *emotions are always learned as components of organized response.*

Dollard and Miller give a very interesting illustration of how emotions depend on the sum total of the organized behavior in whose setting they occur. A man was out for a Sunday drive in his car. He was approaching a place where another highway crossed the highway he was on, and he wanted to make a left-hand turn at the intersection. However, he was blocked by a long line of cars waiting to get across the intersecting highway. He realized that, at the rate the traffic was moving, it would take him fifteen or twenty minutes to get to the turn. He sat at the wheel, occasionally making a slow forward movement, and fussed, fumed, fretted, and swore. Then he noticed that very few cars were coming towards him and passing on his left, because most of the traffic was headed in his direction, and the block was only on his side of the road. After a glance to make sure that his plan was possible, he swung over to the right-hand shoulder, drove clear past the line of waiting cars, past the intersection, made a U-turn, came down on the opposite side of the road, and made his turn. Annoyance and frustration changed to glee and triumph over his cleverness (147, pp. 111–113).

A believer in the theory that emotions are shaped by conditioning might have tried to make the man thoroughly enjoy waiting in the traffic line, perhaps by feeding him candy, or singing him a song, or reciting a poem. Do you think it would have worked? Surely not! His exasperation was not an independent state that could be independently affected. It was part and parcel of his frustration, of his inability to find a successful solution for his problem. The moment the successful technique emerged, exasperation changed to triumph. The man's emotions were logical. They fitted into the sum total of his organized behavior. They made sense in terms of his total organized behavior. It is quite true that, even though the man's emotions were logical, he could not have been talked into feeling differently. Statistics about traffic density would probably not have helped in the least, and it is probable that warnings about the effect of anger on blood pressure would not have helped either. Nevertheless, the man's emotions were not irrational, unless one interprets rationality from the standpoint of some serene and superhuman intelligence who observes the petty strivings of men with a dispassionate eye. When his total behavior-pattern called for irritation, he was irritated. When his total behavior-pattern changed so that it called for glee, he was gleeful.

Now let us apply this analysis to the research findings described above. First, consider the children who had strong feelings about the war but knew little about it. These children had learned certain formulae about the Germans and the British, certain ways of *talking* about the war, certain ways of *thinking* about the war—certain formulae and ways of talking and thinking that would win them the approval of their parents and brothers and sisters and friends and associates. They were able to cope conversationally with the war in a sufficiently satisfying fashion; and, of course, certain emotions went along with this ability.

The same would undoubtedly be true of the students whose feelings about the New Deal overrode the effect of an objective argument. Some were pro–New Deal and others were anti–New Deal, not because they had studied the matter profoundly and balanced all the arguments pro and con, but because being pro– or anti–New Deal was the best way to get on with their associates. For many of these students pro– and anti–New Dealism were social techniques, and successful social techniques too; and such successful techniques could not possibly be broken up by a ten-minute verbal harangue. Those who say that man is an irrational creature because his successful adjustments cannot be changed out of hand by a few bits of information or a brief abstract argument are themselves very irrational and unrealistic.

Certain considerations regarding the nature and management of emotional learning now become clear.

a) All learning is a process of discovering how to deal with problems and challenges, how to attain goals through which basic needs can be satisfied. This is true of so-called "intellectual learning," and also of so-called "emotional learning." Indeed, there is no basic distinction between these two apparently different kinds of learning. Both go on together, and both depend on the same conditions.

Let us say that a social science teacher had charge of some of the students whose attitudes towards and information about the war were investigated in 1940. She might want them to come to know more about the war and to understand it better. Then she would have to work in such a way as to bring home to them the fact that the war involved problems *for them,* problems affecting their personal outlook upon life, and perhaps their future lives and fortunes. To deal with these problems it would be necessary for the students to accumulate and collate information, to think through issues, to reach whatever understandings they could. So far this looks like a purely intellectual process, but in the course of such learning the students' attitudes towards and feelings about the war would certainly be changed along with their changing and deepening insights.

Or again, a college instructor taking hold of some of the students whose pro– and anti–New Deal prejudices were investigated might very well want them to develop more informed and judicious attitudes and feelings about the whole great social experiment. He could only accomplish this by bringing these students face to face with some of the economic, social, and political problems with which the New Dealers themselves had to wrestle, so that the students would find themselves wrestling with these problems too. If this were done—and there would be many ways of doing it—the students would almost certainly learn new ways of feeling about the New Deal, and at the same time they would come to know more about it and to understand it better.

But, you may ask, does not propaganda make a direct attempt to change people's feelings while leaving knowledge and understanding strictly alone? And is not propaganda often remarkably successful in affecting feelings? The answer is that propaganda does not even try to deal with emotions as independent states of mind. It presents an interpretation of events, and proposes a line of action. We are not invited to sit down and hate an enemy, while doing nothing but bite our finger nails. The enemy is represented as a fiend in human form, and a threat to ourselves and our fellow citizens. His fiendishness is often explained at great length, with numerous alleged facts in support of the claim. A way of thinking is set up. A way of acting is proposed—pay taxes, invest in war bonds, take up a job in a war factory, join the armed services. And the hate goes along with everything else.

b) Every real problem or challenge that we face is both intellectual and emotional. It involves relationships, and its solution turns upon insights; and also it involves feeling. A child comes to school for the first time and finds himself frightened and bewildered. That is to say, he suffers from disturbing and even shattering emotions. But his trouble is not merely emotional. He does not know his way around the building. He does not know how to get home. He does not know when his mother will come for him, or whether she will come at all. He does not know how to behave in strange situations. He does not know to whom to turn for guidance. Like the man in the traffic jam, he is caught in a difficult situation and has no clue for coping with it. But as soon as the clue begins to manifest itself, his fear and bewilderment subside, and other emotions take their place. Later on in his school career this same child is told to imagine that he left home that morning with ten cents in his pocket, and that he bought two sticks of candy for three cents each, and then he is asked how much money he would have left. This is what would ordinarily be called an intellectual problem. But it is not a purely intellectual problem. If the child solves it, he will no doubt learn something about arithmetic. But also he will learn a certain amount of self-confidence, and he may get a significant thrill in dealing with the challenge.

c) Emotions are not, in and of themselves, causes of action. They are part and parcel of the patterns of behavior by means of which we deal with the problems of living. A child may hate arithmetic, and if he hates arithmetic, he will probably do very badly with it. But the hate is not the cause of the failure. It is a component of the child's total ineffective response in dealing with situations which demand arithmetic for their resolution. We could not make the child do well with arithmetic even if it were possible to find some psychological magic which would transform his hatred for it into liking without changing anything else. But we can profoundly influence the child's feeling about arithmetic by helping him to succeed with it, and by helping him to realize what far-reaching satisfactions there can be in mastering it. A child may be afraid of other children at school, or he may be aggressively hostile to them. In either case his adjustment to school life is likely to be thrown very much out of gear. But the fear or the hostility are symptoms, not causes, and the way to overcome them is to enable the child to learn how to deal successfully and co-operatively with his schoolmates.

d) It is easy to see why a great deal of the learning that goes on in school classrooms has very little effect upon the emotions. Such learning tends to emphasize routines, memorization, and the challenges set up by marks and tests. Even as intellectual learning it is not effective, for it does not lead to a mastery of curricular material by way of insight and understanding. And when a subject is not understood it cannot be used as a tool for living, and its emotional potentialities cannot be realized. To have a real understanding of natural science, or social science, or history, or mathematics, even though that understanding is very far from complete, is to acquire an outlook on life and on the world which involves both intellect and feeling.

As a simple instance, consider some few of the effects of the nonacademic "subject" of woodworking. A boy in the woodworking shop learns to deal with a wide range of problems. He probably achieves a genuine mastery, even though he may never develop the highly polished skill of an expert cabinetmaker. Looked at from one point of view, this mastery consists of motor skill, i.e. the ability to structuralize a situation and to act accordingly. But there will also be an emotional side to the mastery. Along with his skill the boy will almost certainly learn some pride in good workmanship, some impatience with slovenly workmanship, some admiration for fine craftsmanship in other people. So his experiences with woodworking tend to affect both his motor reactions and his ways of feeling. In just the same way, the study of any academic subject can and should affect ways of thinking, ways of acting, and ways of feeling. If the study of an academic subject does not have this threefold effect, then it is certainly being badly learned, and perhaps not even learned at all in any genuine sense.

GOOD AND BAD EMOTIONAL LEARNING

Emotional learning can grade all the way from very good to very bad. In this it is just like all learning—the learning of golf or quadratic equations, for instance. The similarity between intellectual and motor learning on the one hand and emotional learning on the other hand is obscured because we are so used to expressing the success or failure of motor and intellectual learning quantitatively by a score or mark, something that cannot be done with emotional learning. Yet even with intellectual and motor learning quantitative scores do not tell us much about what is really going on. The poor golfer makes a high score, but his poorness lies in his awkward swing. The bad solver of quadratic equations makes low marks, but his badness lies in his dreadful blunders and misunderstandings. This is an exact parallel with emotional learning, for bad emotional learning means emotional blundering and ineffectiveness, and good emotional learning means emotional effectiveness.

1. Let us briefly describe what is really meant by good emotional learning, which produces good and effective emotional reactions. To make the description specific, let us consider a first-grade child newly come to school. It is well known that a child in this situation faces many problems and challenges which are difficult for him to meet.*

a) We want this child to learn to accept authority without fear or aggressiveness. That is to say, we want him to learn certain feelings about his teacher. To help him with this learning is part of the teacher's responsibility. How can she manage it? In general, she should create a positive and constructive situation in the classroom. The child must be enabled to understand what he is expected to do, and also to understand that these expectations are reasonable. He must feel that the teacher is sympathetically aware of his problems, so that he can turn freely to her for help in finding solutions. He should not be asked to do things that are impossible or incomprehensible; but he should realize that the new situation is challenging, and that he can nevertheless get on in it. If there is a clash of wills between child and teacher, the child will probably be forced into submission. But although he may conform outwardly, there may easily be considerable harm done, for emotional learning will start off along the wrong track (629).

Pressey and Robinson (531) tell a story of the troubles of a young and inexperienced teacher which is a good illustration of the points just made. The class with which this teacher was trying to deal got completely out of hand. The classroom was old-fashioned, and the ceiling was supported by metal pillars. These pillars became focal points for the general disorder. The

* The following analysis is based on Breckenridge and Vincent, bibliography item 69.

children took to shinning up them and hanging on at the top for a surprisingly long time, while general hubbub reigned. The teacher threatened, stormed, scolded, begged, and even wept, but it did no good. Finally an experienced teacher was assigned to take over, and to bring order out of chaos. The day she first put in an appearance the pillar-climbing started off as usual, but the teacher took no notice whatsoever. She sat calmly at her desk, hurled no verbal thunderbolts, seemed to do some work of her own, carried things along as well as she could. It was not long before the antics began to pall. The organized activities of the classroom began to take hold. More and more of the children began to resent interruptions. Within a comparatively short time the whole situation came under control.

This experienced teacher had guided emotional learning wisely. She made it possible for the children to find satisfactions in orderly conduct, and to reduce and finally to obliterate the satisfactions they had previously found in very disorderly conduct. Under the guidance of this teacher, the children learned to accept authority without either fear or aggressiveness. They learned a new set of feelings about this teacher in particular, and probably about teachers in general.

b) Once again, we want our first-grade child to learn to deal with his peers confidently and without aggressiveness. How can this piece of emotional learning be brought about? By creating constructive and guided group situations, both in and out of the classroom! Older people need to remember that a first-grade child is likely to be quite inept in dealing with other children. He has few good working techniques, either of co-operation of competition. He has a deep need to assert himself, to behave like other children, to be admired and respected as a person. But he is not able to set up for himself feasible goals in and through which these needs can be satisfied. Hence he is apt to be either angry or frightened, either belligerent or cringing. To try to change these emotional reactions directly, perhaps by lecturing the child, or even by head-on collision is futile, because such reactions are symptoms—symptoms of frustration and ineptitude. He must be helped to find ways in which he can deal with other children successfully. For instance, a teacher notices that one of the children in her group is isolated, friendless, and withdrawn, and she suspects that he is far from happy. If this child is left to himself, he may make some blundering attempts to get into the swing of things, or he may retreat into a psychological bolt-hole and compensate by developing feelings of inferiority or contempt. All such reactions are, of course, very bad for him. What the teacher ought to do is to create some social enterprise or enterprises in which he can really play a part, and then to help him in making the discovery that the part is possible.

c) We want our newly arrived first-grade child to face a daily stated pattern of activities and tasks with cheerfulness and zest. Here is quite a problem in emotional education. It is not too hard to force a group of young children to conform externally to the daily schedule. But to get them to conform with cheerfulness and zest is a somewhat different matter. Yet feelings of cheerfulness and zest about the day's work are tremendous assets in a first-grade classroom, and tremendous assets all through life; so the emotional lesson is well worth learning.

The lesson is best taught by making the pattern of the day's undertakings as much as possible a matter of choice and decision, rather than an arbitrary and purely imposed routine. This is one of the great values of co-operative planning. To be sure, the co-operative planning of the school day does not mean that the teacher should turn the helm over to the children, and concur in doing whatever they might happen to think it would be nice to do. An inexperienced mariner put in full charge is likely to run the ship on the rocks, and if young children are asked to shoulder too much responsibility, they are sure to make self-frustrating choices. But if children find that they have some real opportunity to reflect about what they ought to do, and within limits to decide on what should be done, they will work more wholeheartedly, they will learn better, and they will tend to acquire emotional reactions which are valuable in the classroom here and now, and which can serve them well in later years.

d) Yet again, we want our first-grade newcomer to learn subject matter. Here too is a far-reaching emotional issue of first-rate importance. We want him to learn subject matter with zest and enthusiasm. We want him to look with new eyes at clouds, and running water, and growing trees and plants, and animals, and people. We want him to discover new and enlarging possibilities in books, and pictures, and music, and numerical symbols. We want him to be proud and happy in knowing and understanding more than he knew and understood before. This is what subject-matter learning should and can mean. It is what such learning does in fact mean when subject matter is made an interpretation of the endless and fascinating problems and challenges which life presents. Subject matter so taught and learned ceases to be a mass of dead material to be meagerly assimilated by half-hearted learners, and becomes a prime agency for establishing a constructive emotional orientation which can carry forward into all the years to come.

2. Next let us consider the characteristics of bad or misdirected emotional learning. Psychiatrists recognize a number of types of emotional disturbance and maladjustment, and I shall discuss some of the most conspicuous of them. All of these types of disturbance, it should be noted, are emotional components of frustration and failure.

a) Aggressive behavior is a common and generally recognized type of emotional disturbance. Aggressive behavior has been defined as behavior in which a person manifests opposition to others coupled with a disposition to attack (208). The tendency to attack may be overt and physical, or it may be indirect, expressing itself in general hostility, the playing of practical jokes, the making of belittling comments, and so forth. Dollard and Miller (148) insist that aggressive behavior is always the result of frustration. Allison Davis (138) maintains that with slum children, aggressiveness is a normal way of acting and feeling. However, it should be noticed that the aggressiveness of underprivileged children tends to crop up very markedly in school; and for such children the school is very often a frustrating environment, not because they lack the ability to do schoolwork successfully, but because the standards, expectations, values, and types of conduct represented by the school are out of tune with the rest of their lives.

Of course, it is often quite possible for teachers and school authorities to suppress obvious manifestations of aggressive behavior by means of penalties and threats. But this covers up the maladjustment rather than curing it. We know that a harsh authoritarian regime in school definitely fosters and tends to create aggressive tendencies. Thus in one field study of a school situation in which very severe and authoritarian measures were used to keep external "good order," a number of the children made a regular practice of "picking" on one of the boys in the class whenever they had a chance to do so (399). So the flames of aggressiveness are often fanned rather than damped down by vigorous direct counter-aggression, even though, on the surface of things, the teacher is the winner. Aggressiveness can be fostered by conditions both in and out of school—by repeated failure in school tasks and undertakings, or by unfortunate home conditions with the teacher becoming the emotional substitute for the resented parent.

In all such cases, treatment by a direct clash of wills is always a poor choice. It may damp down the aggressor, who is usually in a weaker position. But a direct clash of wills is very unlikely to correct the aggressive tendency itself, which is what we want to do if we are thinking in terms of sound emotional education. The proper policy by all means is to organize opportunities for significant success for the aggressive person.

Here I may mention once again the case of the young teacher assigned to a school in a slum neighborhood, who was immediately put in charge of a "problem" group of overage boys. These boys were about as aggressive characters as are ever likely to be found in any school. To quell their aggressiveness by sheer harshness and terrorism would probably have been too much for a champion pugilist. But this young teacher, who was no tremendously husky physical specimen, had a conspicuous success in dealing with them simply because he managed to *teach* them something.

b) Another type of emotional maladjustment is what is known as regression, i.e. a tendency to slip back into more childish modes of response. This is also one of the possible emotional components of frustration and disappointment. For instance, in an investigation, a group of children were occupied in a play situation in which they were free to manipulate various fairly attractive and interesting materials and objects. Their play activities were observed, and individual children were rated for "constructiveness in play." After half an hour in this situation, the children were admitted to a part of the room which they had not seen before, and in which there were materials and objects of a much more interesting and attractive kind. They were not allowed to play with these things, but only to examine and explore them, and then they were returned to the former part of the room. Different individuals reacted differently to the disappointment and "let down," but the general level of constructiveness became definitely less mature. That is to say, the general response of the group now became typical of considerably younger children (30).

Regressiveness manifests itself in a great many different ways, for instance, in lack of response to the suggestions and stimuli presented by the teacher, in persistent boredom, in day-dreaming, or in negativism, i.e. not wanting to do anything that might be suggested, insisting that nothing suggested is worth-while, and so on. Teachers are often puzzled and annoyed by such negative manifestations and relapses into sheer infantility, and perhaps try to overcome them by scolding, or threats, or pressure. But these reactions serve a real purpose in the economy of mental life, for they are often attempts to protect the personality against the impact of failure and frustration. The child retreats emotionally from a situation that he finds too much for him. What he needs is a reassuring sense of sympathy and success. It has been pointed out that regressive and negativistic tendencies are very likely to affect a child's performance on a mental test. A conventional mental test is a formidable emotional challenge, and if the child's first impression is that he cannot handle the series of school-like tasks which make up the test, he is likely to quit either overtly or by ceasing to try, and to give quite a false impression of his mental ability. One reason why children who have spent some time in a good nursery school may do better than other children on a mental test may very well be that school has accustomed the child to handle the kind of tasks that make up the test, so that he attacks them with vim and self-confidence (143).

c) Rationalization is a very common type of maladjustment, that appears often in school situations. Rationalization means inventing plausible reasons for a faulty or frustrating course of action. It may take many forms. One type of rationalization is the "sour grapes" attitude, i.e. saying that success in school, good marks, and so forth, are not worth-while. Another variant is the explanation of failure by saying that one lacks the necessary special ability or "bump." This is a very common excuse for not doing well in mathematics, or language study, or English composition, and unfortunately it is often supported by teachers who perhaps have failures of their own to explain away.

Rationalizations of failure may grade all the way from almost genuine explanations to quite preposterous ones. They are, however, not easily overcome by counter-argument. A teacher may *tell* a pupil that he could do very well, and the pupil may nod his head without really believing a word. What is needed, once again, is the experience of genuine and convincing success. Incidentally, mental tests can sometimes be used to counter rationalizations of failure, for a high test score can have quite an electrifying effect on a pupil who has been stubbornly convinced that he lacks the ability to make good. Mental tests, for better or for worse, have considerable social and emotional prestige, quite apart from their objective value as measuring instruments; and this makes them potent agencies which can do much harm, but also considerable good.

Such emotional disturbances as those we have been discussing, and others like them, can grade all the way from triviality to extreme seriousness. Probably almost everybody manifests them to some extent from time to time. It has been said that 90% of the so-called "emotional problems" of adolescence are "normal" reactions (198). The same probably holds true of younger children and adolescents. But what does "normal" mean? It is a slippery, and indeed a rather dangerous word, which needs clear definition. In one sense all emotional disturbances are normal because they are the logical concomitants of failure and frustration. Aggressiveness, childishness, daydreaming, or rationalization may often seem peculiar, disconcerting, and wild reactions, but when we consider the circumstances which the person concerned is facing, they become quite understandable. However, when it is said that 90% of such disturbances are normal, the word is used in a more restricted and special sense. What is then indicated is that the emotional peculiarity or difficulty can be handled by ordinary means, so that if a reasonable approach is used there is no need for special treatment, and no likelihood of disastrous consequences later on.

For instance, the tendency of many adolescents to dress in sloppy clothes and to be personally unkempt often seems to be a repudiation of parental insistence on cleanliness and neatness. It is self-assertion carried a little beyond conventional limits, a mild form of aggressiveness; and as time passes by, the youngster gets through the phase of dishevelment with no harm done at all. Or again, a teacher may notice that one of the boys in her class seems to be noisy, excitable, and pugnacious. Quite probably it is a case of too much energy and too few outlets. The way to handle the boy is probably not to insist that he "pipe down," but to give him responsibilities in the classroom and the school.

Yet again, a teacher has to deal with a child who is an imaginative liar, and who spins quite untrue yarns of family grandeur and great exploits. One such case was dealt with by telling the child that he had certain qualities not possessed by others, and having him write up his stories as fiction pieces and read them to the class. Quite another kind of lying may come from a desire to keep out of trouble, and then the prescription is to build courage and self-assurance. A juvenile thief is often a have-not. A child with many subjective fears can often be reached by sympathy, reasoning, and assignments which lead him to the experience of satisfying success. Aggression which centers on some particular person or situation is much more likely to be normal, i.e. manageable by ordinary means, than a general and diffused aggressiveness. Persistence in the face of frustration is always a favorable sign. So rating for "effort" is sound enough in principle, although such ratings should not be used for marking, but should be considered as personality indications. These might all be considered as instances and indications of "normal" emotional difficulties.

A certain number of emotional disturbances will be a little further outside the normal range. Such was the case of Dick, who called attention to himself by staying away from school a great deal. When he was questioned, the first thing that rather reluctantly came out was that he was afraid to go to school. Further investigation revealed that he was being bullied by a gang of his classmates. The situation might have been handled by reproving the bullies, but this would probably have made things worse for Dick at that time, and might have developed a lasting and troublesome emotional disorientation. Dick, however, was given a physical examination. It was found that he was in poor condition due to adenoids. The adenoids were removed; Dick was allowed to remain out of school for the rest of the term; and when he returned there was no more difficulty.

Or again, there was the case of Sally. Sally was an angel child, too good and docile to be true. The very absence of every vestige of trouble bothered Sally's perceptive teacher. The case was investigated, and Sally turned out to have a thymus disorder which was impairing her general development, but which could be corrected. These are cases in which something beyond even intelligently organized school procedures is demanded, and which therefore go somewhat beyond the "normal" range as the word is here understood.

Still less normal patterns of emotional reaction are general and diffused aggressiveness, persistent childishness, or silly vocational and educational plans and choices which may be based on personal attachments and crushes, and on nothing else. Emotional disturbances and difficulties of this kind may go beyond the control of the teacher and the school, and call for medical and psychiatric treatment. The reason is partly that special skill and insight may be needed to treat such cases, and partly that an outside expert like a physician or psychiatrist can often do something about underlying conditions when a teacher is powerless.

For instance, an investigation has been made of the relationship between parental overattentiveness at home and the child's social adjustment and work habits at school, the subjects being second-grade and fifth-grade children. The tabulation below shows the outcome of this study.

	Babied at Home		Pushed at Home		Well-adjusted at Home	
	Grade II	Grade V	Grade II	Grade V	Grade II	Grade V
Good social adjustment at school	24%	16%	18%	23%	70%	73%
Good work habits at school	27%	30%	18%	18%	75%	78%

From Hattwick and Stowell (275).

From these figures it is perfectly clear that parental attitudes in the home have a great deal to do with a child's performance and adjustment at school. The practical difficulty in dealing with the situation indicated is that home conditions are often quite inaccessible to the teacher, whereas a physician or psychiatrist may be able to do something about them (16, 198, 637).

ATTITUDES

We have seen that when emotion is defined by the "pointing method," attitudes are among the phenomena we have in mind when we talk about emotions. Attitudes are more or less persistent and lasting emotional trends. However, they do not have an independent existence, nor are they psychological floaters, any more than any other emotional states. Attitudes are always tied up with insights and interpretations and opinions and actions. Otherwise they could not manifest themselves at all, and presumably would not even exist. This always needs to be born in mind when we ask how attitudes are acquired, a question which has been answered very convincingly by Gordon W. Allport (6).

1. Attitudes are acquired by the co-ordination or integration of many similar experiences. If a whole series of experiences all point in the same direction, a child may *discover* that he hates arithmetic, or dislikes playing team games, or is thrilled and excited by the democratic way of dealing with people. A very good illustration of how a sequence of experiences can affect attitudes is provided by a workshop in music and art that was set up for teachers in a summer school. Many of these teachers had had some very sad experiences with music and art in past years, so they enrolled for the workshop with grave doubts and fears. However, the persons in charge did everything possible to make significant success possible, and not only possible but quick in arriving. Materials that were easy to manipulate were provided. No one was forced to do anything against her will, but

everyone was shown how to paint, or draw, or model, or make up tunes in such a way that quick and interesting results appeared. There was a great deal of stimulation and encouragement and a great deal of sharing of problems and methods and of mutual aid. By the end of the session, the various members of the workshop could feel, quite legitimately, that they had begun to get somewhere, that they had been given a real taste of what art and music could mean and of what they themselves could do with music and art. "The studio activities gave me new confidence." "I could not wait each day to get back to the studio. This showed me how excited children could get about the things they were doing if they were really interested." These were two of the typical statements made in a post-mortem roundup of opinions. It was very clear that the cumulative experiences of the six weeks session had brought about profound and probably permanent changes of attitude (170).

You may be interested to notice that there is a certain similarity between the effect of a sequence of experiences in producing an attitude and the effect of repetition in learning the skill. In both cases it is not the mere number of experiences that does the trick. The effect depends on the condition that all the experiences, although they are not identical, point in the same direction, suggest the same outcome, require the same intelligent and intelligible integration. One *discovers* a skill through repeated attempts. One may *discover* an attitude through a sequence of experiences. In both cases learning is a process of discovery, and what is discovered is a new reaction, a new way of dealing with situations, a new tool for living.

2. Attitudes can be established by individualization or differentiation, or to use a more familiar word with the same meaning, by specialization. General peevishness and discontent with life can crystallize into communism. General reluctance to go to school can crystallize into specific dislike for what is often called "culture." General social ambition can crystallize into a violent longing for an expensive car. General en-

thusiasm for outdoor life can crystallize into passionate interest in horses. Attitudes which can affect a person's whole life are often acquired in this way. What happens is that a general diffused disposition, much too vague to be called an attitude or even to be very precisely defined or understood, acquires "a local habitation and a name." It attaches itself to an interpretation or a theory, communism being an instance, and usually to some pattern of activity as well, horseback riding being an instance. What this clearly suggests in a practical way is the great importance of the general atmosphere of the school and the classroom. A child who comes into a pleasant and inviting building and finds himself in an attractive room is at least started towards favorable attitudes towards school and much for which school stands. Notice, however, that it is not merely the pleasantness of the surroundings that is important and effective, but rather the child's feeling that here is a place where it is good to be, where he can feel at home, where he can feel understood and helped, and where all suggestions are that he can achieve success.

3. Attitudes can be acquired by "trauma," i.e. by a single dramatic, impressive, and memorable experience. One disastrous and humiliating experience with singing can cripple a child's vocal efforts for years to come. Conversely, one convincing and thrilling experience of the beauty of poetry or the charm of a picture or the fascination of a mathematical problem can establish a life-long favorable attitude.

In a little book on the teaching of appreciation written many years ago the great point made is that the presentation of a poem to children should be a "red-letter" experience. Interest and anticipation should be built up in advance. Perhaps there should be some preliminary explanations a day or two beforehand, so that the children will not be puzzled and baffled, and therefore repelled. The actual presentation should be carefully staged at a time when there will be no interruptions, and the poem should be read expressively and with feeling and enthusiasm. Such an experience can very well have a profound and lasting effect (280). This is an excellent instance of one extremely important way in which attitudes can be established. It brings out two points which every teacher should have in mind. (*a*) A single qualitative experience can have a momentous and lasting influence. (*b*) That influence depends on something being revealed in the experience, and not on a process of conditioning.

4. Attitudes can be and, indeed, constantly are picked up by the process of imitation which we analyzed in connection with social learning. Children derive attitudes from other children, not because of an instinct to imitate, but because the actions and words of other children constitute a pattern, a model, an interpretation, a revelation of how to act and feel in a situation. This is why the general social atmosphere of a classroom and a school is of such profound importance in determining the learning process. Moreover, children can and do pick up attitudes from their teachers. A teacher who is an enthusiast for what she is teaching, who is thrilled by it and filled with a realization of its value and significance, will teach perhaps far more than she ever imagines by the tone of her voice, by her unstudied words, by the expression of her face. Moreover, attitudes can be picked up from others by way of vicarious experience. Plutarch's *Lives* is one of the great ethical textbooks of all time, and its portrayals of great men have aroused emulation and created moral standards in countless thousands of young people. Here again, and indeed as always in learning, the process is one of revealing how to think, how to feel, how to act, with the revelation made convincing in human flesh and blood.

QUESTIONS FOR DISCUSSION

1. A third-grade boy suddenly develops an intense dislike for school. The school is well conducted. The boy's teacher seems considerate. Yet the emotional disturbance has appeared. How would you go about dealing with it?

2. Most pupils in school, and in fact most human beings, become more or less emotionally upset at one time or another. Usually such disturbances are within the range of what we consider "normal," but sometimes they are not. Just where would you draw the line between a "normal" and an "abnormal" emotional condition?

3. When a child shows an antipathy towards some specific person, this is a far less serious symptom than a manifestation of general hostility or aggressiveness not focalized on anyone in particular. Why is this true?

4. What objections are there to regarding emotion as essentially a disturbed psychological condition?

5. Collect a number of instances in which advertisers and propagandists try to arouse emotion. How are these attempts made? Do they involve anything that could be called a rational process?

6. Do you think that history, as it is taught in our schools, tends to produce any emotional responses? Do you think it should be taught for the sake, among other things, of producing such responses?

7. When certain social science textbooks are criticized as subversive, do you think that the appropriate action would be to rewrite these textbooks in a perfectly cold and objective manner, so that they would have no emotional slant at all?

8. If you wanted to create among a group of children a favorable attitude towards school or perhaps towards some particular subject, what are some of the things you would do?

9. Consider some of your own likings and dislikings and try to see how they were acquired. What would have to happen to change them?

10. In the light of this chapter, would you say that human behavior is controlled by reason or by feeling? Or is neither explanation correct?

SUGGESTED READINGS

Allport, Gordon W., "Attitudes," in Carl Murchison, ed., *Handbook of Social Psychology*. Clark University Press, Worcester, Mass., 1935.

Leeper, Robert W., "A Motivational Theory of Emotion to Replace 'Emotion as Disorganized Response.'" *Psychological Review,* LV (1948), 5–21.

Symonds, Percival M., "Classroom Discipline." *Teachers College Record,* LI (1949), 147–158.

———, "Some Empirical Principles of Child Guidance." *Teachers College Record,* XLV (1944), 307–316.

Tuttle, Harold S., "Two Kinds of Learning." *Journal of Psychology,* XXII (1946), 267–277.

10

Transfer of Training

THE PROBLEM

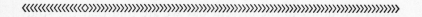

WHEN A person uses an ability in a situation other than that in which he acquired it, he is said to *transfer* that ability from the situation in which he learned it to the situation in which he uses it. Learning French in school and speaking French in Paris, practicing golf shots at a net and playing golf shots on the course would be two instances of transfer. In all such instances what is called a *transfer of learning* or a *transfer of training* is involved.

Transfer of training is the modern and not altogether fortunate name for a very ancient educational doctrine. Indeed that doctrine is the central doctrine of this book, namely that the real effect of education is its effect on human personality. In the great days of ancient Athens a boy's education consisted of gymnastics *for the body* and music *for the soul*, so that he might grow up as a free citizen, an ανθρωρος καλοκαγαθος a "fair and beautiful person." For the motto of his Academy Plato chose the words, "Let none ignorant of geometry enter here," because he believed that geometry trained the mind and the disposition for the study of philosophy. Medieval educators held that grammar, rhetoric, and dialectic (or logic) were a necessary groundwork for the study of theology. The education of the medieval knight was intended to produce courtesy, refinement of manners, kindness towards the weak, respect for women, and loyalty to the Church as well as martial skill. And right down to the present day we are told that the study of geometry will enable a person to reason better, that the study of science will produce exactitude, that Latin can refine literary taste, and so on. It is true that nowadays we tend to concern ourselves with more limited and specific transfer effects, and to ask whether Latin can help to improve a person's English style, or whether algebra can help in the learning of physics. But always the central idea is the same, namely, that any learning experience can have an effect beyond itself, an effect, more or less far-reaching, upon the personality of the learner.

That transfer is possible in some sense and to some extent is bound to be the working credo of every teacher. If what we teach children in the classroom does not affect them outside the classroom, why go on teaching? Why, indeed, continue to maintain schools? So a very considerable shock ran through the educational world when, about forty-five years ago, a series of studies began coming out which proved that many claims about the transfer of training are greatly inflated. It turned out that studying grammar had almost no effect on English style, that Latin had surprisingly little effect on French, that high-school algebra did not carry over well to physics, and that neither geometry nor any other subject seemed to do anything appreciable in the way of strengthening the ability to reason. As a result, the pendulum swung violently away from the doctrine of the transfer of training. As investigations kept coming out, showing disconcertingly little transfer, i.e. showing that learners very often cannot use what they have learned when a new situation arises, many educational workers began to say that there is no such thing as transfer at all. The notion arose that a subject should be taught purely "for its own sake," though it is not easy to say just what this means.

But the true inference from all these negative investigations is, not that transfer of training is impossible, but that it does not take place automatically, that we cannot sit back and count on it, that if we want it we must plan for it intelligently and work for it diligently. If there is no such thing as transfer, if a learning experience can have no effect beyond the situation in which it occurs, then teaching is stultified. So it becomes very necessary to understand the nature of transfer of training and the conditions which bring it about, and to see how such an understanding bears upon our work.

TRANSFER AND LEARNING

The first step in reaching this necessary understanding of the nature and conditions of transfer is to see that the process of transfer of training is even more far-reaching and fundamental than is ordinarily supposed. Certainly we should ask whether the study of one subject can help in studying another subject, how the study of one subject can be made more helpful for the studying of another subject, and whether or how the study of this or that subject can affect a person's power to reason or to judge or to discriminate, and, indeed, influence and mold his personality. These, in the main, are the classic questions which come up when transfer of training is under consideration, and they are important and must be dealt with. But they have to do, in a sense, with special aspects of the general problem of transfer, and the attention that has been lavished on them has tended to obscure the true nature and bearing of that problem. For transfer is basic in all learning and all adjustment. Not until we grasp this can we begin to see how to handle the transfer problem practically and successfully.

1. Transfer has to do, not only with the end results or products of learning, but also with the very process or sequence of learning itself (123). By way of a concrete illustration, consider

what happens when a person learns to throw darts at a target. In a very broad and loose sense he repeats. That is to say, he tries again and again and again. But in a precise sense (as we have already seen) he does not repeat at all. He makes a great many errors, i.e. clumsy throws and misses, which he certainly does his best not to repeat. He has a good many partial successes, and these he tries to improve rather than to repeat. Once in a while, at first, and with increasing frequency later on, everything goes just right. But even these successes are not, strictly speaking, repetitions, for each time the learner succeeds the performance goes more easily and he gains a certain modicum of self-confidence. What our would-be expert dart thrower is trying to do is to create a co-ordination not yet there. Each try, and probably even each error, does something towards creating that co-ordination. Yet when the co-ordination is finally established, the dart thrower's easy certainty is quite a different affair from his anxious tries, even when those tries succeed.

It appears, therefore, that something has to be pulled out from each and all of these tries which the learner makes during practice. A transfer has to take place from the fumbling, anxious, variable tries to the easy and successful skill. We know in general what is involved in this transfer. An organized and structured pattern of action must emerge from the practice. Anything that will make this pattern emerge more quickly and surely, anything that will enable the learner to get a quicker and better transfer from each try he makes, will enable him to learn quicker and better. It is precisely the business of the teacher to speed up the emergence of the pattern, to facilitate transfer during the process of learning.

Learning multiplication is another good illustration which shows very clearly how transfer is involved in the very process of learning itself. The best way to teach multiplication is not to have a child memorize the tables or the "facts." Instead of this, we try to enable the child to discover that multiplying really means combining groups of things. We tell him, for instance, to imagine that he is going to buy six candy bars for five cents each, and that he will need to know how much money he must have. (Notice that I have stated the little problem without using the word "times," which children often use as a tip-off.) Then we give him a handful of play pennies. He picks out five of these pennies, the price of one candy bar; then five more, and so on till he has six groups of five pennies in each group. Here is the concept of six-times-five in concrete form, with the product being thirty. If we like, we can go on to show him that his thirty pennies can be divided up into three groups of ten, and so on.

A great variety of such devices, materials, and procedures have been developed, by using which a child can learn the arithmetical process by manipulation, experiment, and discovery. If you watch a child using play pennies or other such suitable objects while he works at arithmetical problems, the word "repetition" will not seem to you to be a true description of what he does. He makes mistakes and corrects them, he hesitates and decides and then changes his mind, he becomes increasingly sure of what to do, his understanding of and control over the situation emerges bit by bit, now slowly, now with a sudden spurt.

You probably cannot sharply mark off each separate try, as perhaps you can with the dart thrower. But it is clear that something new and different is coming from all these fumblings and hesitations and experimentings. The outcome is different from the endeavors, and so the endeavors must transfer to the outcome, or the child will not learn. The outcome itself is identical in kind with the outcome with the dart thrower, although different words are convenient in the two cases. I called the dart throwing outcome an organized and structured pattern of action. The multiplication outcome is more appropriately called a pattern of understanding.

Now let us try to capture and state the general idea involved in these two illustrations. We have to recognize afresh that learning does not depend on repetition. Each try during practice is somewhat different and often very different from every other try; and the result or outcome itself is different from any of the tries in and through which it is produced. So each try, if it is to be fruitful rather than purely wasteful, must carry something over or transfer to the outcome. So far as we can see, there is only one way in which this can happen. Each try during practice must reveal at least a little something of the pattern of structured action or the pattern of understanding which *is* the outcome. Each try must carry with it at least a little glimmer of the insight which the learner is seeking. Each try must throw at least a little light on the way towards the solution which the learner is endeavoring to find. Only when this happens does each try move the learning forward. This is how each try transfers to the outcome of the whole learning enterprise. So we say that transfer is built into the very process and sequence of learning itself, and that each try transfers to the outcome of the learning by bringing with it a gleam of light, a glimmer (at least) of insight.

This is an enormously fruitful idea. Consider, for instance, the effects of drill on the learning of arithmetic. One common procedure has been to tell children that $7 + 9 = 16$, and $8 \times 9 = 72$, that $8 - 5 = 3$, and so on, and to have them repeat these statements until they can be recited promptly on demand. The procedure might perhaps seem sensible, but we know beyond a doubt that it produces very poor, very wasteful, very uncertain, very temporary learning (84). Why? Because practice is set up in such a way that children are given almost no chance at all to understand. Taking the case of the multiplication, what we want to have happen is that whenever children have to deal with combining eight groups of nine things or nine groups of eight things they will immediately and clearly understand what to do. We wish, in other words, to create an *insight.* But a child can say over "eight times nine are seventy-two" a hundred times without a single glimmer of insight in each or all the repetitions.

Or again, consider formal English grammar. What we want is to enable youngsters to embody their thought in precise, intelligible patterns of language. In order to do this they must be able to use transitive verbs, nouns, pronouns, conjunctions, prepositions, subjunctive moods, and so on as tools. But in much grammar teaching all such concepts are taught only as definitions to be memorized and applied in a small number of examples and problems. So the learning of grammar is organized as an almost meaningless routine, instead of being saturated with insight, as it ought to be. The result is that there is practically no transfer from the routine learning of the grammatical concepts to their natural application as working tools (25).

Or again, as a contrasting instance, consider the teaching of swimming. A great many coaches find it advantageous to teach a great deal of swimming out of the water. Why is it possible for a learner to transfer what he practices on the side of the pool to what he does in the pool? Because each practice try on the side of the pool is aimed straight at creating a patterned and structured co-ordination, so that it transfers to the final outcome.

2. Having seen that transfer is built into the very sequence and process of learning, let us now turn to the relation between transfer and the outcomes or results of learning. That relationship is very close, intimate, and essential. For *whenever we have really learned anything we can transfer it, and if we cannot transfer what we seem to have learned, we have not really learned it.* When a person says that he can throw darts at a target fairly well, he means that he can throw them fairly well at *any* target, not just at one particular target. When a person says that he is a good golfer, he means that he can make a golf shot well under many, if not all, circumstances. When a person

has "mastered" the basic arithmetical operations, it means that he can use them for keeping his personal accounts, figuring supplies needed for a camping trip, or anywhere that he needs to use them. So the very claim that we have learned anything means that we can use or transfer it.

You might be inclined to say that the instances I have just given are instances of application rather than of transfer. But just where is the distinction? In each of these instances the acquired ability is used in new situations, which is the only proof that it really has been acquired. It is in making just such applications or transfers that many people fail. A woman got ready to pay her ice bill at the end of the summer vacation. She found she had bought 1,425 pounds of ice, and she knew the price was fifty cents per hundred pounds. After some considerable figuring, she decided that she owed the iceman $365.25. This seemed rather high, so she recalculated, and brought out her debt to $17.00. The iceman charged her $7.13, which was the right price (304). This woman had certainly been taught arithmetic in school, and probably thought she knew it quite well. Did she really know her arithmetic, or did she not? Decidedly not! What would "knowing" arithmetic mean in this particular situation? It would mean seeing that one must divide 1,425 by 2, and then shift the decimal point two places over. "Knowing" arithmetic, that is to say, meant an act of insight. This woman was unable to use, or apply, or transfer (whichever word you prefer) her arithmetic because she did not really understand it, which is another way of saying that she had never really learned it.

Transferability, to be sure, is a matter of degree. So the more widely any result of learning can be transferred, the more useful and valuable it is. When formal English grammar hardly transfers at all, this means that it is both ill-learned and almost useless. But if English grammar is taught in such a way that it is really understood, it is better learned in itself, and also more useful because it will transfer widely. Typewriting does not seem to transfer to piano playing, and tennis probably does not transfer to baseball. The reason is that different patterns of co-ordination are involved in typewriting and piano playing and in tennis and baseball. But if typewriting and tennis were taught with less emphasis on special routines and more emphasis on rhythm, relaxation, breathing, proper control of the eyes, and so forth, it is very likely that typewriting and tennis would themselves be better learned, and also that they would transfer to piano playing and baseball to a considerable extent. So, too, with any school subject, the more it is learned through insight into its implications, its relationships, its meanings, the better one learns it, the more one gets from learning it, and the more widely it transfers to other situations including other school subjects.

What the argument in this section really comes to is that *whenever anything is really learned, it always affects personality to some extent.* Anyone who has really discovered what English grammar is all about has acquired a new insight into and a new attitude towards language. A woman who has really grasped the inwardness of arithmetic will not be apt to work herself into a frenzy when she tries to calculate the milk bill, or to balance her checkbook, or perhaps to figure her income tax. If a child has really learned and really understood even a little natural science, he has new feelings about things, he looks at the world with new eyes, new curiosities suggest themselves, new ambitions open up. Incidentally, too, a person who really learns one school subject is very likely to find that it has unsuspected bearings on other subjects; or, at least, he can easily be shown that it has such bearings. Learning in school does not transfer because transfer itself is impossible, but because such learning is often exceedingly bad learning, and because teachers simply take transfer for granted instead of planning and working for it.

CAUSATION OF TRANSFER

My last question leads straight to the question: How does transfer take place? What prevents it? What causes it? What are its necessary conditions? In dealing with this issue I shall have to start with a negative statement.

Identical elements

The theory of identical elements is that transfer is caused by similarities or identities between the situation in which an ability is learned and the situation in which that ability is used. Many English words are derived from Latin, so one might expect the study of Latin to help one use, understand, and even spell these words. There is much in common between English grammar and English composition, so grammar study should improve style. There seem to be common elements in being tidy with one's clothes, with one's room, and with one's paper work in school; so perhaps training in neat paper work will make a person neat in general. These instances, whether they seem to you sensible or not, are all suggested applications of the theory of transfer by identical elements, and I mention them to show you what the theory means.

But the theory does not hold water. "Some time ago habit training was introduced into prisons on the assumption that good habits make good citizens. The prisoners were taught hygiene habits, vocational habits, and were paid wages that they were forced to share with their families. During a long period of incarceration the prisoners received an impressive amount of such habit training, which was designed in such a way that identical elements in the world outside the prison should cause these salutary habits to function when the prisoner was freed. . . . The policy did not work out. The study of S. and E. T. Gulick shows that eighty per cent of the men discharged from a reformatory where many approved methods of habit training were in use, were not reformed five to fifteen years later, but continued in their course of crime. The gradual training of habits and reconditioning, with reliance upon identical elements within and without prison walls to effect the transfer, produced few reformations, if any at all. To the prisoner with a dominant anti-social outlook, or other antagonistic traits, such habit training is worthless, for he is in no frame of mind to put it to use. On the other hand, in those rare cases where the dominant attitude and goals are altered, habit training is of secondary importance. The reformed prisoner will find ways of learning to live more hygienically, of taking care of his family, of fulfilling his responsibilities, provided only that his interests and ideals are altered. And they are not altered by mere routine drill" (8, p. 263).

I hope you find this an extremely challenging statement. With a few changes in wording, it is a perfect picture of a great deal that goes on in school. We want to produce thinking people. Science, mathematics, and history contain a great deal of the stuff with which people think; and without available material people will never think very much or very well. Quite true! But we set up learning experiences in science, history, and mathematics which emphasize the memorization of content, and perhaps introduce some "thought questions" and "original problems" which are nothing but empty verbal puzzles.

We want to produce people who have a wide range of living interests. Literature, music, and art can be priceless lifelong interests. True again! But we teach the historical framework of literature and only the techniques and abstract "fundamentals" of music and art. We want our young people to develop an integrating philosophy of life. Every subject in the curriculum can contribute to and reflect upon such a philosophy. But we organize the learning of sheer memory content. We want children to adhere to normal social conventions, among which presumably is neatness. So we drill them on being neat in their paper work. We want the various subjects of the curriculum to bear upon one another, so we set up comprehensive survey courses in which little bits of various subjects are put together in any arbitrary way that we find convenient. We rely, that is to say, on identical elements. But good people, good citizens, strong and effective personalities are not developed by such procedures.

There is a very famous investigation which points straight at the issue raised by the theory of identical elements. The investigator raised the question as to how a change in the form or wording of a problem would affect a person's ability to deal with it, even though the problem remained essentially the same. A number of algebra problems were used, each problem being put in two different ways. The changes ranged from mere alterations of the letters (e.g. using p, q, r instead of x, y, z) to extensive alterations in wording and manner of statement. Here, for instance, is one of the problems stated in two quite widely different forms.

a) "There are two numbers. The first number plus three times the second number equals seven. The first number plus five times the second number equals eleven. What are the two numbers?"

b) $y = ax + b$

When $x = 3 \quad y = 7$

When $x = 5 \quad y = 11$

What does a equal?

Essentially the problem is exactly the same in the two forms; but 16% of the subjects were wrong with form (*a*) and 70% were wrong with form (*b*). That is to say, the identical elements did not affect their mental operations at all (656).

Yet another very interesting investigation was made of the effects of football on character. Playing football calls for team spirit, self-sacrifice, willingness to work hard, honesty, and so forth. Therefore it is said that football players will tend to develop these virtues and to show them everywhere in their lives. But an extensive study showed that taking part in athletics produced no gain in qualities making for good citizenship or in good habits of behavior in school (259).*

Evidently, then, the mere existence of identical elements, even when they are deliberately emphasized and made conspicuous, does not cause transfer. With this negative proposition out of the way, we can now turn to developing a positive answer to our question, How does transfer take place?

Motivation

The vital influence of motivation and attitude in producing transfer was shown in an experiment made with several groups of college and university students. One of these groups was made up of 28 college freshmen who were failing in their work. These freshmen were given special instruction in how to study. Then by way of a test they were called upon to spend 24 minutes reading a passage in general psychology, to spend 10 minutes giving a written account of the content of the passage, and to take a true-false test on it. Half of the 28 students were told to use the study methods they had been taught when they read the passage and tried to reproduce it. The other half were given no such suggestions, but merely allowed to do as well as they might. The previous "how-to-study" instruction seemed to have no effect on the students who were not specially told to use it; but that instruction had a great deal of effect on those who were specially urged to use it.

Another group in the same experiment consisted of 20 freshmen in a course in first-year college Latin. Admission to this course required four years preliminary Latin in secondary school. The 20 students were given a test requiring them to identify and explain 100 English words derived from Latin, 50 of these English words being derived from Latin words they had previously learned, and 50 of the English words being derived from Latin words they had not previously learned. You

* Recent events, one may think, have perhaps made this study needless!

will notice that for these students identical elements were present in 50 of the English words, and not present in the other 50 English words. The presence or absence of identical elements, however, did not seem to affect transfer. But attitude did affect transfer. Ten of the 20 students were advised to "use" their previous Latin in taking the derivation test, and 10 were not so advised. The students who were advised to use their previous Latin did very much better on the derivation test than those who were not so advised. Yet a third group in this same experiment consisted of 100 freshmen engineering students who had just finished a course in descriptive geometry. They were all given a brief test made up of such items as problems in short division, straight line alphabet, mental counting of the number of lines needed to construct certain objects, the forming of five-letter words from a given word, etc. Half of these students were urged to use their descriptive geometry whenever they could in dealing with the test, and the other half were given no suggestions at all. The students who were urged to apply their descriptive geometry to the test problems did much better than those who were not urged to do so (149).

Some very interesting and important conclusions can be drawn from this experiment.

1. An absolutely necessary condition for the transfer of learning to a new situation is that the learner must *want* to transfer it. No doubt high-school and college athletes do manifest many fine moral traits—in their athletic activities. But usually the athletes are not interested in manifesting the same moral traits in studying for their courses, in handling their jobs, in their social activities, in fulfilling their civic obligations, and so on. So there is very little transfer of ethical learning from athletics to life in general. A perverse and anti-social prisoner may learn excellent hygiene habits and vocational habits while he is in prison. But he has not the slightest interest in using these habits when he gets out, and so there is no transfer. A teacher may insist on children doing their paper work for her neatly. But if

they are not interested or concerned about being neat anywhere else, the neatness will not carry over to paper work for other teachers, and still less to dressing neatly or keeping rooms in good order. It so happens that this particular question of neatness was specially investigated many years ago. When a teacher merely insisted on neat work, she got some results when the children were working for her, but the results did not transfer at all. But if the teacher developed the general ideal of neatness, as something to be desired and sought for, then significant transfer took place (556).

2. There is nothing mysterious or obscure about getting people to want to transfer what they have learned to new situations and problems. Still less is there anything impossible about doing so. If you will re-read the account of the experiment on groups of college students you will see that the desire for transfer was brought about by very simple and common-sense means. Each of these groups of students faced a test. Presumably they were more or less anxious to do well with the test. Some of them were told that if they used what they had already learned, this would help them to do well with the test. And the telling was enough.

Of course, if one were dealing with refractory prisoners, the case would be different. To get such men to want to use good hygiene habits when they were released from jail would no doubt be a very formidable problem indeed. But teachers do not usually have to face any such difficulty. Let a teacher suggest to children that they collect and bring to school as many specimens of chemical elements as they can find around their homes, and most of them will do so eagerly. Let her suggest to a student who is taking woodworking that he plan his attack on a geometry problem much as he would plan a setup on the drill press; or conversely let her suggest that he use his geometry in planning the setup, and he will probably accept her suggestion with appetite. When teachers are told that transfer depends on purpose, motivation, attitude, interest (all of these words meaning much the same thing), they are apt to wring their hands and to say that purpose is beyond their control. Nonsense! There are endless possibilities for transfer in every school subject, and in almost every lesson; and all that a teacher need do is to emphasize these possibilities and to challenge pupils to explore them and discover them.

3. There is one kind of transfer that does in fact take place all the time in conventional schoolwork, although teachers rarely recognize it for what it is, and although it receives no notice in educational discussions. This is transfer from daily lessons to ultimate examinations. When the ultimate examination is given by authorities outside the school, as happens with the New York State Regents Examinations or the College Entrance Board Examinations, this kind of transfer is particularly conspicuous. Teachers preparing students for such examinations do not usually realize that they are dealing with a problem of transfer; yet that is precisely what their problem is, and they often deal with it very well in a purely technical sense. In particular, they build up the examination as an imposing challenge, and do everything possible to evoke a powerful motivation. Under these circumstances transfer indubitably takes place, the only question being whether it heads in the right direction. If a course in civics can be made to transfer to the New York State Regents Examination, there is no psychological reason in the wide world why it could not be made to transfer to better citizenship. All that would be needed would be the same businesslike, sensible, effective procedures which bring about the examination transfer. And the most vital element in these procedures is the arousal of a wish to see the connection and to make the transfer.

Insight

Many experiments have shown that transfer depends on insight. Perhaps the most famous and often quoted of these experiments dealt with learning to hit an underwater target with a dart. The difficulty in hitting the target is caused, of course, by the refraction of the water. Two groups of subjects practiced on this performance, one group being taught the theory of refraction, the other not. In the original learning, a knowledge of the theory of refraction did not help. Neither group had any advantage. Both had to learn by actual physical practice, and took about the same time to reach a given standard. Then the depth of the water was changed from twelve inches, which was the original depth, to four inches. In this new situation the group which had no understanding of refraction met with much difficulty and had to do a great deal of further learning. But the group which understood refraction adjusted far more quickly and needed much less additional practice (358). Thirty-five years later this same experiment was repeated. Once more it was found that an understanding of refraction helps a person to learn to hit underwater objects. But this time it turned out that a knowledge of refraction helped with the original learning with the water twelve inches deep as well as with the changed situation when the water was four inches deep. The persons who ran the experiment the second time found that less actual physical practice was needed, and also that thinking about what to do and understanding what to do had much more effect than had originally been supposed (296).

In another experiment dealing with the relation of insight to transfer an initial test and a final test were set up, in both of which the subjects were asked to formulate the moral of fifteen of Aesop's *Fables*. Between the two tests some of the subjects were given twelve twenty-minute lessons in analysis, abstraction, generalization, and on reading for comprehension, the material used in these lessons being quite different from that in the fables. Other subjects received no instructions between the two tests. Two groups of elementary school children who had received this special instruction between the two tests improved respectively 64.03% and 35.52% beyond other elementary school children who had received no instruction. One group of adult subjects who were given the special instruction improved 16.27% beyond other adults who had no instruction before the second of the two tests (31).

Method

The idea that transfer depends on insight or understanding, which was brought out in the experiments just described, has been developed from a somewhat different point of view in a number of other studies which emphasize the importance of method of learning in producing transfer.

One of these experiments dealt with memorizing poetry and nonsense syllables, using college sophomores as subjects. These subjects were divided into three groups. There was a control group which simply took memory tests at the beginning and end of the investigation, a practice group which practiced memorizing poetry and nonsense syllables for a total of 177 minutes divided into 8 periods, and a training group which was given special instruction in methods of memorizing along with practice. The instruction on how to memorize stressed learning by the "whole method," using rhythm and grouping (i.e. conscious structuralization), attention to meaning, mental alertness, and so-called "secondary connections" (i.e. more or less arbitrary associations which might help memory). This instruction took a total of 76 minutes, so that the training group practiced memorizing for only 101 minutes in contrast to 177 minutes for the practice group. But on the final memory tests the training group did on an average 31.6% better than the practice group (744).

Another experiment planned in a similar way dealt with the defining of words. There was an initial test and a final test. Also there were three groups of subjects—a control group which had no instruction or practice, a practice group which simply had routine practice in defining scientific terms, and a training group which had both practice and also instruction on how to make good definitions. This instruction stressed the importance of including everything in the meaning of a word when one defines it, and the importance of not leaving out anything included in that meaning. It was pointed out, with illustrations, that a good definition is not a mere repetition of the word to be defined, and that it ought to be clear and simple. The training group studied these criteria for a good definition, and also discussed them; and once again this group made a big advance in comparison with the practice group, although it had less actual practice in making definitions (450).

The same general result has been obtained in an investigation dealing with manipulative skills. The subjects were required to assemble various parts and details of electric fixtures. They had to assemble screws, strip screws, work with porcelains, wedges, and wiring connections. In this experiment, too, tests were given at the beginning and the end of the work. Practice produced some improvement, but practice plus explanation of principles and methods had a very great effect indeed, even though the explanations took time from the practice (126).

Various investigations have reported similar findings in connection with school work. For instance, it has been shown that lessons and discussions on how to deal with typical textbook material can pay excellent dividends. In one study on this question 30 lessons were set up on seeing important or essential topics when one reads, on separating important from unimportant topics by numbers and other symbols, and on outlining. It was found that there was a marked transfer from these "how-to-study" lessons to speed and comprehension in reading, and also to marks in a number of content subjects which were being taken by the students concerned (559).

Similarly groups of fifth-, sixth-, and seventh-grade pupils were given training in how to read historical materials. This training stressed ways of answering questions from the readings in history, the making of evaluations of what one had read, and outlining and summarizing what one had read. Very definite transfer effects were reported, and it was shown that the value of training and instruction in outlining was particularly great (593).

Another instance of somewhat the same kind is furnished by a special unit on South America. The organization of this unit made it possible to put much emphasis on picking out the most important points from information that had been gathered, on recognizing the contrasting viewpoints of different authorities, on using one's own experience to interpret information, on organizing information that had been gathered, on learning the use and value of maps, pictures, and graphs in interpreting information, and on making drawings, illustrations and graphs to convey knowledge and ideas (140).

As I have already suggested, these experiments which emphasize method in learning as a cause of transfer overlap the experiments which stress the importance of insight. The vital point in both these sets of experiments is that at least a large part of the secret of transfer is to make learning as meaningful, as "insightful," as consciously intelligent as possible.

Transfer, then, depends on motivation and attitude, on insight, and on an intelligent method of learning. These are not three different ideas. They are three aspects of the same idea, and taken together they point to a very definite practical conclusion. *Transfer is produced best when anything is learned in close connection with its applications.* This is sound psychology and also practical good sense. The value of learning general ideas and principles and also physical skills in close relationship with their actual use is recognized in the case method of teaching law, in clinical training in medicine, in golf instruction while the learner is actually going round the course, in the setting up of combat conditions in military training, in the use of relief models on a sand tray in the briefing of combat pilots, in having mechanics learn their skills by assembling and disassembling airplane engines, and so forth. Learning, indeed, is usually organized on a basis of the closest possible application whenever real efficiency and authentic results are earnestly desired.

No sensible person can doubt that the learning of curricular subject matter must be organized on this same basis if children are to transfer it to the problems and issues of actual living, i.e. if they are really to learn this subject matter effectively. Moreover curricular subject matter can be taught and learned in close contact with its applications. Community hygiene has been taught in connection with a local survey of health conditions carried on by the children in a rural school. Local history and a wide range of social concepts have been taught in connection with a year-long study of a local textile industry. Reforestation and the conservation of soil and wildlife have been taught in terms of actual participation in many rural schools. Fractions have been taught in connection with planning menus for parties (119, 301, 439). There is a most curious tendency to call these practices "progressive," and to think of them as very modern inventions. They are really nothing of the sort. They are merely, and, indeed, obviously sound and sensible. They produce an excellent grade of learning, and they tend to make that learning transfer to the very situations on which it ought to have a bearing. Let us pause for a moment to consider just why this is so.

1. When a child sees that something he learns has a bearing beyond the classroom and the school and the examination situation—that it has a bearing on what he wants to do and to understand—he is strongly motivated to learn that something well. A topic in social studies, a mathematical process, a scientific idea ceases to be a mere lesson and is transformed into a tool for living. It becomes an instrumentality by which he can satisfy certain basic needs. When this happens, an essen-

tial condition for effective learning and far-reaching transfer is immediately created.

2. No one can bring to bear a social or scientific concept or a mathematical technique upon the actual problems of living unless he understands it. Indeed the very process of coming to understand any such concept or technique is the process of coming to see how to apply it. A concept or a technique which is only learned in words (if one can really call this learning it) is more or less useless. A concept or a technique becomes useful by being understood. When it is understood, and only when it is understood, it can be brought to bear on genuine challenges, and can serve as a tool for living. When it is understood, that is to say, it transfers.

3. One learns any skill best by learning how to use it. This statement applies to any skill, all the way from such "intellectual" skills as efficient reading, efficient outlining, or efficient computing, to motor and manipulative skills like assembling gadgets and fixing machines, or, for that matter, such skills as hitting tennis balls or shooting baskets in basketball. Such skills are always best learned when one mixes as much intelligence as possible with the learning, because then the learner can use the skills most freely, or (in more technical language) transfer them most widely. A first-rate mechanic applies intelligence rather than mere routine. So does a first-rate mathematician or a first-rate golfer. Insight into the rationale of the skill gives one a far more flexible and extensive command over it than routine ever can.

Notice that the reason why anything transfers best when it is learned in close connection with its applications is *not* because there are then many identical elements in the learning situation and the application situation. The important thing always is not what there is in the situation, but what happens to the learner. Learning in close connection with application tends to evoke purpose, to evoke insight, and to render learning meaningful throughout its course.

TRANSFER AND THE SCHOOL

Our discussion of transfer of training has numerous and many-sided implications for schools and teachers. Some of these implications we must now consider.

1. First let us consider transfer between school subjects. How does the learning of one subject affect the learning of other subjects? How should and can the learning of one subject affect the learning of other subjects? These closely linked questions are the first with which we must deal. They have received a great deal of attention in the research literature. Indeed, they have been discussed and investigated more than they deserve to be, for the problem of transfer in relation to schoolwork involves much wider issues. Still, it is important to consider them, because they throw much light on what teaching is and what it ought to be.

As to the actual influence of learning one subject upon learning other subjects, the facts are very plain and well-established. That influence is usually negligible. Scores and, indeed, hundreds of investigations have reached substantially this conclusion. There is not the least need to describe or even to list any considerable number of these investigations, for the findings that have already been mentioned in this chapter are thoroughly typical, and have been duplicated in effect again and again. Grammar study does not improve the ability to understand and interpret English, to write good English, or even to identify and correct grammatical errors. Latin study may have some effect on English vocabulary, but appears to have none on English style or on the ability to read English. It is true that students taking Latin tend to do better in other subjects than students not taking Latin; but the reason is that students who take Latin tend to be above average in intelligence or "academic aptitude," so that their superiority in other subjects is not due to Latin. The study of the various sciences has remarkably little mutual effect. Learning chemistry does not help students to learn physics. Algebra (as we have seen) prepares very poorly for physics. And to cap the climax, high-school chemistry seems to have very little effect on college chemistry; for when the achievements of large numbers of students were compared, those who had taken chemistry only in college did just about as well in a chemistry test as those who had taken it in both high-school and college (528). One investigator who has summarized and co-ordinated a great many studies on transfer between subjects has reported that there is usually some positive transfer. In a strictly statistical sense this is true. But the amount of transfer is so small as to be negligible.*

Why is there so little transfer between subjects? This is a very easy question! Because in conventional teaching there is no emphasis on interrelationships, and no organized urge to discover connections. As just one revealing and all-too-typical example, consider the following piece of translation produced in an advanced Latin course. "L. Lucullus was able to remedy a part of this grave war and disaster by your united order, part of the army was sent away and part handed over to M. Glabrio because you follow the manner shown by the example" (456). By merely looking at this specimen one can tell just how the learning was slanted. The student was simply trying to hammer out something or other in some approximation to English. He was not thinking about meanings, and probably he did not really care about meanings. Hence transfer from Latin to English style was impossible.

Yet Latin certainly can be taught for transfer. Several quite careful studies have shown that if Latin is taught with an intelligent emphasis on English derivatives, and if learners are motivated to seek and find the connection between Latin itself and Latin-derived English words, English derivatives will be learned through Latin study (127, 262, 272). Whether this

* Readers interested in the detailed facts are referred to bibliography items 499, 500.

particular and quite narrow kind of transfer from Latin is worth bothering with may be a question, but at least we can see how to produce it. As to teaching Latin so that it will improve English style, which is a far more valuable thing to do, there can be no doubt that this is possible, though so far as I know the point has never been formally investigated. One would select or even actually write material in Latin that would have some genuine interest to the learners. One would urge them to turn the Latin into good idiomatic English. One would use class time to compare and criticize the translations produced, more from the standpoint of style and expression than of accuracy wordwise. These procedures would almost certainly have an effect on English style, and they would also add up to a very good way of teaching Latin.

The case is much the same with arithmetic. Indeed, the lack of transfer which has been revealed in the learning of arithmetic is really quite surprising even to a hardened psychologist. Children learn to add columns of two-place numbers, but this seems to help them very little in learning to add three-place numbers. Learning to add does not help with learning to subtract, or multiply, or divide. Apparently all such learnings are in watertight compartments, and have virtually no mutual influence. The reason, of course, is that these so-called "computational skills" are taught by sheer routine memorization; and the cure is to substitute insight. The introduction of insight and the evocation of purpose in the learning of arithmetic involves a vastly greater variety of practices than can be described in this chapter, but here are just a very few samples.

When a column of two-place or three-place numbers is set up for addition, the teacher may discuss with the children why it is important to arrange the numbers so that units, tens, and hundreds are always lined up below each other vertically. This immediately challenges thinking about what addition really is, and why one performs certain manipulations with units, tens, and hundreds. Or in teaching multiplication one may set up the following sum:

$$\begin{array}{r} 89 \\ 47 \\ \hline 623 \\ 356 \\ \hline 4{,}183 \end{array}$$

This sum can be used, not to demonstrate routine, but to focalize thought. Why are the numbers arranged so that the 9 of 89 is above the 7? Why is the 3 of 63 (i.e. product of 7 × 9) written under the 9 of 89? It is a very curious thing that such a packet of challenges to thought as the above sum should so often be taught as a pure routine. Yet here is the reason for lack of transfer.

Or again, one can use concrete objects which children can manipulate in order to reveal that addition, subtraction, multiplication, and division all have to do with grouping—addition involving the combination of things into new, larger groups, subtraction involving the taking away of things from groups, multiplication being repeated addition, and division showing how many times a smaller group is contained in a larger one. It should be perfectly obvious how procedures of this kind will tend to produce transfer. Moreover, all these learnings can go on in situations and in response to challenges which are genuinely important to the learners (250).

Actual formal experiments on increasing the amount of transfer between school subjects are not very numerous considering the significance of the problem—enormously less numerous than experiments demonstrating that conventional teaching produces very little transfer. Yet the general principle on which transfer can be increased is very clear. Do not emphasize sheer drill. Stress relationships, meanings, methods of procedure. Motivate pupils to see the indicated connections and to apply the emerging insights.

2. The transfer of subject matter beyond the school is a far more important problem than the transfer of one subject to other subjects. The following letter, written by a young man on relief to his former high-school principal, puts the issue clearly and even devastatingly.

> I wish I had been taught more about family relationships, child care, getting along with people, paying off a small mortgage, household mechanics, politics, local government, the chemistry of food, carpentry, how to budget and live within the budget, the value of insurance, how to figure interest when borrowing money, how to detect shoddy goods, how to distinguish a political demagogue from a statesman, how to grow a garden, how to paint a house, how to get a job, how to be vigorous and healthy, how to be interesting to others, how to resist high-pressure salesmanship, how to buy economically and intelligently, and the danger of buying on the installment plan (49, pp. 425–426).

Compared to such a challenge, the problems of teaching Latin so that it will improve English spelling, or of teaching children to transfer multiplication to division may seem to pale into insignificance. Yet, psychologically speaking, the issue is exactly the same, and the solution must be sought along similar lines.

We may be reasonably sure that the effective out-of-school transfer of subject matter is extremely meager. The young man who wrote the letter thought so, and there is little doubt but that he was right. Two of the most extensive investigations ever made—they involved over 14,000 subjects—showed that a year's work in high school has very little effect in the way of improving reasoning ability. High-school programs of all kinds, ranging from very academic to very vocational were considered; and it was found that no matter what kind of program a student might take, the improvement in reasoning ability that could be attributed to the program itself was negligible.

The reasoning test used in this investigation called mainly for verbal manipulations of various kinds. It was, therefore, very "schoolwise" in character. Yet curricular studies had very little effect on performance on this test (92, 663). If this is true, then we may take it as an almost absolute certainty that conventional teaching will do very little indeed to help a person with the sort of challenges mentioned by the young man in his letter.

Yet notice that almost all the problems he mentioned are related to the subject matter of the curriculum. Social studies surely ought to help one recognize a demagogue and understand local government. Science is certainly relevant both to physical health and house painting, not to mention the chemistry of food. So far as paying off a mortgage, living within a budget, and recognizing the pitfalls of installment buying are concerned, the basic techniques involved are those of mathematics. So I could go on, but it seems fairly clear that the subject matter of the curriculum does in fact provide means for dealing intelligently with most, if not all, of this young man's life problems. Why subject matter *as taught* does not transfer to these problems is so obvious, both in itself and also in the light of our whole discussion, that I shall not consider the point. The important question is how subject matter must be taught and learned if it is to apply to problems like this.

a) It would not be much use to base teaching on the theory of identical elements. Organizing on the basis of the theory of identical elements would presumably mean setting up units on how to paint a house, how to pay off a mortgage, how to figure interest on installment payments, how to look after one's health, how to judge the claims of insurance agents, and so forth, and giving definite answers in each of the said units. This kind of thing has been tried from time to time, but it does not seem to work out very well. (1) The situation of a youngster in high school is very different from that of a young family man who has lost his job. What is a disastrous challenge to the destitute husband and father may be a mere academic abstraction to the high-school student. So we really could not establish situations with many identical elements even if we tried. (2) We cannot tell how many of the students now before us in high school will ever be in just the pickle of the young man who wrote the letter. Ten years from now many of the adolescents with whom we deal may very well be grappling with entirely different and quite unforeseeable problems. Even if identical elements could be established in any case, they certainly cannot be established unless we can know the future in advance. (3) Few if any of the young man's problems can be met by routine solutions. Doctors keep changing their ideas about how to keep healthy. Laws affecting small installment loans are frequently altered. The advisability of taking on a mortgage depends on one's entire financial status and prospects. Even painting a house is far from a rule-of-thumb process, for what one does depends, among other things, upon the existence of a vapor bar and the condition of the wall. So when this young man or anybody else says in effect, "These are the things I need to be able to do. Please teach me just how to do them," he is asking an impossibility. Putting all this in technical language it amounts to saying that the theory of identical elements will not meet the issue.

b) The only possible way of meeting the challenge of transferring subject matter beyond the school is to teach it as a means of dealing intelligently with problems which are in some measure real and cogent to the learner here and now. No one can learn in terms of what he will be ten years from now. He can learn only in terms of what he now is. Of course, a teacher does not simply accept as limiting conditions the problems of which young people are aware of their own accord. One great duty of every teacher is to make learners sense problems of which they will not otherwise be aware. But these are by no means necessarily the problems which life forces upon the attention of destitute fathers or sixty-five-year-old retirees or women of thirty who have just given birth to twins. Indeed, the vital point is not the actual content of the problem, but its genuineness and vitality for the learner as he is here and now. What we must do is to show learners that subject matter provides ways of thinking about, understanding, and dealing intelligently with some kind of genuine life problems, so that the possibility of transferring subject matter to life is revealed and the disposition to transfer it to life is generated. If this is done, the teacher has done his best. He has discharged his responsibility. And if later on the learner complains that he cannot handle this or that life problem, when the teacher has put the instrumentalities for handling it into his possession, then the learner has himself to thank.

To discuss at length how these generalizations would work out in practice goes far beyond the scope of this book, but a few sample illustrations will serve at least to indicate the kind of thing that can be done.

The first of these illustrations is a rich and varied course in algebra which was set up on an experimental basis as an alternative to the conventional algebra course pointed towards the College Entrance Board examinations. Algebraic techniques were not stressed in this course, although they were taught, usually more or less incidentally. There was much emphasis on great mathematical discoveries, and on the lives and achievements of great mathematicians. Much time in the course was spent in reading about, explaining and discussing the applications of mathematics to industry, science, economics, weather prediction, and so on. The class was shown how to develop mathematical formulae for many common experiences. Numerous mathematical concepts were taken up, studied, and explained, usually in a more or less nontechnical way. Methods of mathematical thinking were also studied and discussed. As may be inferred, there was much collateral and general reading and much general discussion, which made the course very different from the conventional course in algebra.

There was every reason to believe that this experimental course had a far-reaching effect. Some of the students showed a keen interest in finding formulae, or at least in seeing how formulae could be found for the flight of birds, the flowing of water, and suchlike phenomena. Also some of them became interested in possible applications of mathematics to out-of-doors activities. It was quite clear that many members of the class learned something significant about what "straight thinking" means, and gained a new sense of both the greatness and the limitations of the human mind. At the end of the year the members of the experimental course had not developed quite as much computational skill as those in the conventional course; but they had established strong positive attitudes towards mathematics, and real and vital insights into the meaning and value of mathematics in human life (366).

Another illustration is an experimental organization of science instruction carried on in the seventh and ninth grades. The distinctive feature of the plan was the use of a great deal of interesting extensive reading. Forty books on science which seemed likely to be appealing to seventh- and ninth-graders were made available. The books were catalogued, and brief reviews and reading guides were prepared. So the work amounted to a very well-organized and vital reading course in general science, with class time devoted to guiding the students' reading, and to discussing and collating what had been read. The course achieved superior results in the way of scientific knowledge. Also it brought about a very definite development of scientific attitudes, such as an objective outlook expressing itself in the avoidance of superstitions, a sensitive curiosity about reasons for familiar happenings, a tendency to delay one's response and to hold opinions tentatively, a tendency to weigh evidence rather than jumping to conclusions, and increased respect for the opinions of others. The following will indicate the kind of teaching material used in trying to influence and develop scientific attitudes. "Newspaper clippings containing false deductions, problems with insufficient or superfluous data, incomplete demonstrations of experiments permitting prediction of possible solutions, and reports of inventors and other scientists who were forced to struggle for their success against prejudice and narrow minds . . . were introduced and discussed in class" (136).

Two attempts to reduce the susceptibility of students to propaganda also bear on the problem of getting subject matter to transfer beyond the school. One of these attempts measurably succeeded, and the other failed (502). In one of these experimental attempts, quite large numbers of high-school and college students in social studies classes were given a unit on how to organize propaganda, the unit lasting a week. This unit of work did not seem to have any effect on the students' own susceptibility to propaganda. In the other experimental attempt, in which college students were used as subjects, there were nine lessons in the nature of propaganda involving much discussion and practice in recognizing propaganda in published material and on the radio. A special "gullibility" test at the end of the work indicated that susceptibility to propaganda had been reduced. There are three comments to make about these two experiments. (1) Any test on "gullibility," or susceptibility to propaganda will be only suggestive, not conclusive. It can do no more than indicate whether some effect has been produced. (2) When instruction emphasizes the meaning and motives of propaganda rather than techniques in preparing propaganda material, it does seem to have an effect, even though the instruction does not last long and is rather slender. (3) These experiments strongly suggest that social science teaching could transfer very extensively to life, both in helping people to be intelligent about propaganda and in many other ways as well, if it were slanted systematically and sensibly in the desired directions (57).

Now that you have read these three illustrations, go back again to the generalizations set up on pages 291–296. Notice that in all three cases the learners are shown how subject matter can provide ways of thinking about, understanding, and dealing intelligently with genuine life problems, and that these life problems are brought to the notice of the learner by the organized planning of the work.

c) From all that has been said it is clear that our account of transfer bears on the whole pattern of teaching. There can be no doubt that the great barrier to transfer between subjects, and to the transfer of subject matter to life, is the conventional pattern of teaching. If we set up a body of subject matter in a narrow compartment, and point everything towards tests and examinations within the segregated area, it would be a miracle if students would interest themselves much in anything beyond the boundary fence. The experimental instruction in algebra, in general science, and in propaganda which I have just described, proceeds on a radically different psychological basis. So would such a plan as I suggested for teaching Latin to improve English style, and also the various plans for teaching Latin to improve command of English-Latin derivatives. In all these cases the whole setup and motivation of the learning is pointed towards transfer beyond subject-matter boundaries. By way of contrast, the conventional setup and motivation of learning points straight to transfer from daily and fragmentary learnings to an ultimate examination. So long as we adhere chiefly to this latter pattern, talk about transfer of one subject to others and about transfer of subject matter to life will remain largely talk, for we certainly cannot have it both ways.

There are, however, two cogent questions that remain to be considered.

(1) If we organize instruction in any subject with a strong emphasis on transfer beyond its own boundaries, do we not tend to denature the subject? We propose, let us say, to teach Latin with a strong emphasis on English style, or to teach algebra with a strong emphasis on the place of mathematics

in human affairs, or to teach general science with a strong emphasis on scientific attitudes in ordinary living. Very good! But how much Latin, or algebra, or general science will the students "really learn" under any such plan? It all depends on what one means by "really learn." Under an instructional pattern geared for transfer beyond the subject, pupils will perhaps not learn quite as much of the kind of elementary technique and sheer information that is required in the conventional examination as they would learn under a conventional instructional pattern. But can we call the kind of learning that is intended to transfer to the conventional examination "real learning"? Certainly not. Such learning does not apply, and it does not last; and these are two acid tests. To learn any body of subject matter so that it will transfer beyond its own boundaries, students must be motivated to use and apply it; and they must understand it well enough to at least begin to recognize its implications. This, on all rational grounds, is the only kind of learning worth calling real learning. It has been very well said that subjects do not transfer either to one another or to life because they are not genuinely learned at all, i.e. not genuinely understood. So it is the conventional pattern of teaching rather than its proposed alternative that denatures the subject.

(2) If we teach subject matter with our eyes constantly on life problems, are we not going the long way round? If we want better English style, why teach Latin? If we want better house painting, why teach chemistry and physics? If we want better health, why teach physiology and anatomy? These are very pressing questions. In answering them three points must be made.

First, we do not teach subject matter *ad hoc* for this or that life problem or even for some definite predetermined class of life problems. Chemistry and physics can be made fruitful in terms of house painting—and in many other ways as well. Anatomy and physiology can be made fruitful in terms of better personal health—and in many other ways as well. Latin can be made fruitful in terms of better English style—and in many other ways as well. The point is to make subject matter fruitful here and now, and this to reveal to young learners its unending possibilities of further fruitfulness.

Second, when a subject is taught so as to yield legitimate transfer values, it yields its own values best. Latin, algebra, physiology, anatomy, chemistry, and physics are themselves learned best when the learner is brought to recognize and interest himself in at least some of their significant applications.

Third, the question, Why teach English style through Latin? is obviously a sticker, and it raises an issue of principle. Certainly English style can be well-taught without Latin. Indeed, there is usually more than one way of intelligent approach to any life problem. The psychologist does not necessarily make a plea for Latin or, indeed, for any other stated subject, as a uniquely valuable instrumentality.

What he does maintain, however, is that the content of human culture, a selection of which is embodied in the curriculum, can always be made fruitful in terms of more enlightened living, and of methods of dealing with the problems of life which are effective because they involve the application of insight.

QUESTIONS FOR DISCUSSION

1. It is constantly said that our schools ought to teach the ideals and values of the democratic way of life. In other words, what is taught in school should transfer to certain far-reaching ethical and social ideals. To bring this about would it be enough to choose the right textbooks and to offer appropriate explanations? If not, what else would be necessary?

2. A tradition still supported in some quarters is to have elementary-school children study the Constitution of the United States. Presumably the idea is that such study will transfer to better citizen-

ship. What is your opinion of this practice, from a psychological standpoint?

3. If you happened to go to church last Sunday, you probably heard a sermon which the preacher hoped would transfer to life. Did he do anything to make such transfer probable? If not, what might he have done?

4. There is a great deal of evidence that geometry as taught does not improve one's ability to reason in nongeometrical matters. From your recollection of your own courses in geometry, would you have expected this negative outcome? Why? Do you think that geometry could be taught in such a way as to train people to reason better in general?

5. Some psychologists make a distinction between the transfer of learning and the application of learning. Do you think such a distinction is tenable?

6. If you seriously wanted the athletic program of a school to be an agency for moral training, and if you had the power to shape up the program just as you thought best, what would you do?

7. Do you see any reasons why studying a subject primarily to pass an examination should not do much to enable a person to apply that subject in his daily life?

8. It has been said in this chapter that transfer is facilitated if we teach a subject in close contact with its life applications. Does this seem to involve a belief in transfer by identical elements. If not, what are the reasons for the statement?

9. At the opening of this chapter some of the classic tenets of educational philosophy were presented. It is often suggested that we have gone beyond such ideas, and that they are outmoded in modern educational thought. Do you find any support for them in the discussion of transfer here presented?

SUGGESTED READINGS

Cook, T. W., "Repetition and Learning: I. Stimulus and Response." *Psychological Review*, LI (1944), 25–36.

Dorsey, Mattie E., and Hopkins, L. Thomas, "The Influence of

Attitude upon Transfer." *Journal of Educational Psychology*, XXI (1930), 410–417.

Orata, Pedro Tamesis, *The Theory of Identical Elements*. Ohio State University Press, Columbus, 1928.

———, "Transfer of Training and Educational Pseudo-Science." *Mathematics Teacher*, XXVIII (1935), 265–289.

Salisbury, Rachel, "A Study of the Transfer Effects of Training in Logical Organization." *Journal of Educational Research*, XXVIII (1934), 241–254.

11

The Concept of Mental Growth

EDUCATION AND MENTAL GROWTH

HAVING dealt at some length with the process of learning, we now turn to consider the process of mental growth, or mental development. Since some people make at least a slight distinction between what is called "growth" and what is called "development," I should explain that here I use the two words to mean the same thing.

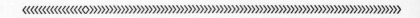

The concept of mental growth has a very important place in modern psychological thinking, and a great deal has been done to bring it to bear on educational planning and procedures. In fact, as I pointed out in the opening chapter, one whole school of psychology undertakes to interpret education precisely as the guidance of growth. Nevertheless, there is nothing inconsistent, still less conflicting, in an emphasis on learning on the one hand and on mental growth on the other. A person's education is always, in reality and in essence, the shaping of his personality. Personality is shaped and molded by facing real challenges and real problems, and by finding ways of dealing with those challenges and problems. In our discussion of motivation we saw what makes a problem or a challenge "real" to anybody—what makes it an ego-involved problem or challenge. In our discussion of learning we saw how solutions to such problems are achieved. Now we are to carry our thinking a step further by introducing the concept of mental growth, and seeing how it bears on the process of adjustment, in and through which personality is shaped and molded, and the character and destiny of human individuals is determined.

1. The terms "learning" and "growth" are not very exactly used or very sharply distinguished, even in technical psychological writings. But there is a very important difference between them. On the whole one thinks of "learning" as pointed towards some more or less specific and definable achievement. A person *learns* to read, to play golf, to multiply, to meet this or that conventional social requirement, to enjoy poetry, to dislike office work. He *learns* Latin or history or algebra. Learning, in short, has a terminal point and a more or less definite outcome.

But when we speak of "mental growth" we have in mind more general and long-term changes in the personality. A person *learns* the binomial theorem, but he *grows* in mathematical insight. He *learns* good English usage, but he *grows* in his ability to express himself well in English. He *learns* to use a knife and fork properly, or not to interrupt when other people are talking, or to take part in a team game; but he *grows* in his general ability to adjust to and cope with social situations. He *learns* English vocabulary, but he *grows* in the capacity to use abstract words as symbols for general concepts.

2. When we think about a person's mental development we think of the future total effect that his specific learning experiences have upon him. In each separate experience in and through which a person learns, he probably achieves or acquires

something fairly specific and definable. But the effect of the learning experience is not limited to its direct outcome. It always has some influence upon his whole development, and tends to some extent to steer that development in some direction. To have learned anything at all, no matter what, is not merely to have achieved a definite result, but also to have gotten oneself ready to learn something else. Every learning experience affects our attitude toward and our aptitude for future learning experiences.

3. Conversely, a person's capacity for adjustment at any given time depends on his maturity, i.e. on how much and what kind of growing and developing he has done. Many adult problems have absolutely no appeal or meaning at all to a child, and if we try to teach him ways of solving such problems, he will only learn empty words without understanding them in the least. So specific learnings both affect mental development and depend upon it.

4. When we think in terms of mental growth we are led to ask ourselves both how far a person is capable of developing and how far he has actually developed. Consider two twelve-year-old children, one very brilliant, and the other quite dull. These two children may be about the same size and may not even look so very different. But they are on quite different levels of development, so that one can be made aware of problems which mean nothing to the other, and is capable of benefiting from learning experiences which would be so much dead wood for the other.

All these four ways of thinking about people come into our mental horizons when we think in terms of mental growth. Yet there is absolutely nothing in them that is in conflict with what has already been said about learning; and also, there is nothing in them which makes it unnecessary to understand, consider, and plan for good learning. One very distinguished authority has drawn a contrast between what he calls a "narrow psychology of learning" and a "liberal psychology of development" (218). But a psychology of learning is only "narrow" if we fail to remember that each specific learning experience, with its definite outcome, is part and parcel of a long sequence of development. And a psychology of development, whether we like to call it "liberal" or not, makes no sense at all if we ignore or slight specific learning experiences. For the only way in which mental development can take place at all is by means of learning experiences.

To recapitulate and summarize, the process of adjustment, in and through which personality is shaped, involves the arousal of the will and the finding of the way. Each specific learning experience reveals a few definite steps of the way, and of course these steps must be taken or a person gets nowhere. But when the steps are taken, new horizons and perspectives open up, and this we call the developmental effect of the specific learning, or the process of mental growth.

GROWTH GRADIENTS

The process of mental growth and development is not nearly so easy to pin down and explain as the process of learning. Yet everyone in educational work ought to have a good, clear understanding of that process. Mental growth has certain well-recognized characteristics. It is brought about and helped along by certain well-understood causes. Also, there are certain influences which can distort, or impede, or even prevent it. Since it is a teacher's business to get children and young people to grow mentally as well as possible, she needs to know about all these things. It is quite possible to give a general explanation of the characteristics of mental growth, and of the influences which tend to favor it or to impede it, and, as a matter of fact, such an explanation will be necessary before we are done. But explanations of this kind are bound to be more or less abstract, and this makes their real meaning rather hard to grasp. What seems the best way to meet this difficulty is to describe a number of actual instances of mental growth before taking up any general explanation and analysis. So in the rest of this chapter I shall describe certain specific lines of growth, or "growth gradients," * about which we have a good deal of quite definite knowledge.

Growth in drawing ability

A child's growth in the ability to draw with a pencil has been analyzed and described in a very interesting way (56). In the first two years of a child's life he manifests nothing that could be called "drawing" according to adult standards. He merely scrawls lines and marks on the paper. Some people would say that when the child does such things he is going through a "scribble stage." But this is a very misleading interpretation. As a matter of fact, the child is simply reacting according to his whole nature and his possibilities and capacities at that age. He cannot make fine, controlled movements with his wrist, hand, and fingers. The movements he makes with the pencil on the paper are large, oscillating arm movements. There is little organization or repetition in these movements. He holds the crayon or pencil in his fist rather than with his fingers. He tends to use the crayon as a general plaything instead of a specialized tool for drawing. For instance, he may put it in his mouth from time to time. Moreover, in his early use of crayon and paper he has no idea at all of representing anything.

It is from this level of behavior that control evolves. The child's movements become less casual and exploratory. The lines he makes become less and less clustered in one part of the paper. The whole paper comes to be used more and more as a total field. Closed lines and space-forms begin to appear, produced partly by the feeling of his own muscular move-

* The term "growth gradient" is used by Arnold Gesell (218). I have suggested and used elsewhere the less technical term "line of growth" (469). Both terms mean the same thing.

ments, and also by his increased noticing of what he is doing. By about the age of three his control of shape and form will probably have developed a good deal. Moreover, a new factor is likely to come in, for he begins to take pride in his work, and to show it to other people with the suggestion, "See what I've done." Now connections between his drawings and actual pictures begin to emerge, and the child gives names to his pictures and may be disappointed if other people can't tell what they are "about."

A further organization of his motor activities goes on, with an increasingly discriminating and conscious use of the whole paper as "picture space." By the age of four, the almost formless activity of two years earlier has at least started to shape up into a definite technique with high personal values. Drawing materials become tools instead of general playthings. The crayon is held and manipulated with the fingers, instead of being grasped in the fist. So the child is in a position to try to represent and to express what he has in mind, and this he proceeds to do. Moreover, his pictures become valued personal possessions, to be cherished, owned, and taken home for admiration. Here is the embryo of all artistic development, and you can easily see that if a teacher wants a child to develop artistic capabilities, the best thing she can do is to favor and foster this evolution in every possible way.

Notice that in this sequence of development (*a*) patterns of response become more and more definite; (*b*) precise and discriminating reactions evolve out of crude ones; (*c*) conscious or "mental" awareness becomes clearer; (*d*) awareness of the implications and relationships of what is being done (e.g. its social implications and effects on other people) steadily expands; (*e*) a technique for satisfying many basic needs is progressively discovered. All these and other general points will be discussed more fully later on, but for the moment I merely call them to your attention.

Social development

At birth a human being is virtually nonsocial. Up to about the age of two months the infant responds to changes in the intensity and quality of stimuli that impinge upon him rather than to the personal origins of those stimuli. The infant's earliest social reactions are to adults, and only later on does he begin to react to and show interest in other children as well. The earliest reactions to other children have been noted as occurring at about four to five months old, and these reactions develop rapidly up to the end of the second year of life.

With responsiveness to other children the beginnings of shyness appear. The first reactions to other children take the form of observation and noticing, and then of "parallel" behavior, i.e. doing what the other children are doing rather than joining in their activities. Co-operative behavior usually manifests itself during the second year. At first this type of behavior is brief, sporadic, and limited to quite small groups. A child of nursery-school age cannot act co-operatively with more than five or six other children, and tends to be better suited with not more than three of them. Not until he is about ten years old will a child's responses to a whole class group of ten or upwards be well established and functional. Competition and co-operation begin quite early, but for a long time they are not sharply distinguished. We usually cannot say whether a child is acting co-operatively with a group or asserting himself competitively in the group, and in fact he is probably doing both at the same time.

Quarreling and scuffling are to be expected as a child learns to deal with others, including his close friends. At first these reactions may take a definitely physical form, including much yelling and scolding, but as subtler techniques and better understandings emerge, better and more effective ways of getting along with others appear. The child comes to acquire his behavior patterns more and more from others, so that the group with which he is associated influences his level of aspiration, and so that he responds to pace-making. With the enlarging and expanding social reactions that arrive soon after the child has entered school, gang tendencies begin to display themselves. These gang influences are very important, for they foster response to social approval, suggestibility, negativism to adults, rivalry, true sympathy involving an understanding of the situation of other people, ideals of good sportsmanship, and snobbishness and exclusiveness. Also the example and personality of the teacher is very influential with children of elementary-school age, and she can do much to counter the tendency of many children ten to twelve years old to consider this or that activity or experience "sissy-ish" (219, 220, 339).

With adolescence the patterning of social behavior grows more definite and elaborate. The simple games of childhood give place to highly organized team games. Even in childhood the behavior of the two sexes is differentiated, and this differentiation grows into highly organized and clearly defined sets of mores and etiquette and expectations. During adolescence leadership relationships establish themselves on a more or less permanent basis, arising to a considerable extent out of skill and achievement in admired activities. Personal evaluations of others shift with age. In one investigation it was shown that seventh-grade boys admired skill and aggressiveness in games, and were indifferent to neatness of appearance. Boys would readily accept girls of the same age-level who were active, but would also admire girls who were not active physically if they were considered friendly and pretty. Ninth-grade boys began to show concern for their physical appearance, held team games and physical skill in high regard, and liked girls who were "good sports." By the twelfth-grade level girls were admired if they played a definitely feminine role. Boys still thought very highly of athletic prowess, but admired a wider range of successful activities than did the younger boys, thinking highly of success in debate, on the school newspaper, and so on (326, 685).

More specifically, growth in the understanding of social concepts has been studied. What happens is that children become able to deal with more and more abstract and inclusive concepts. One investigation dealt with the learning of 25 social concepts by a group of fifth-grade children. The 25 concepts were taught as effectively as possible in a special experimental class in social studies. The children's understanding of these concepts was very thoroughly and carefully tested by interviews, conversations, discussions, written responses, and so on. Eighteen of the 25 concepts were learned by a significant number of children. Seven of them were not grasped at all, even after 4 months of special effort.

The concepts which were successfully understood were those related to actual experience. For instance, a class election enabled many of the children to reach a real understanding of the concept of democracy; and the sight of a harbor full of immobilized ships helped them to understand the concept of a strike. Some of the concepts, however, proved to be unteachable. The concept of conservation of natural resources was taught in connection with pictures and camping and motoring experiences, but it was never really grasped. The same was true of the concept of the industrial revolution, which was approached by discussing the gadgets on the children's bicycles, modes of travel, inventions, and the industrialization of the United States. In spite of all this, the concept "did not penetrate the veneer that lack of real understanding put under it all" (453, p. 28).

It is worth-while pointing out that this interesting, and on the whole successful, attempt to teach social concepts seems to have had a very marked effect on the emotional and personal reactions of the children. For instance, one child suggested that the class might co-operatively write a book to be called "The Great Adventure," which would deal with the part played by ideas in the development of the United States, which she saw as the foremost answer to the problem of human welfare. This young ten-year-old was concerned to know whether we couldn't all do something to help with the problem.

Here again, as with the account of growth in drawing ability, there are a number of points which should be noticed. (*a*) The whole sequence of growth is the emergence of a more and more organized and definite pattern of behavior. (*b*) As the child develops socially, his horizons expand. (*c*) As the child develops socially, he becomes more and more discriminating in his reactions to people around him. (*d*) As the child develops socially, he becomes more and more subtle in his dealing with other people. (*e*) As he develops socially, ideas and concepts have an increasing influence on his conduct. (*f*) Social ideas and concepts which are beyond his level of development are not understood, even though they are carefully and skillfully taught. As I said in discussing growth in drawing ability, I shall deal more fully with these and similar general points later on. But it is well to have them in mind at once.

Intellectual development

Growth in the ability to understand social concepts is, of course, an instance of intellectual development. But intellectual development has been treated in the research studies as a more or less segregated topic. So we may consider it as a definite growth gradient or developmental line.

In connection with intellectual development the claim has been made that the child's mentality is different in kind from that of the adult. This is an old idea, and in many of its popular expressions it takes the form of saying that children are dominated by feeling or imagination rather than by reason, and that they learn by rote or routine or memory rather than by insight. The belief that the mentality of the child differs in kind from that of the adult has been reformulated and defended in the writings of Piaget (521, 522). According to

Piaget, the child never questions whether his ideas about things are shared by others. He thinks always in terms of concrete things, persons, and events, and not in terms of common qualities. What generalizations the child makes are based upon single instances, and are not true inductive or deductive inferences. Such are Piaget's claims.

These claims have been contradicted by virtually all the research work that has been done on the problem since Piaget's day. In one investigation, for instance, a classic experiment that had been done on chimpanzees was tried out with very young children. In the original experiment, a chimpanzee would be placed in a cage with food hung up out of his reach. In the cage there might be boxes which could be piled on top of each other, so that the monkey could get at the food; or there might be a stick in segments which could be fitted together to make it long enough to reach the food; or the string holding up the food might be tied in such a way that it could be undone. It was shown that the chimpanzees were able to solve these little problems by insight, and that they were not limited to mere blind trial and error. In this same situation the human babies too solved the problems by insight, sometimes better than the adult chimpanzees, sometimes not so well (441).

In another investigation subjects were shown a number of identical boxes, one of which contained a doll. Then the boxes were rearranged in various positions, and the problem was to choose the one containing the doll. Four groups of subjects of different ages were used—2½ to 3½ years old, 4 to 5 years old, 6 to 10 years old, and adult. Within this range of ages it was found that the ability to cope with the problem matures. Only 1 three-year-old out of 10 was successful. Three four-year-olds out of 10 were successful. All the children from 6 to 10 years old succeeded. But at every age level the problem was approached by way of reason and insight. The chief difference between younger children, older children, and adults seemed to be the ability to give verbal reasons for what they did. A ten-year-old child or an adult would give a clear and explicit explanation of why he chose the box with the doll in it when the box was in a new position. But a younger child, when asked when he made the right choice, might say, "I knew she was there," or "I just took it" (291).

Yet another investigation dealt with the ability to draw general conclusions from specific data, as this ability manifests itself among children from kindergarten age to the eighth grade. The children were shown live animals at one end of the table and plants at the other end, given eight minutes to observe them, and then asked to state as many differences as they could. They were shown paired pendulums of equal lengths but with different weights, with equal weights but of different lengths, told to watch the pendulums swing, count the swings, and then tell what makes the pendulum go slow or fast. They watched the movement of warm air made visible by smoke, and asked what this showed about warm and cold air. They manipulated teeterboards with different weights, and then they were asked what to do to make a teeterboard balance. They were shown various animals, including birds, and then asked how birds differ from other animals. The number and adequacy of the generalizations the children were able to draw from such data increased with age, and the pendulum and air problems were beyond the range of most of them. But it was clear that even with the youngest children true inductive generalization took place (133). These and many other similar investigations run precisely counter to Piaget's claim that the childish mentality is different in kind from the adult mentality.

As a matter of fact, the thinking of naïve adults is not very different from that of children. In a certain investigation a group of young children and also 35 members of a college faculty were asked to give explanations of various natural phenomena. For instance, the children were asked where waves come from; and some of the answers were that God made them, that they came from Buffalo, or that they came from the water. Also the experimenter moved his finger so that the children could see, and asked them what made it move. Some of them said it moved "because it wants to." Even so, however, most of the explanations given by the children were forthright physical explanations, although they might not always be complete or adequate. Moreover, the children had no monopoly of foolish explanations. The adults saw a wooden ball and an iron ball dropped from a height at the same moment, and the iron ball hit the ground first. At least one of the spectators explained this by saying that it was unfair for the iron to get there first. In accounting for some of the other phenomena grownups might say that the air was "misbehaving," or that nature had changed "since I studied science." So we must not think that because childish explanations are sometimes unreasonable or fanciful, these are special characteristics of the child mind (494).

It is quite true that children's conceptions of physical causality are often animistic, or anthropomorphic, or irrelevant. The thunder is made by an old man in the sky. The rain comes down when somebody opens a trap door or turns on a tap. But the human mind has always run to explanations of this sort when nothing better was available. Such ideas may be primitive, and they are also obviously wrong. But this does not mean that they are irrational, or purely subjective, or different in kind from the ideas of the adult mind (323).

As before, I close this brief account of intellectual development by calling attention to certain points which will be more fully discussed later on. (*a*) We have here an excellent example of the extremely important idea that growth is continuous, i.e. that as a pattern of behavior evolves, it remains essentially the same in kind from its earliest and crudest beginnings to its final and developed form. (*b*) Intellectual development turns quite largely on a growing power to deal with and use verbalisms, language symbols, mathematical symbols, and so forth. (*c*) Along with this growing command of symbols goes an increasing command of abstract ideas or generalizations or concepts.

Language development

There has been a great deal of research on the development of children's ability to use language. Obviously the subject is extremely important. Language is one of the chief instrumentalities of human behavior. It is the characteristic tool of thinking as well as the primary means by which people communicate with one another. So language development affects and is affected by both intellectual and social development. Moreover, language has an important bearing on emotional experience, because words can define and, as it were, crystallize ways of feeling. The subject of language development is so large that only a few of the most outstanding points can be touched upon here.

Piaget brought his doctrine of the special mentality of the child to bear upon language development. He maintained that children differ sharply, not only in degree but in kind, from adults in their use of language. In particular, he believed that the child's use of language is primarily egocentric. By this he meant that very often when a child makes some statement or asks some question, he is really asserting himself or calling attention to himself, and that this egocentric purpose rather than the objective content of what he says is the real point of the child's use of language. More recent research has not supported this view. It is true that the language of children tends to be more egocentric than that of grown-up people. The first person pronoun is much more frequent in the conversations of children than in those of adults. Also children use the first person pronoun in their written compositions more than adults do. However, the egocentric use of language is common enough among adults, though not so conspicuous as among children. So the difference is one of degree, and not of kind. Moreover, it has been found that children tend to use the first person pronoun less in conversations with adults than with other children. So egocentric and self-assertive speech seems to be largely a reaction to situations where the child feels a strong need to assert himself without having any very subtle means of doing so, rather than a general characteristic of children's language as such (234, 504).

From the very first, speech and language are means of emotional expression as well as means for defining, clarifying, and communicating ideas. A few hours after a child is born it already becomes possible to distinguish between sounds which indicate comfort or discomfort. About the third month of life the baby begins to make numerous and rather continuous babblings, lallings, and comfort sounds, which little by little become shaped up by attempts to imitate adult speech sounds, although only very rough similarities are achieved. As speech responses become more and more definitely meaningful in their own right, imitation recedes, and there is a rapid accumulation of phonetic forms and new concepts.

At the earliest stages there is no distinction between speech and song, and the two differentiate out only gradually. Even with a two-year-old child, singing, which means control of vocal behavior by pitch, may not be an entirely independent and specialized way of responding (400). And in any case, language continues throughout life to be a vehicle of emotional expression, a purpose which it conspicuously serves in the behavior of children. A child's questions may often really be comments with a considerable emotional loading. He may use tough language and swearing without meaning or, indeed, understanding what he says, and chiefly as an emotional outburst. And for children as well as for adults, language is a chief means for defining and channeling emotions through appropriate symbols.

Modern investigators of language development agree that language should always be considered as one of the elements in a child's total behavior rather than as a thing in itself. For instance, there have been many studies on the growth of vocabulary. One of the best of these studies reports that on an average a child acquires the use of 3 words in his first year, 272 in his second year, 896 in his third year, and that by the end of the sixth year he will have the use of 2,562 words (602).

Another very careful and authoritative study dealt with the vocabulary growth of elementary-school children. It was based on a count of over six million running words used by children from the first to the eighth grade. The investigator found about 5,000 different words used by first-grade children, of which 2,000 represented 98% of all words actually used, and he reported that by the eighth grade about 18,000 different words in all were used (548). Of course, all these figures are averages derived from counting words used by very large numbers of children, and so they conceal wide individual variations. But the point is that growth in vocabulary is a reflection of an expanding contact with the world, and the steady extension of meanings and concepts. This interpretation of vocabulary growth is an instance which shows what it means to say that language should not be considered as an independent thing in itself but as a factor in the child's total behavior and personality.

It is often said that students in college are likely to have a "recognition vocabulary" of somewhere in the region of 15,000 words. Recognition vocabulary means a list of words whose meanings can be understood, although perhaps not formally and exactly defined; and a person's recognition vocabulary is larger than his "use" vocabulary. The size of the recognition vocabulary is determined by making a test from perhaps 200 words chosen at random from a small dictionary. The test is given to the student, and his score is recorded. If the dictionary itself contains 18,000 words, the student's score on the 200-word test is multiplied by 900, and the product is supposed to show his full recognition vocabulary. This technique has recently come in for some severe criticism. One of the objections has been that most recognition-vocabulary tests are based on small dictionaries, so that the tests themselves are samples of small samples of English words. When this and other defects were corrected, the investigator found reason to believe that college students may have recognition vocabularies of somewhere in the neighborhood of 200,000 words (268, 270). If there is any substantial truth in this claim, it means that a person's awareness of the world and of meanings expands far more widely than has been realized between birth and the twentieth year.

As age increases, there is not only an increase in vocabulary, but also there are many changes in the texture of language. Children use and are able to understand a larger and larger number and proportion of abstract words as they grow older. More and more complex and compound sentences appear in their writings. That is to say, language becomes a more and more flexible tool, more and more effective for dealing with concepts and carrying trains of thought and reasoning. In early language development good English usage, correct grammar, and correct pronunciation have very little place, if any at all. Such techniques in the use of language become important only at later ages and for rather special purposes. The linguistic development of children is not fostered by early insistence on good usage, correct grammar, and correct pronunciation. Linguistic development is fostered best by encouraging and helping children to express themselves as clearly, pertinently, and copiously as possible.

Many of the points to which attention was called in connection with growth in drawing ability, social development, and intellectual development are exemplified in language development, and it will repay you to review these points again in connection with language development. For special emphasis, however, I will call attention to the following points. (*a*) Language development involves differentiation. (*b*) Language development reflects an increasing command of abstract ideas and abstract thinking. (*c*) Language development reflects an expanding awareness of the world about one and of meanings.

Time concepts

The development of time concepts is an interesting and revealing special aspect of the general process of mental growth, and a good deal of attention has been given to it. A young child has little notion of the sequence of time. He has no need to understand time sequences and time concepts even if he could understand them, which he certainly could not. So he lives pretty much in the present. Notions about the future come first into his ken, and particularly notions about the timing of future events that are important to him. When will mother come for him? When is it time to go to bed? How long before his birthday? It is through questions like this that the child begins to develop his awareness of time.

As to more specific time concepts, children will come to understand the parts of the day (morning, afternoon, evening) first; then the days of the week; then the month and the day of the month; then the year. All such concepts are learned incidentally through experience, and because they are necessary in dealing with many of the issues of life. For children and, indeed, for adults too, though perhaps in lesser measure, the future is far more interesting and important than the past; and so children develop working notions of future time far sooner and far better than they develop such notions about past time. This certainly suggests a few questions about the possibility of teaching dates and historical time sequences to elementary-school children.

In any case, a young child's ideas about time are vague and uncertain. A child may say that Mummy will come "pretty soon." He may ask whether "we will do it yesterday." He may remark that somebody "died and died and died." All such uncertainties and vagueness clear up little by little under the molding influence of experience and necessity. Time symbols and time concepts become understood largely through actual life problems than through direct instruction on the uses of clocks and calendars. Time to start out for school, time to get up in the morning, mealtime, time to be getting back home—it is in and through challenges such as these that an understanding of time sequences develops. Hours, minutes, and named and numbered days are the clear-cut symbols and devices by which people control their time with the precision needed in civilized living. There is probably very little use trying to teach these symbols and devices directly to young children, because in advance of much experience and much growth they are simply empty words. Certainly some very earnest and strenuous attempts to give children in the upper grades some real grasp of the sequence of history by using time lines and other visual devices came to precisely nothing at all (12, 267, 493, 523).

The development of time concepts is outstandingly important because of the enormous influence of time concepts on all aspects of human living. It has been said that the clock is the basic machine of civilization; and there is much truth in the statement, for without clocks we could not run our trains, our airplanes, or our factories, we could not navigate our ships, and we certainly could not carry on modern war. A great deal in the social life of individual human beings is determined by the clock and the calendar. A child with very vague time concepts simply cannot conform to numerous adult standards of conduct. It is, for instance, no use punishing a child for unpunctuality if he cannot figure out the number of minutes needed to get to his destination. So the development of time concepts brings before us certain very interesting and significant points. (*a*) It is a development that influences and affects the whole complex of social living. (*b*) The development of time concepts cannot be brought about by the direct teaching of abstract ideas and symbols. (*c*) Abstract time symbols and ideas are means for making the understanding and control of time more precise, flexible, and usable. (*d*) The development of working time concepts is brought about in and through dealing with the actual challenges and problems of living.

Other growth gradients

Arnold Gesell and his collaborators have presented a considerable number of what might be called thumbnail sketches of various growth gradients or developmental lines. A few samples of these sketches are as follows:

1. Prehensory behavior (i.e. the ability to grasp and manipulate objects)
   a) At 12 weeks the child simply looks at a cube when it is presented to him.
   b) At 20 weeks he looks at the cube and "approaches" it.
   c) At 24 weeks he looks at the cube and grasps it crudely with his whole hand.
   d) At 36 weeks he looks at the cube and grasps it deftly with his fingers.
   e) At 52 weeks he grasps the cube with thumb and forefinger and releases it deftly.
   f) At 15 months he looks at the cube, grasps it, releases it, and arranges it so as to build a tower of two cubes.
2. Reading behavior
   a) At 15 months the child pats an identified picture in a book.
   b) At 18 months he points to an identified picture in a book.
   c) At 2 years he names three pictures in a book.
   d) At 3 years he identifies 4 printed geometric forms.
   e) At 5 years he recognizes salient capital letters.
   f) At 6 years he recognizes salient printed words.
3. Acquisitive behavior
   a) At 5 years a child takes pride in his personal possessions.

b) At 6 years he collects odds and ends rather sporadically.
c) At 7 years he collects with purpose and specific sustained interest.
d) At 8 years he collects with zeal and with strong interest in the size of the collection.
e) At 10 years he collects more formally, and with specialized intellectual interests.
f) At 16 years he saves money with discrimination, thrift, and interest in money values (218).

All the general points to which attention has been called in connection with growth gradients previously described apply also to the above three. Notice in particular (*a*) the formation and elaboration of pattern, (*b*) the emergence of more precise and discriminating ways of response, (*c*) the increasing influence of general ideas and general meanings.

It should, I hope, be clear that there are many other developmental lines besides those that have been described. One may speak quite properly of musical growth, artistic growth, literary growth, growth in mechanical ability, growth in mathematical ability, and so on. Always we are speaking of a specialized aspect of the total process of mental growth—an aspect which can be separated out for discussion and study, and which can help to focalize our educational planning.

My intention certainly has not been to describe or characterize all the developmental lines that have been investigated, or even all the most important of them. What I have tried to do is to give you enough concrete and specific descriptions to make the general meaning and nature of mental growth reasonably clear, so that you can at least begin to see what thinking about education in terms of mental growth amounts to. With this much taken care of, we can now go on to discuss the characteristics and conditions of mental growth in more general terms.

QUESTIONS FOR DISCUSSION

1. It is often said that the ability to write good English "grows" instead of being "learned." Consider what such a statement means. Does it throw any light upon the general nature of growth and upon the distinction between growth and learning?

2. The American Historical Association once recommended that instruction in history should be organized with ancient history taught first, medieval history next, and modern history last. Would this be organization in terms of growth, in terms of learning, or neither?

3. One of the persistent problems of teaching is that the elementary parts of many subjects do not seem to offer many chances for "life applications." This would be true of beginning language, beginning algebra, etc., at least if we grant the ordinary systematic organization of these subjects. One must study such subjects for several years, it is said, before one can use them at all. If such subjects were organized in terms of mental growth, might not life applications be much easier to find even from the very beginning?

4. In this chapter there is a description of the growth of drawing ability from the beginning to about the age of four. If a child were to continue on and ultimately become an expert artist, would the further process of growth have the same or essentially different characteristics?

5. Consider and discuss the statement that "all power comes from growth."

6. Discuss some of the ways in which the maturing of time concepts affects a person's general behavior, actions, and feelings.

7. Discuss the interrelationships between intellectual and social development and the relationship of both to emotional development.

8. Under what circumstances would the psychology of learning as applied to education be properly called "narrow."

9. Summarize and list the various common factors among all the various gradients presented in this chapter. Keep your summary for comparison with what is said in the following chapter.

SUGGESTED READINGS

Biber, B., *Children's Drawings: From Lines to Pictures.* Bureau of Educational Experiments, New York, 1934.

Gesell, Arnold, and Ilg, Frances L., *The Child from Five to Ten.* Harper & Brothers, New York, 1946, Chap. 18.

Mursell, James L., *Education for Musical Growth.* Ginn and Company, Boston, 1948, Chap. 1.

Pistor, F., "How Time Concepts Are Acquired by Children." *Educational Method,* XX (1940), 108–112.

12

The Growth-Plan

THE GROWTH-PLAN AND EDUCATION

YOU SHOULD always be careful to remember that the various sequences or gradients of mental growth which were described in the previous chapter are not really separable from each other, although it is often convenient to consider them separately. When a child grows intellectually, his social reactions are also changed. When his ability to draw develops, his social, emotional and intellectual responses are altered by the process. The various developmental gradients are simply aspects of the general process of growth itself; and now we must deal with the characteristics and conditions of that process. It is very necessary to understand these characteristics and conditions if we are to organize education for the effective guidance and promotion of mental growth.

The growth of every living thing follows a certain rhythm, or cycle, or as it is sometimes called, a "plan." An acorn falls from an oak tree, becomes embedded in the ground, sends down roots, sends up a shoot which becomes a trunk from which branches and leaves form; and the whole process goes on through many years as the tree develops, changing in form and increasing in size, until finally there come decline and death. A grub hatches from a fertilized egg, feeds and becomes larger, forms a chrysalis, turns into a butterfly, flits about for a few days, lays its own eggs, and dies. So, too, a human being takes shape in the womb, passes through the crisis of birth, develops and changes through a marvelously complicated sequence, reaches maturity, and moves to the end of the cycle of living. In following out this cycle, this "growth plan," the creature fulfills itself, realizes its potentials, satisfies the basic needs of its nature.

The developmental cycle or sequence of every living creature is predetermined as far as its broad aspects are concerned. The plan is fixed by the creature's in-born growth-potential. Yet this is far from meaning that nothing can be done about the sequence of growth, or that circumstances cannot affect it at all. The reason is that in every growth-plan there is an element, greater or smaller, of *modifiability*. It makes a great difference whether the acorn is planted in fertile soil with plenty of water and plenty of light, or in unsuitable ground shut in by other vegetation. It makes a great difference whether a child grows up in a remote, poverty-stricken, barren country environment, or is surrounded by stimulating, helpful, richly varied influences. We can do much to shape the growth both of the acorn and of the child. Yet all that we can ever do is within the limits of the basic growth-plan itself. The trends or, if you will, the laws of this basic growth-plan must be observed and recognized, or one either accomplishes nothing at all or only does harm.

For instance, one might undertake to graft a different species of oak to the growing tree. But if the graft is not made at the right time of year and in the right way, it will die, and the tree itself may be deformed or even killed. Similarly, one may undertake to teach a child to be respectful to authority or to do fractions in arithmetic; but if the graft is not made at the right time and in the right way, the best that can happen will be nothing at all, and the worst that can happen will be disaster. One must respect the growth-plan, the growth-cycle if one wishes to shape either an oak tree or a human personality. It follows that both for the gardener who wants a good-looking oak tree and for the teacher who wants good citizens in the commonwealth, it is vitally necessary to *understand the growth-plan in order to be able to shape it toward desired ends* (215).

So we are now to consider the growth-plan in general, after having dealt with some of its special aspects. But before going on there are certain limitations in our discussions that should be explained, and a few warnings about terminology that need to be made.

In the first place, we shall be dealing here with psychological or mental growth, and not with physical growth. The phenomena of physical growth are very important for education, and need to be recognized by teachers and schools. Moreover, physical growth always has many and far-reaching psychological effects. But a general book on psychology hardly seems the place to try to tell the whole story of growth, so we shall confine ourselves to mental growth, and touch on physical growth only in so far as it has psychological effects and influences.

As to terminology, I have been consistently using the expression "mental growth." But it is in some ways a rather unfortunate expression, for it tends to make one think only of intellectual processes. What the expression is really intended to mean is the whole psychological side of growth, including the emotional and social processes, and also the processes of motor control. "Behavioral growth" is a more accurate expression than "mental growth," but unfortunately it is rather clumsy. So I shall continue to use the term "mental growth"; and this will do no harm so long as you bear in mind what it is intended to convey.

CHARACTERISTICS

Growth involves the entire personality

There are two senses in which mental growth always involves the whole of the personality.

1. Every specific bit of growing that a person does depends upon his entire personal make-up at the time. The growth-gradients which were described in the previous chapter furnish plenty of instances to explain this statement. When a child works hard at a picture because he wants to take it home and show it to his family, he probably makes an advance in drawing. This may seem like an isolated achievement, but really it is not; for he makes the advance because he has reached a certain level of social awareness. When a child is told to come home at a certain hour and fails to do so, it may seem that what he needs is to be scolded and told to keep track of time. But his capacity to keep track of time depends on his power to understand and deal with abstract concepts and symbols.

A six-year-old child may quite probably collect all sorts of odds and ends, almost like a magpie. But by the time this same child is twelve he may have become an enthusiastic and discriminating stamp collector. This may look like a change in acquisitive behavior, and in a certain sense it is. But this special change is the resultant of an over-all change in the child's personality, for at twelve years old he has developed a command of ideas and a discriminating sense of social and economic values which express themselves in his interest in stamps, an interest that would be impossible for him when he was only six. You could not teach a three-year-old child to keep accurate track of time, or a six-year-old child to take a deep interest in stamps, because in neither case does the child have the necessary personality equipment. In just the same way you cannot teach primary-grade children really to grasp historical events or grammatical techniques and principles, because they lack the necessary personality equipment. Whenever a human being develops mentally in some specific respect, he always does so in terms of his entire personality as it then is. He can develop in no other way.

2. Every specific bit of growing that a person does has an effect on his entire personality. When a child becomes able to tell time by the clock, he thereby becomes better able to fit in to various social plans, he begins to be able to schedule his day, and even his emotions are affected, for the sight of a clock can now start him worrying about getting some place on time. When a child becomes able to read, his personal independence is greatly increased; for he can, for instance, follow printed directions; and he can get a great deal of information and entertainment on his own account. When a child reaches the level of acquisitive behavior where he finds stamp-collecting interesting, he is brought into contact with the political subdivisions of the world, and also into direct social contact with other collectors. Everyone knows that when a youngster learns to drive a car, it makes a tremendous difference in his life and his personality. But the truth is that no one can really learn anything without undergoing at least some total, over-all change. To grow in any specific respect is to gain a new competence, a new control, a new power for dealing with life and the environment. So any and every specific bit of growing affects in some measure one's whole behavior and personality.

But although it is true that growth involves the entire personality, this does not mean giving up the whole notion of distinguishable growth gradients. For growth is not a regular or uniform process. A child may be intellectually advanced and socially retarded, or socially advanced and intellectually retarded. He may be far ahead of his grade in drawing, and far behind it in arithmetic. What causes these irregularities of growth we do not fully know. Often it is said that they are due to special inborn talents and disabilities. The trouble with this explanation, however, is that it explains very little. It amounts merely to putting names to irregularities that we observe. Probably the cause often lies in circumstances. If a child has a gifted and perceptive drawing teacher who helps him to draw as the person he then is, he will do very well with drawing, whereas if his arithmetic teacher insists only on routine memorization, he will be at the same time backward in arithmetic. Such circumstances and conditions certainly have a great deal to do with mental development, but the truth is that we simply do not know enough to explain all the subtle irregularities, the delays, and the sudden spurts of mental growth.

Growth is a continuity

As a mental process develops, its essential character does not change. A child's thinking, in essence, is like the thinking of an adult. A child uses language essentially as an adult uses it. As a child's ability to draw develops, he does not go through a special "scribble stage"; nor does he go through a later stage of what is called schematization, in which he draws things as he knows they are rather than as he sees them (e.g. showing two eyes in a face in profile). His drawing is always an activity in which his whole personality expresses itself through the medium of crayon and paper. A fifteen-month-old child who pats an identified picture in a book may seem to be doing something quite different from fully developed expert reading. But the difference is only in degree, for the child and the mature reader are both reacting to printed visual symbols. Thus the developmental gradients already described provide many instances which show what it means to say that growth is continuous.

But the meaning of that statement carries beyond these specific illustrations. There used to be a belief that a child's whole mentality changed radically as he grew up. The child was supposed to be dominated first by sensation, then by imagination, then by memory, and last of all by reason. From a practical standpoint the memory stage, which was said to be reached at about the age of ten, was thought to be particularly important. That was supposed to be the time to teach subjects with a very heavy memory load, like foreign languages. Moreover, the inference was that in teaching children in the upper grades one should emphasize routine and memorization, because this emphasis was suitable for the children's particular stage of mental development. There is no evidence at all for any such series of separate stages in the sequence of mental growth, and every reason to believe that mental growth is a continuity in which the same basic characteristics and processes appear at all levels, though with varying efficiency.

Evidently the idea that growth is continuous is very important practically. Children, like adults, learn by insight, and teaching should be organized to help both adults and children to learn by insight. Children must be taught to *understand* arithmetic, to grasp some of the *meaning* of historical events, to respond to the *expressive values* of music and art and literature, to appreciate the *reasonableness* and *suitability* of right behavior. Once we recognize that growth is continuous we also have to recognize the mistake of teaching children routine habits and procedures, and leaving an understanding of these habits and procedures to be emphasized only when the children are older.

Growth is the emergence of pattern

Nevertheless changes do take place as a child's mentality develops. In fact changes must take place, or there would be no growth, for growth itself is change. But the changes that take place are not essential or basic. Through the long years during which an acorn turns into a mature oak tree, there are many changes, but in all of them the oak tree is still an oak tree. What happens as the oak tree grows up is that it becomes a more and more elaborately organized structure or pattern. This is just what happens in a child's mentality as he grows up.

The child's mentality—or, if you will, his behavior—becomes more and more elaborately structuralized or organized. As mental growth proceeds, pattern emerges.

Our various growth gradients provide us with plenty of examples of the emergence of pattern as the very core of developmental change. Let us briefly review some of the findings reported in the previous chapter. A little child has very vague and ill-organized ideas of time divisions; but as he matures he becomes able to react to time patterns etched very sharply by clocks and calendars. A child of two holds a crayon in his fist when he is drawing, and is just about as likely to put the crayon in his mouth as to use it on the paper. But two or three years later he has a delicately organized way of holding and manipulating the crayon, and deals with it as an instrument specially for drawing rather than as an all-purpose toy. A child of six may make collections of anything at all; but five or six years later he may be collecting stamps with clear-cut, discriminating planfulness. In all these cases the change that takes place in the process of growth is in the organization, or structuring, or pattern of awareness and response.

It follows, therefore, that if our aim in teaching is to promote, foster, and guide the process of growth, we must organize situations which, over a period of time, favor the emergence of organization, or structuralization, or pattern. The emergence of pattern involves a number of more specific changes in mentality and behavior, and these are the changes which a teacher should recognize as desirable, and should try to make happen.

1. The emergence of pattern involves increasing differentiation or discrimination. A good example is the evolution of vague babblings and lallings first into crude imitative speech sounds, and later into more and more precisely formed speech sounds. This evolution is part of the process by which a child becomes able to talk; and the essence of the change is that he differentiates more and more precisely as he makes his speech sounds.

So a teacher who wants to help children to grow into new abilities must promote these processes of differentiation. Children can develop a better English style by revising a bit of written English so that it will express better just what they want to express, and convey the meaning that they have in mind more clearly to another person. Children can develop a grasp of historical sequences by differentiation. "Story history" may give them an idea that the publication of the Declaration of Independence and the victory at Yorktown happened a long time ago and at about the same time, which may be enough for the moment. Further interesting reading, or perhaps preparation for a pageant, may lead the children to realize that the Declaration came some time before Yorktown. Then later on the exact time relationship can be tied down by specific dates. Projects, demonstrations, and rather informal experiments in general science can given children a broad notion of what happens when an acid is brought in contact with certain metals; and as they go on with further experiences in the field of science this broad understanding becomes more and more discriminating, until it is refined into the symbols of a chemical formula. Improvement in painting is characteristically brought about by painting a picture enthusiastically and as well as one can, perhaps being satisfied with it for the moment, noticing certain awkwardnesses and crudenesses in it, and trying to overcome them in the next picture one does. The general sequence always is to start with broad yet compelling experience, and to get discriminations and refinements to evolve out of it. This sequence is far more promising than any possible attempt to teach the refined or discriminating reaction directly, such as trying to improve style by teaching grammatical constructions, to give children a grasp of historical events by drilling them on dates, to help children understand chemistry by teaching them formulae or having them perform and carefully write up quite intricate experiments.

2. The emergence of pattern in mentality and behavior in-

volves the evolution of precision out of crudeness. This is almost the same process as the increase in differentiation and discrimination which has just been discussed. But there is an important nuance of difference, for teachers should understand that precise responses are best established by being evolved out of a cruder matrix.

In teaching handwriting, for instance, the older method was to have the child use copybook examples as models. It was not a good method for several reasons, one of these reasons being that it meant trying to force very precise manipulations directly. Nowadays we create situations in which a child is able to write "large" without paying much attention to the fine points of what he is doing. His reactions will, of course, be awkward at first, and his writing will not look well. But instead of trying to short-circuit these awkwardnesses, we help the child to clear them up bit by bit, and to substitute more and more refined, delicate, and controlled reactions. In the past many music specialists thought that children should be compelled to sing a new song perfectly from the very first; but now we realize that it is much better for the children to get the general idea of the new tune first, and to clean up the details from that point on. When young people learn to swim (and learning to swim might just as well be called growth in swimming ability), we do not insist on their mastering the stroke-pattern with delicate perfection. On the contrary, we think that a good deal of splashing about, floundering, and experimenting may be quite all right, and we try to get the exact stroke-pattern to evolve out of these flounderings.

So the evolution of any precise and controlled skill is very much like the evolution of a statue out of a block of stone. The general contours and masses of the statue appear first, and until they have appeared no single detail is likely to be smoothed off and finished. On the contrary, all the general contours and masses become more precise as the work goes on.

3. The emergence of pattern in mentality and behavior

means the increasing control of behavior by general principles and by abstract concepts and ideas. For instance, the idea of team loyalty means very little to young children. It is an abstract concept which does not influence their behavior. But when these same children have become adolescents, the concept of team loyalty is very influential indeed. The abstract symbols on the face of a clock mean nothing to most four-year-old children; but when these children are in their middle teens, the clock may have turned into a tyrant. Some time ago an investigation dealt with the personal wishes of children of various ages, each child in the experiment being asked to tell of three such wishes. Fifty-five per cent of the wishes of five- to six-year-old children were for specific material things. But only 14% of the wishes of eleven to twelve-year-old children were for specific material things. These older children had a far more general tendency to wish for money than did the younger children. And money, of course, is a conceptual instrument, a measure of value, a general tool for defining specific values (448).

One of the hardest of all lessons for teachers to learn is that generalizations, abstract statements, formulae, and statements in symbols cannot be grasped out of hand, and that the mind must grow into a realization of their significance. Or if teachers are aware that all this is so, they find it an extremely difficult lesson to apply. We set a so-called "arithmetic problem" about the number of acres in a field; yet many of the children will have not a ghost of a notion about the size of an acre, and some of them will not be too sure about what a field is. We make children read about capes and bays; and yet it has been demonstrated that many of them would not know a cape or a bay if they saw it. We show them a map of the United States; and yet it may be many years before they have a dawning realization of some of the most important things the map can tell them. We make them memorize the statement that any three points define a plane; but very few of them are likely to see that this is the reason why any three-legged stool will sit solidly on the floor while a four-legged stool may wobble.

Yet abstract generalizations, symbols, and ideas have a tremendous effect on behavior. Money, for instance, is a focus of fabulous plannings and actings, and of the most violent emotions. Such a generalization as "the law of supply and demand" has served again and again as a potent political slogan. Such concepts as "average" and "per cent" have been repeatedly used to fool the public with great success. How then does one grasp such abstract meanings? Only by an insight which grows and evolves out of experience! Certainly not by memorizing verbal formulae.

4. The emergence of pattern in mentality and behavior involves a continual widening of the child's range of responsiveness and interest. The child's developing mentality becomes an instrument which can penetrate further and further into his environment, so that he becomes concerned and affected by matters that are more and more remote from him. In babyhood the child's world is very narrow and limited, but as he grows and develops the boundaries of that world continually recede.

This was shown very strikingly in an investigation which dealt with contributions to discussion spontaneously made by children in the second, fourth, and sixth grades. Of the contributions made by second-graders, 61% had to do with the child's own personal activities and experiences, 83% involved the actual personal presence of the child, and only 18% had to do with domestic and world news. Of the contributions made by fourth-graders, 41% had to do with the child's own personal activities and experiences, 52% involved his actual presence, and 29% had to do with domestic and world news. Of the contributions made by sixth-graders, 18% had to do with the child's own personal activities and experiences, 27% involved his actual presence, and 60% had to do with domestic and world news (26). I myself can well remember a child who was almost completely uninterested in the news of the Pearl Harbor attack, and became quite annoyed with adults who would persist in discussing the matter. Doubtless you yourself will have noticed some such confirmatory instances.

The reason for this broadening of the boundaries of interest and concern, which is so characteristic of mental growth, is that as a process becomes more and more highly structured, its relationships beyond itself become more and more evident. When all a child can do in the way of drawing is to make lines on a piece of paper with a crayon held in his fist, he has no instrumentality to bring him much into relationship with things and people. As his drawings become pictures of things he is *ipso facto* brought into relationship with things, and he has in his picture something to show to others, to talk about with others, and to be admired by others. The sort of odd-lots collecting that may go on about the age of six is a very limited social medium indeed; but an enthusiastic stamp collector is interested in material from all over the world, and has colleagues all over the world. An undeveloped mind always has a limited horizon. A primitive tribesman whose whole life and thought are determined by routine and immemorial mores, taboos, and myths does not have the intellectual equipment even to wonder what is beyond the ranges or across the sea. He is like an astronomer with a very weak telescope, or even with no telescope at all. That is exactly how it is with the young child. And the child's development has the effect of extending the range of his mental vision.

That is why the right kind of curricular material for young children is "close-at-hand" material—close at hand either in the actual geographical sense, or in the sense of being intimately related to his immediate interests and concerns. It is hopeless to expect a child to understand or be affected by remote doings and purely adult doings; and doubly hopeless to expect this when we tell him about such doings in formal and abstract language.

SEQUENCE OF THE GROWTH-PLAN

Briefly to summarize what has been said in the preceding section, mental growth involves the whole personality, it is a continuity in the sense that it is a process of expanding and deepening insight from the very first, and its very essence is the emergence of a more and more highly organized pattern. How does this account of mental growth bear upon education? If we propose to apply it practically, what ought we to do and what ought we to avoid when we teach arithmetic, or reading, or history, or when we try to establish sound emotional or social reactions in children? These questions have been very extensively discussed, and we must now come to terms with them.

1. One suggestion has been that what we know about the growth-plan indicates the wisdom of *postponing* many types of learning. If this is our idea, we may think that reading should not be started in the late first grade, that handwriting, too, should be put off, that algebra should not be taught in the ninth grade but kept till later on, and so forth. If it is discovered that a child cannot read by the time he is in the third or fourth grade, advocates of postponement are likely to tell his parents not to worry, because he will come to it when he is a little older.

The most ambitious instance of postponement is the celebrated experiment on arithmetic reported by Benezet (46). In certain elementary schools which were under Benezet's administrative control, no arithmetic was taught until the sixth grade. There seemed to be no deleterious effects. Children in these schools came out knowing just about as much arithmetic as those from schools where arithmetic was started very much earlier. The results of this experiment are often mentioned in defense of postponement as a general educational policy. But there is a catch in this interpretation. Standards of achievement in arithmetic are prevailingly very poor. It is quite believable that older children could be brought up to those standards quite quickly, and in fact this is just what seems to have happened. What this outcome proves, however, is not that postponing arithmetic did any particular good, at least so far as achievement in arithmetic is concerned, but only that it did no harm to an already bad situation.

But surely when we change educational practice to conform to the sequence of mental growth, we hope to do some good, and not merely to avoid doing further harm. The Benezet experiment on postponing arithmetic reminds one somewhat of the famous old experiment on the spelling grind, to which I have already referred. You may remember that in this experiment the investigator showed that children came out spelling just about as well—or rather, just about as badly—whether they were taught spelling ten minutes a day or fifty minutes a day. The most that can be said for Benezet's experiment is that it reveals a lot of needless distress and wasted time in the ordinary teaching of arithmetic. The experiment does not show that children learn arithmetic better when it is postponed.

As a matter of fact, there is solid evidence that children do better with arithmetic when they start it earlier. In one very important investigation tests in arithmetic were given to about 5,000 children in the sixth grade. One-third of these children had begun arithmetic in the first grade, one-third had begun it in the second grade, and one-third had begun it in the third grade. The advantage in the tests was with those who had begun arithmetic in the first grade. This advantage, however, was not very great, which is perhaps some comfort to those who want to believe in postponement (699).

A similar investigation with similar results has been reported from Scotland. Battery A of the Public School Achievement Test was given to 5,961 11-year-old Scottish children. These children surpassed the United States norms on the test by 18 months in computation, and by 15 months in problem-solving. This is an appreciable difference, but not an enormous one. The main reason why the Scottish children did better in arithmetic than American children is thought to be that in Scotland children begin to learn arithmetic when they are five years old (434).

The argument for postponement is that a child's mentality must have reached a certain level of structuralization before he can deal to advantage with such subjects as reading or arithmetic. More specifically, he must have developed a sufficient command of abstract ideas and abstract thinking, and a certain competence in handling language patterns. This is perfectly true as far as it goes. But the weakness in the argument is the assumption that this sequence of mental development happens of its own accord, that nothing can or should be done about it, and that the sound policy is simply to wait until it has taken place. But growth is not promoted best by a laissez-faire policy, and if we simply keep our hands off and wait, growth is likely to take place much more slowly and uncertainly than it need or should. This is the reason why postponement does not seem to improve achievement and may even impair it, and why early beginnings can bring about somewhat better results.

Of course it can be argued that postponing arithmetic and reading removes certain dangerous pressures from children, and makes the school a happier place. This, no doubt, is all to the good; but it seems like shirking a responsibility rather than meeting it. Perhaps the school would be happier still if there were no curriculum at all up to the sixth grade; but it would certainly be less fruitful, and its impact upon personality would be extremely questionable, to say the least. The school does not shape personality best by avoiding difficulties, by avoiding problems, and by dodging certain subjects because they are hard to learn and hard to teach. It shapes personality best by teaching all subjects so that they become real tools for living, and so that the very experience of learning them is strengthening and formative.

2. Advocates of postponement as a general educational policy have been quite vocal about their ideas. But those who believe in the opposite policy of *forcing* have, as a general

thing, gone serenely on their way without defending themselves beyond perhaps remarking from time to time that what they are doing is "just common sense."

"Forcing" may be defined as the attempt to get children to learn some skill or ability by direct pressure, irrespective of the children's general level of mental development. Such disregard of the sequence of growth is, of course, a matter of degree. No one, so far as I know, has ever advocated teaching algebra in the second grade or plane geometry in the third grade. But arithmetic, as conventionally taught in the early grades, is a good example of forcing, because this teaching is not planfully geared to the children's capacity to handle abstract ideas and relationships, or to the development of this capacity.

In the light of everything that has been said in these pages about mental development, one would expect the policy of forcing to produce very poor learning. This expectation is confirmed in general by the very poor results of conventional arithmetic teaching. But so far we only have a theoretical argument. However, certain studies have shown quite specifically just what happens when an attempt is made to high-pressure children into learning some skill or ability prematurely.

In one of these studies the subjects were 63 third-grade children whose competence in arithmetic was investigated at the beginning of the school year. All the children had been taught arithmetic in the first and second grades. More specifically, they had all been taught the 200 standard addition and subtraction combinations. The method used was conventional drill. For instance, a certain combination, such as "5 + 3" would be exhibited. Then the answer would be given. Then there would be practice on the combination, with flash cards, special games, and the like. Some days later there would be a test including the combination. If the children did not know it, i.e. if they could not tell the sum of 5 + 3, they were not allowed to find out for themselves what it was. Instead, the answer was given again, and there would be more drill. (This procedure has been recommended to prevent finger-counting, guessing, etc.) So in general it is clear that the learning of arithmetic in the first and second grades meant repeating and memorizing a large number of verbal formulae.

This was the arithmetical background with which the children entered the third grade, at which point the investigation began. The investigators set up a series of three tests, each test being made up of 100 addition combinations (which the children had previously learned). The first of these three tests was given immediately at the start of the year. The average time the children took on it was 17 minutes, and the average number of errors was 11. This, of course, was an exceedingly bad result. Then the children were given special drill on arithmetic for five minutes daily five days a week for a month, after which the second addition test was run. The average time now dropped to 11 minutes, and the average number of errors to 4. A month later, during which there was no special drill, the third addition test was given, and now the average time had dropped to 7 minutes and the average number of errors was still 4.

So far these findings show that direct high-pressure drill on arithmetic does in fact produce some gain in efficiency. To that extent the findings justify the policy of forcing and of early beginnings. But additional findings in the investigation show that the drillwise teaching of arithmetic which has been described, and which is a type case of forcing, is extremely wasteful. For the investigators raised the question of how the children actually got their results in the three addition tests. This question was answered by interviewing individual children and asking them about their methods of work. In the first of the three tests it was found that 22.2% of the answers were obtained by inwardly counting, 14.1% of the answers were obtained by indirect methods (e.g. getting an answer for 3 + 4 by figuring that it must be 3 + 3 and 1 more, etc.), 23.8% of the answers were obtained by guessing, and 39.5% were directly known. Knowing answers directly and immediately was, of course, the whole aim of the drill procedure. As to the second of the three tests, 17.4% of answers were obtained by counting, 15.6% by indirect methods, 18.2% by guessing, and 48.8% were known directly. As to the third of the three tests, 19.4% of answers were obtained by counting, 12.6% by indirect methods, 15.2% by guessing, and 52.8% were directly known. The conclusion is that sheer drill is a very poor procedure for getting children to learn what should always be learned, namely *a good and effective method of dealing with a situation* (90).

Another famous and sensational investigation of the process of growth points in much the same direction. This is an investigation of two identical twin boys, Johnny and Jimmy. These twins were taken at two years of age. One of them was given intensive special training in several skills, among which were roller skating and tricycle riding. The other twin was given no training at all. At the end of the training period the contrast between the two was very striking. The trained twin had become an astonishingly successful roller skater and tricycle rider, but the other twin could not do these things at all. Four years later, however, when the two boys were at school age, the trained twin had completely lost his roller skating ability, although his tricycle riding ability was still retained. The suggested explanation is that body proportions change so much between the ages of two and six that roller skating becomes quite a different skill while tricycle riding remains much the same (432, 433). From these two investigations we can conclude that while the premature teaching of any skill or ability may produce what looks like a fairly good result, that result will be more or less spurious and will almost certainly fade away quickly. This is just about what we might expect from our general understanding of the characteristics of the growth-plan.

Forcing, therefore, is poor procedure for the following reasons. (*a*) It does not give the learner a firm and sure grasp of the ability he is supposed to learn. This means that he is not likely to be able to use the ability as a genuine tool for living. (*b*) Forcing necessarily means routine repetitive drill with a minimum of insight. To bring about such drill, motivation has to be largely negative, i.e. by penalties and the threat of failure. The only possible positive motives are usually of the superficial sugar-coating kind, such as flash cards with pictures, spelldown type games, and the like. Thus the actual learning of the ability cannot be an inspiring and strengthening experience in itself, and is certain to be accompanied by a great deal of boredom, covert negativism, and hostility.

3. In contrast to both postponement and forcing, much is being made in modern educational discussions of the concept of *readiness*. Psychological and educational readiness is thought of as a stage or level of growth at which the child is ready to take up some study or learn some skill. The concept has been applied chiefly to reading and arithmetic, so that we have the expressions "reading readiness" and "arithmetic readiness." But it has also been brought to bear, though much more vaguely and sketchily, on other subject-matter areas; and the claim has been made that there are readiness levels for all school learnings, which would mean that we could at least in theory, determine just the moment when each one of these learnings should be undertaken.

The idea of readiness is very fruitful and also essentially very simple. That idea is that no one will learn anything well until he has developed to the level at which he will understand what he is learning and see the point of learning it. But also the idea of readiness involves a great and ever-present danger. This is the danger of treating the new learning as a definite stage or a definite change which breaks the continuity of development.

Thus some schools have organized what are called reading-readiness programs in kindergarten and first grade. In these programs children have stories read to them, are given many opportunities to handle printed material, have their attention called to captions and titles underneath pictures, and so on. The general purpose of these programs is to build up the children's interest in reading and their desire to read, and to give them at least some light contact with basic reading techniques such as turning pages, looking at pages from top to bottom and from right to left, and so on. In the readiness program there is no formal instruction; but when the program is over and the child enters the second grade, formal instruction in reading begins, in the belief that the child is now ready for such instruction. As you will see, this plan at least tends to put a kind of psychological watershed between readiness and formal learning. In the readiness program the child moves in one milieu, and in formal instruction he passes into a different one. When this happens it is clear that we have set up a discontinuity in what ought to be a continuous process of development.

A concrete instance will help to explain the idea of readiness, and its fruitful values and possible dangers. A remarkable experiment in teaching arithmetic was carried on a few years ago in the elementary schools of a New England city. No formal arithmetic whatever was taught in the first and second grades, and very little in the third grade. In the first and second grades, and for the most part in the third, social and informational arithmetic was taught. That is to say, there were numerous games, projects, undertakings, and discussions which gave the children a variety of experiences with numbers and numerical relationships, but the customary direct study of addition, subtraction, multiplication and division was omitted, except for a little drill in the third grade. A total of 475 children were involved in this experiment. At the end of the third grade they were given a standard arithmetic test. The national third grade norm for this test was a score of 60, but the average score of these 475 children was 97.8 (730).

This is an extremely spectacular showing. It seems to prove

that arithmetic *can* be well taught and learned in the early grades. Notice that it was not brought about either by (*a*) postponement or (*b*) forcing. The working principle was to bring the children up against real problems and challenges suited to their level of development as a whole, and then to help them deal with these problems and challenges by arithmetical insight and thinking. An understanding of numbers and numerical relationships were built into the growing personalities of the children, and the results were admirable and enviable. One could, if one liked, call the work an unusually ample and intelligent arithmetic readiness program.

But would there not be a fallacy in thinking that all these fruitful experiences were simply getting the children ready for formal arithmetic, with its empty manipulations and spurious textbook problems? If the social and informational projects did so much for the children up to the third grade, why discontinue them at that point? Why the suggested transition? Would not a transition to formal arithmetic kill the interest, destroy the self-confidence, and even break down the competence that many of the children had developed? These children had already gone a good way in developing arithmetical insights, and if we grant that growth is continuous, they should have been allowed to continue developing along the same lines. The danger in thinking about this plan of work as an arithmetic readiness program is that it might then be treated as one stage of development leading to quite a different stage. This would be a mistaken interpretation, yet it is an interpretation very often put upon the concept of readiness. What readiness ought *not* to mean is a preparatory stage leading to a transition to formal study. What readiness *ought* to mean is that all growth simply gets one ready for more growth of the same kind, in which case each specific bit of learning is simply a milestone on a continuing pathway.

A summary of the factors which are nowadays considered essential for reading readiness will throw further light on the concept of readiness itself. Indeed such a summary is quite revealing. In order to be ready to read (*a*) a child must be aware of reading itself and of its possibility for him. (*b*) He must be motivated so that he wants to read. (*c*) If he is to learn to read in school he must be used to the school building and neighborhood and feel more or less at home there. (*d*) He must have an adequate language equipment. This means that he must be able to tell about his experiences, to describe things, to converse, and also that he must be able to discriminate fairly well between word sounds. (*e*) He must be interested in pictures, which of course are themselves symbols. (*f*) He must be able to attend and to keep to the point. (*g*) He must be able to follow stories when they are told to him, and must be interested in them. (*h*) He must be able to handle books with reasonable skill, to turn pages, and to follow lines of print from left to right. (*i*) He must have a mental age of six or over, or better still of seven. (*j*) He must have good eyesight and hearing and no serious health deficiencies. This summary of the factors involved in reading readiness is drawn from several authoritative sources. It is a remarkably varied list, and shows at a glance that reading readiness means vastly more than narrow specific preparation (214, 243, 306, 462). In connection with it, please notice the following points.

a) The ten factors which have just been enumerated amount to a comprehensive picture of a growing personality at a certain level of development. Such a personality will no doubt be ready to read, and also ready for a great many other things. Indeed it has been pointed out that quite young children are, in a real sense, ready for everything offered in the school curriculum. They are ready to deal with relationships such as up and down, before and after, larger and smaller, more and less, but not for formal arithmetic. They are ready to deal in innumerable ways with the physical realities about them, but not for formal science. They are ready for an expanding and significant range of social experiences and understandings, including vicarious experiences such as hero stories, tales of impressive doings, and the like, but not for formal history. They are ready for a vast variety of aesthetic experiences and activities, but not for technical training in art and music.

If it is asked when the formal aspects of any subject should be introduced, the answer in developmental terms is that there is no such fixed point, for formal learning should emerge gradually as horizons expand, insights become more abstract, and controls become more refined. In actual practice, and because of its institutional limitations, the school may have to introduce arithmetic, reading, history, and so forth at some predetermined grade level; but this is always an artificial choice and contrary to the true nature of growth. Such sudden transitions can be largely smoothed out in a flexibly organized modern school, with its tendency to do away with rigid annual grade classifications and to break down arbitrary barriers between subjects (86). Such expressions as "reading readiness" or "arithmetic readiness" are, in fact, almost misnomers, and can very easily be misleading. For the personality factors which make a child ready to read or to study arithmetic also make him ready for almost any kind of significant school learning (568).

b) A child who is really ready to read in the rounded and inclusive sense in which the idea is now understood will probably learn to read with very little formal instruction. Given a little of the right kind of help, he will probably grow into reading almost insensibly and with very little trouble. The same is true of arithmetic also, for the barriers and obstacles that make arithmetic hard to learn and hard to teach come in the main from a lack of rich, varied, and compelling experience in the use of numbers, and from a lack of motivation (463).

c) There is no simple, automatic way of telling when a child is ready to read or ready for arithmetic or indeed for anything else. A good test may reveal a few significant factors, but only a few of them. One cannot say that readiness will be attained at a certain chronological age, or at a certain grade level. The only way to determine readiness is to study and try to understand the individual child, and to make the best estimate that one can of how the new learning will suit his personality and his total level of maturity (754).

d) The question has been raised as to what happens if a child is ready for some learning and then the learning is not provided (339). Does he stay ready indefinitely, or does the condition of readiness evaporate? Or does he, perhaps, become more and more ready? This is an interesting enough question, but an extremely artificial one, and it is based on thoroughly fallacious thinking. Readiness is not a specific state but a general condition, and as a matter of fact we are always psychologically ready to learn infinitely more than we ever actually do learn. To be ready to learn reading or arithmetic is to be ready for a whole range of possibilities, only a few of which can ever be realized in a lifetime. Moreover, it is perfectly true that readiness to learn can be dissipated, but when this happens, the change is in the total personality. A grown-up person may object to starting with the elementary beginnings of a new subject, or he may feel unable to do so. He may have been ready to start the subject once, but he is ready no longer. The reason is that his experiences, his prejudices, his fear of looking foolish, his very successes have made him into a person who hates to compromise his dignity. To become ready for the elementary learning he would have to reorient himself as a person and become as a little child, which is hard to do. Ignatius Loyola, after a considerable military career, learned to read from the beggarly elements onward. His devoted determination to do so created a state of readiness, and that readiness to learn to read was precisely a reorientation of the man's whole personality.

CAUSES OF GROWTH

What are the causes of mental growth? I have postponed this question until now because it seems to me that one cannot deal with it fruitfully until one has a fairly clear, comprehensive, and concrete picture of the growth-plan and its chief characteristics and aspects. However, the question of causation must be considered, because if teachers are to guide and promote the growth process they need to know what makes that process happen.

Maturation and learning

Mental growth is brought about partly by maturation and partly by learning, or experience. Maturation is the physiological ripening of the body, and particularly of the nervous system. Its general effect is to produce more and more organized and patterned and controlled behavior. Maturation, so far as we know, is beyond our control. All that we can do is to wait until it takes place.

The following experiment with two identical twin girls shows the meaning and effect of maturation very clearly. When twin T. was 46 weeks old she began to be trained in climbing a small staircase and in manipulating cube blocks. This training went on for 6 weeks. At first T. was passive and needed help. After 4 weeks of training she climbed the staircase eagerly, and after 6 weeks she climbed it in 26 seconds. By this time twin T. had completed her fifty-second week of life. Meanwhile her sister C. had been given no training at all, but now, at the beginning of her fifty-third week of life, she began to be trained on the staircase and with the cube blocks. At the very beginning C. climbed the staircase in 45 seconds, and in 2 weeks she was able to climb it in 10 seconds. Six weeks additional maturation had brought her behavior patterns to a point at which she could make much more progress in 2 weeks than her sister had made in 6.

As to cube behavior, the 6 weeks training that T. received were accompanied by the emergence of prehension, manipulation, and exploration. But at the end of the training period, when both twins were completing their fifty-second week, C.'s cube behavior was just about on a level with T.'s, although C. had been given no training at all (221, 222). So various performances are impossible or almost impossible below a certain level of maturation, but they may become quite easy above that level. A child of two cannot manipulate a crayon delicately with his fingers, and a child of eighteen months cannot make many precise speech sounds. But above a certain level of maturation there is no particular difficulty in such performances.

The educational policy of postponement, in so far as it has any psychological basis at all, depends on the assumption that maturation is the chief if not the only cause of mental growth. If this were true, then all we could do would be to wait for maturation to take place, and postponement would be justified. But it is certainly not true that maturation is the chief or only cause of mental development. This is not true even with very young children. Certainly we could not teach a two-year-old child to draw like a five-year-old child, if only because he manipulates the drawing materials much more crudely. But what would happen if a child had absolutely no opportunities to draw until he was five—if he had no crayons, no paper, and was even prevented from trying to draw with any hit or miss materials that might come his way? If we suddenly gave him a crayon and a piece of paper on his fifth birthday, would he use them just as well as another child who had had them all his life? Certainly not. The five-year-old would probably "pick up" drawing quite fast, but he would have to pick it up, which would take time. So even between the ages of two and five experience as well as maturation contributes a great deal to development.

With older children and with other types of developmental gradients, the effect of experience is much greater, and the effect of maturation is much less. It would be foolish—indeed, it would be fantastic—to try to teach a child to read before he could focus his eyes properly. But most of the influences which bring about a development of reading ability come from experience and not from maturation, and are therefore more or less under our control. The same is true of the great majority of the growth gradients with which we are concerned in school. With far the most of them maturation is a comparatively negligible factor except in very special cases, and the crucial factor is experience or learning.

Learning and growth

The shaping, or guiding, of mental growth depends upon specific learnings. Indeed the only way in which we can guide or shape the mental growth of a child is to set up situations in which he learns various specific things. For instance, we want him to develop qualities of co-operativeness, responsibility, and leadership which we think are essential for a democratic personality. How can these qualities be developed? Surely the only way of leading the child to develop them is to put him into situations where he will learn many ways and means of getting along with, understanding, and dealing with other people. Some of these situations will be of the face-to-face type, such as committee assignments, study-group assignments, planning assignments, the making of classroom contributions, play-group activities, and the like. When the child is older we will seek to organize situations in which he will learn to deal with others on a more wholesale scale, such as student government activities, junior civic activities, team game activities, and so on.

In all these situations the intention is for him both to learn a whole range of social techniques, and also to grow in a certain direction. In addition we will organize situations where more abstract and verbal learning takes place, and in which the child will come in contact with explanations of the methods, practices, and problems of democratic society. Once again there will certainly be specific learnings, but in and through those learnings there will also be growth in a determinate direction. Or, to take another illustration, we may want a child to grow to some extent in the capacity for scientific thinking. Clearly this is not likely to take place by chance, and it certainly cannot happen by magic. Such a sequence of development can only come about if the child brings to bear scientific thinking on a whole series of specific problems and situations—that is to say, by a whole series of appropriate learnings.

Walter P. Chrysler, in his autobiography,* gives a very interesting illustration of the relationship between specific learning and growth. When he was a young man, Chrysler got a job in a locomotive factory. The foreman, who was somewhat hostile, assigned Chrysler to set the valves on a locomotive which was not working properly. The task, apparently, is a tricky one, and the foreman expected and hoped that the young man would fail. However, he set the valves successfully, for he knew just what he was about. This specific skill stood Chrysler in good stead. It was, of course, useful in itself. But it carried far beyond itself. It gave Chrysler a firm status in the factory. It gained for him the respect of his fellow workmen. It served as an entering wedge for new contacts and relationships. And it opened the way for new insights into engineering.

You can see from this instance that there is nothing mysterious about the relationship of learning to growth. On the contrary, it is quite a common-sense matter. Every genuine bit of specific learning tends to open up new worlds, to reveal new possibilities, to lead a person to feel differently about himself, and to behave differently in a great many ways. These are the long-time effects of every bit of genuine learning, whether that learning takes place in the classroom or anywhere else. When a contrast is made between a "narrow psychology of learning" and a "liberal psychology of growth," this does not mean that learning can be disregarded. It only

* Walter P. Chrysler, *Autobiography of an American Workman*. Dodd Mead & Company, Inc., New York, 1937.

means that we should always consider the long-time and expanding and ramifying effects of any bit of specific learning, instead of thinking only about its immediate results. The "narrowness" comes in when we concentrate only on immediate results, to the exclusion of everything else.

Yet specific learning cannot be slipshod or hit-or-miss if it is to have its proper influence on growth. Slipshod learning tends to produce, not growth, but frustration, at any rate in the long run. If Chrysler had only had a general idea of how to set the valves of a locomotive, he would have failed in his immediate task, and lost all the collateral advantages that came to him. When an intelligent child has failed to learn to read by the fourth grade, it is absurd to say that the failure does not matter (the child himself usually feels that it matters considerably); and it was a mistaken kindness not to have done something about it sooner. When a group leader has never really learned the techniques for dealing with other people in a democratic manner, ideals of democratic action strike him as empty and impractical talk.

In a certain investigation a test on major contemporary problems was given to 4,348 graduating high-school seniors. Some of the issues set up in the test were whether the United States can continue to hold its present important position in international trade, whether trial by jury is on the wane, whether the administrative powers of government should be further increased. The average score was 20.34% and the highest was 58%. The high-school seniors who took the test had information on about one third of the issues, no information on about a third of them, and misinformation on about another third of them (446, 447).

In yet another investigation it was found that 51% of high-school seniors could not name either senator from their own state and that only 20% could name both; that during the war only 50% knew that Henry L. Stimson was Secretary of War; that only 45% of factory workers tested could name the

Secretary of War; that only 44% of union members knew the names of the presidents of the A. F. of L. or the C.I.O.; and that among a random sampling of adults only 39% could give the approximate interest rate of war bonds in spite of the immense publicity on war bond sales (550). No doubt much can be said about such showings. But one thing is very certain. Uncertain skills, vague knowledge, and insight that is mostly fog and mist cannot effectively influence mental growth and the development of personality.

It would, however, be a profound mistake to draw the inference that learning is made an effective means of growth by the pressure of narrow and largely negative motivation brought to bear in routine situations. We may perhaps undertake to teach children to spell by setting up predetermined lists of spelling words, breaking the lists up into smaller segments, drilling on the segments, and instituting periodical reviews. Spelling so taught is not well learned in itself, and does very little to contribute to the process of mental growth and the shaping of personality. The reason is that the motivation is impoverished and limited, so that when children learn, they are not acquiring an effective tool for living.

But if, as one possible instance of contrasting procedures, we set up a project which calls for the writing of reports to be read by other people, perhaps in the school paper or elsewhere, call attention to spelling, indicate the importance of proper spelling, perhaps suggest the use of the dictionary to get words properly spelled, then we have a far broader motivation. Under such circumstances children learn spelling as a genuine tool for living which is related to many basic needs. Or again, we may teach history and try to maintain "high standards" by daily quizzes and weekly true-false tests along with much emphasis on marks. But this will not tend to produce a kind of learning which is fruitful in terms of mental growth. Such procedures point towards study for the passing of tests rather than for the understanding of history. If, however, we do everything possible to make history meaningful, perhaps by suitable extensive readings, the planning of historical pageants, or organizing opportunities for investigation, discovery, and creative self-expression, then the study of history is related to many basic needs, and we can hope for and expect fruitful mental growth in and through the study of history.

Once more, we may produce a semblance of good behavior by rigid regimentation, strict rules, and autocratic discipline. But the learnings that go on under such a regime are not likely to have the desired developmental effect. If, however, we establish worth-while co-operative tasks which themselves create the necessity of orderliness, and if we build around these tasks a pattern of self-discipline and self-government, then the specific social learnings that go on favor healthy mental growth and the effective development and shaping of personality.

Fruitful learning does not take place in isolation, for such learning is always the discovery of new ways of satisfying basic needs. This is why mental growth is depressed and retarded by a barren environment, something that has been demonstrated again and again. In an institutional setting a child is likely to begin to show retarded development during the first year of life, even if the institution is well managed. The reason is the impersonality of the setting. The child lacks personal affection and intimate encouragement, which means that he does not get enough stimulation to try to discover and to establish new behavior-patterns, and not enough intimate appreciation when he does try (216, 217). In an investigation which dealt with "hollow folk," i.e. people living in remote "hollows" in the southern mountains, where the whole cultural environment was very impoverished, very young children lagged only a little behind normal developmental standards, but were retarded more and more as they became older (587, 588).

Yet another investigation, dealing with mentally retarded

children in an orphanage, demonstrates again how much effect the total setting has upon mental development. The orphanage was run in a routine fashion, and although the children were well looked after physically, there was very little mental stimulation, and not much interest was taken in them personally. A plan was set up under which some of the adolescent girls in this institution were given special charge of a small group of the younger children. The girls took a great interest in these children, lavished much affection on them, talked to them, played with them, and helped them in many ways. According to the investigators, this specially treated group of young children showed a gain of 27.5 points in I.Q. (intelligence quotient) in from 6 to 52 months (598). So, although it is true that ineffective learning is not a fruitful cause of mental growth, effective learning is not produced by routine pressure in a narrow setting, but by an environment which stimulates the learner to reach out, to create new patterns of thought, action, and feeling, and to achieve new satisfactions.

It has been very truly said that "the best method of maturing children is to provide them with situations in which they can work out behavior that will satisfy their personality needs as the latter appear. This does not mean stressing drill for mastery of the "fundamental processes"; it does not mean rote learning and recitation; it does not imply the use of regimentation to teach good habits and conformity; it does not permit indoctrinating all children with arbitrarily chosen emotionalized concepts; it does not suggest that teachers should have a bag of tricks for motivating pupils. These methods produce psychological immaturity.

"Instead this means giving children a chance for the progressive accumulation of meaningful experiences that will reveal the world as it is; it means offering experiences that will orient the children in the physical world, in the social world, in time, and in the aesthetic, ethical, and spiritual realities as far as we have discovered them. It means helping children to organize their experiences into generalizations, attitudes, and value concepts. It implies granting them opportunities for significant action in relation to their needs, attitudes, and emerging purposes. It means granting them increasing responsibility to direct their own behavior, and it implies challenging them with the world's unsolved problems as a means of evoking purpose. All of this must be experienced by each child in the company of and with the cooperation or opposition of other children" (530, pp. 194–195).

MEASUREMENT OF GROWTH

If the environment of the school and the classroom is to be organized for the promotion of mental growth, it is essential to have a way of recording and tabulating the mental development of the children. Such a system of records has many specific values. It can help a teacher to deal intelligently with individual children and with groups of children, for she can study the background and development of the children in connection with her planning. It can often be very helpful to her in understanding the special problems and difficulties of individual children. It can throw light on the success or failure of this or that procedure or experiment, and so lead to the improvement of practice. Moreover, the system of records, or of "pupil accounting" always has a great pervasive influence in the life and work of the school, and a great and constant effect on the attitudes of teachers, administrative officers, parents, and pupils. I would not care to say that nothing can be done to shape up the life and work of the school for the fostering of mental growth even when pupil accounting is mainly the recording of marks. But there can be no doubt whatever that the lack of an adequate system of developmental records is a great handicap, or that such a system is an extremely valuable tool both for individual teachers and for the school as a whole. So it is important to understand in general, and without going into much detail, what an adequate system of developmental records would be, and how it can be set up.

A method often used in measuring mental growth is to make a record of the changes that take place in some specific type of achievement over a period of time. These changes in achievement are expressed in scores, and can be plotted in graphic form, the result being called a growth curve. Some typical growth curves are shown below and on pp. 384–386. They show improvement in vocabulary, in mechanical ability, in art ability, and on a series of performance tests.*

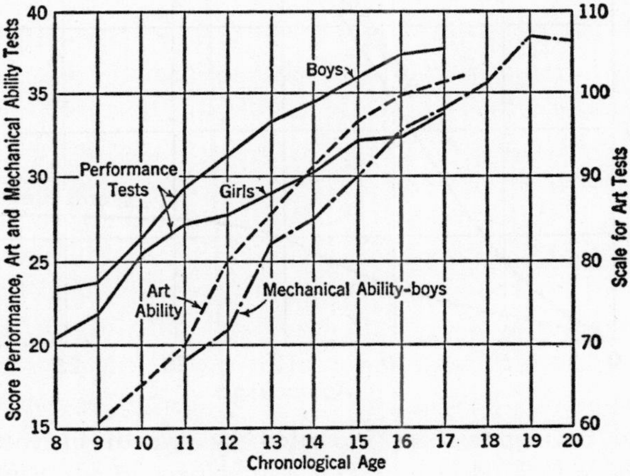

Growth in abilities as shown by (*a*) a series of performance tests (Ferguson Form Boards), (*b*) tests in abilities in visual art (Lewerenz), and (*c*) tests in mechanical ability (Minnesota Mechanical Test Battery A). (Adapted from data of Louise Wood and Edythe Kumin, "A new standardization of the Ferguson Form Boards," *J. Genet Psychol.*, 1939, LIV, 265–284; D. G. Paterson, *Minnesota Mechanical Ability Tests,* p. 345; and the normative data of the Lewerenz tests.)

* Performance tests are intelligence tests which call for some kind of overt performance such as fitting a jigsaw puzzle together instead of for responses that are largely verbal.

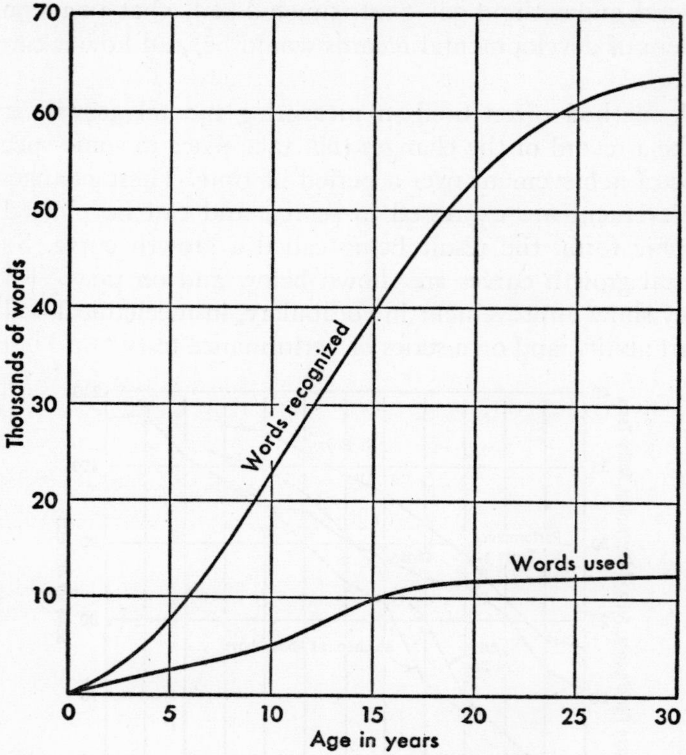

Mental development as indicated by growth in vocabulary. (From John J. B. Morgan, *Child Psychology*, 3d ed., Rinehart & Company, Inc., New York, 1942.)

It should be noticed that these curves express changes in the *average* achievement of considerable numbers of children. This involves a serious limitation, and can lead to a major error. (*a*) The school is interested in the development of the individual child; so a way of recording individual development is needed, even though records of average changes may have some value. (*b*) There is a danger of thinking that such growth curves as those shown above indicate what ought to happen as well as what does happen. This is not necessarily true at all. Even though large numbers of children do show certain average changes in vocabulary, mechanical ability, and so forth, it does not follow that just these average changes are right, proper, and desirable. Still less does it follow that we should judge the growth of any individual child largely with reference to these averages.

The two growth curves shown below and on p. 386 avoid these particular difficulties. They show the growth of two individual children under different circumstances. So they are much closer to the kind of record we need for practical educational purposes, for they tell us at least something of what happens to a person under different types of influence.

But even such growth curves as these last two do not tell us nearly all we need to know if we are to guide the mental de-

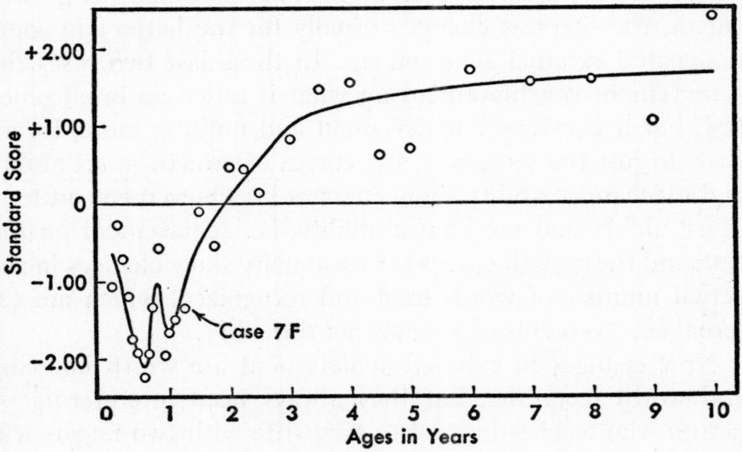

Age curve of relative intelligence of strongly motivated girl. (Berkeley Growth Study.) Her increasing scores are probably due to several factors of which motivation is only one. (From the Institute of Child Welfare, University of California; published in 515 and reproduced by permission of the contributor, Nancy Bayley.)

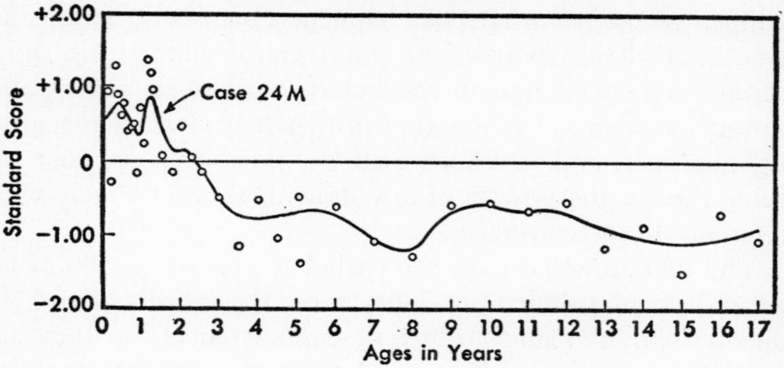

Age curve of relative intelligence of poorly motivated boy. (Berkeley Growth Study, from the Institute of Child Welfare, University of California; published in 515 and reproduced by permission of the contributor, Nancy Bayley.)

velopment of pupils as wisely as possible. Like all other growth curves, they express change (usually for the better) in some designated external achievement. In these last two cases the achievement is achievement on what is called an intelligence test, but it is external achievement and nothing more, for all that. In just the same way, the curves of growth in art ability and mechanical ability show changes in achievement on tests of art ability and mechanical ability, i.e. achievement *on the test;* and the growth curves for vocabulary show changes in the actual number of words used and recognized, which are external achievements of yet another sort (14).

Now changes in external achievement are worth knowing and worth recording, but they always need interpreting. A person who teaches himself to typewrite with two fingers will probably improve quite a good deal. We could make a record of this improvement, express it in a curve, and call the curve a curve of growth. But in dealing with this person it would be extremely important to know that he was using only two fingers on the typewriter. If we wanted him to develop to anything like the limit of his capacity, we would have to reorganize his whole method of typewriting. This simple illustration shows where the real problem in guiding growth is located. Growth is always a change in method, in the organization of response, not merely an improvement in outer efficiency. As children develop mentally they become more and more able to deal with abstract concepts, their motor reactions become more and more precise and controlled, and their perceptions become more and more discriminating. These changes will be reflected in improved performance on intelligence tests, tests of mechanical ability, and tests of artistic appreciation and judgment. But a teacher's business is with the changes themselves, which are not directly revealed by the test scores. As a tree grows, its size increases and so does the circumference of its trunk. But a record of these external and measurable changes would not be nearly enough information for a gardener who wanted the tree to grow into the right kind of shape, and also to grow in such a way that it will continue healthy.

So our developmental records must be made and kept for the sake of understanding pupils *as persons* and not merely as test-takers, or as learners of arithmetic, reading, spelling, and so forth. Such a system of records calls for effort and planning, but it is not impracticable. For instance, elementary-school teachers have found their attitudes towards pupils, and their ideas of what the school can do and of what teaching really means transformed by such simple measures as visiting the homes of all the children early in the session, and setting aside enough time to get well acquainted with everybody in the class. If all the teachers in an elementary school make it a business to get to know the children in a natural and human way, and if all of them contribute what they learn to an organized filing system, a great deal will have been done to create the right kind of developmental records (613).

In high school the problem of getting to understand young people personally is somewhat more difficult, but it can be solved. Thus it has been found very helpful to have each new pupil make out a record card showing his name, his age, his grade, his home address, his nationality and church, the occupations of his father and of other members of his immediate family, his hobbies and ambitions, the clubs to which he belongs and the honors he has won, the names and addresses of two close friends or relatives in school, and whatever after-school work he may be doing. This is only a beginning, but it is a good beginning (392). From such a starting point an adequate cumulative record for each pupil can be built up, bringing together, summarizing, and to some extent interpreting the influence of the pupil's home and social background, his record in other schools, his school history, his mental ability and special capacities, his subject-matter achievement, his out-of-school experiences, his educational and vocational interests, and his future plans. Some such system of records is almost essential for any school which seriously accepts the responsibility of fostering and guiding mental development and shaping personality towards desirable ends (677).

While such comprehensive cumulative records are very necessary, this does not mean that improvement in external achievement which expresses itself in the improvement in test scores is not worth ascertaining and recording. Quite the contrary, indeed. The ordinary marking system does not reveal the individual pupil's sequential growth over a period of years because he is marked separately on each course or subject without any continuous basis of reference. This is a very great defect, and a good testing program can rectify it by revealing how each pupil is improving or not improving in certain specific respects as he moves along through the school. A testing program can become a danger under two conditions: (*a*) if it is organized to give only a snapshot picture of a pupil's test performance as it now is, rather than a picture of the changes in his test performance over a period of years; (*b*) if it is supposed to tell us everything or nearly everything that we need to know about a pupil. But a testing program that follows up the individual pupil and that reveals facts to be interpreted in terms of a wider whole can be very valuable indeed.

QUESTIONS FOR DISCUSSION

1. The basic idea of a plan for organizing the teaching of subjects in high school which has attracted wide attention is to divide each subject up into a number of units, and then to take steps to make sure that each unit is completely mastered by everybody before the next is undertaken. Discuss the psychological aspects of this plan, and particularly its relationship to the process of mental growth.

2. In some school systems the content of United States history is "covered" more or less systematically and completely as many as four times throughout the twelve grades. The main difference is that in the later presentations there are more details, more generalizations, etc. Does this sequence of complete systematic coverage seem to you a good way to organize the subject? If not, what alternative plan would you recommend?

3. If we agree that a good way to start the study of science is to organize learning around various interesting and useful applications of science, does this mean that we deny the importance of reaching an understanding of scientific principles and of science itself as an organized discipline?

4. Why is it that as a child matures mentally, he tends to become more and more interested in and concerned with what is remote from him in time, place, and circumstances?

5. A learning experience may have the effect of promoting mental growth, and also it may not. Under what general circumstances will it have this effect, and under what circumstances will it not? Can formal drill ever have any positive and helpful effect on mental growth? Find from your own experience instances of learning which have and have not had such an effect on your own mental development.

6. A certain junior high-school teacher always makes a great point of getting personally acquainted with her pupils at the start of

each school year. As her classes are large, this takes much time and effort, but she considers it well worth-while. Can you think of any definite practical advantages that this plan would be likely to have when it came to her actual teaching?

7. To what extent can school marks give us any real picture of a child's mental development?

8. Returning to discussion question number 9 from Chapter 11, see whether the various common factors in the growth gradients discussed in Chapter 11 correspond to the characteristics of mental development presented in the present chapter.

SUGGESTED READINGS

Commins, W. D., *Principles of Educational Psychology*. The Ronald Press, New York, 1937, Chap. 2.

Jersild, Arthur T., *Child Psychology*. Prentice-Hall, Inc., New York, 1947, Chap. 2.

McGraw, Myrtle B., *Growth: A Study of Johnny and Jimmy*. D. Appleton–Century Company, New York, 1935, Chap. 10.

13

General Intelligence

ABILITIES AND MENTAL TRAITS

So FAR WE have been consistently thinking of a man's personality as the integrated pattern of his *ways of dealing* with the problems and challenges of life; we have been trying to understand the process of adjustment by which this integrated pattern of behavior is shaped and molded, and have been asking what schools and teachers can do about the process. But it might be said that a man's personality is the integrated pattern of his *abilities and traits.* At first sight this seems like quite a different way of looking at personality. Certainly it is a way of looking at personality that is long-established and widespread. A hundred years ago the doctrine of phrenology was very popular in this country. According to phrenology a man's personality is made up of a large number of abilities—abilities which he "possesses"—such as amativeness, combativeness, musical ability, reasoning ability, and so forth. Moreover, you were supposed to be able to tell how much of these abilities anyone had by noticing the shape of his head, or "feeling his bumps." At one time this doctrine was taken very seriously, even enthusiastically, by many eminent persons, including the great educator Horace Mann. Nowadays no competent person believes in bump-feeling. But because of the great popularity of the testing movement (which is often taken to be bump-feeling gone statistical) a great many people think that everyone "has" certain mental entities called abilities, or talents, or traits, and that the abilities, or talents, or traits that a person "has" make him the sort of person that he is.

This way of looking at personality is certainly very different from the way in which we have been looking at it up to now. If there is any force in the idea that a human being is really a bunch of more or less ready-made abilities, which somehow or other exist inside of him, then all our ideas on the shaping of personality and on what the school can do about it will have to be modified considerably if not completely changed. So it becomes very necessary to consider and analyze the concept of mental abilities and traits, and to find out just where we stand in the matter. In so doing I shall begin with what is called "general intelligence," which is the most famous of all these alleged mental abilities, and the most important for education; and then I shall go on to deal with special abilities and traits.

GENERAL INTELLIGENCE TESTS

The concept of general intelligence has a very important place in present-day educational thought and planning. This is true even though authorities on testing are increasingly interested in more special mental abilities and traits. So it is very desirable for teachers to have an informed understanding of what general intelligence means and implies, for it has a very practical bearing upon their working problems. If we think of education as the shaping of personality, we must consider the relationship of general intelligence to that process.

The concept of general intelligence in modern psychology has developed in connection with testing. Indeed, the importance of this concept depends mainly upon the considerable practical success of general intelligence tests. So I shall begin by dealing with a few typical tests of this kind, both for the sake of giving some information about them, and also to bring out the ideas that are embodied in them.

The testing movement in its modern form originated in the work of Alfred Binet. Binet was not only an originator. He inaugurated a tradition and put forward many ideas which are still focal points for discussion. He published his first syllabus of mental tests in 1905, after some ten years of research. Binet himself revised, extended and rearranged his tests several times, and developed his early syllabus of tests into what is known as a scale. This Binet Scale has itself been adapted and revised in many countries, including the United States, and this widespread movement may be said to have culminated in the important and ambitious revision published at Stanford University in 1935. This was the second revision of the Binet Scale which was made at Stanford, and its full title is the Revised Stanford-Binet Tests of Intelligence. For thirty years the tradition started by Binet and culminating at Stanford University was the core of the mental testing movement, and that tradition is still very influential though new concepts and methods are emerging.

Binet first became interested in mental testing for a practical reason. He was asked officially to try to discover ways and means for identifying academically promising and unpromising children in the schools of Paris. He looked around to see what tests might be available, but none of them were promising. There were indeed many mental tests to be had, but all of them dealt with quite narrow special abilities, such as rote memory for digits, quickness of response, and the like. Probably many of these tests were accurate enough within their limits, but they did not pick out children who succeeded or failed in school, and so for Binet's purpose they were useless.

Accordingly, he had to construct tests of his own, and in doing so he set to work on a new basis. Instead of testing this or that special ability, he proposed to make a general over-all survey (or at least quite a broad survey) of a child's whole mentality. He went about making this over-all survey very simply and directly. He thought of a great many kinds of little tasks and problems which could be set up in test form, and then he ascertained which of these tasks and problems were related to success and failure in school. For instance he tried out a test in handwriting, but this told him nothing about a child's academic prospects. After much winnowing and experimenting, he finally arrived at thirty tests which were related to academic success and failure. Among these thirty tasks or problems were the following: finishing incomplete sentences, making up sentences which would include three given words, knowing the names of various parts of the body, reversing clock hands from memory and telling what time it would be with the hands reversed. Out of thirty tasks and problems like this he made his first syllabus of tests; and since his basic idea was to make an over-all survey of a child's mentality, he considered that his syllabus indicated *general intelligence.*

There are three points in this story which should be noticed particularly. (*a*) Binet did not begin with any preconceived or fixed notion or definition of an entity called general intelligence. (*b*) He attached the name general intelligence to whatever is shown by a many-sided and varied survey of a person's mentality. (*c*) His purpose was practical. He did not choose or construct his tests on the basis of any theory. He merely found out what tests would in fact indicate a child's academic possibilities. All these three points have served as guiding principles in much of the later development of testing. They throw much light upon the nature of mental tests, and also upon the concept of general intelligence in particular, and of human abilities in general (58, 640).

Revised Stanford-Binet

The Revised Stanford-Binet Tests of Intelligence or, as it is often called, the Second Stanford Revision has already been mentioned, but it is so important that a further discussion is in order. It is an immense sophistication and elaboration of Binet's first syllabus of tests which appeared thirty years earlier. But the later work is essentially consistent with what had been done before, and in fact some of Binet's original tests appear in it (642, 643).

The Second Stanford Revision, like Binet's own tests and numerous other revisions, is an *individual* scale. That is to say, children take it one at a time, and not in groups. In contrast to Binet's first syllabus of thirty tests, this latest revision contains 240, divided into two equivalent alternate scales of 120 tests each. The tests are of very varied types. Children are asked to point to the longer of two sticks, to select certain numbers of blocks from a pile of blocks, to give definitions for various numbers of words, to name various objects shown in pictures, to explain why certain pictured actions are foolish, to give reasons in support of an oral statement, to tell in what way pairs of words are alike, and so on. These test items were chosen with the greatest care from thousands of possibilities, partly on the basis of expert opinion, partly by various kinds of tryouts with over 3,000 persons serving as subjects. The resulting 240 tests make up an extremely miscellaneous list. In fact the scale has sometimes been criticized as nothing but a hodgepodge. But however that may be, it certainly embodies Binet's original idea of discovering general intelligence by a many-sided survey of a person's mentality.

A very notable feature of the Second Stanford Revision is the arrangement of the tests on a basis of age. Binet had not done this in his first syllabus, although he did it in his later revisions. The First Stanford Revision also had been arranged in this way, and the Second Revision carries the plan further.

Groups of tests are set up for each six-month interval from the ages of two to five, then for each year up to fourteen, and then there are four adult levels—average adult and superior adult I, II, and III. For instance, one of the tests for age two is to name common objects in two separate pictures; one of the tests for age six is to point to one of five pictured objects that is different from all the others; one of the tests for age ten is to name as many disconnected words as possible in a minute. The Second Stanford Revision, like all other scales thus arranged on a basis of age, is known as an *age-scale*.

You may very well ask how the authorities who made the scale knew that such and such a test would be just right for the age to which it was assigned. The answer is, by using a *standardization group*. The various tests were tried out with children of various ages. The numbers of children used varied from one to two hundred for each separate age level. Roughly speaking, a given test would be designated as suitable for a given age because a majority of the children of that age could pass it. This, essentially, was the procedure for assigning or "scaling" the tests, although there were many refinements in actual practice. Notice particularly that the makers of the scale had no way of knowing in advance which tests would be right for certain ages. They assigned the tests to various age levels by what was really a cut-and-try method.

From this scale and the long tradition back of it many very influential ideas have arisen. Three of these ideas call for comment here.

1. First there is the idea of *mental age*, or M.A. Mental age, as the concept is used in the Stanford Revisions, means the average chronological age at which a certain performance is possible or a certain set of problems can be solved. When a child passes the tests designated for age seven, this means that he is up to the average of the seven-year-old children in the standardization group. It is for this reason that we say that he has a mental age of seven. As you will readily see, this

procedure raises a great many questions. If, for instance, the standardization group of seven-year-olds was unusually bright, their average performance would be better than that of seven-year-olds in general. Then the seven-year-old tests would be too difficult, and the whole scale might even be standardized too high. This was probably the case with the First Stanford Revision, but not with the Second.

2. Then there is the idea of the *intelligence quotient*, or I.Q. This was not one of Binet's own ideas, but was developed at Stanford University. A person's I.Q. is his mental age divided by his chronological age, the quotient being multiplied by 100 for convenience. If a child of twelve passes the twelve-year-old tests, his chronological age is 12, his mental age is 12, and his I.Q. is 100. If he passes the fifteen-year-old tests, his M.A. would be 15 and his I.Q. 125. If he could only pass the nine-year-old tests, his M.A. would be 9 and his I.Q. 75.

There is a great deal of needless mystification about the M.A. and the I.Q. They are both perfectly simple common-sense notions. Parents are usually pleased when children can put up some kind of mental performance "ahead of their age"; and this is simply an informal way of expressing what the I.Q. expresses formally in figures. When a child performs mentally ahead of his age, we say that he is bright. If we had known Francis Galton in his childhood, we would have said that he was almost alarmingly bright, for when he was five he could read, write, multiply by single-place numbers, repeat fifty-two lines of Latin poetry, read a little French, and tell the time. Expressed in numerical terms this indicated an I.Q. of about 200. So in general, the I.Q. is a measure of brightness. The M.A., however, is a measure of maturity, for obviously a child of six may have the same I.Q. as a child of twelve, but the level of maturity of the two children will be quite different, and this difference may be expressed in two M.A.'s of 6 and 12 respectively, if in both cases the I.Q. is 100.

3. One other idea that calls for comment is that of the

age of arrest. This term calls attention to the fact that when age-scales are used, people's performance on such scales does not improve beyond a certain age level (C.A.). An unselected group of people forty years old, merely because they were forty, would not do better on the Second Stanford Revision than a group of people twenty years old. So the question arises as to the actual age at which test performance stops improving. This age is called the age of arrest. There has been a great deal of research on the subject, and somewhat varying answers have been reported. For the First Stanford Revision the age of arrest is set at 16 years C.A. So even if a person of forty took this set of tests and came out with a mental age of 18 (which would mean that he was equal to the eighteen-year-olds of the standardization group), his I.Q. would be figured by dividing 18, *not by 40 but by 16.* In the Second Stanford Revision the age of arrest is somewhat different, and the method of figuring I.Q.'s for people beyond that age is somewhat more complicated, but the variation is not very great. Much has been made of this concept of the age of arrest—in fact, a great deal too much. There is no valid claim whatsoever that mentality cannot develop beyond the designated age of arrest. The only claim that can be maintained is that performance on a given set of tests does not improve beyond the age of arrest established for that set of tests.

Wechsler-Bellevue

This test, which was published in 1939, is, like the two Stanford revisions of the Binet Scale, for individual, not group use. In most other respects, however, it is very different from the Stanford revisions. Instead of containing 120 separate tests arranged according to age, it consists of 10 units, all of which are usually taken by the person being tested. These units call for general information, general comprehension, arithmetical reasoning, the repetition of digits, recognizing similarities between parts of words, the completion of incomplete pictures, the arrangement of pictures to tell stories in sequence, assembling cutouts, reproducing symbols by means of colored blocks, writing code symbols for numbers, and vocabulary. The following are two of the most important special features of this test.

1. It is a test for a very wide range of ages, running from 10 to the age group 60 to 70. In fact, the Wechsler-Bellevue Intelligence Scale is regarded as one of the best general intelligence tests for adults.

2. As I said previously, the ten tests of the scale are not arranged agewise. So one cannot obtain a mental age by using it. What it does give is a numerical score, the total of the scores earned on the ten separate units. This numerical score is called a point score, and the scale itself is an instance of a point score, in contrast to the Stanford Revisions, which are age scales. However, Wechsler (the author of the scale) does supply tables by which the point scores can be converted into what he calls I.Q.'s. But the Wechsler-Bellevue I.Q. is a different sort of measure from the Stanford-Binet I.Q. (708).

Army Alpha

I mention this test chiefly because of its historical importance, for it is the first important group test of general intelligence. (That is, it can be given to a considerable number of people at once instead of one at a time.) It was constructed for use in the United States Army in the First World War. Army Alpha is made up of 8 subsidiary tests (or subtests). In these subtests the subjects are required to follow sets of verbal directions, to solve 20 arithmetic problems, to decide what to do by common sense in 16 described situations, to indicate whether 40 pairs of words are the same or different in meaning, to rearrange 24 disarranged sentences and indicate whether they are true or false, to complete 20 incomplete number series, to complete 40 verbal analogies, and to respond to 40 general information items. It is clear that the intention of this test is to make an over-all survey of mentality as thoroughly as possible in the limited time allotted. Army Alpha has been very widely used. Several civilian revisions have been made from which items and expressions referring to army matters have been removed. On the whole the test is too easy for college students. Its authors were a very distinguished group of psychologists, and it had much prestige and great influence in the development of other group tests. But it is no longer generally employed.

Otis Quick-Scoring

This is a widely used battery of group tests of general intelligence, published sequentially from 1936 to 1939. The battery consists of a series of three sets of tests, for grades 1 to 4, 4 to 9, and 9 to 16. The content of the battery is much like that of other general intelligence tests—vocabulary, rearranging disarranged sentences, reasoning, interpretation of proverbs, indicating the opposites of lists of words, and so forth. The battery yields a point score, which can be converted into an M.A. and an I.Q. by the use of equivalence tables published in the instruction book. I mention these tests here because of their emphasis, both in title and organization, on "quick scoring." They belong, indeed, to an "efficiency" type of tests. They are set up so that one can score them by machine; and even when this is not done, hand scoring is very quick and easy. Each of the three series of the battery takes from twenty to thirty minutes to give. Efficiency and conciseness of this sort is one of the conspicuous advantages of group mental tests. Certainly if one can get any reasonable indication of the mentality of a group of people in twenty or thirty minutes, the time has not been wasted.

Henmon-Nelson. Terman-McNemar

These are two of the best general intelligence tests for high-school age. Both of them are revisions of earlier tests. The Henmon-Nelson was originally published in 1932, and revised in 1946. The Terman-McNemar, which was published in 1941, is a revision of the Terman Group Test of Mental Ability, published in 1921. This is worth noticing, because one point in judging a test is the experience that has accumulated in using it. A very old and unrevised test (like the original Army Alpha) may have been superseded. A brand-new test may be experimental, and in any case experience has probably not indicated just what its findings mean. But a test which has matured through one or more revisions, and which has been used in many hundreds of places and with many thousands of children is prima facie a good one.

In both of these tests the constituent subtests are of the conventional kind—sentence completions, information, picking out synonyms, arithmetical reasoning, logical classification, stating the opposites of listed words, and so on. Henmon and Nelson have given an interesting account of how they decided on what items to include in their test. They began with a general working concept of general intelligence. They collected a much larger number of items than would be needed, all of which seemed likely to reveal some aspect of general intelligence as they conceived it to be. This collection of items was scrutinized and winnowed down by a number of experienced teachers. The resulting reduced list of items was tried out on 500 high-school students; some items which turned out to be inconsistent with the test as a whole were rejected,* and the test was made up of this final list. This is a typical instance of what would be considered sound practice in test construction, so it throws some light on the nature and possibilities of mental tests. This is my reason for including the account here (298).

Wonderlic Personnel

I mention the Wonderlic Personnel Test for two reasons. First, there is its name. Wonderlic, its author, called it a

* An item would be inconsistent if a large number of the tryout group passed the item but did badly on the test, and vice versa.

"personnel test" to avoid the fear sometimes felt by persons who are called upon to take something called an "intelligence test." Here is yet another symptom of the vagueness of the concept of general intelligence. Intelligence-test makers themselves do not usually think that they are measuring any clear-cut, sharply defined psychological entity. A second point of interest in the Wonderlic Test is that it is one of the very few group intelligence tests really well adapted for adults. It is a revision of an earlier test (the Otis Self-Administering Test of Mental Ability) made more difficult by higher standardization (742).

Merrill-Palmer

General intelligence tests suited to adults are rare, but there are plenty for the opposite end of the age range. The Merrill-Palmer Scale is a good example of tests for young children. It is set up for age groups ranging from 18 to 24 months to 66 to 71 months. Clearly one cannot use the same kind of material in a test for young children as for children of school age, for young children cannot read or deal with arithmetic problems or follow complicated directions or hold attention very long on verbal material. So different tasks and problems must be found. Two of the Merrill-Palmer tests for children between 18 and 24 months old are to copy building a tower out of blocks and to copy the folding of a piece of paper. Among the tests for age range 30 to 35 months is classifying capsules of red, green, blue, and yellow in correspondingly colored boxes, and at later ages children are called upon to copy a circle, to copy a cross, and to put together jigsaw puzzles of various types.

The question has arisen whether tests like the Merrill-Palmer Scale, which is fairly typical of many tests for young children, measure the same ability as tests for older children which stress verbal problems such as sentence completion, recognizing analogies among words, giving the opposites of various words, and so forth. No very definite answer has been found, and perhaps no definite answer is possible, for there is no precise definition of what any general intelligence test measures. However, it is true that the ratings made by children on the so-called "baby tests" do not correspond very closely to their ratings on standard intelligence tests later on (623).

Performance tests

It has always been recognized that young children cannot deal well with verbal and symbolic material, and the same is true of many older people also. So tests which are largely verbal in their content and which stress the manipulation of symbols might give quite a false picture of the mentality of many persons. Hence what are called "performance tests" have been developed. Less technically these are sometimes called "do-something" tests, for people who take them are called upon to solve mazes, to assemble patterns out of blocks, to fit cut-outs into their proper places, to assemble disassembled pictures, to choose the right tools for a number of tasks, and so on.

Tests of manual dexterity use many of the tasks which are embodied in performance tests; but the difference is that a performance test is intended to show general intelligence while a dexterity test is intended to show special manual ability. One of the first performance tests was Army Group Intelligence Examination Beta, intended for illiterate draftees in the First World War, which was a companion test for Army Alpha. A good recent example is the Cornell-Coxe Performance Ability Scale, which includes the assembling of a mannikin, block design, picture arrangement, digit-symbol, memory for designs, cube construction, and picture completion (124). Performance tests are supposed to measure general intelligence, but they do not correlate well with verbal tests of general intelligence.

RELIABILITY

Now that we have before us some concrete descriptions of general intelligence tests, we can go on to consider some crucial issues which arise in connection with intelligence testing in particular and the measurement of mental abilities and traits in general. The first of these is the issue of reliability.

The reliability of a test is a technical name for its accuracy. There is always a problem of reliability with any measuring device, mental tests included. Old-time carpenters had a motto, "Always measure six times before you cut," the reason being that they knew from sad experience that any one measurement is subject to error, i.e. far from perfectly reliable. A doctor will usually take your blood pressure several times for the same reason. So the question of the reliability of any method or instrument of measurement is very practical and important, and we need to know about how reliable good mental tests really are.

Two eminent authorities dealt with this question in a very interesting and revealing way. They prepared a hundred cardboard strips of different lengths, and made a rubber ruler which could be adjusted with six different tensions. Then they made two sets of measurements of the cardboard strips, adjusting the tensions of the ruler at random each time they measured a strip. When the two sets of measurements so obtained were compared, it was found that they agreed with one another just about as much as two sets of measurements would agree when a good mental test was given twice to the same group of people (333).

Another investigator has reported an amusing accident which throws considerable light on the reliability of intelligence tests. The American Council of Education Psychological Examination was given one fall to 102 students. The same group was tested again a year later, and by mistake the same test was used again. Half the scores made by the students in the two testings varied more than twenty percentile points (725).

The scanty findings which I have reported are samples from a great deal of research on reliability all pointing in much the same direction. I have chosen the two examples above because they tell the story very strikingly and clearly. Obviously, intelligence tests do not measure with anything like the accuracy of a foot rule, although they are much better than sheer guesswork.

Figures for the reliability of a test are usually given in the instruction book, as they certainly should be. But the mere reporting of such figures does not close the issue. How are these figures obtained? Just what do they mean in a practical sense? And by way of a still further question, *Just how reliable are these measures of reliability themselves?*

One way, and for many years the commonest way of determining the reliability of a test, is to give it twice to the same people, and then to find out to what extent the two sets of scores agree. The extent of this agreement is expressed in what is called a correlation coefficient. Correlation coefficients which express the test-retest agreement for any test are often spoken of as reliability coefficients for the test, but it is more accurate to call them retest coefficients, for there are other ways of determining reliability. As an instance, retest coefficients for the Henmon-Nelson test, as reported by the authors of the test, run in the high eighties and low nineties. This is usually thought very satisfactory, although the correlation for the two sets of measurements with the rubber ruler (333) was 0.869, which at least suggests what the figures really mean.

Let us say, however, that we choose a test and find a statement in the instruction book that it has a retest coefficient of 0.90. Does this mean that the test will always have that much reliability whenever it is used? Most certainly it means no such thing. We give the test once to a group of children. Then we wonder how much the showing would differ if it were given again. The statement in the instruction book may hint at an answer, but it can offer no more than a hint. When the authors tried out their test by repeating it, they did so under the best possible conditions. They used the same room, followed exactly the same procedure, probably ran the retest at the same time of day, and since they were experts, they took care of many technical details. But if you were to repeat the test, you probably could not control conditions nearly so well. The children might be bored at taking the same test over. They might be tired or distracted. There might be more noise in the room. You yourself might be in a different mood, and you might let your mood affect your procedure. So your retest showing might probably differ far more from the original showing than the instruction book says it should. Thus the retest coefficient in the instruction book does not express the automatic or built-in reliability of the test, but only its reliability under optimum conditions which can rarely be duplicated. In other words, the reported reliability coefficient is itself far from reliable.

Whenever a test is repeated with the same group of people, no matter how carefully conditions are controlled, there is always some change in the situation, if only from having run the test previously. This means that test-retest coefficients are always affected by influences which cannot be exactly determined, but which are certainly present. So another method of computing the reliability of a test is often used. The test is split into two halves, each half is treated as if it were a separate test, and the scores on the two halves are correlated. When this is done the obtained correlation has to be boosted because reliability falls as the test is shortened.* But apart from this technical point, the aim of the procedure is to avoid the inevitable problems and doubts which arise when a test is given twice to the same group.

You may be interested in trying out the method on some test of your own. Score the responses on a 100-point objective

* The formula used to boost the correlation is the Spearman-Brown Prophecy Formula, i.e. $r_n = \frac{Nr}{1 + (N-1)r}$ where r_n is the new correlation to be found, r is the obtained correlation, and N is the multiple by which the length of the test is increased. In the above case $N = 2$.

test. Split the test into two halves of 50 items each. Compare the standings of your group on the two halves. This is the basis for determining the reliability of your test by the split-half method, and all that you now need is to know how to compute the correlation between the two halves and to apply the boosting formula. As you will see, the procedure avoids running the same test twice. But the sort of correlation that will be obtained will depend a good deal on how the test is split into two halves. You might split it by putting all the odd-numbered items in one half and all the even-numbered items in another, or by dividing it at the fiftieth item, and in many other ways. But the correlations between scores will certainly be influenced by how the two halves are determined; and this is at least one of the serious limitations of determining reliability by the split-half method.

Yet another method of reporting reliability is to indicate the amount of error in each separate score. This method has been used with the Second Stanford Revision of the Binet Scale. For instance, let us suppose we are dealing with three children of 100 months mental age, then an obtained I.Q. of 100 would mean that the real I.Q. is between 95.8 and 104.2, an obtained I.Q. of 125 would mean that the real I.Q. is between 119.8 and 130.2, and an obtained I.Q. of 75 would mean that the true I.Q. is between 71.6 and 78.4 (436). This shows how much error one must expect in the obtained scores. Statements such as these make the meaning of reliability very clear, but they are not based on any new way of ascertaining reliability. There must still be two runnings of the test, and then the comparison between the two sets of scores is worked up statistically so as to express it in terms of the error of each individual score.

There are many other statistical techniques for determining the reliability of tests (131, 384, 385, 632). But none of these techniques get around one basic difficulty. The moment we give a mental test we change to some extent the very thing, whatever it is, that we are trying to measure. You can measure a board with a foot rule without changing the board in the least. But when you give a child a mental test, he responds to some extent in a special way; and if you test him a second time his response is sure to be altered more or less. So the test itself influences whatever it is that is being tested. This is one of the unavoidable conditions and limitations of all mental testing. The best mental tests are better than guesswork. They are fairly reliable, though just how reliable they are under practical conditions we do not know. This is about all that can be said, in spite of an enormous amount of laborious research on the problem of reliability.

What, then, are the practical implications? (*a*) Never base any important decisions about a child or a group of children upon mental test results alone, still less upon a single testing. It has been said that "group tests are a good rough screen but classify individual children incorrectly often enough to prove serious in the lives of many individual children" (69, pp. 334–335). Individual tests like the Stanford Revisions are probably better, but are not sufficient criteria in and of themselves for important decisions. (*b*) A good testing program should be cumulative, carrying on year after year, and following up individual children. Changes in test performance will often show far more and provide far better bases for judgment than any single test performance. (*c*) It is quite possible to regard a mental test as a sort of clinical instrument rather than as a measuring device. When we give a mental test to a group of children we create a very artificial, special, and unusual situation. For just this once all the children are up against precisely the same challenge in precisely the same way. Their varying responses to the challenge can tell us things about them that almost nothing else will tell. And there is a great deal in these responses which is not shown in the test score—reluctance or eagerness, bewilderment or certainty, resistance or docility, slowness or speed, and so forth. If we frankly use a mental test as a sort of standard challenge which may be revealing, then the fact that it may have a rather low reliability ceases to matter very much (387).

STANDARDIZATION

In the descriptions of tests which were given earlier in this chapter you will have noticed several references to the standardization group of the test. The standardization group is, indeed, the very heart of any test. I have given several instances of how test makers go to work. They collect a large number of items which they think could be used to reveal general intelligence (or whatever other trait or ability they propose to test). They winnow these items, and arrange those that are left tentatively in the form of a test. Then they try out the test with groups of children. This trying-out is quite essential. Some or all of the items might be so difficult that even the brightest children would fail. Some or all the items might be so easy that even the dullest would pass. These, of course, would be the two extreme and limiting cases. But there is no way of finding out how difficult the experimental test is, and therefore of knowing just what a performance on a given level means, except to try the test out with groups of children and to see what happens. These groups taken together are the standardization group of the test.

When the completed test is given, let us say, in some third grade, the performance of the third-grade children is rated in terms of the performance of the children in the standardization group. We have seen that a mental age of 10 on the Second Stanford Revision really means a test performance equivalent to that of the 200 ten-year-old children in the standardization group. All mental test scores are determined in essentially the same way—that is, by reference to a standardization group—whether those scores are expressed in terms of age or in some other way. The standardization group, in fact, is the yardstick with reference to which the test measures.

If the standardization group is large and representative, then the test is so far significant, because comparisons based on such a group mean something. The Revised Stanford-Binet Scale of Mental Tests was standardized on 3,184 persons. This is not a very large number, but the group was very carefully chosen. It included children from seventeen communities in eleven states in the East, South, Midwest, and West with representation from rural and urban localities. All these children were native American whites. The occupational distribution of the families represented was in proportion to the distribution of occupational populations in the United States Census. Many recent group tests have standardization groups of several hundred thousand. On the other hand, many published tests are quite inadequately standardized. The Cornell-Coxe Performance Ability Scale has a standardization group of 301 children from kindergarten to the eighth grade, which is meager for such a wide range. A study published in 1927, in which 127 tests were investigated showed that 25% of these tests had less than fifty in the standardization group, while of the remaining tests, 39.2% ignored sex distribution, 90.2% did not consider racial composition, and 88.2% ignored social composition, although 59% used large numbers in the standardization group (590).

This process of standardization, on which mental measurement depends, always needs to be remembered in deciding how to use tests, what to do about their results, and what interpretations to place on their findings. It has a bearing on some of the most important problems which have arisen in connection with the measurement of human traits and abilities.

1. It has been repeatedly found that rural children rate lower on intelligence tests than city children. For instance, in the celebrated investigation of the "hollow folk" to which I have already referred, the average I.Q. of the "hollow" children was 61.2, while the average I.Q. of the children in a small village in the region was 96.1 (587, 588). Such results have

often been reported in this country and elsewhere. Thus in an elaborate study of the intelligence test performance of children in the county of Northumberland (England), it was found that the highest levels of performance occurred either near the cities or far away from them. The suggested explanation is that the most intelligent children who lived neither too near nor too far from cities tended to migrate to them, leaving the children of lower intelligence in the intermediate area (151).

However, these differences between rural and urban children, although they are commonly found, are not universal. In Scotland it has been reported that there is no difference at all, due, it is thought, to the homogeneous culture of the country and the uniform distribution of educational opportunities (573). Also, in this country, a comparison was made of intelligence test performance of children in a small town in Westchester County and in New York City. The children were classified by family into four socio-economic groups—professional, business, skilled labor, and semiskilled labor; and when these groupings were taken into account there was no difference in test performance between the rural and urban children (24).

There has been a great deal of theorizing about these obtained differences betweeen urban and rural children. Some authorities have said that the city draws the brighter and abler persons from the country. Other authorities have suggested that country life retards the development of intelligence. But a much simpler explanation is that a great many intelligence tests are standardized on urban children and are therefore unfair to rural children. In one investigation a general information test of 25 items was made up in two forms. Form A was standardized for city children, and form B for country children. On form A city children did better and country children did worse; and on form B country children did better and city children did worse (590). In another investigation the items of the First Stanford Revision of the Binet Scale were examined with rural-urban differences in mind. Some items definitely favored urban children, others definitely favored rural children, and at the upper age levels there was definite and serious discrimination against rural children (138). So it appears that much of the apparent difference in general intelligence between urban and rural children is really produced by the tests themselves, and by the method of standardizing them.

2. Ever since the advent of intelligence testing it has been found that the test performance of children from the upper socio-economic levels (i.e. those whose parents have superior occupations, and who have better home conditions and better general social status) is better than the test performance of children from the lower socio-economic levels.

Binet himself remarks on this fact, saying that children from the social classes in "easy circumstances" tested 1.25 years ahead of working-class children (58). A well known tabulation showing the relationship of average I.Q. on the Second Stanford Revision to socio-economic status is reproduced below.

Mean Stanford-Binet I.Q.'s Classified According to Father's Occupation

Father's Occupational Classification	Chronological Ages			
	2–5½	6–9	10–14	15–18
I. Professional	116	115	118	116
II. Semiprofessional and managerial	112	107	112	117
III. Clerical, skilled trades, retail	108	105	107	110
IV. Rural owners	99	95	92	94
V. Semiskilled, minor clerical, minor business	104	105	103	107
VI. Slightly skilled	95	100	101	96
VII. Day laborers, urban and rural	94	96	97	98

From Terman and Merrill (643, p. 48).

In the study already cited on the distribution of intelligence in Northumberland, 1,722 children of "brain workers" had an average I.Q. of 106.6, 10,848 children of "hand workers" had an average I.Q. of 98.6, children of clergymen had an average I.Q. of 121, and children of hawkers and chimney sweeps had an average I.Q. of 91 (151). In another study dealing with retarded children in England, those of gypsy parentage had an average I.Q. of 75.4, and children of canalboat dwellers had an average I.Q. of 71.5. More recently a very comprehensive investigation has been made of the test performance of all children of various ages in a midwestern community, and it was found that the test performance of those from the more favored socio-economic levels was consistently better (237). Finally, in a study of 100,153 individuals in 273 health centers in New York City, very great differences in mental test performance which corresponded to the social and economic level of the local community were found, differences in average I.Q. ranging from 74 to 118 (438).

As with rural-urban differences, there is an extensive literature of debate on the obtained facts about differences in test performance at different socio-economic levels. The very wide issue of heredity versus environment has been dragged into the argument. Some authorities have insisted that there is no evidence showing these differences to be due to heredity—i.e. that children of low socio-economic status and inferior test performance are not "born that way" (479). Others have argued to the contrary, insisting that heredity is the real cause of the differences. There have been various accusations of bias on both sides, and it has been pointed out very truly that no one really knows the answer, for there has never been a crucial investigation to find out whether so-called "socio-economic differences" in intelligence are due to heredity or environment.

Once again the obvious explanation of these urban-rural differences is that they are largely due to the standardization of intelligence tests. Allison Davis has investigated a multiple-choice vocabulary test using items and words often employed in items and instructions of intelligence tests. He says that 70% of these items in his vocabulary test show a bias in favor of the upper social brackets. "Facility in a particular language—in this case the rarer forms of 'standard English'—offers no sound basis for measuring mental capacity. Any language is a highly formalized system of cultural behavior. It must be learned by long experience in that cultural group which possesses the language. The lower socio-economic groups have a different language-culture than the higher groups. They speak various 'nonstandard' dialects. Therefore, their mental capacity cannot be tested by asking them to define such words as 'ambiguous' or 'illumination' or to understand the meaning of such phrases as 'is to' in the statements: 'loud *is to* sound as bright *is to* what?' or 'Zoo *is to* animals as aquarium *is to* what?' or 'Complex *is to* simple as hard *is to* what?' These questions test only one's facility with, and training in, middle-class linguistic culture" (138, pp. 82–83).

There is no doubt that such an analysis very much reduces the far-flung significance that some psychologists like to find in mental test results. A mental test is not a psychological X-ray machine, which reveals the hidden but immutable realities below the surface of life. It is simply a closely controlled and clearly defined challenge; and it interprets the response which individuals or groups make to that challenge by comparison with the response already made by a known and carefully chosen standardization group. If the persons who take the test have a very different outlook and mentality from those on whom it was standardized, all the interpretations and evaluations it offers are undermined.

3. Once again, the influence of standardization procedures must always be remembered in interpreting racial differences in intelligence test performance. It is well established that Negro and Indian children do considerably worse than white children on standard intelligence tests. The extent of the dif-

ference varies in various research reports, but Negroes and Indians usually show an inferiority of from twenty to thirty per cent on verbal intelligence tests, and a smaller but still quite marked inferiority when performance tests are used. These facts have been recognized ever since the great mental testing program set up in the United States Army in World War I.

But do the facts prove that Indians, Negroes, and other races are actually inferior to whites in native intelligence? By no means! Inferior test performance, without any doubt, is largely due to the standardization of the tests.

a) As to language use, there is the same difficulty here as with different social classes. Tests use highly stereotyped and special English, both in their content and their instructions. White children, who usually compose the standardization group, are likely to find this language much more understandable than Negro, Indian, or South European immigrant children.

b) Besides language, there are other cultural factors which are very influential even in performance tests which minimize the use of language. When a group of Yakima Indian children were given a picture completion test, many of them failed to see the net missing in a picture of a tennis court, or the filament missing in a picture of an electric light bulb, or the stamp missing in a picture of an envelope. When they were asked what was missing in a picture of a house without a chimney, many of them said that the crucifix was missing. These children were also given a "common sense" or "what to do" test. One question was what to do if your playmate hits you unintentionally. But primitive reservation Indians do not discriminate between intentional and unintentional injuries. Another question was why all parents should send their children to school. The right answer in the scoring key is that school prepares children for life; but such an idea is relatively meaningless to reservation Indians.

c) The question of rapport is always important, and particularly so in dealing with racial groups unaccustomed to taking tests or suspicious of them. Even to sophisticated white children a mental test can be rather a strain, and to many rural Negro children it can be positively terrifying. Furthermore, many urban Negroes know very well that mental testing has seemed to cast aspersions on their race, and so they are hostile from the beginning. The whole emotional set of children of other races is likely to be very different from that of white children, and particularly of the white children in the standardization group who know they are co-operating in an experiment and have nothing to lose or gain from taking the test.

So, in summary, it is quite certain that we can make no flat statements about differences in racial mentality on the basis of racial differences in mental test performance (176, 374).

VALIDITY

When we speak of the validity of a test, we mean the determination of exactly what it measures. The validity of a test always needs to be carefully defined and well understood if it is to be used to good purpose. For instance, during World War II many experimental tests were developed for air force candidates. It was found that a number of these tests would predict performance during training quite well, but had no relationship at all to performance during actual combat. So the question, *Validity for what?* is always crucial (336).

One would think that people who construct tests would always have an answer to this question, based on ascertained facts, or at least that they would try to find an answer. But this is not so. Quite elaborate tests were used during the war in Germany for Luftwaffe candidates. Many of these tests looked very impressive on paper. But no one made the slightest effort to find out whether they predicted success either in training or in combat. So the tests were worth no more than the paper on which they were printed. Test makers in this country usually accept more responsibility for determining what is being measured than the German test experts seem to have done. But plenty of tests come on the market with a very ill-defined validity.

There is more than one way of ascertaining the validity of a test. What has been called "practical validation" means checking the test against an independent criterion. Thus we may propose to test manual dexterity by having our subjects fit pegs into the round holes in a form board. We devise our test situation, and then we find out if those who do well in the test also do well in other kinds of manipulation. This is basically the method of validating intelligence tests, and the method has been used widely enough to enable us to say pretty well what intelligence tests do and do not measure.*

1. Intelligence test performance has little relationship to learning ability as that ability is demonstrated in experimental and laboratory situations. This may seem rather surprising, since intelligence is often defined as the ability to learn. But the fact is well established (594, 743). The point to remember, however, is that learning that takes place in a psychological laboratory is usually very restricted. Learning to make tallies, to memorize nonsense syllables, and to run pencil mazes does not seem to be related to performance on standard intelligence tests. But if it were possible to make a controlled experiment on the sort of learning that goes on in more normal situations, the outcome might be very different.

2. There is no very close relationship between intelligence test performance and school marks in special subjects. "Brightness," "mediocrity," and "dullness" as revealed in intelligence tests have surprisingly little relationship to marks in history, social studies, English, foreign languages, and mathematics.

3. There can be no doubt that the chief success of general intelligence tests is their ability to predict general school achievement as revealed by average marks in all subjects, grade points, honor points, rapidity of progress in school, and other

* Another type of validation, known as factorial validation, will be discussed in the next chapter.

such criteria. For instance, one important investigation revealed that out of 76 children in kindergarten, 24 failed to make normal school progress is the next two years, that out of 95 first-graders, 45 failed to make normal progress in the next two years, and that out of 90 children in the high first grade, 60 failed to make normal progress in the next two years. As you will see, the school progress of 261 children in all was studied. But out of this 261, only 3 with an I.Q. of 110 failed to make normal progress over the following two years. A total of 129 of the children did not make normal progress, and 84 of this group had an I.Q. of 90 or less (192).

Again, it has been repeatedly shown that performance on a mental test can be a useful criterion for guidance with young children. On a basis of much experimentation it has been found that a mental age of 5 years 2 months is desirable if a child is to do well in kindergarten, and that a mental age of 6 years 2 months is desirable for entering the first grade (312).

Once more, a follow-up study of 1,989 children tested in the sixth grade showed a definite relationship between test performance and school progress. Those not entering high school had a median I.Q. of 96. Those entering high school but not graduating had a median I.Q. of 105. Those who graduated from high school, but did not go to college had a median I.Q. of 114. Those who entered college, but did not graduate had a median I.Q. of 115. Those who took an A.B. degree had a median I.Q. of 123. Those who went on to graduate work had a median I.Q. of 124 (48).

Achievement in college, too, is significantly related to mental test performance. Correlations between intelligence test scores and college achievement are said to center about .52. This, to be sure, is not a very high correlation, but the claim has been made that it is higher than the figure for ten years ago (154). These are samples of a very great many investigations, all pointing in the same direction. Moreover, it should be noted that most of these investigations deal with the relationship of a single testing to school achievement. If, instead of using a snapshot test, we have a really good follow-up testing program, our figures will give us a much better means of foreseeing school achievement (245).

All this strongly suggests that, irrespective of any theorizing, performance on a general intelligence test is more closely related to general achievement in school than to anything else. Moreover, intelligence tests themselves have three characteristics which make such an interpretation very reasonable. If you will look back to the test descriptions earlier in this chapter, you will be able to recognize these characteristics. (*a*) The content of the tests is decidedly school-like. (*b*) Test instructions are given in condensed academic language, very much like the language of textbooks. (*c*) It is obvious that the taking of a mental test calls for a definite and rather special personal orientation, or mental set very much like the mental set needed for success in the conventional school. All in all, then, it would seem that a mental test is a challenge which reveals academic adjustment or academic aptitude. Indeed, Binet himself undertook to sample the academic potentialities of children, even though he called his tests measurements of general intelligence.

Three further considerations support the conclusion that general intelligence tests are primarily tests of academic adjustment or aptitude.

a) These tests are decidedly better for predicting school performance than general success in life. A number of psychologists widely experienced in using intelligence tests were asked to rate such tests in terms of their practical value for classifying people (*a*) in the army (*b*) in schools (*c*) in business. Of these psychologists, 88% thought them decidedly valuable in the army, 67% thought them decidedly valuable in business, and 97% thought them decidedly valuable in school (377).

b) Intelligence tests are best adapted for children of school age, and more specifically for children between grades three and nine. These are recognized as the best ages for mental testing with our present tests. Tests given to very young children do not on the whole predict later school achievement nearly so well as tests given at a more advanced age (39). Even tests administered in the first grade provide a rather shaky basis for prediction (4, 5).

Then, going to the other end of the age range, most mental tests will give quite misleading results when they are used on adults, and particularly on old or elderly adults. It has often been found that there is a rapid and marked decline in mental test performance beyond the middle years of life (454). But it must be remembered that most tests call for small tricks of verbal ingenuity, manipulations that seem petty and annoying to older persons, little jobs of rote memory, and also for quick reactions. These are precisely the types of rather school-bound performance in which older people are not likely to do well. But when we are dealing with such more complex, subtle, and appealing functions as understanding the meaning of words, the efficient reading of paragraphs, or the drawing of conclusions from significant data, older people show no falling off (608). So again it would seem that mental tests are particularly well suited for people of school age who are habituated to the demands of conventional schooling.

c) Tests of general intelligence, so called, and good, comprehensive, many-sided tests of educational achievement seem to measure about the same thing. For instance, the United States Armed Forces Institute Tests of General Educational Development deal with the interpretation of reading materials in social studies and natural science, with the interpretation of literary materials, and with correct and effective expression. The dividing line between such tests and general intelligence tests is certainly very faint, if there is any such line at all.

So we reach the conclusion that general intelligence tests actually measure school adjustment, or academic aptitude, to use the more familiar expression. The tests tend to pick out persons who, because of the total setting of their lives, will do well in an academic environment. Certainly there are other factors which determine academic success besides those revealed by intelligence tests. It has been found that persistence, common sense, and dependability correlate about as high with academic success as intelligence test performance, and that the correlation between punctuality, co-operativeness and honesty on the one hand and academic success on the other is only slightly lower (686). To indicate the other side of the picture, Binet long ago, on seeing the restlessness, boredom, and inattention of a class of subnormal children remarked that it would need genius to learn under such conditions (58).

GENERAL APPRAISAL

We are now in a position to make a brief, clear-cut appraisal of tests of general intelligence. These tests do not reveal a basic universal human ability, the nature of which is sharply defined and well-understood. If we assume that they really do reveal such an ability, and proceed to give them indiscriminately to young and old, and to members of various races and various social groups, the results we get and the conclusions we draw are certain to be dangerously misleading. Even when a mental test is given to children who are comparable to the children in the standardization group, we do not immediately have a secure foundation for planning and guidance, because the reliability of the scores is open to question. A single mental test score is only one datum out of the many that are needed to deal with children constructively. If we have a testing program under which children are tested several times during their school careers, this will tell us a good deal more than even the very best snapshot test result, because a sequential testing program gives us at least a partial picture of growth, and because the tests given at different levels can be checked against each other so that errors tend to cancel out. But even so, the test scores can only tell part of the story, and need to be interpreted in the light of the fullest possible understanding of the child as a whole. *Human beings cannot be dealt with and guided constructively merely on a basis of statistical data.*

Nevertheless, tests of general intelligence have been and are important and valuable. They are important because they predict within reasonable limits a child's capacity to succeed in a situation which is very important in our culture—namely, the academic situation. To put the point more plainly, intelligence tests correlate to a useful degree with success in academic studies. The academic curriculum is stereotyped. Its scope is rather narrow. It is out of touch with many of the concerns of human life. Moreover, it is class-biased.

Not long ago a social survey was made of a typical Northern community which was referred to as "Yankee City." The secondary schools of Yankee City offered four curricula, two of which were college preparatory, one commercial, and one "general," i.e. geared to immediate life needs. The class composition of the children in these curricula was investigated. It was found that 100% of the upper-class children of the Yankee City schools, 88% of the upper middle-class children, 45% of the lower middle-class children, 28% of the upper lower-class children, and 26% of the lower-class children were in the first two curricula, that is to say, the college-preparatory curricula. From all that we know it is a pretty safe guess that if a standard intelligence test were given, the ratings would drop in parallel with these class distinctions.

Furthermore, intelligence tests, as we have seen, tend to predict stay in school. Children who rate high tend to go on. Children who rate low tend to drop out. The usual explanation is that it takes good general intelligence to continue on in school. But if intelligence tests really reveal academic aptitude, or capacity for school adjustment, then the low-rating children who drop out soon after the sixth grade may do so because the school environment is unsuited to them, and because they find in it little to satisfy their basic life needs.

But the ability to get on well in an academic curriculum is

certainly not to be despised. In this country it is not so tremendously important as it used to be in the Old World, where the right academic degree was an iron-clad prerequisite for all the most preferred occupations. But even here academic success helps to open many doors and to make possible many desirable prospects. Moreover, there is a great deal of very rich ore in the academic curriculum itself, in spite of many aspersions; and if not nearly so much of this ore is transmuted into gold as one could wish, that is the fault of the teaching and not of the curriculum itself. So with things as they actually are, any instrument or device which will really help us to decide in advance whether a child is likely to be an academic success is well worth having and using. There is no doubt at all that general intelligence tests can help us in shaping up such decisions. A good testing program almost always reveals unsuspected abilities, and removes bushels which have been concealing surprisingly bright lights. For instance, the potentialities of Negro children can easily be underrated, but when well-chosen intelligence tests are run many of them come out with very high ratings. On the basis of test results, at least, such children are excellent academic prospects, and they ought to be given their opportunity, both for their own sake and for the sake of the social order (337).

It could even be argued that the tests we have been discussing can quite properly be called intelligence tests, in spite of their strong academic and schoolwise slant. Geometry may not strengthen a person's reasoning power, and struggling with elementary Latin may do very little for one's command of English; but no one has ever undertaken to show that a child can make an academic success without a good mentality—and a good mentality is useful anywhere in life. What we must avoid is the thought that so-called "general intelligence" tests reveal a basic faculty, a definable and specific ability, which is essentially the same in all human beings and differs only in degree.

So far in this discussion I have kept close to the tests themselves, and to the issues arising immediately out of them. An informed and intelligent attitude towards mental tests is a proper part of every teacher's professional equipment. Furthermore, it is not possible to deal adequately with the wider question of the nature and significance of human abilities and traits in general without some insight into the testing instruments that are supposed to reveal those abilities and traits. This wider question must certainly be discussed, but I shall postpone it until we have considered a number of types of tests other than tests of general intelligence.

QUESTIONS FOR DISCUSSION

1. Are there any important aspects of human behavior and mental life which are not included in Binet's working method of surveying general intelligence?
2. Can any test ever reveal anything more than behavior or response under a special set of circumstances?
3. Discuss the relationship of "academic aptitude" to general capacity for intelligent behavior in life.
4. Do you think that an intelligence test which would be suitable for and fair to all human beings could be constructed?
5. In what respects do you think mental growth could go on beyond the age of arrest for some given test?
6. Collect and discuss any remarks you may have heard or known of made by parents about their children which seem to embody essentially the idea of the intelligence quotient.
7. Considering the content of intelligence tests, why might one naturally expect that they would predict general school achievement fairly well?
8. Granted that an intelligence test measures by comparing a person who takes it with a standardization group, does this mean that the test score is meaningless or necessarily misleading?
9. What practical inferences about the use of tests and the in-

terpretation of test results might be drawn from the facts about reliability presented in this chapter?

10. In what respect does mental testing resemble and not resemble phrenology?

SUGGESTED READINGS

Cornell, Ethel L., and Coxe, Warren A., A *Performance Ability Scale: Examination Manual.* World Book Company, Yonkers, N.Y., 1934, Chap. 1.

Freeman, Frank N., "The Meaning of Intelligence." *39th Yearbook,* National Society for the Study of Education (1940), Part I, Chap. 1, 11–20.

Kornhauser, Arthur, "Replies of Psychologists to Several Questions on the Practical Values of Intelligence Tests." *Educational and Psychological Measurement,* V (1945), 181–189.

Mursell, James L., *Psychological Testing,* 2nd ed., Longmans, Green & Company, New York, 1949, Chap. 2.

14

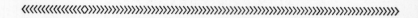

Specialized Abilities and Traits

FACTORIAL TESTS

THE CONCEPT of general intelligence is one of the most fruitful and successful in the whole history of psychology. It has led to the development of tests whose substantial practical usefulness cannot be questioned, even though they do not probe nearly so deeply into the mysteries of the human mental make-up as has sometimes been supposed. Nevertheless, the concept of general intelligence is undeniably quite vague, and so one cannot say what the scores or ratings on general intelligence tests—mental ages, intelligence quotients, and point scores—exactly indicate. For these reasons there has for some time been increasing dissatisfaction both with the concept itself, and with the so-called "global" or over-all scores obtained by general intelligence tests. Is it not possible to analyze mentality with real precision, to find out just what its components are, and to construct tests which will measure these components exactly and economically? This question has been coming more and more to the fore, and the attempt to answer it has given rise to the technical development known as *factor analysis*.

The basic idea back of factor analysis can be explained quite simply. Let us suppose that we give a person a mental test in which he has to solve 15 arithmetic problems, to indicate similarities and opposites among 30 pairs of words, to complete 15 incomplete sentences, to say what he would do in 15 "common-sense" situations, to reply to 20 general information questions, and perhaps to do a number of other tasks of a similar kind. When he has finished, we find that his over-all score is 135. Our tables in the instruction book of the test tell us that this score is equivalent to a mental age of 15; and since his chronological age is also 15, this gives him an I.Q. of 100. So far we have nothing but global scores which indicate the level of the person's general intelligence, whatever the phrase means.

But it would seem that when this person carries through the various tasks in our test, a great many different mental processes are involved. Among these mental processes will be his memory, his power to handle words, his capacity for inductive reasoning, and the like; and if our test included the completion of pictures or some manipulations with blocks, his capacity for space perception would also be involved. If we could pick out all the mental processes which account for the person's performance on the tasks we have set him, and then if we could construct tests which would measure just precisely these processes, we might very well have a much better picture of his mentality than the rather hit-or-miss general intelligence test with its global scores can afford. Moreover, if our new tests are properly constructed, they will be purged of all dead material, for every item in every one of these new tests will bear upon one and only one clearly defined mental process. To use the current technical expression, our new tests will be "purified," whereas there will almost certainly be useless and confusing irrelevancies in the general intelligence test. The technique for singling out the various mental processes involved in performance on tests such as that described above is known as factor analysis. The mental processes themselves are usually called mental factors, although some other names for them are used as well. And the resulting new type tests are known as factorial tests.

There are already a fair number of sets, or batteries, of tests which undertake to measure a certain list of specified and defined mental factors. One of the best of these is the battery known as the Chicago Tests of Primary Mental Abilities. These tests were the work of L. L. Thurstone, and the term "primary mental abilities" is his term for mental factors. I shall have something to say about the suitability of Thurstone's term a little later on. The Chicago Tests of Primary Mental Abilities were the outcome of quite a spectacular and very arduous piece of research. Thurstone gave 54 conventional mental tests of various types to 240 college students, and applied an intricate statistical technique to find out what mental processes were involved in dealing with these tests. Among the mental processes identified by Thurstone in this and later investigations are perceptual ability, space-visualizing ability, verbal facility, memory, ability to reason inductively or to generalize, and ability to reason deductively.

Notice carefully that Thurstone arrived at these mental processes by a statistical analysis of performance on a great many conventional tests, and he believed that they account for the students' performance on those tests. These mental processes, that is to say, were brought into play when the students attacked the tasks presented in the conventional tests. The Chicago Tests of Primary Mental Abilities differ from the conventional tests, because each test in the new battery aims to measure one and only one of the mental processes, and to call for nothing at all except this one defined and specific mental process. So the Chicago Tests do not yield a global or over-all score. They yield a special score for each mental process.

This is often called a profile, because the separate scores can be expressed in a graph, which shows just where a person stands in memory ability, in space visualization, in inductive reasoning, and so forth. Thurstone calls the mental processes "primary mental abilities" as we have seen. Many other workers call them mental factors (671, 674).

This same idea of profile scoring in contrast to global scoring is embodied in much simpler form in the American Council on Education Psychological Examination for College Freshmen, which is one of the most widely used of mental tests. A new form of this test is prepared and published each year. Until quite recently the examination was of the conventional intelligence test type, yielding a global score. But later editions have differentiated a quantitative or Q score, and a linguistic or L score. The quantitative score is obtained by tests on arithmetic problems, the completion of number series, and the analysis of figures; and the linguistic score is obtained by tests on language completions, verbal analogies, and same-opposite problems with pairs of words (673).

Factor analysis bulks so large in present day psychology that teachers ought to understand its general meaning at least, and should have some informed opinion about it. Yet its statistical techniques are quite intricate, and may easily seem quite mystifying to anyone who is not a fairly good mathematician. However, a good enough appraisal is possible without bogging down in mathematical complications. In making such an appraisal the following points seem decisive.

1. Factor analysis is a statistical procedure. (There are, in fact, a number of different techniques used.) So the analyst must have statistical data to start with. That is to say, he must have a set of scores, or he cannot analyze at all. He can go to work with test scores, or with ratings expressed in numerical form, or even with school marks. But there are a great many kinds of mental performance which do not yield a score of any kind; and some of these unscorable mental performances are

exceedingly important—diligence, for instance, or resistance to temptation, or initiative, or originality, or susceptibility to temper tantrums. Of course one might cudgel one's brains and cook up something that might conceivably be called a score on diligence, or resistance to temptation, or initiative, or originality, or bad temper. Indeed, such scores have been concocted; but if anything in this world is certain, it is certain that scores of this kind are preposterous and meaningless. Factor analysis could undoubtedly go to work on such silly scores; but then it would come out with a silly result, for there can be nothing in the outcome that was not first in the data. So analysis can only reveal the factors present in performances that can be scored in a meaningful and sensible way, and clearly this greatly limits its range of application.

2. There is a great deal of disagreement among experts in factor analysis about what the mental factors really are. I have mentioned Thurstone's original list of factors, and it is a conservative one. But new factors keep popping up all the time. You will remember that one investigator counted up all the human instincts which various authorities alleged to exist, and found that there were about 14,000 of them. So far as I know, nobody has yet counted up all the alleged mental factors, but my guess would be that while considerably less than 14,000 have as yet been "discovered," they probably run well up towards the first thousand if not over. Crude considerations like this are usually quite disgusting to experts who burn to apply statistics to everything under the sun, and who seem to think that obscurity is equivalent to a scientific attitude. Also it is quite true that the great and growing diversity of mental factors is accounted for partly because there are several different methods of factor analysis, and partly because analysts start with very different sets of data. But to the naïve onlooker the seemingly uncontrolled proliferation of factors casts at least a shade of doubt upon the concept.

3. Are factorial tests more valid than global intelligence tests? This is a very searching question, because if the new tests do not tell us more that is worth knowing about children than the old tests did, then the best one can say for these new ones is that they are experimental gropings towards an improvement not yet attained.

In explaining how conventional intelligence tests are validated by rating them against an outside criterion, I pointed out that this is only one method of validation, often called "practical" validation. For factorial tests quite another sort of validation is proposed, namely "factorial" validation. Factorial validation means the analysis of a test to determine its "purity," i.e. the extent to which it measures the one factor, such as verbal fluency, space perception, or deductive reasoning, which it was designed to measure (255). If the test turns out to be less valid than it should be in this respect, it is revised by eliminating items which do not bear upon the indicated mental factor.

Factorial validation, clearly, is a process of internal analysis. It is not a process of checking the test against some criterion external to itself. So even with the best and "purest" of factorial tests, the question of their practical validity still remains. Do they or do they not give us more and better information about human beings than conventional global tests? Apparently they do not. Factorial tests such as the Chicago Tests of Primary Mental Abilities do not correlate more closely than conventional intelligence tests with general school achievement, or with special achievement in specific subject-matter areas (235). Nor are the patterns or profiles of mental factors revealed by such tests very closely related to this or that vocation. So it has been said that claims which have been made that on the basis of a battery of factorial tests one can tell any high-school student what his vocation should or should not be, are absurd (1). Factorial tests, then, are experimental. They have not yet demonstrated any unmistakable practical superiority to conventional intelligence tests, in spite of many a priori arguments.

4. Are mental factors psychological realities? We have seen that Thurstone came to the conclusion that verbal fluency, spatial imagination, inductive reasoning, deductive reasoning, memory, and suchlike processes or functions, are involved in performance on a great many mental tests. Moreover, Thurstone called these processes, not factors, but primary mental abilities. This expression implies that the processes are real psychological entities, genuine elements in a person's mental make-up. All the points already made here cast doubt on this proposition. Large numbers of factors have already been uncovered. Which are the genuine ones? Factors are discovered by analyzing scores on scorable mental performances. Are we always sure that the scores really represent the performance? Also, what about performances that cannot be scored? Long before statistical methods were used much in psychology, a great many "mental faculties" were thought to exist, such as a faculty of memory, of reasoning, of emotion, of love for children, of leadership, of writing ability, and so on endlessly. The notion that the mind is made up of such faculties collapsed because it was so obviously possible to invent a faculty to explain anything. It has been suggested that mental factors are simply faculties all over again, the main difference being that factors are discovered by a laborious statistical analysis instead of being made up on the spur of the moment. This is not quite a fair criticism, because the analytic technique does check sheer imaginative invention, but a certain parallel between faculties and factors does strongly suggest itself.

The reasonable position seems to be that mental factors are really working concepts which enable us to classify test responses. In geography the Greenwich meridian and the Equator are classifying concepts. The Greenwich meridian and the

Equator are not real things, like Mount Everest and the Atlantic Ocean; but they are useful, because they enable us to classify things as north and south and east and west of certain imaginary lines. So it may be useful for purposes of test construction to classify responses as pertaining to memory, or inductive reasoning, or space perception. But memory and inductive reasoning and space perception may still be and, indeed, probably are imaginary lines in our psychological world, instead of solid, substantial, permanent, mutually independent realities (1, 104).

PERSONALITY TESTS

There is a large but very ill-defined group of tests which are called "personality tests." Just what any one of these tests is supposed to measure is usually anything but clear, in spite of the explanatory verbiage in the instruction book. The best way to get at least a rough and partial idea of what is involved in the so-called "personality tests" is by a brief description of a few typical examples of various kinds.

Self-rating scales

Self-rating scales, or tests, are questionnaires in which a person answers questions about himself, the questions being framed so that they can be answered very briefly, and often by a mere Yes or No. Two instances of such tests are the Adjustment Inventory and the California Test of Personality. Each of these tests is made up of a large number of questions such as: "Do you daydream frequently? Did you ever have a strong desire to run away from home? Do you take cold rather easily from other people? Do you enjoy social gatherings? Are you often sorry for yourself?" The person taking the test is supposed to answer such questions "frankly and honestly," although they often seem intimate to the point of impudence, and also very vague. The answers are scored according to a key, and the scores are supposed to reveal a person's self-adjustment, or social adjustment, or health adjustment, or home adjustment, or occupational adjustment, whatever these terms may mean (675).

A more complicated self-rating scale than the two just mentioned is the Bernreuter Personality Inventory, which has been quite widely used. The Inventory consists of 125 questions of which the following are typical: "Do you like to bear responsibilities alone? Does it make you uncomfortable to be unconventional or 'different'? Do you often feel miserable? Do you try to get your way even if you have to fight for it?" By means of elaborately worked-out keys the answers to these questions are supposed to indicate the degree to which a person exhibits six traits. The six traits are (*a*) neurotic tendency, i.e. emotional instability (*b*) self-sufficiency, i.e. rarely asking for sympathy, ignoring advice, liking to be alone (*c*) introversion-extroversion, i.e. being imaginative, living in and for oneself (*d*) dominance-submission, i.e. tendency to dominate others in face-to-face relationships (*e*) self-confidence, i.e. wholesome self-assurance (*f*) sociability (52, 411, 412).

By far the most carefully and thoroughly constructed self-rating personality test is the Minnesota Multiphasic Personality Inventory. It is made up of 550 simple declarative statements in the first person singular, to which responses of "true," "false," or "do not know" can be made. Typical among these statements are: "I seldom worry about my health," "My daily life is full of things that keep me interested," "I sometimes feel like swearing." In the individual form of the Inventory each statement is printed on a separate card which is picked up by the person taking the test and classified according to his response. A group form of the inventory has also been prepared. By means of scoring devices, the responses a person makes can be rated for indications of various psychopathological conditions, such as hysteria, paranoia, schizophrenia, and so forth (273, 274).

Projective tests

Projective tests are personality tests of quite a different kind from those just described. The best known of them is the Rorschach Test. It consists of 10 large ink blots, 5 in different shades of gray, 2 in gray with one shade of red, and 3 entirely, or almost entirely, in color. Each ink blot is printed on a separate card. The subject looks at it, and is asked, "What could that be?" or "What do you see here?" That is to say, he may make any interpretation of the ink blot that suggests itself to him. His interpretation is supposed to be a self-projection, a revelation of his personality type. Certain features of his interpretation are specially noted. Thus he may take account of the ink blot as a whole or of only some small detail in it. He may "see" a human figure, an animal, a plant, etc. His response may be very vague, or very accurate and definite. He may "see" some quite common object like a shovel or a dipper, or something very unusual.

The Rorschach Test is not regarded as an instrument of measurement, like all the tests we have so far discussed. On the contrary, it is regarded as an instrument of diagnosis. The interpretations that a person makes of the ink blots are supposed to be self-revelatory or symptomatic, and to show the kind of person that he is. Quite an enormous mass of special literature has grown up dealing with what various interpretations indicate. For instance, if a person persistently concentrates on small details in the ink blots, this may suggest that he is penurious, literal-minded, and unimaginative. On the other hand, if he makes broad, sweeping interpretations he may be generous, rash, and careless. These two illustrations, let me hasten to say, are much over-simplified, and from the standpoint of Rorschach enthusiasts, quite naïve. I offer them merely for the sake of a quick explanation. The literature on the Rorschach Test carries the analysis of the subject's responses to great lengths of refinement and sophistication (43, 375).

So much for a few samples of the very large number of existing personality tests. The great question about them, and indeed the only question that matters much to us is to what extent they are valid. Do they really measure personality characteristics? Can we place any reliance on what they seem to reveal? As to the self-rating questionnaires, the general opinion of psychologists is that their validity is extremely dubious. The best criterion is independent diagnosis of a person by competent and thorough psychiatrists, and usually the results of the tests when applied to this person have little correspondence with such independent diagnoses (161). In one investigation 79 psychologists made ratings of the Bernreuter Personality Inventory. Of these 79, 1.5% found the test highly satisfactory, 13.5% found it moderately satisfactory, and all the others rated it anywhere from doubtful to highly unsatisfactory in practical use (378). It is likely that expert opinion on most, if not all, of the other tests of this type would be equally unfavorable. In fact one authority, summarizing numerous research studies, has said, "Nearly all reputable personality testing outside carefully controlled clinical situations is still frankly tentative and experimental" (161, p. 424). As to the Rorschach Test, it is not possible to be quite so certain. But at least its practical validity has never been indubitably demonstrated on a widespread scale.

The basic trouble with all these tests is the extreme vagueness of what is being measured or indicated. When, for instance, we speak of introversion or emotional instability, we are dealing with something that manifests itself so differently in different persons that in each case it becomes virtually a different thing. We are, in fact, dealing with what has been called a "common trait." "Common traits are those aspects of personality in respect to which most mature people within a given culture can be compared. The trap to be avoided is the erroneous assumption that the common trait ever corresponds exactly to the neuropsychic dispositions of individuals. Perhaps in a few cases there may be a close accidental correspondence; but it is always precarious to measure traits on the assumption that they are direct measurements of personal dispositions. A test has different meanings to different subjects, and their responses may have quite different significance. Time and again subjects in submitting themselves to a personality scale complain that the test does not fit them. They seem to sense that the scale misses their individual traits. There is no convincing reply to these critics. The best the psychologist can do is to assure them that the test is only a 'rough measure' and that in individual cases it may indeed fall wide of its mark" (8, p. 300).

It has been interestingly pointed out that whereas personality tests seem to have very little practical value in everyday life, they have proved fairly valuable in the United States Army. The reason is that the characteristics desired in a soldier or an officer are quite clearly defined, so that a test can be built which will indicate them with at least tolerable accuracy (121).

I should add a note in closing about the use of the term "personality tests" for the kind of tests we have been describing. The term is employed very loosely, and certainly not because there is any clear-cut theory or concept of personality back of the tests, but seemingly because no better cover-all term could be found.

INTEREST TESTS

There are a large number of tests designed to indicate a person's interests. They are, in the main, self-questionnaires, in which the subject reports his liking, disliking, or indifference to numerous school subjects, vocations, avocations, and types of activity. Many of these tests or questionnaires are quite simply constructed, but some have been developed on a basis of extensive research and interpret the subject's responses in the light of elaborate statistical analysis.

A typical interest test which has no very elaborate background of research but which is an excellent one for its purpose is the Interest Questionnaire for High School Students prepared by Percival Symonds. Sixty-eight of the questions have to do with occupations, about which the person taking the test is asked to state his liking, indifference, or dislike; 24 questions are on general activities; 20 have to do with school subjects, 41 have to do with school activities, 12 have to do with prominent men, 26 have to do with things to own, 23 have to do with magazines. The items in the questionnaire were chosen in order to reveal the different interest-patterns of students in academic, commercial, and technical courses. It is reported that the questionnaire can predict a student's success in a specific curriculum better than a general intelligence test.

The two Vocational Interest Blanks by Strong, one for men and the other for women, are much more elaborately developed instruments. The Strong Vocational Interest Blank for Men is a long and varied questionnaire, containing items on 100 occupations, 36 school subjects, and 46 items on the peculiarities and types of people. To all these items the subject responds with "liking," "indifferent," or "dislike." In addition the blank calls for self-ratings on preferences, habits, and traits of character. The distinctive feature of the Strong Interest Blank is the method of interpreting the subject's responses. Strong has been able to show that in each of a large number of occupations there is a distinctive pattern of interests which characterize the men in that occupation. Moreover, he has also found that with many occupations the characteristic interest-pattern is more marked and sharply defined in highly successful than in less successful men. So when a young man answers the questions in the Interest Blank, it is possible to tell the extent to which his interest-pattern coincides with that found in men employed in any of the listed occupations (620). The Strong Interest Blanks have been widely used, and have proved of real service in vocational guidance.

The Kuder Preference Record is another important instrument for the measurement of interests. Its layout and working plan are somewhat different from the Strong Interest Blanks. The Preference Record consists of 14 sets of 3-choice items, and the subject is called upon to indicate which of each three he likes best and least. One such three-choice item is as follows: "Visit an art gallery: Browse in a library: Visit a museum." The responses made to these items are classified to indicate mechanical, scientific, persuasive, artistic, literary, musical, social service, and clerical preferences. Unlike the Strong Vocational Interest Blanks, the Kuder Preference Record is not a vocational scale. The two instruments approach the measurement of interest differently, and can be used to supplement each other (383).

Results from interest tests and questionnaires are not very closely related to immediate achievement in school. This, of course, is quite understandable, because there are other factors besides interest that determine whether a pupil will do well or badly in his studies in general or in any one particular subject. For instance, a person may be very much interested in mathematics or art, and yet not do as well as another person who is less interested but who has a better background and more ability. But looked at in a long perspective, revealed interests are very important indeed. A persisting and continuing interest is a very good indication of where a person can best spend his energies and devote his time; and this is something well worth knowing, even though we may not be able to tell how well such a person will do in comparison to others (184, 619).

ATTITUDE SCALES

There are available a great many tests or scales for the measurement of attitude. Attitude, as it is understood by the makers of such tests and scales, has been defined as "The sum total of a man's inclinations and feelings, prejudice or bias, preconceived notions, ideas, fears, threats, and convictions about any specific topic" (672, pp. 6–7). Scales or tests have been devised for the measurement of such attitudes towards the church, towards other races, towards school, and so on at great length. There are several types of attitude scale. The most familiar type consists of a number of statements which reveal the presence of the attitude in question and its degree. For instance, a scale for measuring attitude towards church contains such statements as: " 'I would rather go to church than do anything else'; 'I like to go to church'; 'Going to church bores me'; 'I would never set foot inside a church.' " In developing the scale each statement of this kind is given a score value, determined by the use of a standardization group. When anyone takes the test, the strength of his attitude in favor of or against churchgoing or whatever it may be, can be expressed as a numerical score (672).

APTITUDE TESTS

There are innumerable tests for special aptitudes—for mechanical dexterity, clerical ability, musical ability, artistic ability, aptitude for law, aptitude for medicine, and so on at great length. In fact, the field is so enormous that only a few comments are possible here.

The best and most successful aptitude tests are more or less of what is called the "work-sample" type. A work-sample test, as the term indicates, is a test made up of items which sample the kind of work that the person being tested has in mind to do. Some clerical tests, for instance, contain items calling for the correction of wrong spellings, such as might be met by a clerical office worker. Tests for various manipulative jobs in factories contain items which are closely similar to some of the actual tasks in these jobs. Such tests are very practical, and their usefulness for the screening of candidates is obvious.

Some aptitude tests, however, are constructed on a basis of psychological theory. One notable instance is the Seashore Measures of Musical Talent. This is not a work-sample test at all; that is to say, it does not contain any of the actual job-items which a practical musician performs. It undertakes to measure, among other things, the sense of pitch and the sense of rhythm, on the theory that a good sense of pitch and a good sense of rhythm are important for musicians. No doubt the theory is quite true in a general sense, but specifically it is very much of a question whether the decisions about pitch and rhythm which one must make in taking the test are at all like those that a musician must make in his actual work. As a matter of fact, the Seashore Measures of Musical Talent in particular, and theoretically-based aptitude tests in general are not very successful, and their validity is open to the gravest doubt.

CONSTANCY OF MENTAL TRAITS

Now that we have completed this quick and admittedly superficial survey of the various kinds of tests, we are in a position to deal with the larger issues involved in the psychology of human abilities and traits. The first of these issues is that of constancy.

To begin, let us define this issue. Suppose we give a person a battery of tests at some given time, perhaps when he is fifteen years old. We find that he has an I.Q. of 100 on the Second Stanford Revision of the Binet Scale; that he is strong in the mental factors of inductive reasoning, deductive reasoning, and word fluency, and weak in space perception and memory; that he tends to prefer working by himself to working with a group; that he has a fondness for outdoor occupations; that he does not do very well with mechanical tasks; that he has strong race prejudices. Here we have a picture of some of this person's abilities, aptitudes, traits, and tendencies. Is the picture likely to remain the same in future years, or is it likely to change? This is the question of constancy.

Obviously it is an extremely important question for test makers, for if tests can give us a picture of a personality, not only as it now is, but also as it is going to be, then they are very valuable instruments indeed. On the contrary, if tests can only indicate present conditions, and cannot tell us much about future developments, they may still be quite useful, but their results can never be decisive. Also, the question of constancy is very important for teachers and guidance workers. Teachers and guidance workers want to change personality. No doubt it is possible to make some changes in a human being's personality. But how far-reaching, how radical can such changes be? What are the limits of reasonably possible change? Our answer to the question of constancy gives us at least a good deal of the answer to these questions too.

Nearly all the work that has been done on the problem of constancy has centered on the constancy of general intelligence, or more specifically, on the constancy of the I.Q. However, as I have suggested by implication in the preceding paragraph, the issue is very much wider than this, and really has to do with the constancy of all mental abilities, aptitudes, and traits. As we proceed we must keep in mind the breadth and inclusiveness of the problem of constancy. But an insight into the research work on the constancy of the I.Q., which is the only important body of research work on the whole problem, will help us to take a reasonable position on the question of the constancy of mental abilities and traits in general.

In spite of the contrary notions of many ill-informed persons, no competent research worker has ever claimed that an obtained I.Q. is absolutely constant. No competent research worker, that is to say, has ever claimed that if a child tests out with an I.Q. of 110 when he is 10 years old, he is certain or even exceedingly likely to have an I.Q. of 110 when he is 15 years old. Terman dealt with this question more than thirty years ago, in connection with his work on the First Stanford Revision of the Binet Scale. He reported results for 315 children who were retested over various periods of time. In only 26 cases was the I.Q. exactly the same on the retest. In 50% of the cases the average change was between 3.3 points decrease and 5.7 points increase. The rest of these changes ran beyond these limits, and might be as large as about 20 points (639).

These early results have often been roughly confirmed. For instance, in one rather recent investigation, 1,367 children were tested and retested between 1924 and 1942. Over 46% of the changes were less than 6 points up and down; 75% of the changes were less than 11 points; and less than 10% of the changes were over 15 points (311). However, some investigators have found a larger number of large changes. In one study dealing with 52 children, 33 of them gained from 2 to 32 points and 18 of them lost 1 to 21 points between testing and retesting (480, 481). Another investigation found the changes below as tabulated among 1,100 private-school children over a period of 2½ years (669).

Changes in I.Q. among 1,100 Private School Children after 2½ Years (669)

Increase		Decrease	
Points	N	Points	N
50	2		
45	3	45	1
40	7	40	1
35	11	35	6
30	15	30	4
25	45	25	8
20	60	20	11

The changes in this tabulation are spectacular and unusual, but still they happen. Taking into consideration all the ascertained data, of which those that have been cited are a representative sample, we may say that in about 50% of the cases the I.Q. is likely to shift not more than 5 points up or down, but that in another 50% of cases the changes will be larger, and often very much larger.

How are these facts to be explained? One very familiar explanation is that the I.Q. indicates the amount of a definite ability called intelligence, and that this amount does not change because it is inborn. There are two difficulties with this account of the matter. First, it does not fit the facts, because the I.Q. remains fairly constant in only about 50% of cases. Second, the I.Q. is certainly not a measure of a well-defined psychological entity or ability. On the contrary, it is a figure which expresses the result of a many-sided survey of a child's academic potentialities. So an alternative explanation becomes necessary, and this is not hard to find. The general psychological environment in one conventional school does not differ enormously from that of another conventional school. One school may be somewhat better or worse than others, but on the whole most schools are run in pretty much the same way, teach similar subjects by similar procedures, maintain similar requirements and expectations. Of course the similarities among schools are not complete, but they are almost surely much greater than the differences, except in a few extreme and unusual instances. Moreover, a child who finds himself at home or at a loss in one school will tend to find himself at home or at a loss in others. True, his adjustment may alter for better or worse as he grows older or changes from one place to another. But the influences around him, including those of the record he builds up from year to year and takes with him when he transfers, favor constancy. So, granted that intelligence tests indicate school adjustment or academic promise, it is quite understandable that intelligence quotients obtained on these tests should be just about as constant and just about as variable as they turn out to be.

This conclusion is strongly supported by what we know about ways in which the I.Q. can and cannot be changed. It seems that a child's intelligence quotient is not likely to be affected very much by various general and often superficial improvements in the conditions of his life—by better diet, removing adenoids and tonsils, special tutoring, or setting up an "enriched curriculum" under ordinary school conditions. But there is good reason to believe that the I.Q. can be affected *by radical changes in school conditions, particularly if these changes are made early in the child's life.* Ever since 1925 there have been persistent reports of very marked increases in I.Q. associated with attendance at preschool. The pioneer investigation on this subject dealt with 43 pupils at the Merrill-Palmer School. During their preschool attendance 27 of these children showed an average increase of 19.7 I.Q. points, 8 showed a decrease of 10.8 points, and the I.Q.'s of 8 of the children remained constant within 5 points (745).

The whole issue has been brought to the fore by reports made by Beth Wellman from the Child Welfare Center of the University of Iowa. Her first report dealt with 600 children who had attended the nursery school of the Center. These children showed an average gain of 15 I.Q. points for two years of attendance. The greatest gains were found among children on the lower I.Q. levels. After two years attendance, below-average children gained 36 points, average children gained 35 points, superior children gained 17.1 points, very superior children gained 7.1 points, and children in the genius category showed a loss of 2.1 points. Children who had only one year in the nursery school showed smaller but in general similar changes (709, 713).

Moreover, in a later investigation, Wellman has contended that these gains which appear in connection with nursery-school attendance are maintained until the children enter college. She was able to find two groups of 21 college students, each member of the one group being matched by a member of the other whose original standing on the First Stanford Revision was equal to his own. The students in one of these groups had attended nursery school, while those in the other had not. Those who had attended nursery school excelled those who had not in all testings at the college level. Thus Wellman concludes that the nursery school can affect mentality permanently (712). There has been an extensive controversy over these reports, and the findings have been subjected to meticulous and often rather hostile analysis. But they have not been disproved, and it has been shown that similar results are produced by other nursery schools besides the one at the University of Iowa (615, 710, 711).

Thus a nursery school project was set up in a large orphanage. Activities began at eight o'clock with vigorous play, then there were quieter doings. At nine-thirty tomato juice and cod-liver oil were served, and there was a rest period. Following this there were constructional activities, music, and stories or excursions until it was time to wash for the noon meal. School continued until three o'clock, with books, music, and so forth, and guided constructional and other activities went on until five, when it was time for supper and bed. The children showed moderate but definite and consistent gains in I.Q., which were proportional to the length of time they remained in the school (599). This is comparable to the study which I have already described elsewhere, in which very remarkable gains in I.Q. were found in young orphanage children who received the affection and care of some of the older girls (598).

Similar results have also been reported with older children. Thus in one instance an experimental attempt was made to deal with 254 boys and girls ranging in chronological age from 12 to 14 years. These children were classed as feeble-minded, and had a mean I.Q. of 51.7. Their specific needs were analyzed, and were identified as being improvement in the tool subjects, growth in responsibility, better understanding of group relationships, better social skills, and so forth. An educational program pointed straight at these needs was organized. This program emphasized group planning, group experiences, the representation or duplication in the school of problems and situations arising out of school, and opportunities in the creative and manipulative arts. In 3 years this feeble-minded group made an average gain of 4.1 years normal gain in educational achievement, and in 8 years 27% of them had completed 4 years in high school (569).

In all these cases the essential thing that was done was to give the children experiences of significant, convincing, and gratifying success in school. Positive motivations were established, self-confidence was built up, a happy and effective adjustment was promoted. The effect of these measures was reflected in gains in I.Q. This is just what we might expect if what intelligence tests really measure is present and prospective adjustment to the school.

Our conclusion then must be that whatever constancy the I.Q. has is due quite largely to the constancy of the conditions adjustment to which is indicated by the I.Q. It is very probable that the same line of thinking applies to the constancy of a great many abilities, traits, and characteristics. We know, for instance, that interests tend to remain fairly stable, at least within broad categories. A person may not remain interested all his life in this or that specific activity, but anyone who is interested in bookish pursuits, or mechanical pursuits, or open-air pursuits is likely to stay interested in such pursuits in one way or another for many years. Indeed, interests seem to become more ingrained as age advances, and the main changes are that older people tend to become interested in quieter activities than those they liked when they were younger (619).

Attitudes, too, do not usually change radically and capriciously. As to special aptitudes, their constancy over long periods of time has never been seriously or extensively investigated, because aptitude tests are usually run with some specific immediate occupation in mind. However, both interests and attitudes can be changed; and they can be changed just as the I.Q. is changed, namely, by giving a person convincing experiences of success or convincing prospects of success in a given direction. So it would seem that the constancy of mental traits is due quite largely to the constancy of the actual environment in which people live their lives. Most of us tend to run in grooves. We find certain ways of thinking, feeling, and acting that suit us at least fairly well, and so there is no great incentive to change, for change requires effort and involves risks. But if teachers, guidance workers, psychiatrists, or other such persons take the trouble to organize radically different conditions, it is quite possible for us to produce a radically different set of response-patterns, and quite probable that we will do so.

Of course there are always limits to what can be done by changing environmental conditions. The most superlatively good school cannot make all children into geniuses, and even very bad schools indeed have failed to turn geniuses into morons. But the limits are far wider, and the flexibility and modifiability of human characteristics is far greater than many people seem to think. The relative constancy of mental characteristics in general is due quite largely to our tendency to get into a rut and to jog along in it comfortably forever after. The relative constancy of the I.Q. in particular largely reflects the fact that schools are on the whole quite stereotyped, and that they rarely make any urgent, creative effort to shape up personality, intensify and deepen motivation, and improve basic adjustment.

HEREDITY AND ENVIRONMENT

In the previous paragraph I remarked that there are limits to the influence of a changed environment. This is quite obvious to ordinary common sense, and no elaborate research is needed to prove it. But the statement raises the whole question of how much in human abilities is due to heredity, and how much to environmental influences. This question has been extensively investigated, and a number of different lines of evidence have been brought to bear on it, and we must now present a brief summary and evaluation of the work that has been done. As with the issue of constancy, nearly all the research on hereditary and environmental influences has dealt with the inheritance of general intelligence, but here too the issue is much wider and bears on all human abilities and mental traits.

1. The alleged constancy of the intelligence quotient has been cited very often as evidence that a person's level or degree of general intelligence is determined by heredity. But as we have seen, the intelligence quotient is very far from entirely constant, and also it can be deliberately modified within quite considerable limits. All the data can be explained by saying that heredity establishes boundaries whose exact location is not known but which are certainly quite wide, beyond which the intelligence quotient cannot be modified, and that within those boundaries the circumstances of life are decisive. In this respect a person's intelligence quotient is not unlike his waistline. A person can expand or contract his waistline by food and exercise, but he cannot do so beyond certain limits.

2. The classic evidence for the inheritance of intelligence has been provided by certain studies of family resemblance. On the one hand there are the Kallikaks and the Jukes, who brought forth imbeciles, defectives, degenerates, and criminal types generation after generation. On the other hand there is the family of Jonathan Edwards, which produced a long succession of eminent men and important scholars (226, 733). These celebrated studies have been supplemented with various accounts of the ancestry of men of genius, who usually seem to have come from what is called "good stock."

It seems a fairly safe guess that in all these cases heredity had a considerable influence. But just how great that influence may have been we simply do not know. The general conditions under which Kallikaks and Jukes were raised generation after generation were very unfavorable. Those surrounding the Edwards family were very good. Most men of genius seem to have had some kind of environmental stimulation in their youth, and often very rich and intimate stimulation. From time to time statements are made about the per cent of influence exercised by heredity on the one hand and environment on the other in determining intelligence. Claims of this kind should not be taken seriously. It seems reasonable to think that both heredity and environment are influential, but just how much is due to either we do not know at all.

3. It has been thought that studies of the resemblances of siblings and twins may throw some light upon the problem of the inheritance of mental traits. That siblings resemble one another in test performance much more closely than do unrelated individuals is undoubtedly true; but how much of this resemblance may be due to similarities of family background we do not know. Twins, and more particularly identical twins, are a crucial case, for here if anywhere the influence of heredity should be apparent. In the most important investigation of twin resemblance part of the work dealt with nineteen pairs of identical twins, the two members of each pair being raised apart from one another. These nineteen pairs of twins were given a number of tests, and the degree of their resemblance on these tests was compared to that of other identical twins raised together and of fraternal twins raised together. The pivotal findings appear in the tabulation below. Three points

Traits	Identical raised together	Fraternal raised together	Identical raised apart
Standing height	.981	.934	.969
Sitting height	.965	.901	.960
Weight	.973	.900	.886
Head length	.910	.691	.917
Binet I.Q.	.910	.640	.670
Binet M.A.	.922	.831	.637
Otis I.Q.	.922	.621	.627
Stanford Achievement Test	.955	.833	.507
Woodworth-Matthews	.562	.371	.583

From Newman, Freeman, and Holzinger (486).

should be noted in connection with these findings. (*a*) Resemblance is much lower in mental than in physical traits. (*b*) Resemblance markedly decreases when identical twins are reared apart. (*c*) The environments in which the separated twins were reared were not extremely different. If some of them had been reared in an impoverished slum setting and others in the best possible conditions, it is likely that the resemblances would have been a good deal less (486). So here again we have the same story. Heredity certainly seems to have a considerable effect, but so does environment; and how much effect either has we do not know.

4. A number of studies of the psychological and cultural influence of foster homes have been brought to bear on the question of hereditary and environmental effects. What happens when children are taken from their true parents and put in foster homes? Do the children go on showing the traits to be expected of the offspring of their true parents, or do they take on the traits of their foster parents? There has been much investigation on this point, and this is not the place for a complete review of it. Here, however, are the results of two fairly recent and typical studies. These studies have shown that if a child is adopted when he is very young, his intelligence correlates more and more closely with the intelligence of his foster mother the longer he stays in the foster home. Also, a group of children whose true mothers had an average I.Q. of 63 were adopted very young, and after 5 years in good foster homes had an average I.Q. of 106, which is certainly not what one would expect (266, 611).

5. Many of the arguments about heredity and environment have centered about social mobility and vocational and social selection. For instance it is known that Northern Negroes tend to do better on mental tests than Southern Negroes, even when they live in the large Southern cities. One pat explanation has always been that the abler Negroes tend to migrate northwards, in which case the social selection of innate intelligence

would be taking place. But it has been very energetically argued, though indeed not proved, that the northward migration of Negroes is nonselective, that the superior test performance of Northern Negroes is due to a more favorable environment, and that their test performance gets better and better the longer they stay in that environment (374).

Much the same kind of back-and-forth argument can be made about occupational selection. It has been shown that there is an occupational hierarchy or ranking in mental test performance, with the professions and superior business occupations at the head of the list, and going downwards through skilled and semiskilled to unskilled occupations. A great deal of debate has gone on as to whether a certain occupation tends to select a certain level of intelligence, or whether the occupation into which a person gets and in which he stays affects his intelligence. In all probability there is some truth on both sides. In any case we must always be careful to bear in mind the bias of the tests that are used. In one important study of occupational intelligence, routine clerical workers tested out on the average higher than skilled mechanics. One may be pretty sure that this result was due to the clerical bias of the tests. So, as to the alleged evidence from occupational intelligence and social selection, the truth seems to be that it gets nowhere, proves nothing, and merely raises questions which cannot be answered (14).

In all probability you will think this whole discussion of heredity and environment and the part they play in determining mental abilities extremely unsatisfactory and indecisive. This is quite true. The plain truth is that we have no exact or certain knowledge on the subject. It would have been easy to detail the results of scores or even hundreds of research studies instead of the few I have cited, but to do so would not have brought an added glimmer of enlightenment. Some years ago a favorite theme of experts on testing was that intelligence tests would reveal the limits of a child's educational possibilities. This is probably true enough, at least if we go on the assumption that the child is going to be educated in accordance with standard and stereotyped school procedures, to which general intelligence tests are tied very closely. But the school stereotype itself limits educational achievement; and there is not one scrap of evidence to deny that if we deal with a child as constructively and effectively as we know how, his educational achievement will go far beyond the limits indicated by standard intelligence tests. There will still be limits. The boundaries of heredity cannot be overpassed. But where those boundaries are, nobody really knows. All this is just as true of special abilities of all kinds as it is of general intelligence. The inheritance of mental factors or "primary mental abilities" is a complete terra incognita. So is the inheritance of special aptitudes or "talents." In spite of all the painstaking research that has been done, we cannot go one step beyond ordinary common sense in any of these directions.

One ingenious investigator has even argued that the positions taken by scientific men on the effect of heredity and environment on mental traits are due chiefly to sheer prejudice. He made a comprehensive study of the work of twenty-four scientists, including biologists, geneticists, statisticians, and psychologists, and tried to show from their writings that a hereditarian position goes with general conservatism and that an environmentalist position goes with general liberalism (512). No doubt many of the specific interpretations of this investigator are open to a good deal of question, but there is an uncomfortable reasonableness about his over-all conclusion.

The great and crucial point to get hold of is that human abilities and traits, general and special, are not psychological entities or things in themselves. What we call general intelligence is simply the name we give to the whole range of a person's responses to a certain kind of situation. A mental factor such, for instance, as verbal fluency, is a name we give to a person's responses to a very limited and sharply defined situation. An aptitude is "a condition symptomatic of a person's general fitness, of which one aspect is his readiness to acquire proficiency—his general ability—and another is his readiness to develop an interest in exercising that ability" (59, p. 18). An aptitude, that is to say, is not a thing in its own right, but a dynamic trend of the personality. When we say that a person has great mechanical aptitude, we mean that he does well with machinery. When we say that he has great musical talent, we mean that he does well with music. If there were no machinery, there would be no mechanical aptitude. If there were no music, there would be no musical talent. And it is pretty safe to say that if there were no schools, no one would ever have invented the concept of general intelligence.

Tests are useful because when they are properly made and properly used they can and do predict future performance under a stated set of conditions. This is a very practical and genuine usefulness, but it is a limited one. If conditions are radically changed, test results become extremely misleading. For tests certainly cannot accomplish what that particular class of fakers called phrenologists claim to be able to do—pick out and measure self-existent abilities determined by heredity and able to operate under all sorts of circumstances.

MENTAL TESTS AND PERSONALITY

The great constructive value of tests is that they can help us to understand human beings, and to see how to deal with human beings wisely and helpfully. Tests cannot reveal abstract abilities. Still less can they reveal just what is due to hereditary and environmental influences in a person's mental make-up. But tests can enable us to locate and understand crucial problems in adjustment. This they can do very conveniently and often very impressively, because in essence they are objective and standardized challenges. When a child is confronted with such a challenge—when he takes a test, that is to say—he is almost certain to reveal certain important things about himself which he might otherwise overlook or at least misinterpret. It follows, therefore, that tests of all kinds should always be used, not for the purpose of crudely classifying children on some predetermined scale, but for the sake of understanding these children better as persons, and serving them more effectively (650).

In discussions of the practical application of tests a very serviceable term has come into use. This is the term "deviate." A deviate is a person who departs significantly from average or normal test performance, either up or down. In what I have to say here about the relationship of testing to the shaping of personality, I shall consider the problem first of the "low deviate" and then of the "high deviate," and then pass on to some common practices for dealing with the differences among children which tests reveal.

The low deviate

Let us suppose that we run a testing program in the sixth grade, and come upon a boy with an I.Q. of 80. We have already had certain questions in our minds about this boy, for he is about a year overage for the grade, and has not been doing very well in school. Now our test shows that while his chronological age is 13½, his mental age is slightly less than 11, which would bring out his I.Q. at 80. How much have we learned about this boy? Nothing, perhaps, so very new. But we have confirmed our suspicions, and to an appreciable extent defined our problem, all of which is well worth doing. Above all, if we know our business, we have at least begun to get the picture of a personality, its potentialities, and its probable future.

1. Let us begin with a sketch of this picture, which has been given as follows:

"The dull child was probably a little later in learning to walk and likely a little slow in learning to talk. He was probably shy in making social contacts. His parents may have tended to push him to do things before he was quite ready. He probably started school at about the same time as the average or bright child but seemed somewhat immature. He adjusted himself to the school situation rather slowly and found it difficult to do first-grade work. As a result, he probably repeated the first or second grade and then went on without any particular difficulty until the fifth or sixth grade, when again he was obliged to repeat half a year to a year. Although he probably was not interested in reading or at least found it difficult, and also sometimes had difficulty with arithmetic, he may have had certain fields of interest in which he did very well. Some years ago this type of person would have dropped out at the end of the fifth or sixth grade unless there was great pressure on the part of parents or friends. Now he enters the junior high school and is offered work of a definitely non-academic character. Sometimes today he gets into the senior high school but fails miserably to do work of the college entrance standard. It is rare that he attempts to enter college. His school experience was discouraging and tended to make him feel the futility of effort. After finishing school, work this slow individual undertakes is apt to be of the unskilled or semi-skilled type. It is sure to be routine and may be of a blind-alley type. He may make good advancement within a limited field if he has special ability and good personal qualifications. He probably belongs to the class of workers that changes jobs frequently. The slow person is apt to be restless in his social contacts, partly because of his low economic level. He will tend to follow blindly any offer of improvement even though it has no sound basis. Provided he has desirable personal qualities and fair economic security, he may appear to be among the stable, semi-skilled classes—a happy, thrifty citizen. It is rare that he shows any qualities of leadership, except in very small groups, and he often shows poor judgment in selecting his companions. He reads very little, possibly looking at the newspapers for the funnies and the ads. He goes to the movies of the cheaper variety. Chance may lead him into wholesome recreational groups, but just as likely he will be led into groups which have an unfortunate influence" (27, pp. 245–246).

To see so much in a single test result may seem rather like discovering the whole universe in a grain of dust; but all this is at least suggested, though of course with innumerable possible variations. From the standpoint of the school, at any rate, we have here a picture of a person for whom the academic stereotype is thoroughly unsuitable. When he is forced to study an academic subject he learns by simple routine methods, needs much drill and repetition, prefers short-term assignments, is not interested in theory. This amounts to saying that when such a person studies an academic subject, *he learns very badly* (27). So the academic stereotype condemns him to continual experiences of failure, and definitely hinders rather than helps the development of his personality. What this boy obviously needs are experiences and learnings in which he can succeed, which lead him into constructive social relationships here and now, and towards fortunate choices later on.

2. Now let us turn to the question of interests and hobbies. Here we may expect our test result to suggest some quite important considerations, for the interests and hobbies of slow learners are likely to be very different from those of quick learners. This has been brought out in an investigation in which a standard intelligence test was given to 45,000 children from many parts of the country, the children ranging from the fourth to the eighth grade. Comparisons of the interests and hobbies of the top and bottom ten per cents of this large group, and the results are tabulated below (p. 458). The figures are percentages reporting a given hobby (403).

As you can see, the retarded children had fewer, poorer, less varied interests than the superior children, and also interests less likely to be helpful to them in later life. Doubtless this was as much due to lack of opportunity and encouragement as to anything else. Yet these low deviates, with their rather poor vocational prospects, are just the sort of people who might find a good hobby a real lifesaver later on. So surely the school ought to set to work to help them develop some such constructive and valuable hobbies and interests. The way these low deviates are likely to learn when they tackle such a hobby

Hobbies	Boys		Girls	
	Superior	Retarded	Superior	Retarded
Reading novels	50	23	60	31
Reading history or science	31	9	22	9
Reading funny papers	49	39	22	9
Active games and sports	67	39	50	41
Quiet games and sports	26	15	29	24
Playing musical instruments	22	10	28	11
Listening to radio	39	30	37	29
Sewing, knitting	3	4	36	34
Housework	7	8	32	40
Going to shows	33	30	34	29
Dramatics—participation	9	4	16	6
Make-believe games	9	6	24	17
Religious activities	17	11	21	15
Building things, shopwork	34	27	4	3
Traveling	13	8	11	8
Driving automobile	7	9	3	3
Studying	9	4	11	8
Working—farm, store	10	17	3	5
Clubs—social, dance	4	2	9	6
Scouting or other serious outdoor activity	13	6	10	4
Collecting	30	9	22	9
None	1	14	1	12

From Lewis and McGehee (403).

is likely to be very different indeed from their learning processes in academic subjects.

3. Our low deviate is quite apt to have rather inferior traits of character. Another part of the investigation cited above dealt with this problem (423). The investigators gave a personality inventory to the children, and then had fifty hygienists rate the indicated traits in the order of their importance for mental health. It was found that the superior children were far ahead in dependability, friendliness, happiness, and honesty, and that

the retarded children showed far more daydreaming, boredom, slovenliness, cheating, etc. You may perhaps ask what the school has to do with such character traits, and in particular how the teaching of subject matter (which is after all in one sense the chief business of the school) is related to them. I hope that by this time the answer is clear. When schoolwork is organized in such a way that it does not satisfy basic needs, and does not open up compelling goals through the experience of success, it is almost certain to produce unfortunate and even disastrous reactions. A school so conducted tends to produce moral weakness rather than strength.

Going beyond such mildly unfortunate traits as those listed above, it used to be thought that low mental test performance was closely associated with downright delinquency. As a matter of fact, there is a connection. The low deviate is more likely to become a delinquent than the normal child or the high deviate, although the probability is not so great as was once supposed. The reason is not chiefly that the low deviate cannot understand ethical principles or foresee the consequences of his acts, but that he is likely to be a frustrated and unhappy person who tries to satisfy his basic needs in terms of socially unfortunate goals. Once more, the challenge for the school is to help such people to find constructive and satisfying ways of living and acting (315).

4. What about the home and family backgrounds of retarded and slow-learning children? It used to be thought that there is a very close relationship indeed between mental test performance and home background. A recent very extensive study has shown that while there certainly is a positive relationship, it is by no means as close as was once supposed. Children with high I.Q.'s tend to come from good homes, but there are many significant exceptions. Retarded and slow-learning children come from all types of homes, although a majority of them have a culturally impoverished home background. This creates a real problem for the school. If our retarded child has

well-educated, ambitious parents, they have to be convinced that forcing him into the academic mold may do him lasting harm, and that quite another kind of education may not and probably will not ruin his life. If the child's home lacks stimulating influences and cultural richness, it becomes the task of the school to do everything possible to make up the deficiency (424).

The high deviate

Now let us take a contrasting case. We find in our group of sixth-graders a child with an I.Q. of 135. In chronological age he is young for his grade, but in mental age he is somewhat beyond it. He is doing good but not superlatively good work. What sort of a person is this child likely to be, and what problems does he present for the school?

1. As before, let us begin by sketching in outline the general picture of what we might expect to find. By far the most extensive study of gifted children is the series entitled *Genetic Studies in Genius* by L. M. Terman and his associates at Stanford University (644). This work was begun in 1921–22 and carried forward for twenty-five years. It is based on a total of 1,528 individuals with I.Q.'s from 135 to 200. One of Terman's motives for carrying through the study was the widespread prejudice which has been felt against mentally precocious children. All possible reasons for such a prejudice were completely contradicted in the opening investigations. These mentally superior children turned out to be well above average in physique and health, and to have many-sided rather than one-sided interests. They were much above the average in intellectual interests, somewhat so in social interests, and about average in activity interests. Six years after the initial investigation the group was studied again. The children had about the same general characteristics as previously found, and most of them made superior high-school records, going through the high school younger than the average.

Twenty-five years after the start of the work, a final set of investigations was made. The individuals were rated for adjustment in general, which was satisfactory in 80.55% of the cases, and somewhat unsatisfactory in 15.26% of the cases, while 3.38% showed some maladjustment. As to their educational history, 90% of the men and 87% of the women had entered college, 70% of the men and 67% of the women had graduated, and 68% of the men and 60% of the women who had graduated had returned for graduate study, 51.2% of the men and 29.3% of the women had taken graduate degrees. As to occupational status, 71% of the men were in professional, semi-professional, or higher business occupations, whereas only 13.8% of the population of California is in these brackets. Moreover, the percentage of the group so employed is considerably higher than the percentage of all college graduates in such occupations. Furthermore, the members of the experimental group had a superior record for continuity of employment.

As to avocational interests, nearly two-thirds of the group were interested in two or more avocational pursuits, and more than one-third in three or more. Among such interests sports came first both for men and women, photography was second for men and music was second for women, music was third for men and gardening was third for women. As to reading interests, 77% of the men and 91% of the women read considerably in the sort of material classified under the Dewey Decimal System as "literature." * Fiction was the most popular reading choice. The reading of history was reported by 51% of the men and 83% of the women. As to social-political attitudes, 45.2% of the men and 41.6% of the women were Republicans or "conservatives," and 40% of the men and 41.3% of the women were "liberal," New Deal, or Democratic. Of this group 91% voted in national elections, as compared to 65% of the whole electorate.

* The Dewey Decimal System is the most widely used system of library classification.

By way of a side comment before we go on, this summary of the facts makes it very clear why a high rating on general intelligence tests is important. Whatever such a rating may or may not tell us about inborn ability, it certainly indicates membership in a successful and elite group in our society.

2. Is our child with his I.Q. of 135 likely to present any particular problem or challenge to the school? Indeed he is! It has been shown again and again that while such children will probably succeed in school, their educational performance tends to be lower than their promise as indicated by the tests. This fact was brought out by Terman himself in the extensive study cited above, and it has often been confirmed. A recently published investigation reports on forty-three children with I.Q.'s of 130 or more who were tested and then followed up and retested eleven years later. Their school histories were often rather disappointing. They showed superior achievement and tended to graduate early, but this seemed to be because of their own initiative rather than because of constructive guidance from the school. Their teachers often penalized them for lack of effort, and also often failed to recognize their superior ability because of their shyness, naughtiness, and so forth. Psychological support and understanding at home were found to be crucially important for these children. Twenty-one of them had good and harmonious conditions at home and reasonable and considerate early training, and these children tended to be active, happy, and full of engrossing interests. Twenty-two of them were less successful because of harshness, over-protection, and quiz-kid exploitation. These less fortunate children often had the attitude that one must be naughty in order to shine (649).

Recognition at school and helpfulness at home are extremely important for the general adjustment and successful achievement of the bright child. This has been well shown in an investigation of bright children who do well and other bright children who do not do well in school. Those who did well excelled in dependability, honesty, originality, self-reliance, ambition, artistic impulses, investigative impulses, all of which are characteristics rated very high by hygienists. Those who were not doing well tended to have traits which were of no great hygienic significance, or which might be actually harmful for school work, such as laziness, boredom, tendencies to quit, and so forth (401).

The child who rates high on an intelligence test is often called a "good school risk." But this does not mean that schools and teachers need do nothing about him except to let the laws of chance work out as they will. A child capable of the highest types of learning does not flourish well under imposed routine learning. A child capable of far-reaching and many-sided growth is apt to be warped and stunted by conditions which persistently thwart growth. It is a great reproach when a brilliant child succeeds *in spite of* his teachers. Clearly the school should provide guidance so stimulating, so expert, so intelligent that he will make far more of himself than he could without his teachers.

APPRAISAL OF CERTAIN PRACTICES AND CONCEPTIONS

1. Classifications of human beings on the basis of tests are dubious and misleading. One of the most famous of these classifications is shown below.

Intelligence Classified by I.Q. Levels

I.Q.	*Classification*
Above 140	"Near" genius or genius
120–140	Very superior intelligence
110–120	Superior intelligence
90–110	Normal or average intelligence
80–90	Dullness, rarely classifiable as feeble-mindedness
70–80	Borderline deficiency, sometimes classifiable as dullness, often as feeble-mindedness
Below 70	Definite feeble-mindedness.

From L. M. Terman (640, p. 79).

This classification was developed by Terman in connection with the First Stanford-Binet (640, p. 79). More recently it has been softened, amended, and revised in connection with the Second Stanford-Binet. Individuals with I.Q.'s from 70 to 79 are now called "borderline defectives," and those from 69 down are called "true mental defectives" (451). So the classification is retained in essence, but the derogatory term "feeble-minded" is avoided. Needless to say, the categories of these and similar classifications ("moron," "idiot," etc.), are bandied about with great freedom, apparently under the impression that the words really mean something definite, even when they are only defined in terms of I.Q. levels.

As a matter of fact, a test score is only an indication. Other characteristics which may or may not be associated with it must be considered in judging and dealing with a human being. Insight, foresight, resourcefulness, shrewdness, originality, emotional stability, volition, temperament, and motility are all very important characteristics which must be taken into account in deciding whether a person is or is not feeble-minded. Feeble-mindedness, in short, is a great deal more than merely the low end of the I.Q. distribution (146). In just the same way, "genius" is not simply equivalent to the high end of the I.Q. distribution. On Terman's own showing, the great creative geniuses have usually been bright, but not always excessively bright. There are probably quite a number of students in any good college who would do better on a mental test than Mozart, Bach, Cezanne, or Tennyson. But these students are not usually men of genius! So once more, a mental test result is only an indication, valuable and helpful to be sure, but very far from a complete appraisal.

2. Should mental test results be announced or kept confidential? This may seem a petty issue, but it deserves a brief discussion. At least two fairly careful investigations have been devoted to it (3, 350). The salient facts brought out in these investigations were as follows: psychological examiners were

12 to 1 against announcing test results, apparently because they thought that these results revealed the heredity of the children tested. Of 164 city superintendents of schools, 43 thought that test results should be given out, and 121 said they had no trouble with parents or children when this was done. Of 179 members of a class in psychology, 14 thought test results should be given out, 42 thought they should not be given out, 41 were inclined to think they should be given out but were not sure, 48 were inclined to think they should not be given out. The real significance of this tempest in a teapot is not that we have a Yes or No answer to the question of giving out test results, but that professional people and the public overvalue tests to quite a preposterous degree. Tests yield no infallible insights. They are only useful tools among many other tools. Anyone who lets a test result determine or even greatly affect an individual destiny simply does not know his business.

3. Is homogeneous grouping desirable? The so-called "homogeneous grouping" of pupils in school is usually based pretty largely on intelligence. It is true that other factors are considered. In a survey made in 1927 it was found that chronological age, educational age on achievement tests, anatomical age, social development, general health, and school marks are considered in varying degrees in classifying pupils, and the same is probably true today. However, intelligence tends to be the paramount consideration, and everybody concerned (including the pupils who are classified) knows this perfectly well, no matter what polite name may be invented for the "slow" groups. A critique and appraisal of homogeneous grouping can be very briefly presented. It turns on the following salient points.

a) Homogeneous grouping does not and cannot produce homogeneity. All the children in a group may be reasonably homogeneous in arithmetic, but just as heterogeneous as ever in reading, art, music, physical education, etc. (101, 364).

b) As a practical device, homogeneous grouping does not produce better learning. A child does not seem to learn subject matter any better when he is with a group of children closely similar to him in ability than when he is with the ordinary unclassified or heterogeneous group.

c) In principle, homogeneous grouping usually implies an entirely wrong conception of the function of the group in relation to learning and mental growth. The idea back of homogeneous grouping is to get together a number of children who can "cover" a certain amount of ground in a certain time, or who can all go a certain distance in a certain direction. But the real educational function of a group is to create stimulus and motivation. The ideal learning group is made up of children who can co-operate and work well together, or at least who can quickly and surely discover how to do so. Such a group will no doubt be homogeneous in a broad sense, but probably not in the narrow sense that all its members will have about the same intelligence test ratings.

d) Homogeneous grouping as usually practiced is a purely administrative device, with very little psychological significance. School administrators are bedeviled by enormous numbers. They have to split up grades and classes somehow. Tests provide at least a rough and ready and apparently reasonable basis for so doing. Thus homogeneous grouping is at least a convenience in running a large school, even if it has no genuine educational advantages.

4. One of the most important outcomes of the modern study of intelligence is the realization that an over-all assessment is far more significant in dealing with a person than any specific pattern of subject-matter studies. This has been shown again and again. Whether or not a youngster has studied a given subject in high school makes astonishingly little difference to his success with that same subject later on in college. The particular subjects that a student takes in high school have very little relationship to his general success in college. The

common college practice of designating and requiring certain high-school subjects for admission is based on nothing better than mythology, except in so far as certain of these subjects (Latin, for instance) may tend to select better "academic risks" (239, 240). Motivation, seriousness, ambition, stability, and the inclination and ability to handle abstract material are by far the best indicators that we have of academic prospects. Intelligence test results are a valuable symptom, but only one symptom among many. Here as always, what we have to consider is not what subjects a student is studying, but what kind of person he is.

5. The most far-reaching and fundamental conclusion to be drawn from the whole discussion in this chapter and the last is that we should never think or plan in terms of a faculty called intelligence, but rather in terms of promoting, fostering and furthering *intelligent behavior*, i.e. rational and successful ways of dealing with the problems of life. The great problem for the school is not how much intelligence a child brings to it, but how intelligently he is able to behave when he leaves it. We may and legitimately can hope to promote more intelligent behavior by means of a more vital and realistic curriculum, and by teaching which is more wisely oriented psychologically (138).

At the beginning of Chapter 13 I raised a question which goes to the very roots of the account of education as presented in these pages. Should we, must we think of a man's personality as made up of an integrated pattern of self-existent abilities, traits, and talents? From everything that has been said in this chapter and the previous one it is clear that the answer is No. General intelligence is not a psychological entity. Mental factors are only classifications of test responses. Far the best way of telling whether a person has an aptitude for a job is to try him out on some sample tasks required in that job. An interest test is useful, but it is useful because in it a person can tell what he likes and does not like. Personality tests are exceedingly dubious at the best. People seem to keep about the same personality characteristics over periods of years quite largely because they tend to get into ruts and stay there. As to heredity and environment, we do not know how much each of them has to do with human behavior, action, and achievement.

What, then, is left? Clearly the only thing left is our concept of adjustment, which is based on the assumption that personality is dynamic, i.e. that it is a pattern of ways of acting, and not in any sense a static pattern of traits and abilities. The concepts of mental ability and of special traits and characteristics are useful, just as many other abstract concepts are useful, because they enable us to deal with human beings more effectively and to understand them better. Tests are useful because they enable us to help people more intelligently. But abilities, traits, and talents are not independent entities, and the testing movement should never be regarded as a new phrenology which is capable of revealing the abilities, traits, and talents which make up human personality.

QUESTIONS FOR DISCUSSION

1. It is sometimes said that our evidence for the inheritance of mental traits is purely "circumstantial." Can you interpret this statement in the light of the present chapter?

2. In what sense would you say that the word "personality" is to be interpreted as it is used in connection with the personality tests that have been described?

3. For what reasons would a very favorable nursery-school experience be likely to improve a child's performance on an intelligence test?

4. Discuss the suggestion that the constancy of a person's mental traits may be largely due to the constancy of his environment. To what extent is a person's actual or "behavioral" environment likely to be constant?

5. Check the generalized descriptions of high and low deviates against some actual cases known to you. How far do the bright or dull individuals you know conform to the generalized descriptions?

6. In what respects are schools likely to hamper the progress of very bright children?

7. Can you see any reasons why interest tests might be likely to indicate good academic and vocational choices?

8. What assumptions about the independent or real existence of psychological entities called aptitudes seem to underlie aptitude tests of the work-sample type?

9. Can you make any essential distinction between mental factors and mental faculties?

10. Summarize and discuss the ways in which a good testing program might help school officials who wished to do their best to shape and develop the personalities of children and young people.

SUGGESTED READINGS

Bingham, Walter V., *Aptitudes and Aptitude Testing.* Harper & Brothers, New York, 1937, Chap. 1.

Kornhauser, Arthur, "Replies of Psychologists to a Short Questionnaire on Mental Test Developments, Personality Inventories, and the Rorschach Test." *Educational and Psychological Measurement,* V (1945), 3–15.

Nemzek, Claude L., "The Constancy of the I.Q." *Psychological Bulletin,* XXX (1933), 143–168.

Thomas, Lawrence G., *Mental Tests as Instruments of Science.* American Psychological Association, Evanston, Ill., 1942. Also Psychological Monographs, LIV (1942), No. 3, Whole No. 245.

15

Subject Matter and Personality

In this chapter and the next I shall bring together the various ideas and lines of thought that we have been developing as they bear on the two great practical problems of the school. These are the problems of subject matter and of teaching. The school is a teaching institution. It is an institution that teaches a body of subject matter. In a practical and realistic sense this has always been the function of schools. It still is their function; and it is likely to remain their function for as far ahead as we can see. Clearly then, the teaching of subject matter must be used as an instrumentality for the shaping of personality. Otherwise we must admit that our conception of education as the shaping of personality is not applicable to the school. This would be a quite disastrous admission, for the school is the chief educative agency recognized and maintained by society.

Throughout this book I have tried to show that personality can be and, in fact, is shaped and molded by the learning of subject matter and by teaching, and also to show how subject matter must be learned and how teaching must be conducted if they are to have their true constructive influence on personality. Now in conclusion it seems well to pull together the various threads of discussion.

THE PROBLEM AND ITS SOLUTION

If one looks at the work of the conventional school, and considers its actual effect upon the lives and personalities of young people, one is immediately struck by the astonishing ineffectiveness with which subject matter is learned. Some of the pertinent facts have already been presented, particularly in the chapter on transfer, but now it is time to bring the problem to a head and to face it explicitly. Let us consider a few sample investigations.

An analysis was made of the arithmetical errors of 860 college freshmen. They were required to answer 18 questions on each of the 4 fundamental processes, i.e. 72 questions in all. Of these 72 items 23 were missed by one-fifth or more of the students, 15 were missed by one-fourth or more, 8 by one-third or more, and 2 by one-half or more. There were 20 items on long division, and on these 10% of the students scored zero. Eighteen per cent scored zero on the multiplication of common fractions. Twenty per cent scored zero on decimals. Fifty-eight per cent could not define in any way such common measures as acre, gallon, peck, and millimeter (252, 532).

Two hundred sixty-seven college students were given a 10-item test on the structural correctness of English sentences, and half of them scored below the twelfth-grade norm (253). Of 1,576 college students, only 53% could locate the verb in simple English sentences, only 53% could find subordinate clauses in sentences, only 73% could find 3 nouns in sentences, and only 69% could find 3 pronouns in sentences (532). Of a group of 331 college students, 58% were below twelfth-grade norms in spelling (254).

A very simple state-wide test in algebra was taken by nearly 10,000 high-school students who had studied the subject. A temperature graph showing thermometer readings at different times in the day was shown, but only 27% of the students could read it to tell at what time the temperature was —8°. Another question was: "If a train runs M miles in 5 hours, how far will it run in K hours if it maintains the same speed?" Again the percentage of success was very small. In summary, out of 62 such simple items, 50% of the pupils got only 10 right, and 75% got not more than 12 right (404).

Students entering college physics might be expected to have reasonably good equipment in arithmetic and algebra. However, in the case of one large group of such students, the mean score on a standard arithmetic test was equivalent to that for the low seventh grade, the mean score on an algebra test was 16.4, whereas the norm for the ninth grade was 21.8, and only 27% of the students were above the high-school norm for algebra. Apart from such showings on standard tests, it was reported that these students showed "hopeless inability" to handle problems in arithmetic and algebra (415).

I have reported here only a very few investigations on the adequacy of subject-matter learning. Those that I have chosen are neither spectacular nor unusual. They could be supplemented by literally hundreds more, dealing with most areas of the curriculum. There is no doubt whatever that the picture of inefficiency which they present is generally quite true. Also, there can be no doubt whatever that subject matter so ineffectively learned cannot possibly have a constructive influence on life and personality.

The obvious question is what to do about it. Here a number of suggestions might be made.

1. It might be said that the ineffective learning of subject matter is a recent phenomenon, and that in days gone by students learned much better. All ascertained facts contradict this idea. In comparisons with education as it was fifty years

ago, we find that children in school today are not less intelligent, and that they seem to learn subject matter rather better (174, 175).

2. One might suggest a complete change in the curriculum. But here there are two formidable difficulties. (*a*) The curriculum as we have it is not a consciously and deliberately planned scheme. It is, in effect, a folk product, a resultant of many forces, supported by a host of vested interests and traditions. It can be modified, but only gradually and bit by bit. Wholesale and radical change is quite obviously impracticable (356). (*b*) Moreover, the undoubted fact that subject matter is badly learned does not prove that we are, in the main, trying to teach the wrong kind of subject matter. We would only have an argument for complete and radical change if the present curriculum were being learned as well as it could and should be learned, which is certainly not so. Also, we might set up an entirely different curriculum, and still have very bad learning.

3. One might argue that the true function of the school is not to promote the learning of subject matter, but to give general over-all guidance. This is a counsel of despair. Woodrow Wilson, when he was president of Princeton University, once drew a distinction between the academic "side shows" and the "main tent." I would not for a moment suggest that guidance is an educational "side show." But the very best of guidance is sure to be frustrated unless and until what goes on in the "main tent" is the learning of subject matter in such a way that it becomes a dynamic influence upon life and personality.

So these three suggestions, which are often put forward in one way or another, do not seem promising explanations or solutions of the problem of subject matter.

While a great many investigations have shown that the learning of subject matter in general is extremely ineffective, there are also some investigations which paint an entirely different picture, and which indicate the true solution to the problem. These investigations go to show that *where a genuine functional outcome is concerned,* subject matter is quite effectively learned and well retained.

Two equivalent tests in Latin syntactical forms were given to all students in a large high school who were taking Latin. One test was given at the end of the school year, and the other was given at the beginning of the next school year. It was found that the students who intended to continue Latin did decidedly better in the second test than the students who did not intend to continue Latin, even though the performance of those intending to continue was not better on the first test than the performance of those not intending to continue. For those intending to continue Latin, knowledge of syntactical forms was a working tool, but for the others it was not. To be sure, a knowledge of syntactical forms for the sake of taking another course in Latin is a meager functional outcome. But even so it had an effect, which gives us at least a hint about where to look for our solution (368).

An investigation was made of the retention of French 11 months after the end of a one-year course. The students concerned had forgotten 66% of the idioms, 70% of the irregular verb forms, had lost 53% of their ability to put English into French. But they had lost only 7% of their ability to put French into English. Where there was a real functional ability, a genuinely usable tool, the loss was negligible even after what must have been quite a superficial course (76).

As to information, it has often been shown that those who know most to begin with retain most both absolutely and relatively. This has been found true in connection with college botany, and with American history (76, 77, 246). As to American history, the material worst retained has to do with names, geographical locations, legal documents, treaties, governmental plans. The material best retained has to do with concrete and personally interesting historical trends and events. This is perfectly understandable, for undoubtedly far more people remember the myth of George Washington and the cherry tree than know the main provisions of the Bill of Rights.

Quite apart from any technical investigations, the true solution of the subject-matter problem should be obvious to anyone who looks at our schools and their work with unprejudiced eyes. Music and the fine arts are quite as difficult as any subject in the curriculum. Yet thousands of schools have admirable orchestras, bands, and choirs, and turn out very creditable work in their studios. Football players often seem like dullards in their classes, yet they manage to learn quite complex tactics and strategy on the football squad. Anyone who doubts whether subject matter can influence personality should consider the effect of a good high-school orchestra or band, or, indeed, of a football team upon its members. Anyone who doubts whether impelling functional outcomes can transform the efficiency of learning should visit a band or orchestra rehearsal, an art studio, a woodworking or metalworking shop, or one of the "skull sessions" conducted by the football coach.

The solution of the problem of subject matter, then, is to organize the learning of subject matter for genuine functional outcomes, for genuine life uses, for the satisfaction of basic needs. This is the solution upon which all the discussions in these pages come to a focus. Let us formulate our solution in a number of specific points.

1. Subject matter should be organized for interest. As we have seen, material becomes interesting when it is a means for successfully achieving goals in and through which basic needs are met and satisfied. Thus it has been found that children make great and encouraging progress in English composition when subjects of community importance are used as topics, and when genuine audience situations are created for the finished product (495). The use of news-outline magazines and a strong emphasis on contemporary events has been found greatly to improve learning in the social studies (367). Arithmetic is much better learned when it is learned as a technique

for dealing with innumerable life problems, ranging all the way from keeping game scores and using good judgment in installment buying to voting on a school bond issue (107). In all such cases, the material is learned as an instrumentality for achieving some significant need-satisfying goal; and this is the condition precedent for interest.

2. Subject matter should be organized for insight. Any organized and co-ordinated body of cultural materials is not a body of information but a kit of tools for thinking. History, in essence, turns, not on a collection of facts, but on interpretation. Mathematics is not computation but analysis. When we make a boy memorize the formula $c = 2\pi r$ (the formula for the circumference of a circle), we are almost certainly organizing learning as a *memoriter* process. But if we have him find out how fast the rear tire of his bicycle goes round under certain conditions, and give him the old craftsman's adage "once around is three times across," we are organizing for insight. When we tell children the date of the burning of the Capitol by the British, we are simply emphasizing a fact. But when we invite them to discover the events in Canada and elsewhere that led the British to burn the Capitol, we are fostering insight. Until and unless subject matter is learned by dint of insight, it cannot play its proper part in human life.

3. Subject matter should be organized for transfer. Transfer, as we have seen, depends on two conditions—an attitude or wish to transfer what one is learning, and an insight into the meaning of what we learn. As an instance of what organization for transfer implies in practice, the curriculum at a certain experimental school was set up to enable the abler pupils to discover the evolution of the common things in our culture, e.g. food, clothing, shelter, transportation, sanitation, timekeeping, illumination, tools and implements, communication, law, government, war, and punishment (314).

4. Subject matter should be organized for mental development. Each specific learning experience should be considered,

not only from the standpoint of its immediate results, but also from the standpoint of its long-term future effects and of its present relationship to the maturity of the learners. Moreover, as we shall shortly see, it is possible to define certain growth gradients or developmental lines within subject-matter areas.

These four points bring to a head the discussions in this book, in so far as they bear on the problem of subject matter. Clearly all four points are closely interrelated. Taken together they clearly indicate that the learning of subject matter can be a dynamic agency for more enlightened living and the constructive shaping of personality. It has been said that "the material in many courses offered in high school is rich with implications for human understanding and only needs a teacher with insight to lift it from dull impersonal academic drabness to living vital material close to the concerns of boys and girls" (444, p. 158). Perhaps this statement somewhat exaggerates what can be done by the individual teacher working alone, but the kind of organization indicated is clear enough, and the attainment of it is feasible.

It is not appropriate in a book of this kind to discuss the various curricular subjects in detail. But in order to make the four points just presented and the general idea that underlies them more meaningful, I shall show how they apply to reading, English expression, mathematics, natural science, social studies and the arts.

READING

There has probably been more research on reading than on any other curricular area. The details, and still more, the techniques of this research are for the specialist. But we can very properly ask what we have learned from all this work about reading in particular and about education in general. The answer to this question is important for every teacher.

Reading involves the whole personality. Reading is not an isolated knack or skill. When a child reads, he reads as a person.

When a child learns to read, a readjustment of his personality takes place. This is one of the outstanding results of research, and it is full of practical significance both for the teaching of reading and for teaching in general.

1. Reading is a very serious challenge for a first-grade child. He is, perhaps, not quite at home in school. He cannot attend for very long at a time. His ability to respond to symbols and to deal with concepts is limited. Yet the school makes him feel that reading is very important. So failure to learn to read may be daunting and humiliating, and will probably be more and more so if the failure continues for some time. For the first-grade child reading is more than just simply reading. It is a big personality issue, and the way he meets it may have a big effect upon him, for better or for worse. This is why experts on reading insist that the basic problem in teaching elementary reading is to help the child to deal adequately with the challenge to his personality. The use of some standard method of teaching, supposed to be "scientifically correct" and applied indiscriminately to everybody thwarts many children, slows down their reading achievement, and produces bad adjustments which may be far-reaching and long-continuing (55).

What should be done is to use varied, simple, interesting materials, to organize many chances for success, and to make all such successes as significant as possible. Thus, instead of using a reading primer with its ready-made lessons, a teacher may jot down titles, names, and little comments on the drawings that children have made. Or she may put brief printed messages on the blackboard and encourage children to recognize and understand them. Or she may write down on the blackboard something that a child has said. Or she may tie reading in with manuscript writing, so that children can recognize their own and others' words (301). In following out such plans, which can be and, in fact, are elaborated endlessly and with many variations, there will be little formalized instruction in reading, but a great deal of actual reading closely related to the actual interests and doings of children.

2. It has been often shown that much failure and retardation in reading is associated with personality problems and maladjustments. For instance, one investigation dealing with 100 children who had serious reading disabilities found the following symptoms and disturbances in the group: 10 cases of nervous tension, 14 cases of "retreat reactions," i.e. general negativism, 18 cases of children who were inveterate practical jokers, 16 cases of general defense reactions, 26 cases of withdrawal (mind-wandering, daydreaming), 33 cases of laziness or passiveness or general indifference, 35 cases of extreme self-consciousness (202). A later important study dealing with a relatively small number of children who were extremely retarded in reading showed that 54.5% of them came from maladjusted homes, and that 41% had serious general emotional problems (549).

Along somewhat the same line Allison Davis insists that many "lower-class" children are retarded readers, because the whole cultural and social setting of their lives make them indifferent to reading (138). The solution Davis seems to suggest is to "de-emphasize" reading for a great many children. But this is a doubtful proposal, unless of course our usual ideas about the importance of reading are mistaken. Granted that reading is important and that failure to learn to read is a serious misfortune, there are obviously two things that the school should do: (1) Take into consideration a child's whole emotional and social adjustment, his personal and social background, his actual working goals, because success or failure in reading often turns on these things. (2) Do everything possible to present the challenge of learning to read as worth-while, intriguing, and interesting, and to give the learner early and convincing experiences of success (53).

3. Reading should always be treated as a functional tool for living rather than as merely a skill to be learned. A vital part of the teaching of reading is to show learners the many uses to which reading can be put, and the endless opportunities for reading that exist. Why to read, what to read, how to read—

these are the questions which the school should help pupils to answer. Such help is very much needed. All studies of the reading interests of adults show that those interests are not nearly as broad and as varied as they might be. Most grown-up people simply do not use reading anything like to the fullest extent (738). So, from the first grade on, there should be a concerted effort not merely to teach a skill, but to show how much reading can do to enrich and enhance a person's life.

Reading is a very definitely patterned and organized kind of motor response. Research, particularly since 1920, has made this very clear.

When a person reads, his eyes make a series of movements and pauses along the lines and from line to line. He actually reads during the pauses, and not during the movements. An ordinary reader, dealing with fairly easy and interesting material, may make three or four pauses per line. He will not spell out each word, or look at each letter. In fact he will not even look at each separate word. He will probably get a clear and complete impression of only about a quarter of what is on the page. Moreover, within limits, the fewer pauses he makes and the less he clearly and completely sees, the better and faster he reads. So reading is quite a different performance from proofreading, where a person has to scan each word and even each letter, or at least to try to do so. This, briefly summarized, is the account of the reading process as a motor reaction which has been established by research.

1. This understanding of the motor aspects of reading has proved to be very valuable. (*a*) It has opened the way to much more efficient instruction in the technique of reading. Older methods of teaching reading used to emphasize the separate letters, the learning of the alphabet, the spelling out of words, and the phonetics of separate syllables. Since words are made up of letters and syllables, such approaches seemed very right and proper. But with the recognition that a reader does not scrutinize details, the teaching emphasis shifted to the word

itself as the basic unit. There are quite a number of "methods" of teaching reading, and each of them has its advocates. But in all of them the essential idea is to organize the learning situation so that the child will come to respond to the whole word as a functional unit, without first studying its separate parts. There is no doubt that these modern methods enable children to learn to read quicker and better than used to be the case (621).

b) Moreover, this shift of emphasis from the separate letters to the whole word as the perceptual unit and the unit of meaning has made possible a much more flexible approach in teaching reading. More interesting reading materials can be used when one is not tied down to a letterwise approach. There can be intelligent diagnosis of such reading impediments as poor vision, or reversal tendencies (i.e. tendencies to read words backwards, for instance "saw" for "was"). Reading difficulties can be attacked when and where they actually arise. And if we see that every child, in learning to read, must learn how to look at the page and to move his eyes over it, intelligent individualized instruction becomes possible.

c) Furthermore, an understanding of the motor aspects of reading shows us just what must be done to supplement what is sometimes called the "experience approach." The "experience approach," in its pure and undiluted form, would mean giving the child plenty of interesting and easy reading material, encouraging him to use this material, and letting him "pick up" reading just as he might. This way of teaching reading, which some people would no doubt advocate, is the extreme opposite of the old-time formal *memoriter* drill on letters and syllables. It rejects any kind of systematic instruction, and relies wholly on motivation. The alternative to it, however, is not sheer empty formalism and routine drill, for once we really understand the motor processes involved in reading, we can see just what we ought to help the child to accomplish in all the free, rich, varied, and interesting reading that he does.

2. However, the great emphasis on the motor aspects of reading that has come from all the successful and impressive research devoted to them, has also created certain dangers.

a) It has brought about an undue emphasis on speed of reading in the teaching of reading, and this emphasis has been reinforced by numerous reading tests which center on speed. For instance, the median norms for grades eight, ten, and twelve of the wisely used Iowa Silent Reading Examinations are 222.08, 234.85, and 260.24 words per minute, and many teachers are likely to judge their own work and the attainments of children by norms of this kind. But the very concept of a basic desirable reading speed is a dubious one. The speed of reading differs very greatly with different kinds of material, and it differs when one reads for different purposes. The same person varies his reading speed very greatly at different times. The idea that it is always best to read fast is true only in an extremely limited sense. The most significant findings from the studies of reading speed, which are numerous, is that there are great individual differences. Thus individuals in selected groups of college and high-school students may vary in the ratio of three or even four to one in reading speed. The slowness with which some such individuals read is far more important as a symptom than for its own sake. It probably indicates far-reaching difficulties in adjustment involved in the reading process.

b) In any case, the heart of reading is comprehension rather than speed, and comprehension is only indirectly and, indeed, inadequately treated if we teach chiefly with an emphasis on the externals, such as speed and eye movement. It is usually said that speed and comprehension in reading are closely and positively related. Recently, however, the studies on which this conclusion is based have been seriously criticized. The point of this criticism is as follows. Tests of reading comprehension are made up of questions on the content that has been read, and the score on such tests is the number of right answers. While no doubt such a score does indicate comprehension, speed of reading is also a factor in determining it. Various attempts have been made to measure comprehension irrespective of speed, and when this is done the relationship between speed and comprehension seems to be negligible. In any case, it is a great mistake to teach chiefly for speed in reading with the thought that comprehension will then take care of itself (621).

c) Furthermore, stress on the externals of the reading process can lead to very dubious conclusions about suitable reading materials. In choosing suitable reading materials for children of various ages, the concept of *readability* has been developed, as well as various formulae for determining the degree of readability of any given item. One of these formulae combines average sentence length, ratio of prepositional phrases to the total number of words, and proportion of hard words (hard words being those not included in a certain standard list of easy words). As an interesting illustration I present below the application of this formula to the Gettysburg Address.

Number of words	269	Average sentence length, words	26.9
Number of sentences	10		
Number of prepositional phrases	26	Ratio of prepositional phrases to number of words	.0967
Number of hard words	43	Ratio of hard words to total number of words	.1599

Formula

26.9 × .07 =	1.8830
.0967 × 13.01 =	1.2581
.1599 × 10.73 =	1.7157
constant	1.6126
Total	6.4694

From Irving Lorge (413).

This final total indicates the grade level of readability of the material. The Gettysburg Address has a readability level of a little below the middle of the sixth grade. At this level one would expect that 75% of the questions on a comprehension test based on the passage would be answered correctly (413). There is, of course, no doubt that readability in this sense is important. Yet it is certainly true that children can deal with and, indeed, thrive on surprisingly difficult material if they find such material interesting and important. On the other hand, a passage might be perfectly suitable for certain children so far as the externals included in the above formula go, and yet be so dull or inane that it would really be almost unreadable (54).

The improvement of reading is a many-sided process of growth. In one of the earlier chapters of this book I cited an experiment in which a large number of students in a course in educational psychology increased their average reading speed from 274.6 to 319.4 words per minute in six weeks by means of some simple instructions and 10 minutes practice per diem (706). In another such experiment a group of students improved their "reading efficiency" * 30–35% in 5 weeks on an average, with some individuals improving 250% (79). Numerous comparable reports have been published. Results like these certainly seem to contradict the statement that the improvement of reading is "a many-sided process of growth," and to suggest that what is really needed is only a little careful advice and a few weeks of directed practice. However, in many of these experiments the individuals concerned were already eager to improve their reading, and more than willing to accept any help that they might get. So the all-important personality setting was already established. If all the basic conditions are right, dramatic improvement of reading is undoubtedly possible when skillful instruction and specifically directed prac-

* By reading efficiency the authors of this experiment mean speed multiplied by score on a comprehension test.

tice is given. But when we think of getting unselected groups of thousands and tens of thousands of children and young people to read better, the practical problem is immensely more complicated.

Expert guidance in the proper techniques of reading is always necessary. But so are varied and stimulating opportunities and experiences. More than twenty years ago attention was called to the values of what is called "extensive reading." Extensive reading means the comparatively loose and quick reading of diffusely written material. It contrasts with the careful, analytic reading required by the sort of closely and compactly written material found in most textbooks, this being called "intensive reading." As compared with intensive reading, extensive reading was found to yield better understanding, better grasp of ideas, better solution of problems, and longer retention—that is to say, it added up to better reading (228–231).

Nowadays we would not think in terms of mere extensiveness, or limit ourselves to planning supplementary reading assignments and liberal collateral. Rather, we would wish to organize rich reading programs, containing many kinds of reading material associated with various activities and various aspects of the school program. We would use book lists, reading discussions, library visits, reading in connection with field trips, the reading of research material, recreational reading, the promotion of more reading out of school; and also, we would wish to capitalize on the peculiar and stimulating values of good oral reading. Along with such a program of rich, varied and stimulating reading experiences would go the organization of aids, suggestions, and guidance on how to read better and more effectively. To sum all this up, we now think that the teaching of reading should center on creating both the ability to read and the inclination to do so (242, 243, 331).

If we are to deal intelligently with the practical problems of reading, it is absolutely necessary to remember that the improvement of reading is both the development of a skill and the development of interest and inclination, and that both are essential. Some very sweeping statements are often made about the reading inadequacies of high-school boys and girls. For instance, it has been said that about one-third of these young people cannot read up to the fifth-grade level, and from this it is concluded that such pupils belong to what is called the "non-verbal type," whatever that may be. The fact itself is open to dispute, and the conclusion still more so. The unsuitability, dullness, and difficulty of school reading, and the narrowness of the conventional reading tests accounts for a great deal of the apparent trouble (739). If students were tested on comprehension in reading the comics, the picture would probably be entirely different, considering the enormous popularity of the comics among children on all levels of intelligence (735, 737). As to remedial reading, which is so often advocated, it may indeed be valuable, but only if it is geared to growth rather than to tricks, devices, and drill; for growth in reading comes chiefly from much and varied and interesting free reading rather than from special exercises, even though such exercises may have some occasional usefulness (659).

The relationship of this brief account of the modern teaching of reading to the various points set up in the preceding section is perhaps fairly obvious, but in closing I will try to make it explicit. (*a*) The act of reading itself, as a motor performance, is an intelligible pattern of response the nature of which is understood. (*b*) The teaching of reading must foster and promote interest in reading. (*c*) The teaching of reading must seek to bring about the widest possible transfer of reading to life, i.e. to make reading an instrumentality for adjustment. (*d*) The improvement of reading is essentially a developmental process. It may be thought of as a growth gradient or developmental line, centering on the development of ability to comprehend language symbols. All specific learnings and experiences bearing on reading can and should be organized to promote this line of development in its many-sided applications.

ENGLISH EXPRESSION

For reasons of space I shall confine myself here to written expression, although the use of oral English is also profoundly important. The following are the outstanding points in the teaching of written English expression.

The ability to express oneself in English is not an isolated skill. It is a manifestation of the personality, and of the organization and maturity of the personality. Moreover, the acquisition and improvement of that ability is itself a means for the shaping and development of the personality.

Here is a letter written to a friend by a ninth-grade pupil. "How are finds thats good. Bill, do you remember the lot across from the fire department they're building a garage there now and its like the best one in prairie city but they aren't enough yet. We had a lot of football game our boys get hurt all the time out of town" (627). The defects of this letter are not mere weaknesses in grammar and good usage. They are defects in clarity of thought. Moreover, the inability to produce a better piece of writing than this is much more than an immediate practical disadvantage, for it is an inability to clarify ideas and to convey ideas. Such an inability cannot help but profoundly affect any person in many of his or her transactions with life. Thus English expression is clearly a reflection of the quality of a person's thought, an externalization of the way in which his mind deals with the problems and challenges of living. English expression turns on the ability to know what one means and to say what one means. This is the controlling viewpoint of all sound teaching in this area (560).

To improve English expression we must organize writing situations which enlist the genuine participation of children and young people—situations in which motivation is created and established, situations in which children and young people really *want* to say something as well and clearly as they can. Such situations may include social and business correspondence, the writing of telegrams, bulletin board notices, and announcements to be read aloud, writing reports to be read in class, keeping records and minutes of class discussions, writing stories, essays and poems, writing news reports for class and school newspapers, keeping vacation diaries for report in school, interpreting the moods of music, keeping records of expeditions, summarizing and commenting on news reports, keeping logs and records of class projects, and so forth (111, 247). The organization of such a wealth of really significant writing situations is a tremendous contrast to the old-style course in English Composition, with its stereotyped essay and limited range of topics.

To improve English expression we must have a clear-cut conception of the function or process that we want to improve. What we want to produce is *growth in clarity and adequacy of expression.* We want to help children to be clear about what they have in mind, so that they can convey whatever it is to other minds. This, indeed, is the very essence of English expression, all the way from the little third-grader to the most gifted and distinguished of writers. So here we define our contemplated developmental line.

1. To emphasize clarity and adequacy of thought and expression in the teaching of English expression is very different from emphasizing good English usage. So-called "good usage" is not always very closely related to clarity and effectiveness, for it is really a literary-social convention or set of conventions. The conventions of "good language manners" are certainly important for various purposes, but they are not the basis of style. Emphasis on good usage can be and often is arbitrary, superficial, and finnicky. For instance, when a certain pupil wrote, "a horse who fairly danced with pride," his teacher corrected it to, "a horse which danced with pride"; and when another pupil wrote, "poles and lines and sinkers," the teacher

corrected it to, "poles, lines, and sinkers" (394). Whatever such learning experiences may or may not be worth, they certainly do not foster growth in clear thinking and clear expression. For instruction in good usage is of secondary importance, and should come in situations where such usage is normally expected and demanded, such, for instance, as business correspondence or the preparation of public notices.

2. Once again, a central emphasis upon clarity and adequacy of thought and expression does not mean an approach through grammatical principles and rules of punctuation. Quite probably the writer of the letter quoted above had been given a good deal of instruction in grammar and some in punctuation, and this instruction had done very little good. This is exactly what we would expect on the basis of practically all the research studies, which show that the teaching of grammar and punctuation in the hope of improving English expression is amazingly ineffective.

But perhaps, after all, one should not be surprised at these disconcerting findings. As to grammar, the conventional grammatical approach to English has come down to us from time-honored methods of teaching Latin and Greek. But English, unlike Latin and Greek, is an uninflected language with which such a grammatical approach is fundamentally unsound. Thus, in the statement, "I bought two new dresses," the topical and grammatical subjects are different. Again, the grammatical definition of a sentence is that it expresses a complete act of thought; but there can be perfectly good sentences which do no such thing, as for instance, "She couldn't find one in a week." Nor can one simplify matters, as some textbook writers have tried to do, by defining a sentence as a statement that "makes sense"; for non-sentences also can make sense, e.g. "Life with father." Once more, non-sentences and run-on sentences are condemned in grammar textbooks and blue-penciled in many student compositions, but if they are intended they may be perfectly all right, as for instance, "The way was long, the wind was cold, the minstrel was infirm and old" (536, 560).

As to punctuation, when one looks at the quite appalling array of abstract, technical and difficult rules in which its operation is set forth, one cannot wonder too much that young people usually get nothing from studying it. But punctuation can and should be taught quite differently. For instance, consider the sentence, "If the hot weather continues, there will be no crop." The rule book says that the comma is needed because the sentence opens with an introducing adverbial modifier, which must be set off with a comma. But so does the sentence, "When we got to the mountains Dad let me drive." The reason why a comma is needed in the first sentence but not in the second is that it has the effect of delaying the forward movement, and thus clarifying the pattern of meaning. So in general, punctuation should be taught and learned as a system of symbols that enables one to set forth one's meaning clearly—which obviously is also one of the ways of discovering just what one's meaning is (561).

3. If you will return once more to the letter quoted above, you will probably see that what its writer needs is the clearing up of the expressive pattern and the thought pattern. The enigma of the first five words, the lack of any separation after "fire department," the vagueness of the statement "they aren't far enough" are far more serious than the lack of a question mark after "fire department" or the writing of "game" instead of "games." Yet it is precisely such minor and really trivial details which are constantly emphasized. What a teacher ought to do with this letter-writer is to lead him to see the need for greater clarity and adequacy, to lead him to ask himself more critically just what he has in mind. This is the direction in which growth should take place.

The fostering of growth in clarity and adequacy of expression is a perfectly practicable teaching undertaking. For instance, our illustrative letter was one of several produced by a number of pupils. These letters might have been sent to the recipients or exchanged among members of the class, so that the writers could have seen just where clarity broke down. Or a smaller number of letters could have been produced in class discussion. In one teaching situation where class discussion was used, the statement, "Betty plays a good game of tennis, and she makes excellent cake," came up for consideration. The children realized that it was not very good because two unrelated ideas were combined without anything to set them off. Another statement that was discussed was "Mr. W. was our adviser. He grasped the seriousness of the situation. He immediately called a meeting of the officers." The objection here was that the language, although clear, was very choppy, and so the idea was reformulated in a single sentence with dependent clauses in place of the three short sentences (196). We know from our experimental reports that this combination of concrete, interesting, significant endeavor with understanding and insight is what gets results. Mere practice on correct forms is not effective; nor is the study of abstract rules and principles. The successful answer is the application of the general principle to improve specific endeavor (634). This, indeed, is the core of modern practice in teaching English expression (359).

MATHEMATICS

For anyone who believes that the central psychological reality of education is the shaping of personality, mathematics presents a most intriguing and challenging problem. Mathematics is of incalculable and immense importance for civilization. Our conceptions of the physical universe, our innumerable inventions and devices, our systems of financing and insurance and government would all be impossible without mathematics; and all of them profoundly condition our lives and determine our feelings. Also, mathematics is an intensely interesting and satisfying study for those who understand it. I well remember a graduate student who was taking his first elementary course in calculus, and who exclaimed in amazement at the wonderful techniques he was discovering.

Yet when we visit a conventional class in second-grade arithmetic or ninth-grade algebra, what do we see? For many of the children the work is all too evidently a hateful endeavor, an experience of sheer bewilderment and failure. For such children mathematics, which might mean so much, is a sort of psychological poison, a focus of frustration and dismay in their immediate living. If we could be perfectly sure that later on all these children would be compelled to use what they are being taught, we might be justified in trying to force them to learn it, just as we would be right to force them not to cross crowded parkways or play with sticks of dynamite or scratch the back of a tiger at the zoo, whether they wanted to or not. But life as it is actually lived does *not* call for complicated mathematical skills. Addition and subtraction and some simple multiplication and division will serve nearly all ordinary purposes, as numerous studies and surveys have shown (695, 731).

Obviously, the tempting conclusion is that only the very simplest of mathematical rudiments should be taught to everybody, that these rudiments should be taught largely by routine, and that everything beyond the rudiments is only for the few. This is the point of view of numerous practical educators—many of whom, by the way, are probably mathematical cripples themselves, so that they have a prejudice. These educators often defend their position by saying that a child must have a certain I.Q. or even a certain special ability if he is to make anything of mathematics. Such contentions may be true if we are thinking of mathematics *as ordinarily taught;* but they are at least very questionable when we begin to think of mathematics *as it should be taught.*

Moreover, the undeniable fact that most people use very little mathematics in their lives is not conclusive, because most people have very little mathematics that they could use in any case. A living insight into mathematical principles, processes, and ways of thinking can certainly be brought fruitfully to bear on many of the problems of human life, all the way from a whole host of practical matters to such far reaching yet momentous concerns as resistance to unscrupulous propaganda and advertising, intelligent attitudes on many public problems, or a recognition of the relationship of the physical universe to individual human destiny. Moreover, the learning of mathematics, if properly organized, can be a success experience of great hygienic value. So we can reply that if people do not and cannot use much mathematics in their lives, they are the worse and the poorer for it, and that if these people had at least some gleam of genuine mathematical insight, their lives would thereby be more enlightened and successful.

Mathematics, indeed, is the prime example of a subject with great but unrealized educational possibilities. How can these possibilities be realized? This is the practical problem. The solution to this problem is found in the combination of two approaches in the teaching of mathematics, the "meaning approach" and the "social approach."

The meaning approach

The meaning approach to the teaching of mathematics takes off from the proposition that the heart of mathematics is the understanding of relationships, or relational thinking, and that gain in mathematical competence is growth in relational thinking or the understanding of relationships. Mathematics is defined and taught, from start to finish, as "the science of necessary relationships" (263, p. 2). In other words, the meaning approach treats gain in mathematical competence as a well defined growth gradient or developmental line, focusing on relational thinking.

The meaning approach to mathematics has been worked out extensively and in detail, but a few examples will suffice to show what is involved, and how this approach differs from conventional teaching. Thus addition is ordinarily taught as the memorization of the "addition facts," without emphasis on understanding. Such teaching favors errors, uncertainty, and impermanence. What should be done is to help children to discover and understand that addition really means the combination of groups of things, so that the statement $5 + 3 = 8$ means that if we take a group of 3 things and another group of 5 things and combine these two groups we then have a group of 8 things (84).

Again, it has been found that certain number combinations are specially difficult. Among these difficult combinations are $7 + 9$, $5 + 9$, $9 + 8$, $16 - 9$, $13 - 8$, $11 - 3$, $14 - 6$, 8×7, 9×6, 7×8, $54 \div 9$, etc. Moreover, it is said that altered methods of teaching do not remove these difficulties or make the combinations easier to learn (117, 701). But the changed methods that have been tried out are only superficially altered. They amount to no more than changes in the order of presentation, or in the devices that are used. The underlying memory routine remains the same. But if the learning of the number combinations is approached, not through memory, but through insight, so that children are able to understand what they are doing when they add, subtract, multiply, and divide, then the designated combinations are no harder to learn than any others (648).

Once again, the meaning approach does not involve abandoning standards of speed and accuracy in arithmetic. Rather, it involves basing speed and accuracy on insight and good procedure. In interviews with one hundred and fifteen pupils in grades two to five on how they found answers in doing simple multiplication, it was shown that these pupils used no fewer than eleven different methods in this very simple and straightforward kind of work. The methods included rote memory, guessing, various kinds of counting, and starting at the bottom on the multiplication table and going on up till the right answer was found. Pupils may get a right answer by a bad method, but they will have no certainty about the answer, and the getting of it will certainly be no help to them in relational thinking (85).

This same emphasis on insight and relational thinking which is exemplified in teaching the number combinations is continued throughout the teaching of mathematics. Fractions, for instance, are a bugbear to many pupils. The concepts of numerator and denominator are never grasped by many of them. Gross errors are made, and often pupils have no idea that there is any error. It is found that many pupils may think that $1/16$ is larger than $1/2$, that they do not know that $3/4$ equals $6/8$, and may not realize that $3/4$ means 3 out of 4 equal parts. All such troubles stem from the routine teaching of fractions, and they are largely alleviated when children are helped to understand what a fractional expression really means (478).

So too, a lack of understanding of the significance of tens causes very frequent trouble in "carrying" in addition and subtraction. But a first insight into the meaning of tens can be developed when children encounter the numbers from 10 to 19, for instance by showing them how to sort 18 cards into one group of 8 and another of 10, and then to write down the corresponding symbols, 8 and 10, with the 8 and the 1 in the right places (646). The same general idea is applied also in the teaching of geometry, which, as we have already seen, can be presented as a method of thinking and reasoning (171). In algebra, too, the same emphasis applies. Algebra is not essentially different from arithmetic, but only more generalized. It should not be treated as a sequence of unrelated topics and of meaningless techniques such as the reduction of very complicated fractions or the manipulation of brackets. Rather, pupils should discover through the study of algebra how it is possible to clarify, understand, and control relationships by means of positive and negative signs, the use of tables and graphs and formulae, and the employment of the language and symbolism of variation, etc. (70).

This meaning approach is often called the "mathematical

approach." It centers upon the logic of relationships, more or less does away with such subdivisions as arithmetic, algebra, geometry, trigonometry, calculus, etc., and turns on the idea that the great essential is always genuine mathematical thinking. The central idea of this approach is that meanings in mathematics at all levels must be sought for in the structure of the subject itself (648).

The social approach

The so-called "social approach" means teaching arithmetic in the setting of various practical situations, such as telling time, laying out measurements, planning recipes, recording temperatures, weighing the members of the class, providing enough books and papers for everyone in the room, making change, taking subscriptions, figuring costs, and so forth. Those who advocate this approach make much of the fact that mathematics is not much used in ordinary life, and so they propose to set up in the classroom a variety of common situations in which it is used. Advocates of "social arithmetic" often make violent attacks upon the meaning approach or mathematical approach, which they call unrealistic and a return to formalism (731).

Yet there need be no conflict between these two approaches, and indeed there certainly should not be. Undoubtedly the use of intriguing practical and social problems can and should lead to an understanding of abstract relationships and to growth in relational thinking. For instance, the laying out of a tennis court, the figuring of the proper constituents of a cement mixture, planning menus, figuring the costs of a party, laying off angles in a workshop, computing gear ratios, or studying a proposed personal budget create opportunities for more and better relational thinking than almost any standard textbook. But a purely *ad hoc*, projectwise, social approach to mathematics, which leaves learning pretty much to chance and which relies almost wholly on motivation and nothing else, sacrifices some of the greatest potential values of mathematics. For these values are dependent upon the achievement of genuine insight and upon growth in insight (715, 716).

Furthermore, the claim of enthusiasts for social arithmetic that the meaning approach is a new formalism is entirely unjustified, as can be seen from the following points.

1. In the conventional organization of mathematics teaching, a series of topics is set up and rigidly followed, and drill and application materials are provided under each topic. This virtually blocks off genuine and varied social applications. For instance, the laying out of a tennis court would have to wait until the unit on angles had been studied; and the planning of recipes and menus could not be undertaken before fractions and decimals had been "covered." The meaning approach, on the other hand, is not tied to any specific or predetermined sequence of topics. Its basic proposal is to foster mathematical or relational thinking wherever and whenever opportunities occur. This at once opens the way to innumerable applications, which can have real social value and genuine interest. Thus any store can provide a very wide range of just such applications, as, for instance, the study of price lists to reveal and record price ranges, the discovery of fixed prices for standard brands, the effect on prices of quantity buying, the effect of credit arrangements on price, the discovery of the units in which articles are sold, including the concept of net weight and the importance of reading what is said on a standard package, techniques and problems connected with weighing things, the value of making a rough estimate as well as a precise calculation of the amount of a total bill, and so forth (565). All these are intriguing and important problems, out of which can come growth in relational thinking (96).

2. The conventional approach, with its rigid order of topics, creates an insoluble problem of individual differences. The meaning approach makes great flexibility possible. There is no need to take each topic in a fixed order, or for everybody to "cover" or "master" each separate topic completely before

going on to the next. The reason is that the meaning approach operates in terms of the continuous growth of a central and well-defined function, rather than in terms of a set sequence of items to be learned perfectly one by one (91, 95).

3. The conventional approach separates problem-solving from the routines of computation. The meaning approach treats the basic computational routines as challenges to thought, insight, and understanding. One of the worst consequences of conventional teaching, with its separation of computation from problem solving, is that pupils so taught tend to be completely baffled by unfamiliar problems which are not stated in the expected language and style of the textbook (700). The meaning approach, however, treats the learning of mathematics as problem solving from start to finish, and constantly uses practical and social problems which have very little resemblance to the pale travesties of mathematical problems with which so many textbooks are burdened.

NATURAL SCIENCE

The basic mental process in natural science is *objective thinking*. The scientist is, par excellence, the man who accepts reality as it is, and undertakes to deal with it on its own terms. Galileo and Darwin got themselves into trouble, not because they were masters of obscure and mysterious techniques which made people think that they might be dealers in black magic, but simply because they insisted on an objective attitude towards facts and evidence, and were therefore compelled to take a stand against the innumerable precious prejudices and superstitions which so amazingly beset mankind. Natural sciences, therefore, represents the objective attitude towards life and experience. There is no need for me to do more than mention the enormous values which society has reaped from this attitude. But also, it is of great value for the sound and healthy adjustment of individual human beings. Nevertheless, the objective attitude and objective thinking are not attained by chance. It is altogether necessary to inculcate them, and of great importance to do so. Thus the true focus of science teaching is not on useful information or on experimental techniques as such, but rather on the development of objective thinking.

A certain organized plan for the teaching of science was based on a formulation of scientific attitudes or "scientific mindedness" which was drawn from an examination of a large number of books dealing authoritatively with scientific method. In the summary derived from these writings, scientific attitudes were described as follows:

> I. Belief in universal basic cause-and-effect relationships, which renders untenable (*a*) superstitious beliefs in general, such as belief in signs, or good luck, or in charms (*b*) belief in unexplainable mysteries (*c*) undue credulity and tendencies to magnify the importance of coincidence.
>
> II. Sensitive curiosity concerning the reasons for happenings, coupled with ideals (*a*) of careful and accurate observation and equally careful use of data collected by others (*b*) of patience in the collection of data (*c*) of persistence in the search for adequate explanations.
>
> III. The habit of delayed response, the holding of views tentatively, and the willingness to alter views relatively to the matter in hand. This to permit (*a*) adequate consideration of alternatives (*b*) formulating a conscious plan of attack on a problem.
>
> IV. The habit of weighing evidence with respect to its (*a*) pertinence (*b*) soundness (*c*) adequacy.
>
> V. Respect for another's point of view, open-mindedness, willingness to be convinced by evidence. (136, p. 48)

These five points and their subdivisions may be taken as a particularization of what is meant by "objective thinking" or "objective-mindedness."

Thus the entire science program from the first grade on may be conceived and planned as a growth gradient centering in objective thinking. The core of such a program would be a continuous development from objective thinking and understanding that is simple, inadequate, limited, and vague, towards precision, adequacy, generality, abstract controls, and depth of insight. Many simple experiences with friction before studying the coefficient of friction, many simple but revealing comparisons between animals and plants and inanimate objects before dealing with the technicalities of physiology and biology, many simple but revealing experiences with sound before dealing with the technicalities of acoustics—these few suggestions at least indicate how a developmental program of science teaching can be organized.

Such a program differs very markedly from the ordinary scheme of science instruction which is set up to teach standard scientific content and elementary scientific techniques. The conventional scheme is open to the following objections. (*a*) Science is treated as an informational and technical subject, which virtually eliminates it from the elementary school. (*b*) Learning in the field of science is organized more or less arbitrarily as a sequence of topics without much internal continuity or relatedness. (*c*) Far too much emphasis is placed upon remembering facts and details, and far too little upon good methods of thinking. (*d*) The material taught is not closely related to daily life, and cannot be because of its internal topical arrangement. (*e*) Last but not least, conventional science instruction has to depend largely upon textbooks which are usually more or less outmoded even before they are published, and which often contain surprising amounts of out-of-date, misleading, and even downright false material (100).

Furthermore, a program of science instruction which centers on the development of objective thinking differs from various proposals now being made to teach science simply for the sake of immediate practical utility. There are organized courses in general science which undertake to tell people how to take care of their health, how to cure colds, how to pick out a proper diet, how to tell shoddy goods when one sees them, how to fix electric motors, how to make and use cleaning fluids and soaps, and so forth. The units or separate lessons of such courses often consist of just such "practical" topics. The most obvious objection to plans of this kind is that they put the teacher in the position of giving advice, backed by all the authority of science, on all sorts of matters about which she cannot possibly know a great deal. To take just one example, think of the question of diet. The teacher finds in the textbook various positive statements about diet, with the intimation that these statements are scientifically valid. But unless she is a very naïve person, she knows very well that dietary experts disagree and seem to change their minds quite often, and also that the more expert they are, the more careful they will be about advising in individual cases. So she fears, and with good reason, that she may easily do harm instead of good.

But there is another and deeper objection to science instruction geared simply to immediate practical helpfulness. It is perfectly true that science should be learned in connection with familiar matters of everyday life, and that it should be brought to bear on them—on cleaning windows, and choosing textiles, and fixing electric circuits, and mixing concrete, and heating one's home, and so on endlessly. But out of experiences and dealings with such problems should grow an attitude towards the world about us and to ourselves, a respect for facts and evidence, a resistance to prejudice and superstition, a capacity for objective thinking. The case is exactly parallel with that of "social arithmetic" which I have already discussed. Mathematics instruction should undertake, not simply to teach children useful tricks with numbers, but to develop in them the mathematical way of thinking. In the same way science instruction must seek to develop the scientific habit of mind, and not simply to teach an array of practical accomplishments.

Yet a continuous emphasis at all levels upon the development of objective thinking enables one to bring science instruction very close to common experiences and everyday problems. One very authoritative and influential statement on the planning of science instruction recommends that local resources should be studied for their educational possibilities. "Often such a study will reveal richer resources than one usually is aware of. Even in regions which often seem entirely barren, it is surprising what materials and relationships are revealed when one turns over stones, boards, or logs, examines the surfaces of apparently bare rocks or cliffs, digs up roots of plants in waste places, probes decaying logs, examines compost piles, and hoes the family garden. Fence corners, roadsides, and waste places are equally as rich in science materials as are the forest, the field, the pond, or the seashore" (537).

Just to give a few practical illustrations, very good opportunities for science teaching have been found in the following: a brook in the school grounds; a home assignment on the responses of plants to stimuli such as light or heat or gravity; a simple study made in school of how people breathe; health issues in local restaurants; a study of how electric fans move air—whether by pushing or by pulling it; the effect of noise on efficiency; the local waterworks. A great variety of published material can also be used for the purposes of science instruction. Such material includes consumer research publications, newspaper stories, advertising, material from numerous government bureaus, including the weather bureau, biographies and personal revelations of great scientists. All this, as you will notice, is "live" material. It deals with obviously genuine, important, and interesting issues. Yet in using it, the idea is not to present a series of ready-made solutions for practical problems, although vital science teaching will have plenty of practical references. But the prevailing idea is to inculcate the scientific habit of mind and to promote the development of objective thinking (477).

SOCIAL STUDIES

Two controlling approaches are possible in the organization and teaching of the social studies. The focus may be either the accumulation of information, or the promotion of growth in social understanding. Some people might say that the proper choice is not "either-or," but a judicious combination of both; and in a sense they would be quite right. But as a matter of fact, a great deal of teaching of social studies has emphasized information for its own sake and very little else. Some years ago an extensive investigation was made of the tests prepared and given by teachers of history. It was shown that there was an enormous preponderance of fact questions and only a meager scattering of questions that could be interpreted as thought questions. This shows pretty clearly what really goes on in the various courses, for test questions reveal what pupils will work for and what teachers consider important when the chips are down (503).

Another investigation of numerous textbooks in the field also showed a prevailing emphasis on facts and information (204). In contrast to this, present-day authorities on the teaching of the social studies strongly insist that the central focus should be upon understanding, the grasp of meanings, and the development of a capacity for critical thinking about social issues (19, 320). In the light of our whole psychological discussion it is obvious that this second approach is the right one if we want the social studies to serve as an agency for more enlightened living and as a constructive influence for the shaping of personality.

If this approach is to amount to anything more than words, wishes, and hopes, it must be built into a practical program. A few instances from actual practice will suggest how this can be done. An eighth-grade group undertook to carry through a year's study of the origin and development of their home town. A group of college freshmen in a social studies course undertook to investigate the problem of the use of bicycles in town and on the campus, and to make proposals for regulations which were sorely needed. A sixth-grade group devoted some time to the study of different kinds of United States paper currency by examining various types of bills, thus at least opening up the far-reaching and complex problems connected with money. Another sixth-grade group co-operatively organized a unit on sensationalism in advertising. A tenth-grade social studies class made a co-operative study of the school cafeteria, about which there had been some dissatisfaction. A fifth-grade group set about collecting and assessing information about a dangerous traffic problem at a corner near the school. In a tenth-grade social science class a very successful attempt was made to promote international-mindedness by the use of stories, pictures, letters, and recorded interviews (112).

In all these instances, which are only a scatter of samples of an enormous number of others of the same kind, you will notice certain points that have already become familiar. (*a*) There is always an informational content, yet the idea is not to work for the retention of information for its own sake. (*b*) There is, or at least there certainly can be and should be, a constant emphasis on insight, intelligence, and understanding brought to bear on social issues. (*c*) Activities and materials are closely related to the life-concerns and daily experiences of the learners. Thus social understanding is constantly related to, and developed in connection with, genuine life needs. One further comment on this point is in order. Materials and activities must be related to the needs, concerns, and problems of the *pupils*. When teachers undertake to set up what they call activities, they very often put much value on reading, listening to lectures, group discussions, locating information, and making oral reports. These are, of course, activities in a certain sense, but they are not always good ones from the standpoint of the pupils, or for the sake of bringing about the type of mental growth we want. They are school-bound activities, rather than activities which bring a way of thinking into real contact with life concerns (534).

The working principle of the social studies program, then, should be to develop social understanding in a setting of actual life concerns. Let us see how a program so organized will cope with some practical difficulties and problems of instruction.

1. One such problem is the difficulty of many social studies concepts, such as conservation, the industrial revolution, Greek civilization, or the Renaissance. We meet this problem by emphasizing the *development* of understanding, rather than the complete mastery, once and for all, of a stated array of concepts. No sixth-grade pupils can really understand the problem of money, but this is no reason why they should not be aware that there is such a problem and have a few gleams of insight about it.

2. Another problem has to do with teaching materials. A first-hand contact with a social issue is always ideal, but such contacts are very often impossible. So we have to rely on verbal materials, maps, charts, and so forth, which have great psychological limitations. There is only one way to meet this problem, and that is to break away from the convention of the compendious textbook, which is a very poor instrument psychologically speaking, and to use the widest possible range of printed and written materials of all kinds. If we constantly emphasize growth in social understanding rather than the covering of an array of set topics, the use of a great variety of informal and unconventional materials becomes quite possible.

3. Other problems have to do with the limitations of the pupils. (*a*) Pupils are limited in background, which means that general statements and abstract formulae may mean little or nothing to them. We meet this difficulty by dealing very largely with social issues that are close at hand. (*b*) Pupils do not usually have much spontaneous interest in social studies materials or, indeed, in social issues themselves. We meet this difficulty by revealing to them that they are, in fact, surrounded by innumerable and very pertinent life issues, by challenging them to recognize these issues, and by showing them how solutions can be sought best by the application of social intelligence and critical thinking (320).

4. The teaching of history presents a special psychological problem in the field of social studies. The essence of history is the arrangement of events in time, yet we know that the time concepts of children and young people are very uncertain and vague. When a child thinks that anybody over twenty is really quite ancient, and feels that a birthday six months ahead is aeons away, it is simply fantastic to suppose that dates and historical periods can possibly have any definite meaning for him. This is a very stubborn difficulty, and it cannot be solved by such devices as time charts and time lines, or by the plan that is sometimes tried of teaching history backwards, beginning with the present. The proper psychological approach to history is by way of interest and significance. The early content of history should consist of interesting and significant stories, doings, personalities, and events. Chronology need not be ignored, but it had better be left quite vague at first, to be cleared up and made definite in the course of time. Dates and periods are elements in a framework which hold events together in an intelligible pattern, and a real understanding of this framework can be achieved only by the gradual fitting of events into it (204).

THE ARTS

To speak of "the arts" is to use a rather indefinite term. Defining the term "art" by the "pointing method," it means as here used, music, the visual arts, the literary arts including poetry, fiction, and drama, and the so-called "applied" arts. Although the various arts use different media, the basic psychological process in all of them is the same. That process is *the embodiment of feeling in design.* A blueprint is an organized design, but it is not a work of art in the defined sense, because it conveys intellectual meanings rather than emotional values. A picture, too, is a design, but the design has quite a different psychological function from that of a blueprint, for the picture embodies and conveys that artist's emotional intimations. An expository argument or a mathematical proof, again, is an organized design or pattern, and so is a poem. But the argument or the proof convey intellectual meanings, while the poem conveys emotional values. So in general, every true work of art, all the way from the simplest creative effort of a little child to the elaborate achievement of the greatest artist, is a pattern of symbols whose meanings are emotional meanings. From this it follows that the focus of education in and through the arts is responsiveness to the emotional meanings and possibilities of organized design. This kind of responsiveness is what may more briefly be called *aesthetic responsiveness.*

Aesthetic responsiveness manifests itself in three distinguishable but related ways—in aesthetic production, aesthetic reproduction, and aesthetic enjoyment. Instances of aesthetic production are the painting of pictures, the writing of poetry, and the composition of music. Instances of aesthetic reproduction are the reading aloud of a poem, the playing of a piece of music, or the acting of a play. Aesthetic enjoyment probably explains itself pretty well, and it may go on either in connection with production or reproduction or independently, as when one listens to music, looks at pictures, or reads poetry. The three expressions "aesthetic production," "aesthetic reproduction," and "aesthetic enjoyment" are not very familiar in this country, although they have been used rather extensively by German educators and psychologists. They have the great advantage of being precise, and enabling us to avoid the ambiguities of the term *creative activity* in speaking of the arts. Creative activity really means a great deal more than producing a new art work, for reproduction and enjoyment can also be creative. So when we speak of aesthetic *production,* we know exactly what we mean and do not mean.

So the core of education in and through the arts is the development of aesthetic responsiveness in and through production, reproduction, and enjoyment. This is another and more precise way of saying what is so often said, namely, that the true outcome of education in and through the arts is appreciation. When children paint pictures, make drawings, enjoy looking at pictures, write or read or enjoy poetry or stories, dramatize some idea or theme, produce a play, compose or perform or enjoy music, sing songs, or play instruments, all these activities should be organized to deepen, enrich, and intensify the appreciation of beauty—or putting the idea in other words, to deepen, enrich, and intensify aesthetic responsiveness (113, 475, 538).

How does aesthetic responsiveness operate in human life? Certainly in the production, reproduction, and enjoyment of works of what are called the fine arts, but in many other ways as well. So a program of education in and through the arts, psychologically conceived, can and should touch human life and experience on many sides. Room arrangement, flower arrangement, the choice of furnishings, the choice of pictures, the choice and designing of costume, explorations of the local architecture, the discovery and appreciation of near-by scenes of natural beauty, the elimination of eyesores, the choice of music suitable for various occasions, informal and formal musical participation, the writing and reading of poetry, camera club activities, dramatization and play production, dancing of various types—these are only a few of the possibilities for revealing to children and young people how much aesthetic values and aesthetic responsiveness can mean in their lives both now and later on. As with the other curricular fields I have discussed, as soon as we have managed to define the intelligible way of responding that we want to promote, an endless range of significant applications opens up. For aesthetic responsiveness is most certainly woven into the texture of human life, and children and young people can find in it a means for better living.

I will bring this brief discussion of the arts to a close with three more concrete instances of an educational emphasis on aesthetic values and responses.

The first of these instances is a famous project carried

through some time ago by Hughes Mearns at the Lincoln School of Teachers College in New York City. Mearns actively encouraged a group of young people at the Lincoln School to write poetry. His methods, if such they could be called, were extremely informal. There was a great deal of general stimulation through reading, discussion, and the making of suggestions. No schedule was set up, and poetry could be written at any time. Mearns used to go about the building keeping one pocket of his jacket empty so that anyone who felt shy could slip a poem into it unobtrusively. If someone were suddenly gripped with an idea and wanted to work it out, he might be excused from school for the day in order to do so. Many of the results of this project are published by Mearns in his book, *Creative Youth,* and there is no doubt that they are impressive. But what really mattered was the human side of the undertaking. None of Mearns' pupils have turned out to be writers of genius, but most if not all of them were profoundly and permanently affected. Aesthetic values and aesthetic responsiveness grew to have an important place in their lives, and they themselves were made into different people because of this (443).

My second instance is a decidedly more formal and conventional project in the teaching of literature. The purpose was to embody and apply the aesthetic attitude in this field of teaching. Great poems, great plays, and great novels, it is pointed out, are great because they embody and symbolize the supreme emotional meanings and issues of life. So the aim of teaching should be to help young people to recognize and respond to these symbolized meanings. For instance, Shakespeare's *Antony and Cleopatra* was taken up with a class of high-school girls. The girls' first reaction was antagonism to Cleopatra as a home wrecker, an unscrupulous female cheat. So the teacher's task became helping them to see the wider issues and the true meaning of the play—how the interaction of all the characters produced a profound and moving tragedy (551).

My third instance is based on some recommendations for the teaching of appreciation, particularly of poetry, which were made a good many years ago by an official of the schools of London, named Frank Hayward. I have already referred to this plan, but it is pertinent here. Hayward recommends that when a poem is to be presented in class, the event should be made what he calls a "red-letter lesson." There should be an announcement several days beforehand. If any parts of the poem are likely to be hard to understand, these difficulties should be inobtrusively cleared up in advance. The presentation should be well-rehearsed and carefully staged, so that the poem itself can make its own distinctive effect. Then, after the presentation, there should be what Hayward calls "aesthetic discussion," i.e. discussion dealing with why one has liked or not liked the poem, what parts one particularly likes, etc. The whole idea is to present the poem as an expressive work of art, without any distractions, and with only enough emphasis on its content to be sure that the children are not blocked in understanding it (280).

In each of these three instances, as you will readily see, we have a central emphasis upon appreciation approached in various ways—otherwise put, a central emphasis upon aesthetic responsiveness, which is responsiveness to the emotional values and meanings embodied in and symbolized by organized design.

QUESTIONS FOR DISCUSSION

1. Apply the four statements as to how subject matter should be organized to some subjects not mentioned in this chapter.
2. Can one infer from what is said in this chapter that any subject in the curriculum can be taught in such a way that it will have value for anybody and everybody?
3. Consider some specific and practical ways in which bad teaching in a school can nullify the efforts of the guidance counsellor.

4. Bring together and discuss any arguments, whether explicit or implied, to the effect that the learning of subject matter is irrelevant to the shaping and development of personality.

5. Bring the suggestions in this chapter about the organization of subject matter into relationship with our earlier discussion of basic needs, and show how the various subjects as organized can help to satisfy basic needs.

6. Bring the discussions in this chapter into relationship with our earlier discussion of the kind of personality we want to develop, and consider to what extent the various subjects, when organized as indicated, might contribute to this desired outcome.

7. In the case of each subject discussed, show how the proposed organization is related to the four general points about the proper organization of subject matter.

8. What single issue or principle is involved in proposals for purely social arithmetic, for teaching science on a basis of immediate practicality, and for a pure "experience" program in reading?

SUGGESTED READINGS

Betts, Emmett Albert, "Developing Basic Reading Abilities." *Elementary English Review*, XX (1943), 312–320.

Hollingworth, Leta S., "An Enrichment Curriculum for Rapid Learners at Public School 500: Speyer School." *Teachers College Record*, XXXIX (1938), 296–306.

Thiele, C. L., "Arithmetic in the Lower Grades from the Point of View of Interrelationships in the Number System." *16th Yearbook*, National Council of Teachers of Mathematics (1941), Chap. 4, 45–79.

Wilson, Guy M., "The Social Utility Theory as Applied to Arithmetic, Its Research Basis, and Some of Its Implications." *Journal of Educational Research*, XLI (1948), 321–337.

16

Teaching and Evaluation in Relation to Personality

EVERYTHING in this book bears more or less directly—and for the most part more directly than less—upon the process of teaching. Moreover, I have tried, by means of comments and illustrations, to show the relationship of the psychological ideas that have been discussed to the practical business of teaching. Yet it is not the purpose of this concluding chapter merely to recapitulate or summarize what has already been said, or indeed to present a complete analysis of all the chief aspects of teaching. Rather I shall try to bring everything to a focus in terms of the following question: *What should be the teacher's controlling point of view, in the light of all that has been said in these pages, and on the assumption that the reality of all education is the shaping and molding of personality?*

It may be well to explain in advance how I shall endeavor to deal with this very large, very general question. First of all, it seems evident that a teacher needs a good, clear, working idea of the nature of teaching itself; and so we shall have to see just what interpretation of the nature of teaching emerges from all that has gone before in this book. Then there are three major phases of a teacher's work that need to be considered, and that serve very well as focal points for our present discussion. A teacher must organize and deal with subject matter; she must organize and deal with social situations and activities; and she must organize and conduct some system of evaluation. Each of these aspects of teaching have been touched upon frequently in previous chapters, but now it will be helpful to look at them directly. For, to repeat, our purpose here is not merely to summarize, or indeed to deal extensively with detail, but rather to bring everything into perspective, and to achieve a rounded understanding of the broad meaning of psychology for the practical work of the teacher.

THE NATURE OF TEACHING

In the first place, a teacher needs to have a clear, distinct, and correct understanding of the nature of teaching itself. Teaching has been defined as "the process of structuring the environment of an individual and organizing his activities so as to produce the desired behavior" (683). Putting the idea in other words, the essential business of a teacher is to create and organize situations in which human beings respond, learn, develop, and achieve fruitful adjustment.

This is a very simple idea, yet it is a very fruitful one, and every teacher will do well to return to it again and again. Every teacher, young or old, inexperienced or experienced, constantly tends to forget essentials in the press of her daily routines. She has lessons to prepare, records to keep, papers to mark, recitations to conduct, "ground" that she wishes to "cover" by some stated date. These exacting tasks and duties easily come to overshadow everything else, and to loom up as the be-all and end-all of teaching. Then the teacher becomes the slave of the schedule, the clock, the stated lesson, the textbook, and the marking system, so that her real effectiveness is compromised, and her own sense of the significance and the possibilities of her work evaporates.

If Thursday's lesson does not come on Thursday, if time which was to have been devoted to some designated topic is taken up by some side issue, if some of the material set up at the beginning of the term is still untouched at the end of it, how much does it matter? When one spends hours of hard work with a blue pencil dealing with pupil's themes, how much is one really serving and helping the pupils? When one totes up the figures in one's class book and decides that Jack's mark is B—, to what extent will the B— be a true picture of at least one small segment of Jack's education, and, above all, to what extent will the mark and the process of arriving at it really help Jack? These are questions of the kind that should be in every teacher's mind if she believes that the essential significance of her work is its effect on human beings. Of course there is no one simple answer to such questions. Of course one cannot advocate slovenliness or lack of plan. But the routines and tasks are not ends in themselves, although they very easily become so. In and of themselves the routines and tasks do not constitute the true inwardness of teaching, which is always the influence brought to bear on personality.

There is only one way in which we can influence any living being, and that is by creating and organizing a situation in which that living being will respond. A gardener cannot shape a flower by any kind of direct action. He can only provide soil, and fertilizer, and water, and protection from frost, weeds, and insect enemies. So too, a teacher can influence a child only by creating and organizing a situation in which that child will respond, and learn, and grow.

TEACHING AND LIFE PROBLEMS

The ultimate purpose of all teaching is to enable children and young people to discover ways of thinking, feeling, and acting which will constructively satisfy their basic needs. Putting the statement in the terminology which has been developed in these pages, the ultimate purpose of all teaching is to reveal need-satisfying goals to children and young people, and to help children and young people to discover how they can achieve such goals. Let me try to make this very general statement concrete.

Third graders in one city school carried on a unit study of ancient man. They learned about children of the cave men, the tree dwellers, and early herdsmen. Gradually their study expanded as they began to consider how the earth was formed, how coal was made, the formation of rocks and mountains. They gained some rudimentary geographic concepts of the earth, and learned to use maps. Their class obtained collections of fossils, minerals, and petrified wood. They drew pictures of dinosaurs they had seen represented at the museum. This project laid the foundation for more extensive studies in natural science, history, and geography the following year (301, p. 160).

Fourth graders in one school set up a weather bureau in their classroom, kept weekly and monthly weather records on a prepared chart, and studied the work of the United States Weather Bureau. They collected weather reports and weather bureau maps over a period of a month to test the accuracy of predictions in their locality.

Among the things they learned were:

1. How to use a thermometer.
2. How to use a barometer.
3. How to interpret a weather vane made by a pupil.
4. How to use a chart which gives simple ways to determine wind speeds.
5. To measure snow and rain accurately in a flat pan with ruler.
6. To determine the degree of blueness of paper dipped in cobalt chloride, the blueness depending on the amount of moisture in the air.
7. To recognize four main types of clouds: to describe the sky, day and night.

8. To keep an accurate daily record of weather conditions on the master chart (301, p. 161).

One teacher, in the poetry hour she conducts every week, tells the children to bring their favorite poems and asks them to take turns reading or reciting them. The teacher then proceeds to read other selections the children have requested. Then she teaches a new poem. She has the children list their chosen poems under headings: sad, action, stormy, and the like (301, p. 171).

A group of ten-year-olds studied the development of transportation in America since pioneer days and in modern times. Culminating ideas were expressed in dramatic form. From experiences growing out of the unit emerged various historical, social, geographical learnings, and many new concepts. They gained an appreciation of increasing speed in transportation, familiarity with outstanding figures in American history, better understanding of the complexity of life today as compared with the simplicity of life in other days, knowledge of the contributions of the Old World to the New, better understanding of what life was like in olden times, knowledge of the geographical divisions of the United States, the relationship between climate and topography, vegetation, and animal life, the westward march of the people, in other words an appreciation of how the American has changed himself and his country (301, p. 150).

In a junior high-school course in general science a unit was organized on methods of telling time. The uses of water clocks, hourglasses, and sundials were discussed, and some of the pupils made working models which were brought to class and demonstrated. The limitations of ancient as contrasted with modern methods of time-telling were analyzed. There was a visit to an international airport where clocks showed the time in various parts of the world. Running records of the accuracy of various time-keepers which were installed in the classroom were made, and in connection with these records there was extended consideration of the difficulties of early navigators in ascertaining distance due to defective time-keeping instruments.

These few instances of actual teaching, together with others which have been previously presented, bring out certain crucial points.

1. In each case a new possibility is revealed, a challenge is set up. Moreover, in each case it is a challenge which has some meaning and relevance to the lives and experiences of the children. The weather affects everybody. All of us use transportation and are dependent on it. All of us look at clocks and calendars. But very few of us think of the weather, or the clock, or the family automobile as a problem—or at least as representing a problem—worth considering and finding out about. Books of poetry fill many shelves in our libraries, but the existence and possibilities of poetry are not brought home to many children or, indeed, to many older people either. To refer to earlier instances that I have cited, children may be born and brought up next door to a textile mill, and all of them certainly move about in space; but it may never dawn on them that there is anything to be discovered or worth discovering about the textile industry or about space. So the first step in teaching is to bring to life for one's pupils at least a few of the problems, challenges, and possibilities with which the world abounds.

2. In each case that we have been considering, very varied processes of exploration and discovery were set going. Information was collected, reports were prepared, models were constructed, drawings were made; and very clearly the purpose of everything that went on was to bring insight to bear on the challenges that were presented. Children were helped and encouraged to explore poetry—that is to say, to find out what sort of poems there are in the world, and also to find out how to enjoy a poem.

3. In each of these cases there was a multitrack pattern of activities instead of the one-track pattern of the conventional teaching stereotype. Always there were many different things that different people could do—visiting libraries to get data,

making drawings, making models, formulating and editing final reports for display, choosing various poems, and so forth. The importance of multitrack activities is that they give many and varied opportunities for significant success. If everyone in a class has to do the same thing in the same way at the same time, we are bound to come out with a one-dimensional scale of success and failure, and probably with far more failure than success. So in the conventional teaching stereotype the most basic of all conditions for the shaping of motives is very meagerly fulfilled, whereas in the instances before us that condition is very well fulfilled.

4. In all these instances a wealth of subject matter is involved. Without subject matter none of the possibilities would be possible, none of the goals attainable, and, indeed, the undertakings could not even begin.

5. It is important to grasp the relationship of the undertakings that have been described, and of others like them, to basic needs. All of them have an obvious bearing on "integrative" or "ego" needs—on the need to understand experience, to symbolize experience (as in the case of poetry), to establish a working and integrating philosophy or point of view. Notice in particular that in each of the instances I have cited, there is involved some segment or aspect of life and experience, which is to be interpreted and understood in terms of available cultural materials. This is surely a very different matter from presenting a block of apparently isolated content, a lesson to be learned for its own sake out of relationship to anything else. To be sure, even the drabbest and most isolated of textbook assignments has a *potential* relationship to life, and can *potentially* serve as an agency for the better control, comprehension, and symbolization of experience. But the vital point is to bring the relationship directly home to the learner, so that he is at least dimly aware that he is not merely learning arithmetic, or grammar, or history, but also learning how to understand the

circumstances of his life more intelligently and how to deal with them more adequately.

But undertakings such as those I have described are not related only to integrative needs. A child's sense of achieving something, of coming to know and understand something, can certainly reinforce his self-confidence, and thus has an intimate bearing upon status needs. From the standpoint of mental hygiene a mark of C on a uniform one-dimensional scale may do a child very little good at all, even though it is a passing grade. But to have found out even a little about clocks, or money, or what the automobile has done to our national life, and to have done so through efforts that are largely self-directed, can be very reassuring indeed.

Moreover, undertakings such as those I have described lend themselves very well to group experiences of a constructive and helpful kind. In the unit on the telling of time, for instance, some of the children might make simple working models, others might visit a museum and bring back reports to the class, others might consult and report on library sources, others might prepare charts and graphs and sketches. All these diversified activities can figure as contributions to the group undertaking, and quite apart from the content of what is discovered and reported on, they can be very valuable experiences. They are experiences of belonging to and actively functioning with other people. They are experiences which help the individual to "find himself" in a social situation. Such experiences, we have every reason to believe, are highly satisfying to all human beings.

Furthermore, all the undertakings we have been describing are tied into the process of mental development. They are starting points. Moreover, they are *dynamic* starting points. Much of their value depends, not merely on the immediate results achieved, but on the continuing interests aroused. So we must take into account, not only their immediate, but also their prospective possibilities in the way of need satisfaction. In every case we can see the satisfaction of genuine needs here and now, and also the prospect of still richer satisfactions later on.

THE HUMAN SITUATION IN THE CLASSROOM

If we grant that the effectiveness of teaching turns upon its influence on personality, then one of the great responsibilities of the teacher is to make good use of the human situation in the classroom. We have already seen the great importance of encouragement, helpfulness, and positive motivation generally. All these ideas come together in the statement that the effective teacher will make all possible use of the dynamics of the classroom group. During the last ten years or so much attention has been given to the potentialities and values of group activities, and in fact a whole new field of study seems to be emerging, although somewhat hazily as yet, which goes by the name of *group dynamics*. The study of group dynamics deals with the social and psychological forces operating when a group of people work and act together (297). Although this subject of group dynamics is hardly more than an embryo, certain quite definite conclusions are possible which relate directly to teaching.

1. A series of very striking experiments in school and industry show the remarkable effect of what has been called a "democratic" attitude and orientation in a group. Thus three groups of ten-year-old children were engaged in making masks, doing mural-painting and soap-carving, constructing model airplanes, etc. These activities were associated with various clubs in the school and were quite familiar to the children and accepted by them as normal. One of the groups worked under an "authoritarian" policy, i.e. techniques were indicated by the leader, assignments were made by him, and all criticisms came from him. A second group worked under a "laissez-faire" policy, i.e. the leader simply passed out material, offered help

only when asked, did not participate. A third group worked under a "democratic" policy, i.e. the leader organized group decisions on assignments, techniques and methods of work, and also organized, encouraged, and guided group discussions and criticisms. Under the authoritarian policy the children were submissive, but kept demanding attention. There was very considerable covert aggressiveness and hostility both against the leader and the task, and much overt aggressiveness as between different children in the group. Under the laissez-faire policy the situation was even worse. There was much aggressiveness and quarreling among the children because of unresolved conflicts of motives and goals, and also a general tendency to criticize the leader as too easy-going. The democratic group presented a picture of happy effectiveness. There were very few conflicts. The leader was praised as a "good sport" who worked right along with everybody else, and the whole experience of co-operation was enjoyed. At the end of the time allotted for the experiment the "democratic" group wanted to go on with the work, but the "authoritarian" group most decidedly did not (398, 399).

This experiment will no doubt remind you of the similar experiment on factory efficiency, in which the workers were divided into small groups or teams and given much responsibility and freedom of choice (705). Another similar, though more limited, experiment used as subjects five girls at the Hawthorne Plant of the General Electric Company. These girls were segregated to find out the effect on worker-productivity of rest periods, a shorter working day, light refreshments, etc. It was found that changes in the physical conditions had very little effect unless those conditions were changed for the worse to an intolerable degree. But when a growth of group spirit was promoted by letting all the girls know what each one did, showing them group averages and so forth, there was a steady increase in productivity (721).

An experiment on problem-solving shows a very great effect produced by group work. Six puzzle problems were set up, and these problems were given to twenty-one students to work on individually, and to five groups of four students each. So far as could be told, the individual workers and the group workers were of equal ability. But in one part of the experiment the individual workers got an average of 5.7% of correct solutions while the group workers got an average of 27% (584).

In yet another experiment in which large numbers of high-school students were involved, they dealt with the problem of proper procedure and principles for the release of convicts from a near-by state prison. One of the students studied the problem and then discussed it. Other students studied the problem, and then instead of discussing it, restudied it. The former procedure yielded a much better understanding of the problem, and had much more effect in shaping attitudes towards it (676).

Once again, it was shown that pupils in the fourth, fifth, and sixth grades would study much more effectively for a history test when they themselves had made the questions, the teacher choosing from the total pool of suggested questions (748).

So in general, it is perfectly clear that a democratically organized co-operating group has a great effect on learning and achievement, as well as a more far-reaching and general beneficial effect on the personalities of the group members. Any task for which an individual feels a genuine shared responsibility tends to be made "ego-relevant."

2. Group management and group leadership is definitely an art. It calls for skill, insight, and understanding as well as amiability and kindliness. A good group leader will have certain definite considerations in mind; and many of these considerations have been clarified by investigation.

a) First, the effectiveness of any working group depends very much on the prevailing attitude and behavior of the leader. So far as the children are concerned, the sort of teacher they like best and for whom they will work best is one who is kind, sympathetic, considerate, good tempered, who does not shout or holler, who joins in games, tells stories, supplies interesting school projects, and who likes and praises *each one* of them. The sort of teacher liked least is unkind, unsympathetic, uses ridicule, is cross and cranky, has rigid discipline, is too strict, is inconsistent in her dealings, doesn't know much, and gives too much homework. These likes and dislikes are not arrived at by guesswork, but by extensive questionnaire studies involving large numbers of children (343).

Children's opinions are important and well worth considering, but they are not likely to be very penetrating. However, a rather elaborate investigation in which comparisons were made between twenty-seven good and forty-seven poor teachers comes to pretty much the same conclusions as those drawn from children's answers to questionnaires. According to this investigation a good teacher motivates her work indirectly by competition, rewards, and penalties, but chiefly uses direct motivation based on interest in the subject, by problem procedures, and in terms of the interests and experiences of the pupils. A poor teacher, on the other hand, tends to follow the textbook rigidly, makes little attempt to socialize or motivate the class, and tends to have bad discipline due to negative motivation (34).

All this gets us to a certain point, but a series of investigations of what have been called the "classroom personalities" of certain teachers carries the analysis a good deal deeper and points to some very interesting practical conclusions. These investigations dealt with "dominative" behavior on the one hand, and "socially integrative" behavior on the other. Dominative behavior is defined as an attempt to constrain another person to conform to one's wishes by force, orders, or attacks on status. Integrative behavior means getting cooperation by requests, explanations, suggestions, and so forth.

Dominative and integrative behavior may differ in degree. There may be domination with overt conflict or without overt conflict; and integrative behavior may vary from a more or less neutral condition to highly co-operative leadership. If a teacher says to her class, "I am going to sing you a song," this would be an instance of rather mild dominative behavior. If she says, "Would you like me to sing you a song now?" this would be a mild instance of integrative behavior; and if she goes on to ask what song it shall be, her integrative behavior would be still further developed.

It seems very clear from the results reported in the investigations, that integrative behavior is definitely more effective in producing good group and individual reactions. Under dominative behavior children were less attentive to their work, and there were more irrelevant pupil contacts and more aggressive responses. But the great practical point is that socially integrative behavior is a specific technique that can be learned. One teacher's soft voice did not prevent her classroom behavior being predominantly of the dominative type. Teachers tended to be prevailingly and rather consistently dominative or integrative in the classroom behavior.

It was found that teachers under observation tended to carry on their prevailing attitudes into another school year, when they would be dealing with a new group. There tended to be more dominative behavior in the afternoon than in the morning, probably because by afternoon the teachers were tired. Contacts initiated by the teacher tended to be dominative, but when contacts were initiated by pupils, there was more likelihood that the behavior of the teacher would be socially integrated. So we see that socially integrated behavior means more than the amiability and kindness which are noticed and valued by children. Such behavior amounts to a definite policy for getting along with people and getting them to do what one wants. You can undoubtedly set yourself to learn the techniques of socially integrative behavior with good prospects of increasing success; and such techniques are part of the equipment of a first-rate teacher (16, 17, 18).

b) Another point that a good group leader will have in mind is the social structure of the group with which he is dealing. An interesting technique, called the sociometric technique, has been developed for analyzing group structures. This technique consists essentially of asking group members some simple questions about their personal preferences for other members—whom they would like to go to lunch with, to work with, to play with, and suchlike. Usually a person is asked to give a first, second, and third choice in answering such questions. Then the answers are plotted in graphic form in what is known as a sociogram. A typical sociogram is shown below (p. 526). There are various refinements of the sociometric technique, but the essential idea of it is all that matters to us.

The practical value of the sociometric technique is that a leader who knows the social structure of a group can deal better both with the group as a whole and with the individuals in it. For instance, two children who have few friends or no friends can be seated together. Or an isolated child can be moved away from a closely knit subgroup whose members are so interested in one another that they ignore him. Or potential friendship groups can be put on committees or maneuvered into club memberships. Or a retiring child can be "brought out" by asking him to look after a newcomer in the class. Also, a teacher who knows her group can help isolated children to build social skills and acceptability, for instance, by a little coaching on playground games. In one case a teacher found that a boy was socially isolated because he smelled badly, and she was able to deal with the situation. In another case a teacher was able to build up the self-confidence of an isolated child by getting him to do some special work for the principal, for which he got many compliments and a good deal of recognition. In another case a teacher retained in her room the eight most isolated children when a grade reorganization took

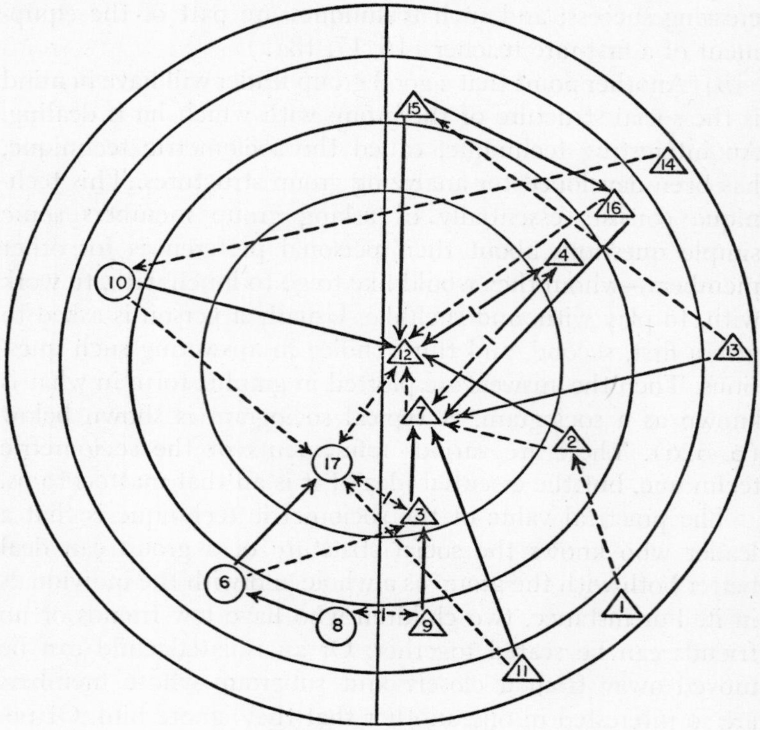

A TYPICAL SOCIOGRAM

This graph shows the luncheon preferences (i.e. the preferred luncheon companions) of 12 boys and 4 girls in a third grade. Solid lines indicate first choices, broken lines indicate second choices. Arrows indicate the person chosen. Double arrowheads indicate mutual choices. From Urie Bronfenbrenner, *The Measurement of Sociometric Status,* Sociometry Monographs, No. 6, New York, Beacon House, 1945, p. 38).

place. Furthermore, a knowledge of the structure of the group can be very helpful in managing interpersonal relationships. For instance, it often happens that an isolated child who cannot be reached directly by the teacher can be reached and influenced by some of the other pupils (135, 160, 344, 460).

c) Anyone who wants to become skilled in the art of group leadership should remember that patterns of group behavior do not come into being ready-made, and that, in fact, they often take considerable time to establish themselves. These patterns mature and develop with time and experience. Very little is known about the evolution of social and psychological patterns in working groups; but a good guess would seem to be that the members of the group come to define their functions (as leaders, followers, contributors, etc.) as time goes on (47, 408).

d) How large should a group be? Educational associations and state departments of education set up various external standards for class size; but psychologically speaking these regulations mean very little. The only possible answer is that a group should not be too large or too small to function together as a group—which is vague enough, to be sure. Small groups are certainly desirable with young children, and the same is probably true when we are dealing with many problem children from unstable or broken homes with whom it is important for a teacher to have as much personal contact as possible (295). On the other hand, Pressey has reported that large groups of students in educational psychology can be effectively socialized. But these people were, of course, undergraduates with an already existing common interest (532). Certainly the type of group that we want is entirely different from the type of fixed, "homogeneous" group often set up for special coaching under the most misleading name of remedial teaching. Instead of being remedial in any reasonable sense, group organization of this latter type can be extremely harmful and limiting. For instance, we may find a group of backward sixth-graders segregated to be coached in the special skills required in junior high-school, and forced to give up gymnasium, household arts, music and art, and much recreation. A practice like this is an educational atrocity which cannot but have baneful effects on the personality and future development of the pupils concerned. The very things that these children must give up are what they ought to have in the richest possible abundance. The very things on which they are forced to concentrate are the things likely to do them the least good (303).

e) Does emphasis on group behavior mean neglect of individual differences? Quite the contrary! If we use our group simply for educational mass production, i.e. as an opportunity to teach everyone the same thing in the same way at the same time, we have automatically created a problem of individual differences for which there is no possible good solution. But if we organize a functional, flexible group, each of whose members can co-operate on a joint enterprise in his own way, then the problem of individual differences is well on its way towards solution. Such a group fosters initiative, gives differential opportunity, reveals differential abilities, and points up the need for individual help where that need exists.

f) How much responsibility should be given to children in a democratically organized and functioning group? Just as much as possible, considering their maturity and experience. There can be no doubt whatever that teachers in general tend to put far too little trust in the judgment and good sense of children and young people. The working principle of good group leadership is certainly not laissez faire. But there is no doubt whatever that human beings of all ages work better when they feel a responsibility for their work, and when their choices and decisions are asked for and respected. I have already mentioned the case of the rather questionable play which was rehearsed extraordinarily well because it was the personal and group choice of the pupils themselves. There are many other instances pointing in the same direction, and in one striking case a group of high-school students under the leadership of their teacher were given freedom to plan an entire year's work, including materials, projects, and evaluation procedures, and did so successfully (223). Moreover, it is certainly true that if we wish to develop originality, initiative, and responsibility in general, we can only do so by creating situations in which these qualities can be exemplified (655).

3. Finally, let us summarize the values of effectively organized group behavior. To be specific, we want a group (*a*) which has a common aim (*b*) in which different individuals can make their own characteristic contribution (*c*) which has strong emotional bonds of affection and trust (*d*) whose members have a sense of oneness and belonging (391). What are the psychological values and advantages of such a group?

a) To begin with, such a group creates a very powerful positive motivation. To share in and contribute to the activities of such a group constitutes a goal which deeply satisfies status needs. The experience of belonging to it can be very valuable indeed. Opportunities for success are opened up, and success is recognized and accentuated in many ways and on many fronts (225).

b) Such a group is an ideal psychological setting for the learning of subject matter as it should be learned, i.e. by exploration, discovery, and insight. If you will refer back to the teaching undertakings described in the preceding section, you will see that, by implication, each and every one of them is a co-operative group project. A well-managed poetry hour certainly requires socially integrative behavior on the part of the leader. The study of time-telling, or of transportation, or of the weather, or of ancient man, as described, obviously involves a pattern of varied but co-operative activities. In fact, I would have not the least hesitation in saying that *subject matter is always best taught and best learned in a co-operative group situation.*

c) The experience of belonging to, working with, and learning with such a group can have a profound effect on the development of a child. In this experience the child can discover how to live and deal with others, and what democratic relationships and attitudes can really mean. Thus a seed is planted, a spark is kindled, and the stage is set for future developments of a very propitious kind.

EVALUATION

Evaluation, as the word is used in connection with teaching, means the appraisal of the efforts and achievements of pupils, the rating of those efforts and achievements in terms of some scheme of values. The proper management of evaluation is one of the vital responsibilities of every teacher; and to manage evaluation properly, it must be properly understood.

In the minds of many teachers, evaluation has to do simply and solely with the construction and administration of various types of tests, and the techniques for working out marks. They take it for granted that evaluation can be improved chiefly by better methods of test construction, and better statistical techniques for computing marks. No doubt technical competence in these phases of a teacher's work is desirable and important. But the idea that such competence is equivalent to good and effective evaluation is a most dangerous fallacy.

The real function of evaluation in teaching is *to develop the learner's own capacity for self-judgment and self-guidance.* A few concrete illustrations will make clear the meaning of this idea, and its essential soundness.

The teacher in charge of the woodworking shop in a certain school always starts a new class out on the construction of small bookshelves. Some people might argue that the pupils should be allowed, from the very first, to choose what they would like to do. But the teacher has a definite reason for his policy. The project is an easy one, yet it is not so easy that there is no challenge. It is something that the pupils can carry through successfully *if they try.* In particular, the teacher insists on the most meticulous perfection. The wood must be cut and grooved exactly right. The joints must fit to a hair's breadth. All surfaces must be sanded satin-smooth. The purpose is not so much to develop high skill at an early stage, as to reveal what standards of workmanship really mean. The pupils are constantly judging their own efforts, and the teacher is showing them how to make valid judgments. Moreover, the pupils are learning a great deal more than merely how to make an acceptable bookshelf. They are learning a lesson in how to judge themselves, how to overcome impatience, in being dissatisfied with anything less than the best they can do, in recognizing and coping with their own limitations. Such experiences can have and do have profound effects on personality, and they typify very well the true meaning of evaluation in education.

Again, a certain man in his early middle years has spent a good deal of time and effort in trying to teach himself to sing. He has a fairly good natural voice and a love of singing. No doubt it is a praiseworthy effort; but the trouble is that he entirely lacks any power of self-criticism. He is willing, nay eager, to sing on any and every occasion, and frequently manages to cause other people a good deal of pain and distress. Of all of this he is supremely oblivious. He is forth-putting, self-satisfied, and strikingly incompetent. Certainly one of the first tasks, and perhaps the most important single task of any teacher who might work with him would be to enable him to make a juster self-appraisal. Such self-appraisal would not necessarily mean discouragement so that all the rest was silence. What it ought to bring about would be a much better self-direction of effort, and a far-reaching change of attitude.

These two instances are typical of countless others. They show very clearly the true role of evaluation in the life and doings and experiences of human beings. Evaluation is important because, when it is valid and well founded, it enables one to do better and to learn better whatever one is trying to do or to learn. Furthermore, the critical self-judgment that one brings to bear on this or that particular undertaking can transfer widely and affect one's ways of dealing with many other challenges and problems—can, that is to say, have a pervasive effect on personality. It is in this sense that all teachers should understand and try to foster and promote evaluation. What, then, are the practical implications?

1. Teachers must help learners to evaluate themselves and their endeavors in relationship to the aim to be achieved. A boy who is making a bookcase has a definite aim, a definite purpose. He has, potentially at least, a criterion against which he can judge himself and his work. If he is left alone without any guidance, he may not use this criterion adequately. Very likely he will be satisfied with something quite slovenly and crude. The teacher's business is decidedly not to impose a purely external standard—not to tell the boy to do thus and so because the teacher says so, or because it is the "right way," or because the outcome will otherwise be a poor mark. What the teacher has to do is to enable the boy to see more clearly the true meaning, the true challenge of the boy's own purpose.

The function of a teacher who is trying to help a learner to improve his English style is exactly the same. The great majority of young people have very little idea of what it means to express themselves clearly and well in the English language, or how to set about learning to do so. They are content with outcomes which are probably far below their potential capacities. What then ought a teacher to do? What, indeed, can he do? What has to be done is first of all to create a situation where the learner *wants to say something,* and then to show him what must be accomplished in the way of planning, care, revision, and polishing if that "something" is to be well and clearly said. The conventional course in English composition does not fulfill these conditions. Such a course commonly seems to rely on quantity production. Large numbers of themes on topics of indifference to the writers are produced in a semester, and these themes are blue-penciled for the most crude and obvious of errors. So very little is done to stimulate the self-judgment and self-criticism which are absolutely vital for progress in English expression.

So the first and indispensable condition for good evaluation is that the learner himself must have an impelling goal. This is tantamount to saying that good evaluation is possible only in a well organized learning situation; for the process of learning, as we have already seen, is the process of discovering how to deal with a problem or challenge. Many instances of well organized learning in school have been presented in these pages—the working out of a theory of space by a group of students, the carrying on of a junior weather bureau, grappling with the mathematics of a class luncheon for parents and teachers, and so on. In all such instances there is obviously "built in" evaluation. The learners have a definite criterion by which to judge their own achievements and with reference to which they can guide and rectify their efforts. In such situations the function of the teacher is not to impose external standards, but to be sure that the children fully recognize the implications and demands of their own purposes.

2. Evaluation properly conducted is something in which both the teacher and the learners share. This is a condition that is often violated in conventional instructional practice. For instance, teachers very often give homework assignments consisting of such and such a body of material to be studied or such and such tasks to be done. The pupils are left to their own devices to deal with the assignment as best they can; and the next and concluding phase of the cycle is for the teacher to check up on how well they have succeeded, and to make a record which is often kept private. The effect is that the pupils do not really know how to cope with the assignment, and do not really know when or whether it has been dealt with adequately. Here is one of the root causes of ineffective study. On a larger scale, many courses are pointed towards examinations the nature and content of which are concealed from the learners. Thus the

learners are expected to work with an undefined and uncertain purpose, and without any clear criterion for self-guidance and self-criticism. In general, as long as a teacher regards evaluation as her own exclusive province, she is not doing what needs to be done to develop the learners' own power of self-judgment.

There are, however, many practical ways in which a teacher can transform evaluation into what it ought to be, namely a shared undertaking. For instance, a unit on the history of the local community was set up in a social studies course. Much of the class time was devoted to planning. Where could sources of material be found? What books were available in the local library? Could anything relevant be obtained at the state capital? Were there any old residents who could be interviewed? What about the origins of long-established business firms? When did the first railroad come to town? Such questions as these were carefully canvassed. Responsibilities for tapping various sources and collecting information were distributed among the pupils. As data came in they were examined and criticized. Some of the material was disappointing at first, or else it was inadequately reported, and the investigator was sent back for more. The nature of an appropriate final report was carefully and quite extensively considered, and the report itself went through a number of stages of development. Both the teacher and the learners were constantly evaluating the work in hand by a process of critical consideration and review which was shared by all concerned.

There can be much less ambitious and yet thoroughly sound applications of the idea of sharing responsibility for evaluation. For example, it is often found desirable to have a class discuss and decide upon the kind of test or examination that would seem appropriate. Or again, when a test or examination has been given, a considerable amount of time can often be profitably spent in studying and discussing its outcomes. Pupils can learn a great deal from coming to understand where and to what extent they have succeeded or failed. You should, to be sure, be warned that if you intend to try any such plan, you as the teacher must exert careful leadership. A teacher should certainly be able to make better and sounder evaluations than her pupils can; but it is not her business to judge the pupils as though they were factory products, but rather to help them to develop better evaluative standards of their own.

3. In all vital and purposeful learning, evaluation is continuous. It does not confine itself to end results. You will probably find this obvious from what has already been said, so I shall not develop the idea at great length.

By continuous evaluation we mean the continuous application of critical standards to what one is trying to do. Am I looking in the right place for information about the cave dwellers? Are my techniques for selecting and recording this information satisfactory? Is this news item about the weather bureau relevant to what our group is trying to accomplish? Have I a good plan for my poster showing the contrast between transportation now and a hundred years ago? Is this detail of my poster working out as it should? Is the report that I am developing about water clocks clear enough to be understood, and does it deal with everything that should be considered? These are the sort of questions that learners should ask themselves all the time while they are learning; for learning is a process of discovery, and discovery involves continual self-questioning, and such self-questioning is the heart of evaluation.

4. Good evaluation is many-sided. This is one of the places where the teacher can help most effectively, because often a child's self-evaluations are too narrow to be good.

For instance, a boy in the fourth grade cannot "carry a tune" when he sings. All he can see is his own inability to sing, and he judges that he is "unmusical" (though probably not in just those words). However, the teacher realizes that this boy has been badly humiliated in the third grade by being made to get up alone and try to "match tones," so that his inability to sing is due to a psychological block. Instead of pressing and forcing him, and giving him a low mark in music, she may give him the chance to learn and play some simple instrument. The teacher is able to take into account more than the boy could take into account, and so she is able to help him to deal with his problem better than he could deal with it all by himself. Furthermore, it is very likely that the teacher will help the boy not only to deal with his immediate problem, but also to achieve juster and more adequate standards of self-judgment.

We have here a single instance of a very general truth, namely, that a good teacher cannot disregard any aspect of a learner's personality in judging him or his endeavors. Such many-sided evaluation is in the sharpest possible contrast with the conventional narrow and one-sided evaluation which judges simply on the basis of test performance.

5. What is the place and function of teacher-made tests in evaluation? Here we come to an extremely practical and down-to-earth issue, for no matter what any psychologist may say, the making and giving of tests and examinations is an unavoidable part of the work of almost every teacher.

From the discussion so far it might seem that we are committed to the denial of any proper place at all to tests and examinations in the scheme of evaluation. This is by no means the case. Everything depends, however, on how tests are made and used and on the purposes they are intended to serve.

Let us try to look at the problem very simply and directly. Any expert and experienced learner who really knows his business and who is directing himself is likely to give himself tests of one kind or another from time to time. A fine golfer is trying to improve his swing. Most of his work is done at the net or perhaps on the practice tee or the practice green. But once in a while he plays a test round to see how things are coming along. A virtuoso pianist is learning a new piece. For the most part he studies its detail and its specific problems very analytically. But from time to time he takes a trial run through it. A man is teaching himself to read a new language. Again, for the most part he reads along as best he can, using grammar and dictionary when and as he needs them. But from time to time he may test himself out on an unfamiliar passage, or perhaps make a general trial review of his working vocabulary. Expert learners find such periodic self-testings very valuable as real and effective aids to better learning.

This shows how a teacher should think about the tests and examinations which she herself makes and uses. A *good test is an aid to learning.* This is its most essential and central characteristic. Once this idea is clearly grasped, a number of practical consequences become at once apparent.

a) A good test must have a clear-cut purpose. It is not enough to run a test for the sake of a vague "check-up," or to find out how much pupils know about material that has been "covered," or merely to make them work harder. A test must be directed towards some specific achievement, or it cannot be good.

One may want to find out whether learners can recall a large number of facts quickly and accurately, in which case one probably gives some kind of "objective" or short-answer test. One may want to find out whether they can produce a well-organized and well-expressed statement on some issue. One may want to find out whether they can indicate a method of dealing with mathematical problems, without perhaps working out complete solutions, in which case one may assemble a large number of problems and let the learners exercise choice. One may want to find out whether they can read and interpret material adequately, in which case the test may consist of a paragraph or even of many paragraphs to be read and interpreted. These are just a few illustrative samples of the explicit purposes for which tests can be made and used. In each and every such case the clear purpose is what makes possible the construction of a good test; and also the purpose, well understood, is what makes the taking of the test a constructive experience. If the purposes for which tests are constructed are developed in co-operative discussion with the learners, a teacher is likely to produce better tests in particular, and more effective evaluation in general.

b) The purpose of a test or an examination is more important than its form. There has been, and indeed still is, considerable debate in educational circles about the relative values of essay tests on the one hand and so-called "objective tests" on the other. Experts in measurement have tended to favor the "objective" type of test, and many teachers have followed their advice rather unthinkingly. But the matter cannot be decided in general or in the abstract. For everything depends on what the teacher is trying to *test for*, and of the actual effect of the test upon the purposes, processes, and future development of the learners.

The chief pros and cons of the issue may be summarized as follows:

(1) It is said that essay tests are extremely subjective, i.e. that in marking them a teacher is greatly influenced by purely personal feelings and opinions. This, however, is only true when essay-test questions are carelessly framed, and when teachers and learners are not clear about just what the questions are intended to elicit. "Discuss" questions, or "tell what you know" questions inevitably lead to subjective ratings. But when a broad question is carefully and clearly framed, and when all concerned understand its intention, then the situation is entirely different. Responses to such questions can be rated very objectively; and this, in practice, means that such responses can be rated in such a way that there will be substantial agreement as between the teacher, the learners, and everyone else concerned.

(2) It is said that objective tests are objective. This seems like a truism, because when we have actually called a test "objective" we have already begged the question of objectivity. But the issue is an important one, nevertheless. Objective tests are doubtless objective in outward form. But they often have a great deal of concealed subjectivity. One objective test on a

given body of material may concentrate largely on footnotes, statistical tables, proper names, and small inconspicuous details. Another objective test on the same body of material may concentrate on broad issues and generalizations. These differences are probably due to the personal opinions of the test makers about what is important. Thus they amount to a "built in" subjectivity which exists in spite of the outwardly objective form.

(3) Technically competent objective tests are extremely hard to make. To produce completion items which are meaningful, but which can be answered in only one way is a very difficult task. Also, it is very difficult to produce statements that are indubitably false, and yet not obviously so to a flagrant degree. Published objective tests, when they are properly made (which is not always the case) have gone through a long and painstaking process of tryout and revision, but very few teachers are either willing or able to take such pains with their own tests.

(4) Objective tests can be scored quickly and easily, whereas essay tests can be rated only by dint of care and hard work. This is quite true, yet it may actually work to the disadvantage of objective tests. The true function of a test is not merely to rate the learners, but to help them. A careful and thorough study and discussion of test responses can be a very valuable learning experience.

(5) Objective tests can cover more ground in a given time than essay tests. This also is true, but again it may not be an advantage. The appropriate purpose may precisely not be to cover ground, but to challenge learners to exercise some specific type of mental process—to think, to co-ordinate, to appraise, to find illustrations and applications.

From all this it is possible to derive two conclusions. First, the value of objective tests has certainly been overrated, and the value of essay tests has been underrated. Second, there is no clear general decision as between essay and objective tests.

The form of the test depends wholly upon the contemplated purpose.

c) The purpose of a test is more important than its statistical characteristics. Teachers are often told that the tests they make should be (1) *objective* and (2) *reliable.* The meaning of these two ideas is as follows. (1) A test is objective when the rating of it does not depend on the personal whims and opinions of the person who rates it. (2) A test is reliable when it would yield the same results if it were repeated one or more times with the same people and in the same situation.

What teachers need to understand is that objectivity and reliability are not general structural characteristics of the tests they make. They are characteristics entirely dependent on purpose. When teacher and learners jointly understand what a test is intended to reveal, and why and how it is intended to reveal this "something," then all concerned can reach a substantial agreement on the ratings. This is the true practical meaning of objectivity in connection with teacher-made tests. As to reliability, the issue is much more theoretical. A teacher-made test can never be given twice in the same situation, because once the test has been given the situation is changed. What teachers should aim at is to produce tests which will give a reasonably true picture of achievement as it now is—a picture true enough to help learners to guide themselves better and to help the teacher to guide them better.

Another general characteristic of tests is *validity,* i.e. the characteristic of actually measuring what it is intended to measure. Here we come straight back to our overriding notion of purpose. Unless a test has a clear-cut purpose, it cannot be valid in any significant sense, because no one really knows what the test is intended to reveal.

d) Everything connected with the administration of a test must be keyed to its purpose. Should a test be announced far in advance, or close to the date when it will be given, or not announced at all? Should a list of study questions be presented, or perhaps developed in class discussion, with the understanding that some of them will be used in the test? Should there be a choice of questions? Should pupils be allowed to use notes and references while taking the test, or is the more ordinary procedure of excluding the use of such materials preferable? There is no general answer to these or similar questions. It all depends on what the test is intended to achieve, and on the effect it is intended to produce on the learners.

One general statement, however, can be made. It is always very desirable to return any test and spend a good deal of time and care in discussing the responses that it has elicited. The reason should be perfectly clear. The constructive educational value of any test is the influence that it has on learning. A test is an instrument of evaluation; and no evaluation is what it ought to be unless it has the effect of developing the learners' capacity for self-criticism, self-judgment, and self-guidance.

e) In thinking about evaluation, teachers should always remember that the great danger in using tests and examinations is that these instrumentalities become objectives in their own right. Beyond any doubt a great deal of work in school is motivated primarily for the sake of "passing" examinations. Certainly there is no quick and easy cure for this weakness, for a primary weakness it most surely is. The best way to guard against it is to treat evaluation as a continuous process, as a shared process, as a many-sided process, so that tests and examinations only function as crucial or nodal challenges set up for definite and well-understood purposes, instead of being made in effect equivalent to evaluation as such.

6. What is the place and function of standardized educational tests in evaluation? There are enormous numbers of such tests on the market, and they are of many different types. There are very broad general survey tests, such as the Gray-Votaw General Achievement Tests, which deal with all the academic areas of the elementary-school curriculum. There are more specialized achievement tests in all the school subjects. There

are diagnostic tests which undertake to reveal the individual strengths and weaknesses of pupils. An instance of a diagnostic educational test is the Progressive Reading Tests, which are set up to show command of vocabulary and power of comprehension. Also there are a number of practice tests on the market. A typical instance of a practice test is the Courtis Practice Tests in Arithmetic. The first stage in this series is a set of tests on the first twelve lessons in arithmetic (assuming a certain course of study). A pupil who makes a satisfactory score can skip all these lessons, but any pupil whose score on one or more lessons is not satisfactory works at that lesson individually until he has raised his level of achievement.

In the hands of a well-informed and skillful teacher, standardized educational tests can be used to good effect. The best of these tests are the outcome of much research, and are very skillfully constructed. A good spelling test, for instance, consists of words which occur commonly in the language, and the words are graded for difficulty. A good test of English usage will center on the most frequent and, therefore, presumably the most important instances of good usage. In the same way, all such tests are made up of a *standard* selection of items, with *standard* instructions for administration, and a *standard* pattern of item presentation. In the case of many educational tests two or more forms equivalent in difficulty are available. Furthermore, norms are worked out based usually on large numbers of children, by means of the standardization group technique outlined in connection with intelligence testing. All these features make the best educational tests technically very convenient instruments.

Educational tests have numerous uses that are chiefly administrative. They make it possible to run comparisons of curricular achievement in different schools in the same school system, or as between different school systems. They can help to reveal weak and strong spots in a city-wide curriculum, and so to justify requests for financial readjustment, and so forth.

But what is of interest for us here is rather the value of educational tests in the classroom, as instrumentalities for good evaluation.

a) Educational tests can certainly help in the proper classification of pupils. It often happens that a pupil will do better work and get more out of school if he can be shifted to another group, either more or less advanced. Achievement tests can be very helpful in determining when such a decision may be wise.

b) To some extent educational tests can be used to show progress during the year. The reason for this is that equivalent forms of many tests are available, so that they can be given several times to the same children. The limitation here is that the test can only show progress in terms of what the test itself contains; and it may reveal either very imperfectly or hardly at all the sort of achievement that the teacher is trying to bring about.

c) By running a battery of well-chosen educational tests early in the year, a teacher can be helped in getting a picture of the abilities and disabilities of the group of children with whom she is dealing. She must, however, guard against the belief that any such tests can possibly give her all the information that she needs. The test is a *standardized* test, and what it reveals is a standardized pattern of achievement. This is its strength, but also its weakness. It can offer the teacher helpful suggestions and intimations, but in and of itself it certainly cannot define her instructional problem with anything like completeness.

d) Educational tests can do a good deal to reveal the effectiveness of various instructional procedures. For instance, when it is shown that a group of children who have done nothing but "social" or "projectwise" arithmetic right to the end of the third grade actually go far beyond the national norms on a standard arithmetic test, something very important seems to have been proved or at least strongly suggested.

e) Diagnostic tests can reveal weaknesses in a pupil's

equipment that might not otherwise be suspected. If a child is failing in arithmetic chiefly because he has never really grasped the technique of "carrying," it is important to know that this is so; and a good arithmetic test of diagnostic type is very likely to get to the root of the trouble.

f) Practice tests can be helpful in individualizing the work of groups of children. These tests first reveal individual weaknesses, and then provide practice material to overcome such weaknesses. So these instruments make possible a very efficient type of supervised study, in which as many as forty children in a room may each be working individually at his own weaknesses, while the teacher supervises and gives help as needed.

These are all constructive and desirable purposes. But there is one great and ever-present danger in using standardized educational tests. This is the danger that the tests may come to dominate the teaching. In schools where they are widely used, there is a strong temptation for teachers virtually to coach pupils for the tests. The teacher has reason to think that she can make a showing in and through her pupils' test performance, and naturally she tends to act accordingly. Moreover, when standardized tests are used on a state-wide basis, which seems to be an increasing tendency, the danger is even greater; for the tests can easily have a very considerable influence upon the curriculum itself. Most certainly it is not desirable to allow makers and publishers of standardized tests to determine what American children shall study, when they shall study it, or how they shall be taught.

7. What is the relationship of the marking system to evaluation properly understood? This is a question which every practical teacher is bound to raise, because the giving of marks is one of her major responsibilities. Yet unfortunately, there is no satisfactory answer.

The marking system in American education is essentially an administrative device. High-school graduation and college graduation are defined in terms of the accumulation of a stated number of "credits," i.e. separate courses. Moreover, these credits must be transferable from one institution to another. Hence a method of academic bookkeeping or accounting which will show the number of credits a student has accumulated at any given time becomes necessary. The marking system is the mechanism by which this method of accounting operates.

Administratively the marking system is very convenient. But as a device for recording human characteristics and achievements it has very grave defects. (*a*) The basis on which marks are assigned by teachers is extremely vague and ill-defined. A teacher's marks may be influenced by a pupil's effort, or his good or bad behavior, or the regularity of his attendance, or his showing on written tests, or the neatness of his work, and so on at great length. From the records in the registrar's office no one can be at all certain how it happened that a given individual got a given mark in such and such a course. (*b*) The basis of marking is usually quite narrow. Most teachers will agree that there are many aspects of a pupil's personality and behavior that they simply cannot take into account in assigning a mark. This, of course, precisely contradicts our claim that evaluation should be comprehensive and many-sided. (*c*) A mark indicates only relative standing, and usually relative standing in the class group. Thus a mark of A in French does not indicate any recognized level of achievement in speaking or reading French, but only that the student stands high in his class. So the same mark may mean quite different things for different teachers, or in different classes, or in different schools. All this means that as a system of psychological records the marking system is extremely ambiguous, to say the least.

Yet marks are extremely important. They have great prestige value. They are powerful motivators. Good marks open the way to many privileges in a school, to opportunities to go on with one's education, to scholarship awards, and perhaps to jobs and careers. Good marks are badges of distinction for which students are very willing to strive. To urge students "not to work for marks" while at the same time doing everything possible to make them primary rewards and incentives has an unpleasant suggestion of hypocrisy.

Now if anything is clear from these pages, it is that the influence of the school on personality depends essentially on setting up the right motivations. What, then, can be done to make the marking system a constructive influence for the shaping of personality and the determination of goals?

Improvements in the technique of marking are not likely to accomplish a great deal. Still, the most important of these improvements should be briefly reviewed for whatever they may be worth.

a) One suggestion is that marks should be assigned on some predetermined proportional distribution. A good many colleges have adopted some such plan. For instance, teachers may be instructed to give 5% of the students in their class A's, 20% B's, 50% C's, 20% D's, and 5% F's. Other percentages are also recommended and used in various institutions. No doubt a plan of this kind does something to regularize marking. But it is really quite arbitrary and has no logical foundation. The usual argument for some such scheme as that just described is that it forces marking into the normal probability distribution. This is supposed to be "scientific." As a matter of fact, it is nothing of the kind. A normal probability distribution appears when events occur according to pure chance. For instance, if one keeps on throwing a collection of ten pennies at random, there will be very few throws all heads or all tails, and the results will be about 50% heads and 50% tails. If, however, the pennies are worn at the edges or otherwise irregular, the normal distribution will not appear, because the operation of pure chance has been disturbed. But surely the whole endeavor of any teacher in dealing with learners is to disturb the operation of chance just as far as she can. She tries to get the learners to learn. The more high achievement she produces, the better she has succeeded. Hence a good teacher ought to produce in her class far more high marks than low ones. So the arbitrary application of a normal distribution to marks is a piece of sheer statistical nonsense.

b) Another suggestion is to "coarsen" the marking system, i.e. to avoid very fine distinctions between different marks or grades. From this point of view a marking system of A+, A, A–, B+, B, B–, C+, C, C–, D+, D, D–, F is preferable to a marking system running from 100 to 0 with a passing mark of 60. The reason is that in the former scheme there are fewer classifications. A straight "letter" system (A, B, C, D, F) would be better yet. A reduction in the number of grade classifications is undoubtedly an improvement, since the meaning of marks is very vague in any case, and when we use the system to register very small differences all its weaknesses become more serious.

c) Another suggestion is to require teachers to mark only on "achievement." Achievement in this sense usually means showing on formal written tests. There is a good deal to be said for this suggestion, because it tends to give marks a very definite meaning. The practical difficulty is that any teacher with even a glimmer of human insight knows perfectly well that many factors in a pupil's personality and development are at least as important or even more important educationally than his "achievement" on written tests.

Is there, then, any solution? None that is quick and easy! The way out is to organize the kind of comprehensive cumulative system of records that has been described elsewhere in this book. Such a system of records furnishes a far better basis for college admission, for promotion and grouping, for special treatment, and, in fact, for all educational purposes than a record that is entirely in marks. In the course of time a good system of comprehensive records can come more and more to overshadow the marking system. This seems to be the way out of the dilemma, for internal reforms of the marking system itself do not promise much in the way of genuine and substantial improvement.

So, in closing, it must be clear that evaluation is a most crucial educational issue, for on it depends ultimately the planned arousal of purpose and the direction of the will. Technically competent methods can never compensate for misdirected motivation; and if motivation is constructively directed, the problem of methodology is more than half solved. In the management of evaluation, as everywhere else in education, teachers should remember that "An environment can be set up to train either for stability of response, obedience, narrowness and rigidity of attitude, or for versatility of response, the exercise of judgment, self-reliance, and a broad attack on life's problems. Such directional tendencies seem not to be given by experiences with any single bit of subject matter or the mastery of any single skill; they are rather life patterns which become set from the general context in which the educational venture is carried forward. They depend in part at least, upon the range of stimulation, the attitudes common to experience, the context in which experience is had, and the capacity to tie together the elements of a life into an integrated whole" (23, p. 76).

Bibliography

1. Adkins, Dorothy C., *The Relation of Primary Mental Abilities to Vocational Choice*. American Council on Education Studies, Series 5, IV (1940), No. 2.

2. Aiken, Wilford M., *The Story of the Eight-Year Study*. Harper & Brothers, New York, 1942.

3. Allen, Clinton M., *Some Effects Produced in an Individual by Knowledge of His Own Intellectual Level*. Bureau of Publications, Teachers College, Columbia University, New York, 1940.

4. Allen, Mildred M., "Relationship between the Indices of Intelligence Derived from the Kuhlmann-Anderson Intelligence Tests for Grade I and the Same Tests for Grade IV." *Journal of Educational Psychology*, XXXVI (1945), 252–256.

5. ———, "Relationship between Kuhlmann-Anderson Intelligence Tests in Grade I and Academic Achievement in Grades II and IV." *Educational and Psychological Measurement*, IV (1944), 161–168.

6. Allport, Gordon W., "Attitudes," in Carl Murchison, ed., *Handbook of Social Psychology*. Clark University Press, Worcester, Mass., 1935.

7. ———, "Effect: a Secondary Principle of Learning." *Psychological Review*, LIII (1946), 335–347.

8. ———, *Personality: A Psychological Interpretation*. Henry Holt & Company, New York, 1937.

9. ———, "The Psychology of Participation." *Psychological Review*, LII (1945), 117–132.

10. Alsop, G. F., "How to Recognize Psychoneurotic Pupils," *Education Digest*, XI (March, 1946), 44–47.

11. American Association of School Administrators, *Youth Education Today*. National Education Association, Washington, D.C., 1938.

12. Ames, Louise Bates, "The Development of the Sense of Time in the Young Child." *Journal of Genetic Psychology*, LXVIII (1946), 97–125.

13. Ames, Viola, "Factors Related to High School Achievement." *Journal of Educational Psychology*, XXXIV (1943), 229–236.

14. Anastasi, Anne, *Differential Psychology*. The Macmillan Company, New York, 1937.

15. Anderson, Harold H., and Brandt, H. F., "A Study of Motivation, Involving Self-Announced Goals of Fifth-Grade Children and the Concept of Level of Aspiration." *Journal of Social Psychology*, X (1939), 209–232.

16. Anderson, Harold H., and Brewer, Joseph E., *Studies in Teachers' Classroom Personalities: I. Dominative and Social Integrative Behavior of Kindergarten Teachers*. Applied Psychology Monographs, No. 6 (1945).

17. ———, *Studies in Teachers' Classroom Personalities: II. Effects of Teachers' Dominative and Integrative Contacts on Children's Classroom Behavior*. Applied Psychology Monographs, No. 8 (1946).

18. ———, and Reed, Mary Frances, *Studies of Teachers' Classroom Personalities: III. Follow-up Studies on the Effects of Dominative and Integrative Contacts on Children's Behavior*. Applied Psychology Monographs, No. 11 (1946).

19. Anderson, Howard R., "Teaching Basic Skills in the Social Studies." *Elementary School Journal*, XXXVI (1935–1936), 424–435.

20. ———, *Teaching Critical Thinking in the Social Studies. 13th Yearbook*, National Council for the Social Studies, The Council, Washington, D.C., 1942.

21. ———, Forsyth, Elaine, and Morse, Horace T., "The Measurement of Understanding in the Social Studies." *45th Yearbook*,

National Society for the Study of Education (1946), Part I, Chap. 5, 71–103.

22. Anderson, John E., "The Development of Spoken Language." *38th Yearbook,* National Society for the Study of Education (1939), Chap. 10, 211–224.

23. ———, "Child Development and Education," *School and Society,* L (1939), 72–76.

24. Armstrong, Clairette P., "A Study of the Intelligence of Rural and Urban Children." *Journal of Educational Sociology,* IV (1931), 301–305.

25. Asker, William, "Does Knowledge of Formal Grammar Function?" *School and Society,* XVII (1923), 109–111.

26. Baker, Harold V., *Children's Contributions in Elementary School General Discussion.* Child Development Monographs, No. XXIX. Bureau of Publications, Teachers College, Columbia University, New York, 1942.

27. Baker, Harry J., *Introduction of Exceptional Children.* The Macmillan Company, New York, 1944.

28. Ballard, Phillip Boswood, *Obliviscence and Reminiscence.* British Journal of Psychology Monograph Supplement, I, No. 2 (1913).

29. Barker, Roger G., Kounin, Jacob S., and Wright, Herbert F., eds., *Child Behavior and Development.* McGraw-Hill Book Company, New York, 1943.

30. Barker, Roger G., Dembo, T., and Lewin, Kurt, *Frustration and Regression: an Experiment with Young Children.* University of Iowa Studies in Child Welfare, XVIII (1941), No. 1.

31. Barlow, M. C., "Transfer of Training in Reasoning." *Journal of Educational Psychology,* XXXVIII (1937), 122–128.

32. Barnes, Emily, and Young, Bess, *Children and Architecture.* Bureau of Publications, Teachers College, Columbia University, New York, 1932.

33. Barnes, Melvin W., "Gains in the A.C.E. Psychological Examination during Freshman-Sophomore Years," *School and Society,* LVII (1943), 250–252.

34. Barr, A. S., *Characteristic Differences in the Teaching Performance of Good and Poor Teachers in the Social Studies.* Public School Publishing Company, Bloomington, Ill., 1929.

35. Bassett, Sarah Jane, *Retention of History in the Sixth, Seventh and Eighth Grades with Special Reference to the Factors that Influence Retention.* Johns Hopkins University Studies in Education, No. 12 (1928).

36. ———, "Factors Influencing Retention of History in the Sixth, Seventh and Eighth Grades." *Journal of Educational Psychology,* XX (1929), 683–690.

37. Bavelas, A., "Morale and Training of Leaders," in Goodwin Watson, ed., *Civilian Morale.* Houghton Mifflin Company, Boston, 1942, 143–165.

38. Bayley, Nancy, "Factors Influencing the Growth of Intelligence in Young Children," *39th Yearbook,* National Society for the Study of Education (1940), Part II, 49–79.

39. ———, *Mental Growth during the First Three Years. A Developmental Study of Sixty-one Children by Repeated Tests.* Genetic Psychology Monographs, XIV (1933), No. 1.

40. ———, "Mental Growth in Young Children." *39th Yearbook,* National Society for the Study of Education (1940), Part II, 11–47.

41. ———, *Studies in the Development of Young Children.* University of California Press, Berkeley, Calif., 1940.

42. Bell, Howard M., *Youth Tell Their Story.* American Council on Education, Washington, D.C., 1938.

43. Bell, John Elderton, *Projective Techniques.* Longmans, Green & Company, New York, 1948.

44. Bender, Lauretta, and Frosch, John, "Children's Reactions to the War." *American Journal of Orthopsychiatry,* XII (1942), 571–586.

45. Bender, I. E., and others. *Motivation and Visual Factors.* Dartmouth College, Hanover, N.H., 1942.

46. Benezet, L. P., "The Story of an Experiment." *Journal of the National Education Association,* XXIV (1935), 301–303.

47. Benne, Kenneth D., and Sheats, Paul, "Functional Roles of Group Members," *Journal of Social Issues,* IV (1948), 41–49.

48. Benson, Viola E., "The Intelligence and Later Scholastic Success of Sixth Grade Pupils," *School and Society,* LV (1942), 163–167.

49. Bent, R. K., and Kronenberg, H. H., *Principles of Secondary Education*. McGraw-Hill Book Company, New York, 1941.

50. Bernard, L. L., *Instinct: A Study in Social Psychology*. Henry Holt & Co., New York, 1924.

52. Bernreuter, Robert G., "The Theory and Construction of the Personality Inventory." *Journal of Social Psychology*, IV (1933), 387–405.

53. Betts, Emmett Albert, "Developing Basic Reading Abilities." *Elementary English Review*, XX (1943), 312–320.

54. ———, "Readability: Its Application to the Elementary School." *Journal of Educational Research*, XLII (1949), 438–459.

55. ———, "Social and Emotional Readiness for Reading." *Educational Administration and Supervision*, XXX (1944), 65–86, 139–164.

56. Biber, B., *Children's Drawings: From Lines to Pictures*. Bureau of Educational Experiments, New York, 1934.

57. Biddle, W. W., *Propaganda in Education*. Bureau of Publications, Teachers College, Columbia University, New York, 1932.

58. Binet, Alfred, and Simon, Therese, *The Development of Intelligence in Children*, trans. by Elizabeth S. Kite. The Williams & Wilkins Company, Baltimore, 1916.

59. Bingham, Walter V., *Aptitudes and Aptitude Testing*. Harper & Brothers, New York, 1937.

60. Blair, Glen M., "The Content of Educational Psychology." *Journal of Educational Psychology*, XL (1949), 267–274.

61. ———, *Educational Psychology, Its Development and Present Status*. Bureau of Research and Service, College of Education, University of Illinois, Urbana, Ill., 1948.

62. ———, "The Psychological Basis of the Modern Curriculum: 6. How Learning Theory is Related to Curriculum Organization." *Journal of Educational Psychology*, XXXIX (1948), 161–166.

63. Bond, G., and Bond, E., *Developmental Reading in the High School*. The Macmillan Company, New York, 1941.

64. Bonney, Merl E., "Personality Traits of Socially Successful and Socially Unsuccessful Children." *Journal of Educational Psychology*, XXXIV (1943), 449–472.

65. Book, William F., *Learning to Typewrite*. The Gregg Company, New York, 1925.

66. ———, *The Psychology of Skill: with Special Reference to Its Acquisition in Typewriting*. University of Montana Publications in Psychology: Bulletin No. 53, Psychological Series No. 1, Missoula, Montana, 1908.

67. ———, and Norvell, Lee, "The Will to Learn." *Pedagogical Seminary*, XXIX (1922), 305–362.

68. Bordin, E. S., "A Theory of Vocational Interests as Dynamic Phenomena." *Educational and Psychological Measurement*, III (1943), 49–66.

69. Breckenridge, Marian E., and Vincent, E. Less, *Child Development: Physical and Psychological Growth through the School Years*, 2nd. ed. W. B. Saunders Co., Philadelphia, 1949.

70. Breslich, E. R., "Measuring the Development of Functional Thinking in Algebra." *7th Yearbook*, National Council of Teachers of Mathematics (1932), 93–118.

71. Brickman, William W., "Educational Psychology: a Review." *School and Society*, LXVIII (1948), 218–223.

72. Briggs, Thomas H., "Formal English Grammar as a Discipline." *Teachers College Record*, XIV (1913), 1–93.

73. ———, "Praise and Censure as Incentives." *School and Society*, XXVIII (1927), 596–598.

74. ———, "Sarcasm." *School Review*, XXXVI (1928), 685–695.

75. Brooks, Fowler D., "Intellectual Development from Fifteen to Twenty-two," in *Growth and Development, the Basis for Educational Programs*. Progressive Education Association, New York, 1936, 105–111.

76. ———, *The Psychology of Adolescence*. Houghton Mifflin Company, Boston, 1929.

77. ———, and Bassett, Sarah Jane, "The Retention of American History in the Junior High School." *Journal of Educational Research*, XXVIII (1928), 195–202.

78. Brown, Francis, "Knowledge of Results as an Incentive in Schoolroom Practice." *Journal of Educational Psychology*, XXIII (1932), 532–552.

79. Brown, L., Lauer, A. R., and Uhl, E., "A Study of the Improvement of Reading Rate and Comprehension." *Proceedings of the Iowa Academy of Sciences*, LI (1944), 367–370.

80. Brown, Warner, "Whole and Part Methods of Learning." *Journal of Educational Psychology*, XV (1924), 229–233.

81. Brownell, William A., *The Development of Children's Number Ideas in the Primary Grades*. University of Chicago Press, 1928.

82. ———, "Educational Research on Learning." *Educational Outlook*, VIII (1934), 210–219.

83. ———, "Learning Theory and Educational Practice." *Journal of Educational Research*, XLI (1948), 481–497.

84. ———, "Psychological Considerations in the Learning and Teaching of Arithmetic," *10th Yearbook*, National Council of Teachers of Mathematics (1935), 1–31.

85. ———, "Rate, Accuracy, and Process in Learning." *Journal of Educational Psychology*, XXXV (1944), 321–337.

86. ———, "Readiness and the Arithmetic Curriculum." *Elementary School Journal*, XXXVIII (1938), 344–354.

87. ———, "Remedial Cases in Arithmetic." *Peabody Journal of Education*, VII (1927), 100–107.

88. ———, "When Is Arithmetic Meaningful?" *Journal of Educational Research*, XXXVIII (1945), 481–498.

89. ———, and Carper, D. U., *Learning the Multiplication Combinations*. Duke University, Research Studies in Education, No. 7 (1943).

90. Brownell, William A., and Chazal, Charlotte B., "The Effects of Premature Drill in Third-Grade Arithmetic." *Journal of Educational Research*, XXIX (1935), 17–28.

91. Brownell, William A., and Sims, Verner M., "The Nature of Understanding." *45th Yearbook*, National Society for the Study of Education (1946), Chap. 3, 27–43.

92. Broyler, Cecil R., Thorndike, E. L., and Woodyard, Ella, "A Second Study of Mental Discipline in High School Studies." *Journal of Educational Psychology*, XVIIII (1927), 377–404.

93. Bruce, Robert W., "Conditions of Transfer of Training." *Journal of Experimental Psychology*, XVI (1933), 343–361.

94. Bruce, W. F., "The Psychological Basis of the Modern Curriculum: 5. How a Psychological Approach to Human Values Clarifies Educational Objectives." *Journal of Educational Psychology*, XXXIX (1948), 157–160.

95. Brueckner, L. J., "The Development of Ability in Arith-

metic." *38th Yearbook,* National Society for the Study of Education (1939), Part I, Chap. 15, 275–298.

96. ———, "The Social Phase of Arithmetic Instruction." *16th Yearbook,* National Council of Teachers of Mathematics (1941), Chap. 7, 140–156.

97. Bruner, Herbert B., *The Place of the Unit in Course of Study Construction.* State Department of Education, Pierre, S.D., 1930.

98. Bryan, William Lowe, and Harter, Noble, "Studies in the Physiology and Psychology of the Telegraphic Language." *Psychological Review,* IV (1897), 27–53.

99. ———, "Studies in the Acquisition of the Telegraphic Language. The Acquisition of a Hierarchy of Habits." *Psychological Review,* VI (1899), 345–375.

100. Burnett, Will R., "The Science Teacher and His Objectives." *Teachers College Record,* XLV (1944), 241–251.

101. Burr, Marvin Y., *A Study of Homogeneous Grouping.* Bureau of Publications, Teachers College, Columbia University, New York, 1931.

102. Bursth, James F., *Home and Community Conditions Related to Pupil Maladjustment. 15th Yearbook,* National Elementary School Principals, XV (1936), No. 6.

103. Burt, Cyril, "The Development of Reasoning in Children." *Journal of Experimental Pedagogy,* V (1919), 68–77.

104. ———, "Mental Abilities and Mental Factors." *British Journal of Educational Psychology,* XIV (1944), 85–94.

105. ———, "Personality, a Symposium: I. The Assessment of Personality." *British Journal of Educational Psychology,* XV (1945), 107–121.

106. ———, "Symposium on Personality: V. Reply to Criticisms and Conclusions." *British Journal of Educational Psychology,* XVII (1947), 6–19.

107. Buswell, Guy Thomas, "The Function of Subject Matter in Relation to Personality." *16th Yearbook,* National Council of Teachers of Mathematics (1941), Chap. 2, 8–19.

108. ———, *Fundamental Reading Habits: A Study of Their Development.* University of Chicago Press, Chicago, 1922.

109. ———, "Psychology of the Newer Methods of Teaching." *Elementary School Journal,* XLIV (1945), 14–22.

110. California State Curriculum Commission, *Teachers Guide to Child Development in the Intermediate Grades*. California State Department of Education, Sacramento, 1936.

111. ———, *Teachers Guide to Child Development. Manual for Kindergarten and Primary Grades*. California State Department of Education, 1933.

112. Campbell, Don W., and Stover, G. F., "Teaching International-mindedness in the Social Studies." *Journal of Educational Sociology*, VII (1933), 244–248.

113. Carritt, Edgar Frederick, *What Is Beauty?* Oxford University Press, New York, 1932.

114. Carrothers, George E., "It Takes Time for Children to Learn." *School and Society*, LXVIII (1948), 169–171.

115. Carter, Harold D., *Vocational Interests and Job Orientation*. Stanford University Press, Stanford University, Calif., 1944.

116. Chapin, H. Stuart, "A Quantitative Scale for Rating the Home and Social Environment of Middle Class Families in an Urban Community: a First Approximation to the Measurement of Socio-Economic Status." *Journal of Educational Psychology*, XIX (1928), 99–111.

117. Clapp, Frank L., *The Number Combinations: Their Relative Difficulty and the Frequency of Their Appearance in Textbooks*. University of Wisconsin Press, Madison, Wis., 1924.

118. Cleveland, Ohio, Board of Education, *Science Course of Study, Cleveland Elementary Schools*. Cleveland, Ohio, 1945.

119. Collings, Ellsworth, *An Experiment with a Project Curriculum*. The Macmillan Company, New York, 1923.

120. Commins, W. D., *Principles of Educational Psychology*. The Ronald Press, New York, 1937.

121. Conrad, Herbert S., Chairman, "Psychological Tests and Their Uses." *Review of Educational Research*, XVII (1947), 1–128.

122. ———, Freeman, F. N., and Jones, H. E., "Differential Mental Growth." *43rd Yearbook*, National Society for the Study of Education (1944), 164–184.

123. Cook, T. W., "Repetition and Learning: I. Stimulus and Response." *Psychological Review*, LI (1944), 25–36.

124. Cornell, Ethel L., and Coxe, Warren W., *A Performance*

Ability Scale: Examination Manual. World Book Company, Yonkers, N.Y., 1934.

125. Coryell, Nancy G., *An Evaluation of Extensive and Intensive Teaching of Literature.* Bureau of Publications, Teachers College, Columbia University, 1927.

126. Cox, J. W., "Some Experiments on Formal Training in the Acquisition of Skill." *British Journal of Psychology,* XXIV (1933), 67–87.

127. Coxe, W. W., *The Influence of Latin on the Spelling of English Words.* Journal of Educational Research Monograph, No. 17 (1924).

128. Crissey, Orlo L., *Mental Development as Related to Institutional Residence and Educational Achievement.* University of Iowa Studies in Child Welfare, XIII (1937), No. 1.

129. Cronbach, Lee J., "Educational Psychology." *Annual Review of Psychology,* I (1950), 235–254.

130. ———, "Norms and the Individual Pupil." *Proceedings of the 1948 Conference on Testing Problems,* Educational Test Service (1949), 75–78.

131. ———, "Test 'Reliability': Its Meaning and Determination." *Psychometrika,* XII (1947), 1–16.

132. Crossland, H. R., *A Qualitative Analysis of the Process of Forgetting. Psychological Monographs,* XXIX (1921), No. 1, Whole No. 130.

133. Croxton, W. C., "Pupils' Ability to Generalize." *School Science and Mathematics* XXXVI (1936), 627–634.

134. Cuff, Noel B., "The Law of Use." *Journal of Educational Psychology,* XX (1929), 438–447.

135. Cunningham, Ruth, *How to Construct a Sociogram.* Bureau of Publications, Teachers College, Columbia University, New York, 1947.

136. Curtis, Francis D., *Some Values Derived from Extensive Reading of General Science.* Bureau of Publications, Teachers College, Columbia University, New York, 1924.

137. Dashiell, J. F., "A Survey and Synthesis of Learning Theories." *Psychological Bulletin,* XXXII (1935), 261–275.

138. Davis, Allison, *Social-Class Influences upon Learning.* Harvard University Press, Cambridge, Mass., 1951.

139. Davis, R. A., "Testing for Aptitudes," *Journal of Educational Psychology,* XXXVI (1945), 39–45.

140. DeLima, Agnes, Baxter, Thompsie, and Francis, Thomas J., *South of the Rio Grande.* Bureau of Publications, Teachers College, Columbia University, New York, 1942.

141. Department of Rural Education of the N.E.A., *Community Resources in Rural Schools.* National Education Association, Washington, D.C., 1939.

142. Deputy, E. C., "Knowledge of Success as a Motivating Influence in College Work." *Journal of Educational Research,* XX (1929), 327–334.

143. Despert, J. L., and Pierce, M. O., *The Relation of Emotional Adjustment to Intellectual Function.* Genetic Psychology Monographs, XXXIV (1946), 3–56.

144. Dewey, J. C., *A Case Study of Reading Comprehension Difficulties in American History.* University of Iowa Studies in Education, X, No. 1 (1935).

145. Dietze, Alfred G., and Jones, George Ellis, "Factual Memory of Secondary School Pupils for a Short Article which They Read a Single Time." *Journal of Educational Psychology,* XXII (1931), 586–598, 667–676.

146. Doll, Edgar A., "The Nature of Mental Deficiency." *Psychological Review,* XLVII (1940), 395–415.

147. Dollard, John, and Miller, Neal E., *Personality and Psychotherapy.* McGraw-Hill Book Company, New York, 1950.

148. Dollard, John, and others, *Frustration and Aggression.* Yale University Press, New Haven, Conn., 1939.

149. Dorsey, Mattie E., and Hopkins, L. Thomas, "The Influence of Attitude upon Transfer." *Journal of Educational Psychology,* XXI (1930), 410–417.

150. Douglass, Harl R., and Spitzer, Herbert F., "The Importance of Teaching for Understanding." *45th Yearbook,* National Society for the Study of Education (1946), Part I, Chap. 2, 7–26.

151. Duff, J. F., and Thomson, Godfrey H., "The Social and Geographical Distribution of Intelligence in Northumberland." *British Journal of Psychology,* XIV (1923–1924), 192–198.

152. Dunlap, Knight, "A Revision of the Fundamental Law of Habit Formation." *Science,* LXVII (1928), 360–362.

153. ———, "The Technique of Negative Practice." *American Journal of Psychology*, LV (1942), 270–273.

154. Durflinger, G. W., "The Prediction of College Success—a Summary of Recent Findings." *Journal of the American Association of Collegiate Registrars*, XIX (1943), 68–78.

155. Durost, Walter N., "What Constitutes a Minimum School Testing Program?" *Educational and Psychological Measurement*, VII (1947), 45–60.

156. Eaton, M. T., *A Survey of the Achievement in Social Studies of 10,220 Sixth Grade Pupils in 464 Schools in Indiana*. Bulletin of the School of Education, Indiana University, Bloomington, Ind., XX (1940).

157. Edgerton, H. A., and Britt, S. H., "The First Annual Science Talent Search." *American Scientist*, XXXI (1943), 55–68.

158. ———, "The Science Talent Search." *Occupations*, XXII (1943), 177–180.

159. Edwards, A. L., "Rationalization in Recognition of a Result as a Political Frame of Reference." *Journal of Abnormal Psychology and Social Psychology*, XXXVI (1941), 224–235.

160. Elliott, Merle H., "Patterns of Friendship in the Classroom." *Progressive Education*, XVIII (1941), 383–390.

161. Ellis, Albert, "The Validity of Personality Questionnaires." *Psychological Bulletin*, XLIII (1946), 385–440.

162. Elwell, J. L., "The Effect of Knowledge of Results on Learning and Performance." *British Journal of Psychology*, XXIX (1938), 39–54.

163. Engelhart, Max D., "How Teachers Can Improve Their Tests." *Educational and Psychological Measurement*, IV (1944), 109–124.

164. Engle, T. L., "Study of the Effect of School Acceleration upon the Personality and Social Adjustments of High School and University Students." *Journal of Educational Psychology*, XXIX (1938), 523–539.

165. English, H. B., Welborn, E. L., and Killian, C. D., "Logical Learning: a General Review of Experiments with Meaningful Verbal Materials." *Psychological Bulletin*, XXXIV (1937), 1–20.

166. ———, "Paradoxical Forgetting or Learning without Overt Practice." *Psychological Bulletin*, XXX (1933), 697–698.

167. ———, "Studies in Substance Memorization," *Journal of Genetic Psychology*, XI (1934), 233–260.

168. Eskridge, T. J., *Growth in Understanding of Geographic Terms in Grades IV to VII*. Duke University Press, Durham, N.C., 1939.

169. Fahey, G. L., "What Every Teacher Can Do for Guidance." *School Review*, L (1942), 516–522.

170. Faulkner, Ray N., and Davis, Helen E., *Teachers Enjoy the Arts*. American Council on Education, Washington, D.C., 1943.

171. Fawcett, Harold P., *The Nature of Proof. 13th Yearbook*, National Council of Teachers of Mathematics, 1938.

172. Fenton, Norman, *Mental Hygiene in School Practice*. Stanford University Press, Stanford University, Calif., 1943.

173. ———, "Mental Test Scores and Self-Regard." *Educational Administration and Supervision*, X (1924), 103–108.

174. Finch, F. H., "Are High School Pupils of the Present Day Inferior to Those of an Earlier Period?" *School Review*, LII (1944), 84–91.

175. ———, and Gillenwater, V. W., "Reading Achievement Then and Now." *Elementary School Journal*, XLIX (1949), 446–454.

176. Fitzgerald, J. A., and Ludeman, W. W., "The Intelligence of Indian Children." *Journal of Comparative Psychology*, VI (1926), 319–328.

177. Florence Louise, Sister M., "Mental Growth and Development at the College Level." *Journal of Educational Psychology*, XXXVIII (1947), 65–82.

178. Flory, Charles D., Alden, Elizabeth, and Simmons, Madeline, "Classroom Teachers Improve the Personality Adjustment of Their Pupils." *Journal of Educational Research*, XXXVII (1944), 1–8.

179. Forlano, G., *School Learning with Various Methods of Practice and Rewards*. Bureau of Publications, Teachers College, Columbia University, New York, 1936.

180. Fowler, B., "An Appraisal of the Eight-Year Study of the Progressive Education Association." *Educational Records Supplement* (1941), 106–110.

181. Fox, Edith, "G-Men Chase the Outlaws." *Journal of the National Education Association,* XXVIII (1939), 122.

182. Fox, William H., "The Stability of Measured Interests." *Journal of Educational Research,* XLI (1947), 305–310.

183. Francis, K. V., and Fillmore, E. A., *The Influence of Environment upon the Personality of Children.* University of Iowa Studies in Child Welfare, IX (1934), No. 2.

184. Frandsen, Arden, "Interests and General Educational Development." *Journal of Applied Psychology,* XXXI (1947), 57–66.

185. ———, "Appraisal of Interests in Guidance." *Journal of Educational Research,* XXXIX (1945), 1–12.

186. Frank, Jesette, "The People in the Comics." *Progressive Education,* XIX (1942), 28–31.

187. Frank, J. D., "Recent Studies of the Level of Aspiration." *Psychological Bulletin,* XXXVIII (1941), 218–226.

188. ———, "Some Psychological Determinants of the 'Level of Aspiration.' " *American Journal of Psychology,* XLVII (1935), 285–293.

189. Frank, Lawrence, "The Fundamental Needs of the Child." *Mental Hygiene,* XXII (1938), 353–379.

190. Franklin, E. E., *The Permanence of Vocational Interests of Junior High School Pupils.* Johns Hopkins University Press, Baltimore, 1924.

191. Freeman, Frank N., "The Meaning of Intelligence." *39th Yearbook,* National Society for the Study of Education (1940), Part I, Chap. 1, 11–20.

192. ———, *Mental Tests: Their History, Principles, and Applications,* rev. ed., Houghton Mifflin Company, Boston, 1939.

193. Freeman, Frank S., "The Challenge of the Individual Child." *19th Yearbook,* Department of Elementary School Principals, National Education Association (1940), 235–257.

194. French, J. R. P., Jr., "Retraining an Autocratic Group Leader." *Journal of Abnormal Psychology and Social Psychology,* XXXIX (1944), 224–237.

195. Friedman, Kopple C., "Time Concepts of Junior and Senior High School Pupils and of Adults." *School Review,* LII (1944), 233–238.

196. Frogner, Ellen, "Grammar Approach versus Thought Ap-

proach in Teaching Sentence Structure." *English Journal,* XXVIII (1939), 518–526.

197. Fults, Anna Carol, "Improving Learning through an Emphasis on Human Relations." *Childhood Education,* XXIV (1948), 305–307.

198. Gardner, George A., "The Mental Health of Normal Adolescents." *Mental Hygiene,* XXXI (1947), 529–540.

199. Garrett, Henry E., "A Developmental Theory of Intelligence." *American Psychologist,* I (1946), 372–378.

200. ———, "The Effects of Schooling upon I.Q." *Psychological Bulletin,* XLIII (1946), 72–76.

201. Gates, Arthur I., "Connectionism: Present Concepts and Interpretations." *41st Yearbook,* National Society for the Study of Education (1942), Chap. 4, 141–164.

202. ———, "Failure in Reading and Social Maladjustment." *Journal of the National Education Association,* XXV (1936), 205–206.

203. ———, "The Nature and Limit of Improvement Due to Training." *27th Yearbook,* National Society for the Study of Education (1928), Chap. 23, 440–460.

204. ———, "Psychological vs. the Chronological Order in the Teaching of History." *Historical Outlook,* XI (1920), 227–230.

205. ———, *Recitation as a Factor in Memorizing.* Archives of Psychology, XL (1917).

206. ———, Batchelder, M. I., and Betzner, J., "A Modern Systematic vs. an Opportunistic Method of Teaching." *Teachers College Record,* XXVII (1926), 679–700.

207. Gates, Arthur I., and Bond, G. L., "Some Outcomes of Instruction in the Speyer Experimental School (P.S. 500)." *Teachers College Record,* XXXVIII (1936), 206–217.

208. Gates, Arthur I., Jersild, Arthur T., McConnell, T. R., and Challman, Robert C., *Educational Psychology.* The Macmillan Company, New York, 1942.

209. Gates, Arthur I., and Taylor, G. A., "An Experimental Study of the Nature of Improvement Resulting from Practice in a Mental Function." *Journal of Educational Psychology,* XVI (1925), 583–592.

210. ———, "An Experimental Study of the Nature of Improve-

ment Resulting from Practice in a Motor Function." *Journal of Educational Psychology* (XVII), (1926), 226–236.

211. Gates, G. S., and Risland, L. Q., "The Effect of Encouragement and Discouragement upon Performance." *Journal of Educational Psychology,* XIV (1923), 21–26.

212. Geddie, Leona, and Hildreth, Gertrude, "Children's Ideas about the War." *Journal of Experimental Education,* XIII (1944), 92–97.

213. Gellerman, William. *The American Legion as Educator.* Bureau of Publications, Teachers College, Columbia University, New York, 1938.

214. Gesell, Arnold, *The First Five Years of Life: A Guide to the Study of the Pre-School Child.* Harper & Brothers, New York, 1940.

215. ———, "Growth Potentials of the Human Infant." *Scientific Monthly,* LXVIII (1949), 252–256.

216. ———, "Stability of Mental Growth Careers." *39th Yearbook,* National Society for the Study of Education (1940), Part II, 149–159.

217. ———, and Amatruda, Catherine S., *Developmental Diagnosis.* Paul B. Hoeber, Inc., New York, 1941.

218. Gesell, Arnold, and Ilg, Frances L., *The Child from Five to Ten.* Harper & Brothers, New York, 1946.

219. ———, *Infant and Child in the Culture of Today.* Harper & Brothers, New York, 1943.

220. Gesell, Arnold, and Thompson, Helen, *Infant Behavior.* McGraw-Hill Book Company, New York, 1934.

221. ———, *Learning and Growth in Identical Twins.* Genetic Psychology Monographs, VI (1929), 1–24.

222. ———, *The Psychology of Early Growth.* The Macmillan Company, New York, 1938.

223. Giles, H. H., *Teacher-Pupil Planning.* Harper & Brothers, New York, 1941.

224. Gilliland, A. R., "The Rate of Forgetting." *Journal of Educational Psychology,* XXXIX (1948), 19–26.

225. Glad, Donald, "Grouping for Development." *Childhood Education,* XXV (1949), 354–356.

226. Goddard, H. H., *The Kallikak Family.* The Macmillan Company, New York, 1912.

227. ———, "What is Intelligence?" *Journal of Social Psychology,* XXIV (1946), 51–69.

228. Good, Carter V., "The Effect of Extensive and Intensive Reading on the Reproduction of Ideas or Thought Units." *Journal of Educational Psychology,* XVIII (1927), 477–485.

229. ———, "The Effect of a Single Reading versus Two Readings of a Given Body of Material." *Journal of Educational Method,* V (1926), 325–329.

230. ———, "The Relation of Extensive and Intensive Reading to Permanency of Retention." *Pedagogical Seminary,* XXXIII (1926), 43–49.

231. ———, *The Supplementary Reading Assignment.* Warwick & York, Inc., Baltimore, 1927.

232. Goodenough, Florence, *Developmental Psychology,* 2nd ed. D. Appleton–Century Company, New York, 1945.

233. ———, "New Evidence on Environmental Influence on Intelligence." *39th Yearbook,* National Society for the Study of Education (1940), Part I, 307–364.

234. ———, "The Use of Pronouns by Young Children: a Note on the Development of Self-awareness." *Journal of Genetic Psychology,* LII (1938), 333–346.

235. Goodman, Charles H., "Prediction of College Success by Means of Thurstone's Primary Abilities Tests." *Educational and Psychological Measurement,* IV (1944), 125–140.

236. Gopalaswami, M., "'Intelligence' in Motor Learning." *British Journal of Psychology,* XIV (1923–1924), 274–290.

237. Gordon, Hugh, *Mental and Scholastic Tests among Retarded Children.* Educational Pamphlets 44, Board of Education, London, 1923.

238. Gough, Harrison G., Factors Relating to the Academic Achievement of High School Students. *Journal of Educational Psychology,* XL (1949), 65–78.

239. Gowen, John W., and Gooch, Marjorie, "The Mental Attainments of College Students in Relation to the Preparatory School and Heredity." *Journal of Educational Psychology,* XVII (1926), 408–418.

240. ———, "The Mental Attainments of College Students in

Relation to Previous Training." *Journal of Educational Psychology,* XVI (1925), 547–568.

241. Grant, E. I., "The Effect of Certain Factors in the Home Environment upon Child Behavior." University of Iowa Studies in Child Welfare, XVII (1939), 61–94.

242. Gray, William S., "Education of the Gifted Child with Special Reference to Reading." *Elementary School Journal,* XLII (1942), 736–744.

243. ———, "Reading." *38th Yearbook,* National Society for the Study of Education (1939), Chap. 9, 185–209.

244. ———, and Holmes, E., *The Development of Meaning Vocabularies in Reading.* Publications of the Laboratory Schools of the University of Chicago, 1938, No. 6.

245. Greene, Edward B., *Measurement of Human Behavior.* The Odyssey Press, New York, 1941.

246. ———, "The Retention of Information Learned in College Courses." *Journal of Educational Research,* XXIV (1931), 262–273.

247. Greene, Harry A., and Gray, William S., "The Measurement of Understanding in the Language Arts." *45th Yearbook,* National Society for the Study of Education (1946), Part I, 175–200.

248. Gregory, W. S., "A Study of Stereotyped Thinking: Affective Reactions to Persons as Bases for Judging Their Nationality." *Journal of Social Psychology,* XIII (1941), 89–101.

249. Grener, N., and Raths, L., "Thinking in Grade Three." *Educational Research Bulletin* (Ohio State University), XXIV (1945), 38–42.

250. Grosnickle, F. E., "Transfer of Knowledge of Multiplication Facts to Their Use in Long Division." *Journal of Educational Research,* XXIX (1936), 677–685.

251. Gruen, Emily W., "Level of Aspiration in Relation to Personality Factors in Adolescents." *Child Development,* XVI (1945), 181–188.

252. Guiler, W. S., "Computational Weaknesses of College Freshmen." *Journal of the American Association of Collegiate Registrars,* XX (1944–1945), 367–382.

253. ———, "Disabilities of College Freshmen in Sentence Structure." *School Review,* LIV (1946), 480–487.

254. ———, "Spelling at the College Level." *Journal of the American Association of Collegiate Registrars,* XX (1944–1945), 96–105.

255. Guilford, J. P., "New Standards for Test Evaluation." *Educational and Psychological Measurement,* VI (1946), 427–438.

256. ———, "The Role of Form in Learning." *Journal of Experimental Psychology,* X (1927), 415–423.

257. Guthrie, E. P., "Conditioning: a Theory of Learning in Terms of Stimulus, Response, and Association." *41st Yearbook,* National Society for the Study of Education (1942), 17–60.

258. ———, and Powers, Francis F., *Educational Psychology.* Ronald Press, New York, 1950.

259. Hackenberg, J. L., Yeich, E. B., and Weisenfluh, L. A., "The Effect of Athletics on Certain Character Studies." *Journal of Educational Sociology,* VII (1933), 264–268.

260. Hake, Dorothy Terry, and Ruedisili, C. H., "Predicting Subject Grades of Liberal Arts Freshmen with the Kuder Preference Record." *Journal of Applied Psychology,* XXXIII (1949), 553–558.

261. Haggard, Ernest A., and Rose, Gilbert J., "Some Effects of Mental Set and Active Participation on the Conditioning of the Autokinetic Phenomenon." *Journal of Experimental Psychology,* XXXIV (1944), 45–59.

262. Hamblen, A. A., *An Investigation to Determine the Extent to which the Effect of the Study of Latin upon Knowledge of English Derivatives Can Be Increased by a Conscious Adaptation of Method and Content to the Attainment of the Objective.* Ph.D thesis, University of Pennsylvania, Philadelphia, 1925.

263. Hamley, Herbert Russell, *Relational and Functional Thinking in Mathematics. 9th Yearbook,* National Council of Teachers of Mathematics, 1934.

264. Harap, H. L., and Mapes, E., "The Learning of Decimals in an Arithmetic Activity Program." *Journal of Educational Research,* XXIX (1935–1936), 686–693.

265. ———, "Learning the Fundamentals in an Activity Program." *Elementary School Journal,* XXXIV (1933–1934).

266. Harms, Irene E., *Children with Inferior Social Histories: Their Mental Development in Adoptive Homes.* M.A. thesis, University of Iowa, Iowa City, 1941.

267. Harrison, Lucile M., "The Nature and Development of Concepts of Time among Young Children." *Elementary School Journal,* XXXIV (1933–1934).

268. Hartmann, George W., "A Critique of the Common Method of Estimating Vocabulary Size, Together with Some Data on the Absolute Word Knowledge of Educated Adults." *Journal of Educational Psychology,* XXXII (1941), 351–358.

269. ———, "The Field Theory of Learning and Its Educational Consequences." *41st Yearbook,* National Society for the Study of Education (1942), Chap. 5, 164–214.

270. ———, "Further Evidence of the Unexpectedly Large Size of Recognition Vocabularies among College Students." *Journal of Educational Psychology,* XXXVII (1946), 436–439.

271. ———, "Insight vs. Trial and Error in the Solution of Problems." *American Journal of Psychology,* XLV (1933), 663–677.

272. Haskell, R. I., *A Statistical Study of the Comparative Results Produced by Teaching Derivation in the Ninth Grade Latin Classes and in the Ninth Grade English Classes of Non-Latin Pupils in Four Philadelphia High Schools.* Ph.D. thesis, University of Pennsylvania, Philadelphia, 1923.

273. Hathaway, S. R., and McKinley, J. C., *Manual for the Minnesota Multiphasic Personality Inventory.* University of Minnesota Press, Minneapolis, 1943.

274. ———, "A Multiphasic Personality Schedule: I. Construction of the Schedule." *Journal of Psychology,* X (1940), 249–254.

275. Hattwick, L. A., and Stowell, M., "Relation of Parent Over-Attentiveness to Children's Work Habits and Social Adjustment." *Journal of Educational Research,* XXX (1936), 169–175.

276. Havighurst, Robert J., and Breese, Fay H., "Relation between Ability and Social Status in a Midwestern Community: III. Primary Mental Abilities." *Journal of Educational Psychology,* XXXVIII (1947), 241–247.

277. Havighurst, Robert J., and Davis, A., "Child Socialization and the School." *Review of Educational Research,* XIII (1943), 29–37.

278. Havighurst, Robert J., and Janke, L. L., "Relations between Ability and Social Status in a Midwestern Community: I. Ten-year-

old Children." *Journal of Educational Psychology*, XXXV (1944), 357–368.

279. Havighurst, Robert J., Kuhlen, Raymond G., and McGuire, Carson. "Personality Development." *Review of Educational Research*, XVII (1947), 333–344.

280. Hayward, Frank H., *The Lesson in Appreciation: An Essay on the Pedagogy of Beauty*. Macmillan & Co., Ltd., London, 1917.

281. Hazlitt, V., "Children's Thinking." *British Journal of Psychology*, XX (1929–1930), 354–361.

282. Heidbreder, Edna, "The Attainment of Concepts: VII. Conceptual Achievements during Card Sorting." *Journal of Psychology*, XXVII (1949), 3–39.

283. ———, "The Attainment of Concepts: a Psychological Interpretation." *Transactions of the New York Academy of Sciences*, VII (1945), 171–188.

284. ———, "The Attainment of Concepts: VI. Exploratory Experiments on Conceptualization at Perceptual Levels." *Journal of Psychology*, XXVI (1948), 193–216.

285. ———, "The Attainment of Concepts: II. The Problem." *Journal of General Psychology*. XXXV (1946), 191–223.

286. ———, "The Attainment of Concepts: III. The Process." *Journal of Psychology*, XXIV (1947), 93–138.

287. ———, "The Attainment of Concepts: I. Terminology and Methodology." *Journal of General Psychology*, XXXV (1946), 173–189.

288. ———, Bensley, Mary Louise, and Ivy, Margaret, "The Attainment of Concepts: IV. Regularities and Levels." *Journal of Psychology*, XXV (1948), 299–329.

289. ———, and Overstreet, P., "The Attainment of Concepts: V. Critical Features and Contexts." *Journal of Psychology*, XXVI (1948), 45–69.

290. ———, *An Experimental Study of Thinking*. Archives of Psychology, LXXIII (1924).

291. ———, "Problem Solving in Children and Adults." *Journal of Genetic Psychology*, XXXV (1928), 522–545.

292. ———, "Reasons Used in Solving Problems." *Journal of Experimental Psychology*, X (1927), 397–414.

293. ———, "A Study of the Evolution of Concepts." *Psychological Bulletin*, XXXI (1934), 673.

294. Heil, Louis M., Kambly, Paul E., Mainardi, Marons, and Weisman, Leah, "The Measurement of Understanding in Science." *45th Yearbook*, National Society for the Study of Education (1946) Part I, Chap. 6, 104–137.

295. Helseth, Inga Olla, "How Large Should a Class Be?" *Childhood Education*, XXIV (1948), 214–218.

296. Hendrickson, Gordon, and Schroeder, W. H., "Transfer of Training in Learning to Hit a Submerged Target." *Journal of Educational Psychology*, XXXII (1941), 205–213.

297. Hendry, Charles E., ed., *A Decade of Group Work*. Association Press, New York, 1948.

298. Henmon, V. A. C., and Nelson M. J., *The Measurement of Intelligence*. Houghton Mifflin Company, Boston, 1937.

299. Henry, Nelson B., *Science Education in American Schools. 46th Yearbook*, National Society for the Study of Education (1947).

300. Heyer, A. W., Jr., and O'Kelly, L. J., "Studies in Motivation and Retention: II. Retention of Nonsense Syllables Learned under Different Degrees of Motivation." *Journal of Psychology*, XXVII (1949), 143–152.

301. Hildreth, Gertrude, *Child Growth through Education*. The Ronald Press Company, New York, copyright 1948.

302. ———, "The Difficulty Reduction Tendency in Perception and Problem Solving." *Journal of Educational Psychology*, XXXII (1941), 305–313.

303. ———, "Hazards of 'Straight Promotion'" *Educational Administration and Supervision*, XXXII (1946), 19–26.

304. ———, *Learning the Three R's*. Educational Publishers, Inc., Minneapolis, 1947.

305. ———, "Personality Traits and Learning at School," in *Education for the Preservation of Democracy*. American Council on Education Studies, Series 35, XIII (1949), 90–92.

306. ———, *Readiness for Learning*. Association for Childhood Education, Washington, D.C., 1940.

307. ———, "Speech Defects and Reading Difficulties." *Elementary School Journal*. XLVI (1946), 326–332.

308. Hildreth, M. M., "Single Item Tests for Psychometric

Screening." *Journal of Applied Psychology,* XXIX (1945), 262–269.

309. Hilgard, Ernest R., *Theories of Learning.* Appleton-Century-Crofts, Inc., New York, 1948.

310. Hill, L. B., "Quarter Century of Delayed Recall." *Pedagogical Seminary,* XLIV (1934), 376–377.

311. Hirt, Zoe I., "Another Study of Retests with the 1916 Stanford Binet Scale." *Journal of Genetic Psychology,* LXVI (1945), 83–105.

312. Hobson, James R., "Mental Age as a Workable Criterion for School Admission." *Elementary School Journal,* XLVIII (1948), 312–321.

313. Hollingworth, Leta S., *Children above 180 I.Q. Stanford-Binet: Origin and Development.* World Book Company, Yonkers, N.Y., 1942.

314. ———, "An Enrichment Curriculum for Rapid Learners at Public School 500: Speyer School." *Teachers College Record,* XXXIX (1938), 296–306.

315. ———, "Personality and Adjustment as Determiners and Correlates of Intelligence." *39th Yearbook,* National Society for the Study of Education (1940), Part I, 271–305.

316. ———, and Cobb, M. V., "Children Clustering at 165 I.Q. and Children Clustering at 146 I.Q. Compared for Three Years in Achievement." *27th Yearbook,* National Society for the Study of Education (1928), Part II, 3–33.

317. ———, and Terman, Louis M., "The Significance of Deviates." *39th Yearbook,* National Society for the Study of Education (1940), Part I, 43–89.

318. ———, and Witty, Paul, "Intelligence as Related to Race." *39th Yearbook,* National Society for the Study of Education (1940), Part I, 257–269.

319. Hopkins, L. Thomas, "Exploring New Avenues of Measurement." *Curriculum Journal,* VI (1935), 22–25.

320. Horn, Ernest, *Methods of Instruction in the Social Studies.* Charles Scribner's Sons, New York, 1937.

321. Horn, Thomas D., "The Effect of the Corrected Test on Learning to Spell." *Elementary School Journal,* XLVII (1947), 277–285.

322. Hoyt, Franklyn S., "The Place of Grammar in the Ele-

mentary Curriculum." *Teachers College Record,* VII (1906), 467–500.

323. Huang, J., "Children's Concepts of Physical Reality: a Critical Summary." *Journal of Genetic Psychology,* LXIII (1943), 71–121.

324. Hull, Clark L., *Principles of Behavior.* D. Appleton–Century Company, New York, 1943.

325. ———, *Quantitative Aspects of the Evolution of Concepts.* Psychological Monographs, XXVIII (1920), No. 1, Whole No. 123.

326. Hurlock, Elizabeth B., *Child Development.* McGraw-Hill Book Company, New York, 1942.

327. ———, "An Evaluation of Certain Incentives Used in School Work." *Journal of Educational Psychology,* XVI (1925), 145–159.

328. ———, "The Psychology of Incentives." *Journal of Social Psychology,* II (1931), 261–289.

329. ———, "The Use of Group Rivalry as an Incentive." *Journal of Abnormal Psychology and Social Psychology,* XXII (1927–1928), 278–290.

330. ———, *The Value of Praise and Reproof as Incentives for Children.* Archives of Psychology, LXXI (1924).

331. Hyatt, A. V., *The Place of Oral Reading in the School Program.* Bureau of Publications, Teachers College, Columbia University, New York, 1943.

332. Jackson, J. A., "A Survey of the Psychological, Social, and Environmental Differences Between Advanced and Retarded Readers." *Journal of Genetic Psychology,* LXV (1944), 113–131.

333. Jackson, Robert W. B., and Ferguson, George A., *Studies on the Reliability of Tests.* Department of Educational Research, University of Toronto, Toronto, 1941.

334. Janke, L. L., and Havighurst, Robert T., "Relations between Ability and Social Status in a Midwestern Community: II. Sixteen-year-old Boys and Girls." *Journal of Educational Psychology,* XXXVI (1945), 499–509.

335. Jayne, C. D., "The Integrated versus the Non-Integrated Use of Motion Pictures in the Classroom." *Journal of Experimental Education,* V (1936), 7–16.

336. Jenkins, John G., "Validity for What?" *Journal of Consulting Psychology*, X (1946), 93–98.

337. Jenkins, M. D., *A Socio-Psychological Study of Negro Children of Superior Intelligence*. Ph.D. thesis, Northwestern University, Evanston, Ill., 1935.

338. Jensen, Kai, "The Social Studies." *38th Yearbook*, National Society for the Study of Education (1939), Chap. 17.

339. Jersild, Arthur T., *Child Development and the Curriculum*. Bureau of Publications, Teachers College, Columbia University, New York, 1946.

340. ———, *Child Psychology*, Prentice-Hall, Inc., New York, 1947.

341. ———, "Education in Motor Activities." *38th Yearbook*, National Society for the Study of Education (1939), Chap. 2, 57–83.

342. ———, "Examinations as an Aid to Learning." *Journal of Educational Psychology*, XX (1929), 602–609.

343. ———, and Holmes, F. B., "Characteristics of Teachers Who Are 'Liked Best' and 'Disliked Most.'" *Journal of Experimental Education*, IX (1940), 139–151.

344. Johnson, A. D., "An Attempt at Change in Inter-Personal Relationships." *Sociometry*, II (1939), 43–48.

345. Johnson, B. E., "The Effect of Written Examinations on Learning and on the Retention of Learning." *Journal of Experimental Education*, VII (1938–1939), 55–63.

346. Johnson, Donald M., "A Modern Account of Problem Solving." *Psychological Bulletin*, XLI (1944), 201–229.

347. Johnson, Elsie P., "Teaching Pupils the Conscious Use of Technique in Thinking." *Mathematics Teacher*, XVII (1924), 191–201.

348. Johnson, M., *Verbal Influences on Children's Behavior*. University of Michigan Press, Ann Arbor, 1939.

349. Johnson, Palmer O., "The permanence of learning in elementary botany." *Journal of Educational Psychology*, XXI (1930), 37–47.

350. Johnston, John R., and Lehman, H. C., "Should College Students Be Informed of Their Intelligence Ratings?" *Educational Administration and Supervision*, XVI (1930), 609–624.

351. Johnstone, E. R., "Discipline." *Training School Bulletin,* XL (1943), 118–120.

352. Jones, Arthur J., *Principles of Guidance,* 3rd ed. McGraw-Hill Book Company, New York, 1945.

353. Jones, Harold Ellis, *Development in Adolescence.* D. Appleton-Century Company, New York, 1943.

354. ———, and Conrad, Hert S., *The Growth and Decline of Intelligence.* Genetic Psychology Monographs, XII (1933), 223–298.

355. ———, and Blanchard, M. B., "Environmental Handicap in Mental Test Performance." *University of California Publications in Psychology,* V (1937), 63–99.

356. Judd, Charles H., *Education and Social Progress.* Harcourt, Brace and Company, Inc., New York, 1934.

357. ———, *Education as Cultivation of the Higher Mental Processes.* The Macmillan Company, New York, 1936.

358. ———, "The Relation of Special Training to General Intelligence." Educational Review, XXVI (1908), 28–42.

359. Kaplan, Louis, "Modern Trends in Teaching Language Arts in the Elementary School." *Elementary School Journal,* XLVIII (1948), 476–483.

360. Katona, G., *Organizing and Memorizing.* Columbia University Press, New York, 1940.

361. ———, "The Role of Order of Presentation in Learning." *American Journal of Psychology,* LV (1942), 328–353.

362. Keen, A., *A Study of the Growth of Concepts and of Reasoning Concerning Physical and Psychological Causation.* Ph.D. thesis, University of California, Berkeley, 1934.

363. Keister, Mary Elizabeth, "The Behavior of Your Children in Failure." University of Iowa Studies in Child Welfare, XIV (1937), 29–82.

364. Keliher, A. V., *A Critical Study of Homogeneous Grouping.* Bureau of Publications, Teachers College, Columbia University, New York, 1931.

365. Kelley, Truman L., "The Reliability Coefficient." *Psychometrika,* VII (1942), 75–83.

366. ———, "Values in High School Algebra and Their Measurement." *Teachers College Record,* XXI (1920), 246–290.

367. Kelty, Mary G., and Moore, Nelle E., "An Experimental Study of the Teaching of Current Events in the Middle Grades." *Elementary School Journal*, XXXII (1932), 417–425.

368. Kennedy, Leo R., "The Retention of Certain Latin Syntactical Principles by First and Second Year Latin Students after Various Time Intervals." *Journal of Educational Psychology*, XXIII (1932), 132–146.

369. Keys, Noel, "The Effect of True-False Items on Specific Learning." *Journal of Educational Psychology*, XXV (1934), 511–520.

370. ———, "The Influence on Learning and Retention of Weekly as Opposed to Monthly Tests." *Journal of Educational Psychology*, XXV (1934), 427–436.

371. Kilby, Richard W., "Relation of a Remedial Reading Program to Scholastic Success in College." *Journal of Educational Psychology*, XXXVI (1945), 513–534.

372. Kirkpatrick, E. A., "An Experiment in Memorizing vs. Incidental Learning." *Journal of Educational Psychology*, V (1914), 405–412.

373. Klineberg, Otto, *An Experimental Study of Speed and Other Factors in "Racial" Differences*. Archives of Psychology, XCIII (1928).

374. ———, *Negro Intelligence and Selective Migration*. Columbia University Press, New York, 1935.

375. Klopfer, B., and Kelley, D. McG., *The Rorschach Technique*. World Book Company, Yonkers, N.Y., 1942.

376. Knight, F. B., and Remmers, H. H., "Fluctuations in Mental Production when Motivation Is the Main Variable." *Journal of Applied Psychology*, VII (1923), 209–223.

377. Kornhauser, Arthur, "Replies of Psychologists to Several Questions on the Practical Values of Intelligence Tests." *Educational and Psychological Measurement*, V (1945), 181–189.

378. ———, "Replies of Psychologists to a Short Questionnaire on Mental Test Developments, Personality Inventories, and the Rorschach Test." *Educational and Psychological Measurement*, V (1945), 3–15.

379. Krueger, W. C. F., "The Effect of Overlearning on Retention." *Journal of Experimental Psychology*, XII (1929), 71–78.

380. ———, "Further Studies in Overlearning." *Journal of Experimental Psychology,* XIII (1930), 152–163.

381. ———, "Rate of Progress as Related to Difficulty of Assignment." *Journal of Educational Psychology,* XXXVI (1946), 247–249.

382. Kubie, Laurence S., "The Psychiatrist Considers Curriculum Development." *Teachers College Record,* L (1949), 241–246.

383. Kuder, G. F., *Manual of the Preference Record.* Science Research Associates, Chicago, 1946.

384. ———, and Richardson, M. W., "The Calculation of Test Reliability Coefficients Based on the Method of Rational Equivalence." *Journal of Educational Psychology,* XXX (1939), 681–687.

385. ———, "The Theory of the Estimation of Test Reliability." *Psychometrika,* II (1937), 151–161.

386. Kuhlen, Raymond G., and Lee, Beatrice J., "Personality Characteristics and Social Acceptability in Adolescence." *Journal of Educational Psychology,* XXXIV (1943), 321–340.

387. Kuhlmann, F., *Tests of Mental Development.* Educational Test Bureau, Minneapolis, 1939.

388. Lamson, Edna Emma, *Study of Young Gifted Children in High School.* Bureau of Publications, Teachers College, Columbia University, New York, 1930.

389. ———, "To What Extent Are Intelligence Quotients Increased by Children Who Participate in a Rich Vital School Curriculum?" *Journal of Educational Psychology,* XXIX (1938), 67–70.

390. Lane, Howard A., "Child Development and the Three R's." *Childhood Education,* XVI (1939), 101–104.

391. Lane, Robert H., *The Teacher in the Modern Elementary School.* Houghton Mifflin Company, Boston, 1941.

392. Larkin, G. Y., "How to Know Your Pupils," *Educational Method,* XXI (1942), 181–187.

393. Leeper, Robert W., "A Motivational Theory of Emotion to Replace 'Emotion as Disorganized Response.'" *Psychological Review,* LV (1948), 5–21.

394. Leonard, S. A., "How English Teachers Correct Papers." *English Journal,* XII (1923), 517–532.

395. Lewin, Kurt, "Field Theory of Learning." *41st Yearbook*, National Society for the Study of Education (1942), Part II, 215–242.

396. ———, "Intelligence and Motivation." *39th Yearbook*, National Society for the Study of Education (1940), Part I, 297–302.

397. ———, "Untersuchungen zur Handlungs und Affketpsychologie." *Psychologische Forschungen*, IX (1927), 1–85.

398. ———, Lippitt, Ronald, and Escalona, S. K., *Studies in Topological and Vector Psychology*. University of Iowa Studies in Child Welfare, XVI (1940), No. 3.

399. ———, Lippitt, Ronald, and White, R. K., "Patterns of Aggressive Behavior in Experimentally Created Social Climates." *Journal of Social Psychology*, X (1939), 269–299.

400. Lewis, M. M., *Infant Speech: A Study of the Beginnings of Language*. Harcourt, Brace & Company, New York, 1936.

401. Lewis, W. Drayton, "A Comparative Study of the Personalities, Interests, and Home Backgrounds of Gifted Children of Superior and Inferior Educational Achievement." *Journal of Genetic Psychology*, LIX (1941), 207–218.

402. ———, "Some Characteristics of Very Superior Children." *Journal of Genetic Psychology*, LXII (1943), 301–309.

403. ———, and McGehee, William, "Comparisons of Interests of Mentally Superior and Retarded Children." *School and Society*, LII (1940), 597–600.

404. Lindquist, E. F., "The Gap between Promise and Fulfillment in Ninth-Grade Algebra." *School Review*, XLII (1934), 762–771.

405. ———, "Norms of Achievement by Schools." *Proceedings of the 1948 Conference on Testing Problems*, Educational Test Service (1949), 95–97.

406. Lippitt, Ronald, "An Experimental Study of the Effect of Democratic and Authoritarian Group Atmospheres," University of Iowa Studies in Child Welfare, XVI (1940), No. 3, 45–195.

407. ———, "Field Theory and Experiment in Social Psychology: Autocratic and Democratic Group Atmospheres." *American Journal of Sociology*, XLV (1939), 26–49.

408. ———, "Socio-Psychological Research and Group Work,"

in Hendry, Charles E., ed., A *Decade of Group Work*. Association Press, New York, 1948, 166–177.

409. Lloyd-Jones, Esther, "Some Current Issues in Guidance." *Teachers College Record,* XLIX (1947), 77–88.

410. Lorge, Irving, "Intellectual Changes during Maturity and Old Age." *Review of Educational Research,* XVII (1947), 326–332.

411. ———, "Personality Traits by Fiat. I. The Analysis of the Total Trait Scores and Keys on the Bernreuter Personality Inventory." *Journal of Educational Psychology,* XXVI (1935), 273–278.

412. ———, "Personality Traits by Fiat. II. The Consistency of the Bernreuter Personality Inventory by the Bernreuter and the Flanagan Keys." *Journal of Educational Psychology,* XXVI (1935), 427–434.

413. ———, "Predicting Readability." *Teachers College Record,* LXV (1944), 404–419.

414. ———, "Schooling Makes a Difference." *Teachers College Record,* XLVI (1945), 483–493.

415. Lueck, William R., "How Much Arithmetic and Algebra Do Students of First Year College Physics Really Know?" *School Science and Mathematics,* XXII (1932), 998–1005.

416. McCarthy, Dorothea, "Personality and Learning." American Council on Education Studies, XIII, Series 1, No. 35 (1949), 93–96.

417. McClelland, T. N., *Overlearning and Review*. M.A. thesis, University of Iowa, Iowa City, 1940.

418. McClusky, H. Y., "An Experimental Comparison of Reading the Original and Digest Versions of an Article." *Journal of Educational Psychology,* XXXI (1940), 603–615.

419. McConnell, T. R., *Discovery vs. Authoritative Identification in the Learning of Children*. University of Iowa Studies in Education, IX (1934), No. 5.

420. ———, ed. *The Psychology of Learning. 41st Yearbook,* National Society for the Study of Education, 1942.

421. ———, "Reconciliation of Learning Theories." *41st Yearbook,* National Society for the Study of Education (1942), Chap. 7, 243–286.

422. McDaniel, J. W., and Reynolds, W. A., "A Study of the Use of Mechanical Aptitude Tests in the Selection of Trainees

for Mechanical Occupations." *Educational and Psychological Measurement,* IV (1944), 191–197.

423. McGehee, William, and Lewis, W. Drayton, "Comparisons of Certain Personality Characteristics of Mentally Superior and Mentally Retarded Children." *Journal of Educational Research,* XXXV (1942), 600–610.

424. ———, "The Socio-Economic Status of the Homes of Mentally Superior and Retarded Children and the Occupational Rank of Their Parents." *Journal of Genetic Psychology,* LX (1942), 375–380.

425. McGeoch, Grace O., "The Conditions of Reminiscence." *American Journal of Psychology,* XLVII (1935), 65–89.

426. ———, "The Factor of Degree of Learning in Reminiscence; a Second Comparative Study of Preschool Children and College Students." *Journal of Genetic Psychology,* XLVI (1935), 455–462.

427. ———, "The Intelligence Quotient as a Factor in the Whole and Part Problem." *Journal of Experimental Psychology,* XIV (1931), 333–358.

428. ———, "Revaluation of the Whole and Part Problem of Learning." *Journal of Educational Research,* XXVI (1932), 1–15.

429. ———, "The Whole-Part Problem." *Psychological Bulletin,* XXVIII (1931), 713–719.

430. McGeoch, J. A., "The Comparative Retention Value of Maze Habits and Nonsense Syllables." *Journal of Experimental Psychology,* XII (1929), 392–414.

431. ———, "The Comparative Retention Values of a Maze Habit, of Nonsense Syllables, and of Rational Learning." *Journal of Experimental Psychology,* XV (1932), 662–679.

432. McGraw, Myrtle B., *Growth. A Study of Johnny and Jimmy.* D. Appleton–Century Company, New York, 1935.

433. ———, "Later Development of Children Especially Trained during Infancy: Jimmy and Johnny at School Age." *Child Development,* X (1939), 1–19.

434. McGregor, Gregor, *Achievement Tests in the Primary School.* Publications of the Scottish Council for Research in Education, VI. University of London Press, Ltd., London, 1934.

435. McKenzie, Gordon, "Implications for Teachers and Coun-

sellors." *43rd Yearbook,* National Society for the Study of Education (1944), Part I, 300–331.

436. McNemar, Quin, *The Revision of the Stanford Binet Scale: an Aanlysis of the Standardization Data.* Houghton Mifflin Company, Boston, 1942.

437. Maller, J. B., *Cooperation and Competition.* Bureau of Publications, Teachers College, Columbia University, New York, 1928.

438. ———, "Vital Indices and Their Relation to Psychological and Social Factors." *Human Biology,* V (1935), 94–121.

439. Mapes, Charlotte, and Harap, Henry, *Six Activity Units in Fractions.* George Peabody College for Teachers, Nashville, Tenn., 1933.

440. Mason, M. M. "Effects of Attitudes of High School Teachers of Social Studies upon Attitudes of Their Pupils." *Purdue University Studies in Higher Education,* XLV (1942), 45–67.

441. Matheson, Eunice, "A Study of Problem-solving Behavior in Pre-School Children." *Child Development,* II (1931), 242–262.

442. Maurer, O. H., "The Law of Effect and Ego Psychology." *Psychological Review,* LIII (1946), 321–334.

443. Mearns, Hughes, *Creative Youth.* Doubleday, Page & Company, New York, 1926.

444. Meek, Lois H., Chairman, *The Personal-Social Development of Boys and Girls with Implications for Secondary Education.* Committee on Workshops, Progressive Education Association, New York, 1940.

445. ———, *A Study of Learning and Retention in Young Children.* Bureau of Publications, Teachers College, Columbia University, New York, 1925.

446. Melbo, Irving R., *Graduating High School Seniors' Information on Contemporary Social, Political, and Economic Problems and Issues.* Ph.D. thesis, University of California, Berkeley, 1934.

447. ———, "Information of High School Seniors on Contemporary Problems." *Social Studies,* XXVII (1936), 82–86.

448. Meltzer, H., *Children's Social Concepts.* Bureau of Publications, Teachers College, Columbia University, New York, 1925.

449. Melvin, A. Gordon, *Methods for New Schools.* The John Day Company, Inc., New York, 1941.

450. Meredith, G. P., "Consciousness of Method as a Means of Transfer of Training." *Forum of Education,* V (1927), 37–45.

451. Merrill, Maud A., "The Significance of I.Q.'s on the Revised Stanford-Binet Scales." *Journal of Educational Psychology,* XXIX (1938), 641–651.

452. Meyer, George, "An Experimental Study of the Old and New Types of Examinations: II. Methods of Study." *Journal of Educational Psychology,* XXVI (1935), 30–40.

453. Michell, F. C., "Ability of Fifth Grade Pupils to Understand Certain Social Concepts." *California Journal of Elementary Education,* IV (1935–1936), 20–28.

454. Miles, Catherine Cox, and Miles, Walter R., "The Correlation of Intelligence Scores and Chronological Age from Early to Late Maturity." *American Journal of Psychology,* XLIV (1932), 44–78.

455. Miles, Walter R., "Age and Human Ability." *Psychological Review,* XL (1933), 99–133.

456. Miller, George R., and Briggs, Thomas H., "The Effects of Latin on English Translations." *School Review,* XXXI (1923), 762–765.

457. Miller, Neal E., and Dollard, John, *Social Learning and Imitation.* Yale University Press, New Haven, Conn., 1941.

458. Mitchell, J. C., "A Study of Teachers' and Mental Hygienists' Ratings of Certain Behavior Problems in Children." *Journal of Educational Research,* XXXVI (1942), 292–307.

459. Monroe, Walter Scott, *How Pupils Solve Problems in Arithmetic.* University of Illinois, Urbana, Ill., 1929.

460. Moreno, J. L., *Who Shall Survive? A New Approach to the Problem of Human Interrelations.* Nervous and Mental Diseases Publishing Co., Washington, D.C., 1934.

461. Morgan, John J. B., *Child Psychology,* 3rd ed. Rinehart and Company, Inc., New York, 1942.

462. Morphett, M. V., and Washburne, Carleton, "When Should Children Begin to Read?" *Elementary School Journal,* XXXI (1931), 496–503.

463. Moser, Harold E., "Advancing Arithmetic Readiness through Meaningful Number Experiences." *Childhood Education,* XXIV (1948), 322–326.

464. Mowrer, O. H., "Authoritarianism vs. Self-Government in the Management of Children's Aggressive (Anti-Social) Reactions as a Preparation for Citizenship in a Democracy." *Journal of Social Psychology*, X (1939), 121–126.

465. Muenzinger, K. F., "Motivation and Learning. II. The Function of Electric Shock for Right and Wrong Responses in Human Subjects." *Journal of Experimental Psychology*, XVII (1934), 439–448.

466. Murphy, Gardner, *Personality*. Harper & Brothers, New York, 1947.

467. Murphy, L. B., "The Nursery School Contributes to Emotional Development." *Childhood Education*, XVI (1940), 404–407.

468. Murray, H. A., "Facts Which Support the Concept of Need or Drive." *Journal of Psychology*, III (1937), 27–42.

469. Mursell, James L., *Developmental Teaching*. McGraw-Hill Book Company, New York, 1949.

470. ———, *Education for Musical Growth*. Ginn and Company, Boston, 1951.

471. ———, *Music and the Classroom Teacher*. Silver Burdett Company, New York, 1951.

472. ———, *Psychological Testing*, 2nd ed. Longmans, Green & Company, New York, 1949.

473. ———, and Glenn, Mabelle, *Psychology of School Music Teaching*, 2nd ed. Silver Burdett Company, New York, 1936.

474. Mursell, James L., *Using Your Mind Effectively*. McGraw-Hill Book Company, New York, 1951.

475. ———, Pitts, Lilla Belle, and Young, Arthur, "The Measurement of Understanding in the Fine Arts." *45th Yearbook*, National Society for the Study of Education (1946), Part I, 201–212.

476. Myers, Garry C., *A Study of Incidental Memorizing*. Archives of Psychology, XXVI (1913).

477. National Committee on Science Teaching, *Redirecting Science Teaching in the Light of Personal-Social Needs*. National Education Association, Washington, D.C., 1942.

478. National Council of Teachers of Mathematics, "Second Report of the Commission on Post War Plans." *Mathematics Teacher*, XXXVIII (1945), 191–221.

479. Neff, W. S., "Socio-Economic Status and Intelligence." *Psychological Bulletin,* XXXV (1938), 727–757.

480. Nemzek, Claude L., "The Constancy of the I.Q." *Journal of Applied Psychology,* XVII (1933), 475–477.

481. ———, "The Constancy of the I.Q." *Psychological Bulletin,* XXX (1933), 143–168.

482. Nestrick, W. V., *Constructional Activities of Adult Males.* Bureau of Publications, Teachers College, Columbia University, New York, 1939.

483. Neuman, E. B., "Forgetting of Meaningful Material during Sleep and Waking." *American Journal of Psychology,* LII (1939), 65–71.

484. New York Meeting of the American Anthropological Association, *Science* (N.S.) 1939, 89.

485. Newburn, H. K., *The Relative Effect of Two Methods of Vocabulary Drill on Achievement in American History.* University of Iowa, 1934.

486. Newman, Horatio H., Freeman, Frank N., and Holzinger, Karl J., *Twins: a Study of Heredity and Environment.* University of Chicago Press, Chicago, 1937.

487. Nichols, M. Louise, "The High School Student and Scientific Method." *Journal of Educational Psychology,* XX (1929), 196–204.

488. Noll, Victor H., "The Habit of Scientific Thinking." *Teachers College Record,* XXXV (1933), 1–9.

489. ———, "Teaching Scientific Thinking." *Teachers College Record,* XXXV (1933), 202–212.

490. ———, "Measuring Scientific Thinking." *Teachers College Record,* XXXVI (1934), 685–693.

491. Northway, Mary L., "The Study of 'Difficulty'; with Reference to a Study of 'Whole-Part' Learning." *British Journal of Psychology,* XXVII (1937), 399–403.

492. Norton, Cecile I., *The Value of Theme-Correction in High School Composition Classes.* M.A. thesis, University of Southern California, Los Angeles, 1924.

493. Oakden, E. C., and Sturt, Mary, "The Development of Knowledge of Time in Children." *British Journal of Psychology,* XII (1922), 309–336.

494. Oakes, M. E., *Children's Explanations of Natural Phenomena.* Bureau of Publications, Teachers College, Columbia University, New York, 1946.

495. O'Brien, F. P., *An Experiment in Supervision of English.* University of Kansas, Lawrence, Kans., 1926.

496. ———, "The Vocabulary of High-School Pupils in Written Composition." *Journal of Educational Research,* XI (1925), 344–350.

497. Ogden, R. M., *Psychology and Education.* Harcourt, Brace & Company, New York, 1926.

498. Olson, W. C., and Hughes, B. O., "Concepts of Growth—Their Significance for Teachers." *Childhood Education,* XXI (1944), 53–63.

499. Orata, Pedro Tamesis, *The Theory of Identical Elements.* Ohio State University Press, Columbus, Ohio, 1928.

500. ———, "Transfer of Training and Educational Pseudo-Science." *Mathematics Teacher,* XXVIII (1935), 265–289.

501. Ordahl, Louise Ellison, "Consciousness in Relation to Learning." *American Journal of Psychology,* XXII (1911), 158–213.

502. Osborn, W. W., "An Experiment in Teaching Resistance to Propaganda." *Journal of Experimental Education,* VIII (1940), 1–17.

503. Osburn, W. J., *Are We Making Good at Teaching History?* Public School Publishing Company, Bloomington, Ill., 1926.

504. ———, "A Study of the Conversation of First Grade Pupils during Free Play Periods." *Journal of Educational Research,* XXIV (1931), 135–139.

505. Osgood, Ellen L., and Beall, Cornelia M., "Experimenting with the High School Misfit." *School Review,* XXXVI (1928), 779–786.

506. Otto, H. J., and Melby, E. O., "An Attempt to Evaluate the Threat of Failure as a Factor in Achievement." *Elementary School Journal,* XXXV (1935), 588–596.

507. Overman, J. R., *An Experimental Study of Certain Factors Affecting Transfer of Training in Arithmetic.* Warwick & York, Baltimore, 1931.

508. ———, "An Experimental Study of the Effect of Method

of Instruction in Transfer of Training in Arithmetic." *Elementary School Journal,* XXXI (1930–1931), 183–190.

509. ———, "The Problem of Transfer in Arithmetic." *10th Yearbook,* National Council of Teachers of Mathematics (1935), 173–185.

510. Panlasigui, I., and Knight, F. B., "The Effect of Awareness of Success or Failure." *29th Yearbook,* National Society for the Study of Education (1930), Part II, 611–621.

511. Pasamanick, B., "A Comparative Study of the Behavior Development of Negro Infants." *Journal of Genetic Psychology,* LXIX (1946), 3–44.

512. Pastore, Nicholas, *The Nature-Nurture Controversy.* Kings Crown Press, New York, 1949.

513. Pegram, Edna Lee, *A Study of Environmental Stimulus Reevaluated in Terms of Changes Made by Individuals.* M.A. thesis, University of Iowa, Iowa City, 1940.

514. Perrin, F. A. C., "Conscious Analysis versus Habit Hierarchies in the Learning Process." *Journal of Comparative Psychology,* I (1921), 287–308.

515. Peterson, Harvey A., *Educational Psychology.* The Macmillan Company, New York, 1948.

516. ———, "Recitation or Recall as a Factor in the Learning of Long Prose Selections." *Journal of Educational Psychology,* XXXV (1944), 220–228.

517. Peterson, John C., *The Higher Mental Processes in Learning.* Psychological Monographs, XXVIII, No. 7, Whole No. 129 (1920).

518. Peterson, Joseph, "The Effect of Attitude on Immediate and Delayed Reproduction." *Journal of Educational Psychology,* VII (1916), 523–532.

519. ———, "Learning when Frequency and Recency Factors Are Negative." *Journal of Experimental Psychology,* V (1922), 270–300.

520. Phearman, Leo T., "Comparisons of High School Graduates Who Go to College with Those Who Do Not." *Journal of Educational Psychology,* XL (1949), 405–414.

521. Piaget, J., *Judgment and Reasoning in the Child.* Harcourt, Brace & Company, New York, 1928.

522. ———, *Language and Thought of the Child*. Harcourt, Brace & Company, New York, 1926.

523. Pistor, F., "How Time Concepts Are Acquired by Children." *Educational Method,* XX (1940), 107–112.

524. *The Place of Mathematics in Secondary Education*. Final Report of Joint Commission of the Mathematical Association of America and the National Council of Teachers of Mathematics. Bureau of Publications, Teachers College, Columbia University, New York, 1940.

525. Poffenberger, A. T., "The Effect of Continuous Mental Work." *American Journal of Psychology,* XXXIX (1927), 283–296.

526. ———, "The Effect of Continuous Mental Work upon Output and Feelings." *Journal of Applied Psychology,* XII (1928), 459–467.

527. Postman, L., and Senders, V. L., "Incidental Learning and Generality of Set." *Journal of Experimental Psychology,* XXXVI (1946), 153–165.

528. Powers, S. R., "The Achievement of High School and Freshmen College Students in Chemistry." *School Science and Mathematics,* XXI (1921), 366–377.

529. ———, "A Comparison of the Achievement of High School and University Students in Certain Tasks in Chemistry." *Journal of Educational Research,* VI (1922), 332–343.

530. Prescott, Daniel, *Emotion and the Educative Process*. American Council on Education, Washington, D.C., 1938.

531. Pressey, Sidney L., and Robinson, Francis P., *Psychology and the New Education,* rev. ed. Harper & Brothers, New York, 1946.

532. Pressey, Sidney, and others, *Research Adventures in University Teaching*. Public School Publishing Company, Bloomington, Ill., 1927.

533. Preston, R. C., *Children's Reactions to a Contemporary War Situation*. Bureau of Publications, Teachers College, Columbia University, New York, 1942.

534. Price, Ray A., *The Use of Activities in the Social Studies*. Doctor's thesis, Harvard University, Cambridge, Mass., 1938.

535. Probst, K. A., and Benton, A. L., "A Comparison of Psy-

chiatric Ratings with Minnesota Multiphasic Personality Inventory Scores." *Journal of Abnormal Psychology and Social Psychology,* XLI (1946), 75–78.

536. Progressive Education Association, Commission on Secondary School Curriculum, *Language in General Education.* D. Appleton–Century Company, New York, 1940.

537. ———, *Science in General Education.* D. Appleton–Century Company, New York, 1936.

538. Puffer, Ethel D., *The Psychology of Beauty.* Houghton Mifflin Company, Boston, 1905.

539. Reed, H. B., "The Learning and Retention of Concepts: IV. The Influence of Complexity of the Stimulus." *Journal of Experimental Psychology,* XXXVI (1946), 252–261.

540. ———, "Meaning as a Factor in Learning." *Journal of Educational Psychology,* XXIX (1938), 419–430.

541. ———, "Why Do Some Colleges Reach a Higher Level of Achievement than Others?" *Journal of Educational Research,* XXXVIII (1944), 161–172.

542. Remmers, H. H., and Silance, Ella Belle, "Generalized Attitude Scales." *Journal of Social Psychology,* V (1934), 298–312.

543. Rice, J. M., "The Futility of the Spelling Grind." *Forum,* XXIII (1897), 163–172, 409–419.

544. Rice, P. B., "The Ego and the Law of Effect." *Psychological Review,* LIII (1946), 307–320.

545. Rice, R. S., "Extensive Reading Versus Intensive Textbook Study as a Means of Acquiring a Knowledge of Scientific Facts and Principles." *Journal of Experimental Education,* IV (1936), 376–402.

546. Riess, Anita, "An Analysis of Children's Number Responses." *Harvard Educational Review,* XIII (1943), 149–162.

547. ———, "Numerical Quantification versus Number Sense." *Journal of Psychology,* XV (1943), 99–108.

548. Rinsland, H. D., *A Basic Vocabulary of Elementary School Children.* The Macmillan Company, New York, 1945.

549. Robinson, Helen Mansfield, *Why Pupils Fail in Reading.* University of Chicago Press, Chicago, 1949.

550. Roper, Elmo, "What People are Thinking." *New York Herald Tribune,* January 4, 1945.

551. Rosenblatt, Louise, *Literature as Exploration*. D. Appleton-Century Company, New York, 1938.

552. Ross, C. C., "An Experiment in Motivation." *Journal of Educational Psychology*, XVIII (1927), 337–346.

553. ———, "The Influence upon Achievement of a Knowledge of Progress." *Journal of Educational Psychology*, XXIV (1933), 609–619.

554. ———, *Measurement in Today's Schools*. Prentice-Hall, Inc., New York, 1941.

555. Ruch, Theodora C., "Factors Influencing the Relative Economy of Massed and Distributed Practice." *Psychological Review*, XXXV (1928), 19–45.

556. Ruediger, W. C., "The Indirect Improvement of Mental Functions through Ideals." *Education*, XXXVI (1908), 364–371.

557. Ruger, Henry A., *The Psychology of Efficiency*. Archives of Psychology, XV (1910). Reprinted, Bureau of Publications, Teachers College, Columbia University, New York, 1926.

558. Ryans, D. G., *The First Step in Guidance: Self-Appraisal*. Cooperative Test Service Publications on Measurement and Guidance, 1941, No. 1.

559. Salisbury, Rachel, "Integration and Transfer in the Junior High School." *Junior-Senior High School Clearing House*, IX (1935), 423–427.

560. ———, "The Psychology of Composition." *English Journal*, XXV (1936), 356–366.

561. ———, "The Psychology of Punctuation." *English Journal*, XXVIII (1939), 794–806.

562. ———, "Some Effects of Training in Outlining." *English Journal*, XXIV (1935), 111–116.

563. ———, "A Study of the Transfer Effects of Training in Logical Organization." *Journal of Educational Research*, XXVIII (1934), 241–254.

564. Sandin, A. A., *Social and Emotional Adjustments of Regularly Promoted and Non-Promoted Pupils*. Child Development Monographs, XXXII (1944).

565. Sauble, Irene, "Enriching the Arithmetic Curriculum: Utilizing Supplementary Materials and Devices." *16th Yearbook*, National Council of Teachers of Mathematics (1941), 157–195.

566. Saunders, A. W., *The Stability of Artistic Aptitude at the*

Child's Level. Psychological Monographs, XLVIII (1936), 126–154.

567. Schaeffer, Grace C., "An Informational Unit on Time." *Elementary School Journal*, XXXVIII (1937–1938), 114–117.

568. Schindler, Alvin W., "Readiness for Learning." *Childhood Education*, XXIV (1948), 301–304.

569. Schmidt, Bernadine G., "The Rehabilitation of Feeble-minded Adolescents." *School and Society*, LXII (1945), 409–411.

570. Schmidt, Hermann, O., *The Effects of Praise and Blame as Incentives to Learning*. Psychological Monographs, XLIII, No. 3, Whole No. 240 (1941).

571. Schorling, Raleigh, "Trends in Junior High School Mathematics." *Mathematics Teacher*, XXXV (1942), 299–343.

572. Schulman, Mary Jean, and Havighurst, Robert J., "Relations between Ability and Social Status in a Midwestern Community: IV. Size of Vocabulary." *Journal of Educational Psychology*, XXXVIII (1947), 437–442.

573. Scottish Council for Research in Education, *The Intelligence of Scottish Children: A National Survey of an Age Group*. University of London Press, London, 1933.

574. Seagoe, M. V., "Additional Laboratory Experiments on Qualitative Wholes." *Journal of Experimental Psychology*, XX (1937), 155–168.

575. ———, "Influence of the Degree of Wholeness on Whole-Part Learning." *Journal of Experimental Psychology*, XIX (1936), 763–768.

576. ———, "Qualitative Wholes: a Re-evaluation of the Whole-Part Problem." *Journal of Educational Psychology*, XXVII (1936), 537–545, 612–620.

577. Sears, P. S., "Levels of Aspiration in Academically Successful and Unsuccessful Children." *Journal of Abnormal Psychology and Social Psychology*, XXXV (1940), 498–536.

578. Sears, Robert R., "Success and Failure," in *Studies in Personality*. McGraw-Hill Book Company, New York, 1942.

579. Segel, David, "State-wide Testing Programs." *School Life*, XXX (June, 1948), 25–26.

580. Shaffer, L. F., *The Psychology of Adjustment*. Houghton Mifflin Company, Boston, 1936.

581. Shaw, C., *Delinquency Areas.* University of Chicago Press, Chicago, 1929.

582. Shaw, Duane C., "A Study of the Relationships between Thurstone Primary Mental Abilities and High School Achievement." *Journal of Educational Psychology,* XL (1949), 239–249.

583. Shaw, Lena, and Crumpton, Claudia E., "The Attitude of the Child in Matters of Skill." *Elementary School Journal,* XXX (1929), 218–222.

584. Shaw, M. E., "Comparisons of Individual and Small Groups." *American Journal of Psychology,* XLIV (1932), 491–504.

585. Shearer, Elga M., and Fannin, Lois, "Reading for the Bright Child." *Library Journal,* LXXIV (1949), 1289–1291.

586. Sherman, Mandel, *Intelligence and Its Deviations.* Ronald Press, New York, 1945.

587. ———, and Henry, T. R., *Hollow Folk.* Thomas Y. Crowell Company, New York, 1933.

588. Sherman, Mandel, and Key, C. B., "The Intelligence of Isolated Mountain Children." *Child Development,* III (1932), 279–290.

589. Sheviakov, George W., and Redl, Fritz, *Discipline for Today's Children and Youth.* Department of Supervision and Curriculum Development, National Education Association, Washington, D.C., 1944.

590. Shimberg, Myra E., *An Investigation into the Validity of Norms with Special Reference to Urban and Rural Groups.* Archives of Psychology, CIV (1929).

591. Shuttleworth, F. K., *The Adolescent Period: A Graphic and Pictorial Atlas.* National Research Council, New York, 1938.

592. Sifert, E. R., *A Comparative Study of the Abilities of Eighth Grade Children to Spell Studied and Unstudied Words.* M.A. thesis, University of Iowa, Iowa City, 1926.

593. Simpson, Robert Gilkey, "The Effect of Specific Training on the Ability to Read Historical Materials." *Journal of Educational Research,* XX (1929), 343–351.

594. Simrall, Dorothy, "Intelligence and the Ability to Learn." *Journal of Psychology,* XXIII (1947), 27–43.

595. Sims, Verner M., "Educational Measurement and Evaluation." *Journal of Educational Research,* XXXVIII (1944), 18–24.

596. ———, "The Relative Influence of Two Types of Motivation on Improvement." *Journal of Educational Psychology,* XIX (1928), 480–484.

597. Skaggs, E. B., "Ten Basic Postulates of Personalistic Psychology." *Psychological Review,* LIV (1947), 255–262.

598. Skeels, Harold M., and Dye, Harold B., "A Study of the Effects of Differential Stimulation on Mentally Retarded Children." *Proceedings of the American Association for Mental Deficiency,* XLIV (1939), 114–136.

599. Skeels, Harold M., Updegraff, Ruth, Wellman, Beth L., and Williams, Harold M., *A Study of Environmental Stimulation: An Orphanage Preschool Project.* University of Iowa Studies in Child Welfare, XV (1938), No. 4.

601. Smith, M., and Macdougall, William, "Some Experiments on Learning and Retention." *British Journal of Psychology,* X (1919–1920), 199–209.

602. Smith, M. E., *An Investigation of the Development of the Sentence and the Extent of Vocabulary in Young Children.* University of Iowa Studies in Child Welfare, III, No. 5 (1926).

603. Smith, M. K., *Measurement of the Size of General English Vocabulary through the Elementary Grades and High School.* Genetic Psychology Monographs, XXIV (1941), 311–345.

604. Smoke, Kenneth L., "Negative Instances in Concept Learning." *Journal of Experimental Psychology,* XVI (1933), 583–588.

605. ———, *An Objective Study of Concept Formation.* Psychological Monographs, XLII, No. 4, Whole No. 191 (1932).

606. Snoddy, George S., *An Experimental Analysis of a Case of Trial and Error Learning in the Human Subject.* Psychological Monographs, XXVIII, No. 2, Whole No. 124 (1920).

607. ———, "Learning and Stability. A Psychological Analysis of a Case of Motor Learning with Clinical Applications." *Journal of Applied Psychology,* X (1926), 1–36.

608. Sorenson, Herbert, "Mental Ability over a Wide Range of Adult Ages." *Journal of Applied Psychology,* XVII (1933), 729–741.

609. ———, *Psychology in Education,* 2nd ed. McGraw-Hill Book Company, New York, 1948.

610. Sparkman, Colley F., "An Analysis of the Fundamental

Problem in Learning to Read a Foreign Language." *Modern Language Journal,* XIII (1928–1929), 1–14.

611. Speer, George S., "The Intelligence of Foster Children." *Journal of Genetic Psychology,* LVII (1940), 49–55.

612. Spitzer, H. F., "Studies in Retention." *Journal of Educational Psychology,* XXX (1939), 641–656.

613. Staff of the Division on Child Development and Teacher Personnel, Commission on Teacher Education, American Council on Education, *Helping Teachers Understand Children.* American Council on Education, Washington, D.C., 1945.

614. Stern, Catherine, *Children Discover Arithmetic; An Introduction to Structural Arithmetic.* Harper & Brothers, New York, 1949.

615. Stoddard, George B., "Intellectual Development of the Child: an Answer to the Critics of the Iowa Studies." *School and Society,* LI (1940), 529–536.

616. ———, *The Meaning of Intelligence.* The Macmillan Company, New York, 1943.

617. Strang, Ruth, "Group Work in Schools and Institutions of Higher Learning," in Charles E. Hendry, ed., *A Decade of Group Work,* Association Press, New York, 1948, 95–104.

618. ———, "Why Children Read the Comics." *Elementary School Journal,* XLIII (1943), 336–342.

619. Strong, E. K., Jr., *Changes of Interests with Age.* Stanford University Press, Stanford University, Calif., 1931.

620. ———, *Vocational Interests of Men and Women.* Stanford University Press, Stanford University, Calif., 1943.

621. Stroud, James B., *Psychology in Education.* Longmans, Green & Co., New York, 1946.

622. Stumpf, Carl, *Die Anfänge der Musik.* Barth, Leipzig, 1911.

623. Stutsman, Rachel, *Mental Measurement of Preschool Children.* World Book Company, Yonkers, N.Y., 1931.

624. Sumption, Merle B., *Three Hundred Gifted Children.* World Book Company, Yonkers, N.Y., 1941.

625. Super, Donald E., "The Kuder Preference Record in Vocational Diagnosis." *Journal of Consulting Psychology,* XI (1947), 184–193.

626. Sward, K., "Age and Mental Ability in Superior Men." *American Journal of Psychology*, LVIII (1945), 443–479.

627. Swenson, Esther J., and Caldwell, Charles G., "The Process of Communication in Children's Letters." *Elementary School Journal*, XLIX (1948), 79–88.

628. Sylvester, Emmy, and Kunst, Mary S., "Psychodynamic Aspects of the Reading Problem." *American Journal of Orthopsychiatry*, XIII (1943), 69–76.

629. Symonds, Percival M., "Classroom Discipline." *Teachers College Record*, LI (1949), 147–158.

630. ———, "Comparisons of Problems and Interests of Young Adolescents Living in the City and the Country." *Journal of Educational Sociology*, X (1936), 231–236.

631. ———, "Education for the Development of Personality." *Teachers College Record*, L (1948), 163–169.

632. ———, "Factors Influencing Test Reliability." *Journal of Educational Psychology*, XIX (1928), 73–87.

633. ———, "Life Problems and Interests of Adolescents." *School Review*, XLIV (1936), 506–518.

634. ———, "Practice vs. Grammar in the Learning of Correct English Usage." *Journal of Educational Psychology*, XX (1931), 81–95.

635. ———, *Psychology of Parent-Child Relationships*. D. Appleton–Century Company, New York, 1939.

636. ———, "A Second Approximation to the Curve of the Distribution of Intelligence of the Population of the United States, with a Note on the Standardization of the Stanford Revision of the Binet-Simon Scale." *Journal of Educational Psychology*, XIV (1923), 65–81.

637. ———, "Some Empirical Principles of Child Guidance." *Teachers College Record*, XLV (1944), 307–316.

638. ———, and Chase, D. M., "Practice versus Motivation." *Journal of Educational Psychology*, XX (1929), 19–35.

639. Terman, L. M., *The Intelligence of School Children*. Houghton Mifflin Company, Boston, 1919.

640. ———, *The Measurement of Intelligence*. Houghton Mifflin Company, Boston, 1916.

641. ———, "Mental and Physical Traits of a Thousand Gifted

Children," in Barker, R. G., Kounin, J. S., and Wright, H. F., eds., *Child Behavior and Development*. McGraw-Hill Book Company, New York, 1943, 279–306.

642. ———, and Merrill, Maud, *Directions for Administering Form L: Revision of the Stanford-Binet Tests of Intelligence*. Houghton Mifflin Company, Boston, 1937.

643. ———, *Measuring Intelligence*. Houghton Mifflin Company, Boston, 1937.

644. Terman, L. M., and Oden, Melia H., *The Gifted Child Grows Up*. Stanford University Press, Stanford University, Calif., 1947.

645. Terry, Paul W., "How Students Study for Objective and Essay Tests." *Elementary School Journal*, XXXIII (1933), 592–603.

646. Thiele, C. L., "Arithmetic in the Lower Grades from the Point of View of Interrelationships in the Number System." *16th Yearbook*, National Council of Teachers of Mathematics (1941), Chap. 4, 45–79.

647. ———, *The Contribution of Generalization to the Learning of Addition Facts*. Bureau of Publications, Teachers College, Columbia University, New York, 1933.

648. ———, "The Mathematical Viewpoint Applied to the Teaching of Elementary Arithmetic." *10th Yearbook*, National Council of Teachers of Mathematics (1935), 212–233.

649. Thom, D. A., and Newell, N., "Hazards of the High I.Q." *Mental Hygiene*, XXIX (1945), 61–77.

650. Thomas, Lawrence G., *Mental Tests as Instruments of Science*. American Psychological Association, Evanston, Ill., 1942. Also Psychological Monographs, LIV (1942), No. 3, Whole No. 245.

651. Thompson, G. G., and Hunnicutt, C. W., "The Effect of Repeated Praise or Blame on the Work Achievement of Introverts and Extroverts." *Journal of Educational Psychology*, XXXV (1944), 257–266.

652. Thompson, J. Clifford, "A Study of the Socialized versus the Academic Method of Teaching Written Composition." *School Review*, XXVII (1910), 110–133.

653. Thorndike, E. L., "The Abilities Involved in Algebraic Com-

putation and Problem Solving." *School and Society*, XV (1922), 191–193.

654. ———, *Adult Learning*. The Macmillan Company, New York, 1928.

655. ———, "Education for Initiative and Originality." *Teachers College Record*, XVII (1916), 405–416.

656. ———, "The Effect of Changed Data upon Reasoning." *Journal of Experimental Psychology*, V (1922), 33–38.

657. ———, *Fundamentals of Learning*. Bureau of Publications, Teachers College, Columbia University, New York, 1932.

658. ———, *Human Learning*. The Century Company, New York, 1931.

659. ———, "Improving the Ability to Read." *Teachers College Record*, XXXVI (1934), 1–19, 125–144, 229–241.

660. ———, "The Influence of Irrelevant Rewards." *Journal of Educational Psychology*, XXIV (1933), 1–15.

661. ———, "The Influence of Primacy." *Journal of Experimental Psychology*, X (1927), 13–29.

662. ———, "Measurements of the Influence of Recency." *American Journal of Psychology*, XLVII (1935), 294–300.

663. ———, "Mental Discipline in High-School Studies." *Journal of Educational Psychology*, XV (1924), 1–22, 83–98.

664. ———, "The Permanence of School Learning." *School and Society*, XV (1922), 625–627.

665. ———, *The Psychology of Wants, Interests, and Attitudes*. D. Appleton–Century Company, New York, 1935.

666. ———, Cobb, Margaret, Orleans, Javob S., Symonds, Percival M., Walk, Elva, and Woodyard, Ella, *The Psychology of Algebra*. The Macmillan Company, New York, 1923.

667. Thorndike, E. L., and Forlano, George, "Influence of Increase and Decrease of the Amount of Reward upon the Rate of Learning." *Journal of Educational Psychology*, XXIV (1933), 401–411.

668. Thorndike, E. L., and Woodyard, Ella, "Differences within and between Communities in the Intelligence of Children." *Journal of Educational Psychology*, XXXIII, (1942), 641–656.

669. Thorndike, Robert L., "Retest Changes in the I.Q. in Cer-

tain Superior Schools." *39th Yearbook,* National Society for the Study of Education (1940), Part II, 351–361.

670. ———, "Words and the Comics." *Journal of Experimental Education,* X (1941), 110–113.

671. Thurstone, L. L., *Primary Mental Abilities.* University of Chicago Press, Chicago, 1938.

672. ———, and Chave, E. J., *The Measurement of Attitude.* University of Chicago Press, Chicago, 1929.

673. Thurstone, L. L., and Thurstone, T. G., *Psychological Examination for College Freshmen, 1946 Norms.* American Council on Education, Washington, D.C., 1947.

674. Thurstone, T. G., "Primary Mental Abilities of Children." *Educational and Psychological Measurement,* I (1940), 105–116.

675. Tiegs, Ernest W., Clark, W. W., and Thorpe, L. P., "The California Test of Personality." *Journal of Educational Research,* XXXV (1941), 102–108.

676. Timmons, W. M., *Decisions and Attitudes as Outcomes of the Discussion of a Social Problem.* Bureau of Publications, Teachers College, Columbia University, New York, 1939.

677. Traxler, A. E., "The Cumulative Record in the Guidance Program." *School Review,* LIV (1946), 154–161.

678. ———, "Evaluation of Aptitude and Achievement in a Guidance Program." *Educational and Psychological Measurement,* VI (1946), 3–16.

679. ———, "Measurement in the Field of Personality." *Education,* LXVI (1946), 424–430.

680. Trow, W. C., "A Child Who Feared Teachers." *Journal of Educational Sociology,* III (1930), 590–601.

681. ———, *Educational Psychology,* 2nd ed. Houghton Mifflin Company, Boston, 1950.

682. ———, "Educational Psychology." *Review of Educational Research,* XII (1942), 345–355.

683. ———, "Educational Psychology Charts a Course." *Journal of Educational Psychology,* XL (1949), 285–294.

684. ———, "Who Are the Gifted?" *University of Michigan School of Education Bulletin,* XIII (1941), 8–11.

685. Tryon, C. M., "The Adolescent Peer Culture." *43rd Year-*

book, National Society for the Study of Education (1944), Part I, Chap. 12.

686. Turney, Austin A., "Intelligence, Motivation, and Achievement." *Journal of Educational Psychology,* XXII (1931), 426–434.

687. Tuttle, Harold S., *Dynamic Psychology and Conduct.* Harper & Brothers, New York, 1949.

688. ———, "Two Kinds of Learning." *Journal of Psychology,* XXII (1946), 267–277.

689. Tyler, Ralph W., "Some Findings from Studies in the Field of College Biology." *Science Education,* XVIII (1934), 133–142.

690. ———, "The Relation between Recall and the Higher Mental Processes," in C. H. Judd, *Education as Cultivation of the Higher Mental Processes.* The Macmillan Company, New York, 1936, 12–16.

691. Ulmer, G., "Teaching Geometry to Cultivate Reflective Thinking." *Journal of Experimental Education,* VIII (1939), 18–25.

692. Updegraff, Ruth, Heiliger, Louise, and Learned, Janet, *The Effect of Training upon Singing Ability and Musical Interest of Three, Four, and Five-Year-Old Children.* University of Iowa Studies in Child Welfare, XIV, New Series No. 346 (1938), 85–131.

693. Vandell, R. A., Davis, R. A., and Clugston, H. A., "The Function of Mental Practice in the Acquisition of Motor Skills." *Journal of General Psychology,* XXIX (1943), 243–250.

694. Vernon, P. E., "Changes in Abilities from Fourteen to Twenty Years." *Advancement of Science,* V (1948), 138.

695. Wahlstrom, Ebba L., "The Computational Arithmetic of Social Experiences of Third Grade Children." *Journal of Educational Research,* XXX (1936–1937), 124–129.

696. Waltimeyer, Verne E., *Pictured Punctuation.* Gregg Publishing Company, New York, 1945.

697. Warner, W. L., *Educative Effects of Social Status.* Supplementary Education Monographs, University of Chicago (1942), 16–28.

698. Washburne, Carleton W., "The Attainment of Gifted Children under Individual Instruction." *23rd Yearbook,* National Society for the Study of Education (1924), Part I, 247–261.

699. ———, "When Should We Teach Arithmetic?—a Com-

mittee of Seven Investigation." *Elementary School Journal*, XXVIII (1928), 659–665.

700. ———, and Morphett, Mabel Vogel, "Unfamiliar Situations as a Difficulty in Solving Arithmetic Problems." *Journal of Educational Research*, XVIII (1928), 220–224.

701. ———, "Are Any Number Combinations Inherently Difficult?" *Journal of Educational Research*, XVII (1928), 235–255.

702. Washburne, John N., "The Use of Questions in Social Science Material." *Journal of Educational Psychology*, XX (1929), 321–359.

703. Waters, R. H., "The Influence of Tuition upon Ideational Learning." *Journal of General Psychology*, I (1928), 534–549.

704. Watson, Goodwin, ed., *Civilian Morale*. Houghton Mifflin Company, Boston, 1942.

705. ———, "The Surprising Discovery of Morale." *Progressive Education*, XIX (1942), 33–41.

706. ———, and Newcomb, Theodore M., "Improving Reading Ability among Teachers College Students." *Teachers College Record*, XXXI (1930), 535–539.

707. Webb, L. W., and Shotwell, Anna Markt, *Testing in the Elementary School*. Farrar and Rinehart, Inc., 1939.

708. Wechsler, David, *The Measurement of Adult Intelligence*, 3rd ed. The Williams & Wilkins Company, Baltimore, 1944.

709. Wellman, Beth L., "The Effect of Pre-School Attendance upon the I.Q." *Journal of Experimental Education*, I (1932), 48–69.

710. ———, "Iowa Studies on the Effects of Schooling." *39th Yearbook*, National Society for the Study of Education (1940), Part II, 377–399.

711. ———, "I.Q. Changes of Preschool and Nonpreschool Groups during Preschool Years: a Summary of the Literature." *Journal of Psychology*, XX (1945), 347–368.

712. ———, "Mental Growth from Pre-School to College." *Journal of Experimental Education*, VI (1937), 121–138.

713. ———, "Some New Basis for Interpretation of the I.Q." *Journal of Genetic Psychology*, XLI (1932), 116–126.

714. Wells, F. L., "Mental Factors in Adjustment to Higher Education." *Journal of Consulting Psychology*, IX (1945), 67–86.

715. Wheat, Harry Grove, "The Fallacy of Social Arithmetic." *Mathematics Teacher*, XXXIX (1946), 27–34.

716. ———, "A Theory of Instruction for the Middle Grades." *16th Yearbook*, National Council of Teachers of Mathematics (1940), Chap. 5, 80–118.

717. Wheeler, Lester R., "A Comparative Study of the Intelligence of East Tennessee Mountain Children." *Journal of Educational Psychology*, XXXIII (1942), 321–333.

718. ———, and Wheeler, Viola D., "The Relationship between Reading Ability and Intelligence among University Freshmen." *Journal of Educational Psychology*, XL (1949), 230–238.

719. Wheeler, Raymond H., *The Science of Psychology*, 2nd ed. Thomas Y. Crowell Company, New York, 1940.

720. White House Conference, *Preliminary Reports*. Century Company, New York, 1930.

721. Whitehead, Thomas North, *The Industrial Worker*. Harvard University Press, Cambridge, Mass., 1938.

722. Whitted, D. J., and Carpenter, H. M., "Readings They've Liked." *English Journal*, XXXII (1943), 440–444.

723. Wickman, E. K., *Children's Behavior and Teachers' Attitudes*. The Commonwealth Fund, New York, 1938.

724. Willcockson, M., "How Ability Groups Improve Social Climate." *Education Digest*, XII (1946), 28–31.

725. Willet, G. W., "Reliability of Test Scores on Seven Tests." *Journal of Educational Research*, XLIII (1949), 293–298.

726. Williams, A. M., *Children's Choices in Science Books*. Bureau of Publications, Teachers College, Columbia University, New York, 1939.

727. Williamson, E. G., and Foley, J. D., *Counseling and Discipline*. McGraw-Hill Book Company, New York, 1949.

728. Williamson, S. J., *Retroactive Inhibition as a Function of Similarity Between Primary and Interpolated Material*. M.A. thesis, University of Iowa, Iowa City, 1942.

729. Willoughby, Raymond R., "Incidental Learning." *Journal of Educational Psychology*, XX (1929), 671–682; XXI (1930), 12–23.

730. Wilson, Guy M., "New Standards in Arithmetic: a Con-

trolled Experiment in Supervision." *Journal of Educational Research*, XXII (1930), 351–360.

731. ———, "The Social Utility Theory as Applied to Arithmetic, Its Research Basis, and Some of Its Implications." *Journal of Educational Research*, XLI (1948), 321–337.

732. Winch, W. H., "Should Poems Be Learnt by School Children as 'Wholes' or in 'Parts'?" *British Journal of Psychology*, XV (1924–1925), 64–79.

733. Winship, A. E., *Jukes-Edwards: A Study in Education and Heredity*. Meyers Publishing Company, Harrisburg, Pa., 1900.

734. Witherington, Henry C., *Educational Psychology*. Ginn and Company, Boston, 1946.

735. Witty, Paul A., "Children's Interest in Reading the Comics." *Journal of Experimental Education*, X (1941), 100–104.

736. ———, "New Evidence on the Learning Ability of the Negro." *Journal of Abnormal Psychology and Social Psychology*, XL (1945), 401–404.

737. ———, "Reading the Comics—a Comparative Study." *Journal of Experimental Education*, X (1941), 105–109.

738. ———, "Reading Interests and Habits of Five Hundred Adults." *Education*, LII (1932), 554–562.

739. ———, "Reading Problems in the Secondary School." *School and Society*, LXV (1947), 113–116.

740. ———, and Decker, A. I., "A Comparative Study of the Educational Attainment of Negro and White Children." *Journal of Educational Psychology*, XVIII (1927), 497–500.

741. Wolf, Theta Holmes, *The Effect of Praise and Competition on the Persisting Behavior of Kindergarten Children*. University of Minnesota Press, Minneapolis, 1938.

742. Wonderlic, E. F., and Howland, C. I., "The Personnel Test: A Restandardized Abridgement of the Otis S-A Test for Business and Industrial Use." *Journal of Applied Psychology*, XXIII (1939), 685–702.

743. Woodrow, Herbert, "The Ability to Learn." *Psychological Review*, LIII (1946), 147–158.

744. ———, "The Effect of Type of Training upon Transference." *Journal of Educational Psychology*, XVIII (1927), 159–172.

745. Woolley, Helen T., "The Validity of Standards of Mental

Measurement during Young Childhood." *School and Society,* XXI (1925), 476–482.

746. Worcester, D. A., "The Permanence of Learning in High School Subjects—Algebra." *Journal of Educational Psychology,* XIX (1928), 343–345.

747. ———, "Retention after Long Periods." *Journal of Educational Psychology,* XIV (1923), 113–114.

748. Wright, Louise B., "The Value of a Motivated Assignment: an Experiment in Directed Study." *University of Pittsburgh School of Education Journal,* V (1929), 64–67.

749. Wrightstone, J. Wayne, *Appraisal of Experimental High School Practices.* Bureau of Publications, Teachers College, Columbia University, New York, 1936.

750. ———, *Appraisal of Newer Elementary School Practices.* Bureau of Publications, Teachers College, Columbia University, New York, 1938.

751. ———, *Appraisal of Newer Practices in Selected Public Schools.* Bureau of Publications, Teachers College, Columbia University, New York, 1935.

752. ———, "Comparison of Newer with Conventional Practices in English." *English Journal* (High School Edition), XXIV (1935), 399–403.

753. ———, and Campbell, Doak S., "Social Studies and the American Way of Life," in *Evaluation of Growth in Social Education,* Part III. Row, Peterson and Company, Evanston, Ill., 1942.

754. Wrightstone, J. Wayne, Nifendecker, E. A., Wade, J. E., and Buck, E., *Determining Readiness for Reading.* Educational Research Bulletin, Board of Education, New York, 1943.

755. Yoakam, G. A., "The Effect of a Single Reading." *University of Iowa Studies in Education,* II (1924), No. 7.

756. Young, F. M., "Causes for Loss of Interest in High School Subjects as Reported by 651 College Students." *Journal of Educational Research,* XXV (1932), 100–115.

757. Zachry, Caroline B., "The Growth Process," in Harold Rugg, *Democracy and the Curriculum.* D. Appleton–Century Company, New York, 1939, Chap. 12.

758. ———, "Personality Growth." *Journal of Educational Sociology,* XVII (1943), 85–89.

Index